W9-CNC-783

MARRYING WELL

Evelyn Eaton Whitehead
and James D. Whitehead

MARRYING WELL

Possibilities in
Christian Marriage Today

1981
DOUBLEDAY & COMPANY, INC.
GARDEN CITY, NEW YORK

Unless otherwise indicated, excerpt(s) from *The Jerusalem Bible*, copyright © 1966 by Darton, Longman & Todd, Ltd., and Doubleday & Company, Inc. Used by permission of the publisher.

Library of Congress Cataloging in Publication Data

Whitehead, Evelyn Eaton.
Marrying well: possibilities in Christian marriage today.

Bibliography: p. 452.
Includes index.
1. Marriage—United States. 2. Marriage—Catholic Church. I. Whitehead, James D. II. Title.
HQ734.W57   306.8
ISBN: 0-385-17130-7   AACR2
Library of Congress Catalog Card Number: 81-43046

COPYRIGHT © 1981 BY EVELYN EATON WHITEHEAD AND
JAMES D. WHITEHEAD
ALL RIGHTS RESERVED
PRINTED IN THE UNITED STATES OF AMERICA
FIRST EDITION

for
J. GORDON MYERS
among friends, the best

CONTENTS

INTRODUCTION

This is a book about the demise of marriage as a state and its survival as a journey. Its theme is fidelity in change—our efforts as believers to be faithful to our God, to our partner and to ourselves in a time of both great promise and considerable confusion for the relationship of marriage. Its intent is to explore the journey of married Christians today, charting where we have been and attempting to glimpse where we may be going.

The metaphor of journey will serve us well, for it has deeply religious roots. It reminds us of the perils and revelations to be experienced along the way. It recalls tests of faith and celebrates —in burning bushes and manna in the desert—the ambiguous signs that God is still with us. But the metaphor is useful only if it can be de-romanticized. The journey of marriage is not just a honeymoon. But neither is it meant to be a forced march.

When marriage is understood chiefly as a state and as an institution it seems relatively secure, with clear and protective boundaries. And until recently marriage, and indeed Christianity itself, has been seen as such a "state" in which believers could expect to live with confidence and clarity of purpose. In the City of God the rules of marriage were clear and consistent and there was much support for observing them. Family, society and the Church reinforced and guarded these rules. In such a stable era, Christians had little personal empathy with Old Testament images of change and transition. The Exodus and the Israelites'

long travail in the desert were past history, superseded by the
New Jerusalem of the Christian Church, its doctrine and moral
principles providing firm walls of support. But today both Christianity as a secure city and marriage as a stable state are gone.

Marriage is in trouble today. As an institution it is criticized
from the left and the right. On the right are those who mourn
the passing of the patriarchal family, with its clear structures of
order and authority. On the left are others who fault marriage for the structures that remain, who judge its formal commitments of permanence and exclusivity to be restrictive and out
of date. Most of us who are married are uneasy with the ideological fervor of much that is said on both sides of the public
debate. But we, too, know marriage to be troubled. We often see
unhappiness in the marriages we know best, perhaps even in our
own. Spouses seem suddenly incompatible or gradually come to
the painful realization that they have never been well matched.
One partner changes in ways that are disconcerting or unacceptable to the other, or they each change, but in directions that
lead them away from one another. It seems that marriages are
no longer "for a lifetime." Fewer and fewer couples seem able
to, or willing to, stay together "for better and for worse, until
death do us part."

Social scientists assure us that the proportion of marriages
broken by separation or death or divorce has increased only
slightly during this century, but this fact gives little consolation.
Divorce seems to be everywhere—in our families, among our
friends, in the neighborhood, among our colleagues at work, in
the Church. For most of us it is no longer "unthinkable" that our
own marriage might end in divorce. Divorce functions in our
consciousness as one of the outcomes of marriage—perhaps an
outcome we repudiate, perhaps an outcome we fear, but one of
the possibilities, nevertheless.

Confronted by these challenges to the stability of marriage,
Christians find new appeal in the Old Testament images of transition and dislocation. We sense ourselves, in the 1980s, less a
people in secure possession of God and more a people in pursuit
of God's sometimes shadowy but continuing presence in our
lives. We know exodus and exile as our own. Both as Christians

and as married persons, we find fidelity a new and unexpected challenge. This virtue, at the core of religious faith and of marriage, makes different demands on a journey than in a stable state. We try now to be faithful to a moving God, alert for the contemporary equivalents of the "cloud by day and pillar of fire by night" that will guide us on this uncertain journey. We try to be faithful not only to the person we married but to the person we continue to be married to. As renegotiation and reconciliation become more frequent demands, we experience the need for new resources of maturity and integrity if we are to manage the stresses of the journey.

As our Christian faith and our married life become more a journey, we find ourselves forced to travel light. Some of our cherished convictions must be left behind. We come to see that some of these have hardened into idols—God as "problem solver," a last defense against having to take personal responsibility for my life; my marriage partner as conforming neatly to my expectations and stereotypes of the opposite sex. But even as we learn to let go some of this baggage, we face another danger of the journey—our exhaustion as the trip continues over time. We begin our marriage in the enthusiastic conviction that our love shall last. But we know marriages that have failed, even marriages well begun as is our own. More than the dramatic events of death or tragic accident, we fear the gradual deterioration of the quality of our relationship and the erosion of our mutual love. This deterioration is particularly alarming since it often seems to be beyond the control of the spouses. People change, couples fall out of love, one of them meets "someone new"—how do we prepare for or manage these apparently mysterious happenings? How do we allow for growth and development in our marriage while we guard against changes that could destroy our love?

As the journey of our marriage continues we may also come to wonder if we have left too much behind. Christians live not just as individuals but as a community. Community requires some sense of shared value, some experience of common purpose. With the loss of much of our former clarity about God, with a changing sense of the meaning of sexuality and mutuality and fidelity in marriage, are we still Christians? As we understand our own relationship in more personal terms does our marital journey become only a private trip? How can we avoid the isolation of the nuclear family's separate enterprise? How shall we be able to travel together as part of a people larger than just our family, as a part of a community of faith? It is these questions about the journey that is marriage for Christians today that we will examine in the chapters ahead.

We are writing a book on marriage for married people and those who minister to them. It is not primarily a book of research facts. We will draw on the social sciences and the findings and interpretations of current research, but our goal will be to draw out insights and interpretive schema to help illumine the contemporary experience of marriage among Christians. With this goal in mind we will list at the end of each chapter the resources on which we have drawn, along with other useful references, rather than burden the text with footnotes.

Ours is a book about marriage as a religious reality. It addresses the shape and possibilities of Christian marriage in a time of enormous change. It explores the religious significance of marriage as it is experienced in the lives of believers today. Our conviction is that Christian marriage exists most concretely in the thousands of couples who are attempting to realize the joys and responsibilities of their lives together, as believers, for more than themselves. We want to acknowledge this reality of Christian marriage—a reality to be celebrated not only to the extent that it fits existing formulations and established norms but also as it suggests the hopes and challenges that will shape marriage for Christians in the future.

Our intention in the chapters ahead is to establish a conversation about marriage among three sources of information, each offering significant insight into its complex and exciting reality. These sources are: (1) the images and understandings of devoted love and marriage that come to us through the heritage of Christianity, (2) the findings and interpretations of marriage today that are available in the social sciences, and (3) the ongoing experience of marriage as lived by Christians today. We approach no one of these sources in the expectation that here alone we shall find full and final answers. The compelling questions that accompany marriage today are multi-faceted. They involve too many aspects of ourselves and are influenced by too many factors of our larger world to be easily resolved or even properly understood from a single perspective. We are aware that our reflection on marriage today takes place in a period of cultural and religious transition. The social sciences present no settled understanding of sexuality or marriage or family life. Christians continue to disagree concerning the tradition's orientation to the body, to women, to married love. One's personal experience of marriage can seem atypical or insignificant or simply confused. But our hope is that the dialogue—or trilogue—among these sources will provide insight to illumine the experience of marriage today.

This book may be seen as a contribution to the Christian spirituality of marriage. Our route to the development of a contemporary spirituality will be to explore the religious invitations that await Christians in the psychological and social challenges of married life today.

To write a book on marriage today is to be impressed with the vastness and complexity of the topic. Initial choices must be made if the writing is to begin; others must be made if it is ever to end. These choices focus the discussion; they likewise limit it. Our book focuses more on marriage than on family, more on the relationship between spouses than on the dynamics between parents and children. This choice allows us to consider in some depth the movements of challenge and consolation that, expectably, mark the experience of married love over a lifetime. It also reflects the context of our own direct experience of marriage, since we have no children.

Our discussion focuses on the factors and trends that characterize marriage among the broad middle range of American adults, that social and economic group in which most American Catholics are found. We are aware that this experience, while dominant, is not "all there is" to marriage. For different reasons, patterns of marriage among certain groups differ notably from the patterns that describe marriage for most Americans. The economic and emotional strains of chronic poverty, for example, have profound effect on what marriage is among the poor. Marriage among the very rich, likewise, takes a shape of its own. Americans among whom European or Hispanic or Asian heritage is strong are likely to experience different pressures and priorities in marriage and family life. Many of these differences are not just trivial. Some reflect cultural preferences, others point to more fundamental strains in our social and economic system. Our goal in this book, however, is not to cover the complete range of social and cultural factors affecting marriage. Its more limited focus is the experience of marriage among most American Catholics today and the factors and trends that promise to influence its shape over the near future.

A final word of introduction to the book. We imagine that few readers will want to move through the chapters in strict sequence, from first to last. It is more likely that a reader will find some chapters more significant than others, some topics of greater personal interest, some issues of more immediate concern. We encourage this selective approach. There is a logic in our overall design and a progression in the flow of the discussion, but we have tried to present each chapter "on its own," so that it may be useful to the reader who chooses to move through the book in a different order.

Some comments from us may help this process of selection. Those especially interested in the contemporary theological discussion on marriage will find Chapters 4, 5, 7 and 20 helpful. To trace recent developments in the social form of marriage, readers might turn to Chapters 2, 3, 16 and 17. Part Two looks at the changing shape of the marriage relationship over the years a couple is together. Spirituality is the focus of Part Three and Part Five. Part Four examines several themes that often emerge as "issues" in the controversy concerning the current shape of married life.

As we move into our discussion of marriage, we are pleased to acknowledge those colleagues and friends who have in a special way helped us to write this book. John Breslin brought us Doubleday's invitation to undertake the project. It was with Gordy Myers that we first took counsel, in this as in much else, as we considered our response. With his characteristic competence and grace, Jim Zullo reviewed our initial outline in detail and made several valuable suggestions that we have incorporated into our final text. Dan Dillabough welcomed us to California: through his good offices we received hospitality and housing at the University of San Diego as we wrestled with the first draft during the early months of 1980. Hildegard Cox typed this manuscript for us, as she has others, with great care and consistent good humor.

We are especially grateful to our parents—Aurea and Ed Whitehead, Evelyn and Red Eaton—from whom we have learned our first and most enduring lessons about marriage. It is from our friends that we have learned most about what it is to be a parent today. We salute these experienced and wise teachers: Mary and Gene Ulrich, Jackie Trehearne, Barbara and Lucien Roy, G. V. Egan, Mary Good and Bill Harman, Toots and Bill Foy, Patricia Livingston, Carol and Jack Lawyer. We have been taught, as well, by John and Megan and Laura. To all these delightful and generous companions on the journey, we offer our sincere thanks.

Part One:

MARRYING—
AMERICAN AND CHRISTIAN

Marriage is undergoing an extraordinary transformation. Forces in contemporary American culture are reshaping this central commitment of adult life. And these changes are complemented by significant developments in Christian understandings of marriage. Focusing on marriage as a relationship, a commitment and a lifestyle, we examine the cultural and religious forces shaping marriage in the United States in the 1980s. Of special importance are shifts in Christian attitudes toward sexuality, fruitfulness and the relationship of women and men. As we review these changes, we will suggest the future shape of this Christian commitment: this will describe a spirituality of marriage that is both contemporary and Christian.

I

CHRISTIAN MARRIAGE—
THREE PORTRAITS

Marriage is a most elastic term today. It embraces very different expectations and lifestyles. We begin our consideration by looking at three couples approaching or living marriage. Each portrait is a composite of couples familiar to us and, we expect, to the reader. In their different concerns and ambitions, we gain introductory glimpses of marriage in America and something of the challenge for Christian marriage in the 1980s.

Molly and Doug, both in their early twenties, are planning to get married next summer. Both have grown up as Catholics in a large Midwestern city, though Molly has not "been to Church" since she finished high school. Three years of dating and an increasingly intimate relationship have convinced Doug and Molly that they want to make a life together. They have found themselves resisting their parents' combined enthusiasm—and advanced planning—for a church wedding. Part of this, they admit, is their struggle against their parents' efforts to manage their lives. But other questions and doubts have arisen for this young couple, as they ask what it means to be married in the Church today.

They differ considerably in their attitudes toward the Church. For Doug, the Church is a confusing but changing place. He remembers some peculiar and harsh instructions about sexuality as a child. But his religion teachers in high school were honest

and approachable and he feels they gave him an appreciation of
what Christianity can be as a way of life. His parish today
doesn't have many activities for young adults but it is involved
in a number of excellent outreach programs which show a real
concern for people in need.

Molly brings very different experiences to their discussions
about a Catholic marriage. Her unpleasant memories are more
persuasive to her than Doug's assurances about a changing
Church. To Molly, the Catholic Church seems terribly "male."
And it still seems to be very much in the business of making
rules for people, especially rules about sexuality. Molly sees herself as a believer and a Christian but is unsure if she is still a
Catholic. "Doesn't being a Catholic mean staying a child all your
life, waiting for some authority to tell you what to do and how
to live?"

Recently Doug and Molly have had some good talks about
their life together—what they hope for from each other; when
they look forward to beginning their family; the values around
which they want to shape their marriage. Neither one of them
can tolerate being just a nominal Catholic; what is the alternative to this? They feel they need to talk more about what a
Catholic marriage would mean for them. The word among their
friends is that the marriage preparation program in both their
parishes is bad. Doug and Molly would enjoy talking with other
couples who are trying to make sense out of Christian marriage
these days.

Steve and Catherine have been married for nineteen years and
have four children between the ages of eleven and eighteen.
Growing up in the "old Church," they were married the year
that the Second Vatican Council began. The changes in the
Church in the late sixties and seventies were, for the most part,
invigorating for them. (Though some of the liturgical changes,
like the enforced socializing at the "Kiss of Peace," seemed
strained for a long time.) The furor in the late sixties over the
Church's teaching on contraception escaped them, as Catherine
was pregnant with their third child.

Catherine, who is forty-three, has only in the past year been thinking about her marriage and family. With the children so independent now, she has begun to question her own usefulness: "What do I do now?" She would like to be good at something, but doesn't know what. She feels, at times, like a very old child of her husband. Emotions she has not felt before, feelings of impotence and resentment, are awakening and these frighten her. It seems that Steve and she have been about such different things for the past years that they don't know each other very well anymore. Her three women friends in the neighborhood talk to her about being more independent and assertive; such talk feels, at once, both true and unchristian. Is it foolish to be looking for something special in her marriage now? Is it immature to be thinking these thoughts?

Steve senses a growing uneasiness in Catherine but does not know how to ask about it. Intensely proud of his children, he still shudders at a recent enigmatic remark by Catherine: "We have a much better family than we do a marriage." Something needs to be done, but what? Last month a parish announcement was made about a Marriage Encounter Weekend for couples married more than ten years. Steve is uneasy with what he has heard goes on at these events. There seems to be so much focus on feelings; he senses he would feel uncomfortable and embarrassed. He doesn't quite want counseling but would like the Church to be a help in some way. What can the Church offer Catherine and Steve?

Martina and Walter are in their late sixties now and enjoying life a great deal. Married forty-five years ago, they had three children who now live in other parts of the country. Perhaps the major religious event in their years of marriage has been their daughter's divorce. Devout Catholics, Walter and Martina had always assumed divorce was a sinful act of selfish people. Yet when Christy, their daughter with two small children, was divorced, they were forced to reevaluate their thinking. They shared Christy's sorrow and were both confused and grateful when she remarried. They assumed that this meant she could no longer be a Catholic and the treatment she received in her parish confirmed this. Yet when, a year later, Christy and her family

moved to a new parish, they were welcomed there with a surprising warmth. A group of divorced and remarried Catholics invited them to join the group. One of the parish's ministers asked
if she wanted to investigate the possibility of "regularizing" this
second marriage. When this "regularizing" (Martina and Walter
never did fathom what this meant) proved impossible, Christy
was still welcomed in the parish's liturgies and other activities.
Walter and Martina were again confused and grateful. The
Church seems more interested in people with marriage problems
than it used to be.

In the newfound leisure of their retirement years, Walter and
Martina would like to do something at the parish. But what?
They hope something comes of the talk about a program of
bringing groceries to shut-ins and to poor families. They could
do this together and think they would enjoy it. Martina has also
been pushing for a discussion group for older people in the parish, to talk about both their own lives and what is happening in
the Church these days. She keeps telling the pastor that the
older folks want more than bingo. She knows it is ambitious but
still wishes there were some way for these older married couples
to encourage those just beginning marriage. If the Church can
act so differently today with divorced people, Martina tells herself, anything is possible.

The concerns that arise in these portraits underscore the psychological and religious challenge of marriage in the 1980s.
These concerns can be gathered into three common questions.

"How are we to be together?" This is the special concern of
Catherine and Steve in mid-life, and it is a concern of many
other marriages as well. What does marriage mean today? What
are the factors that influence or determine how we are together?
What can we expect and ask of each other? How does our culture's changing understanding of women, for instance, challenge
or threaten our relationship?

Being together in marriage entails a commitment, but what
kind of commitment is possible in the 1980s? If I change or you
change, will our commitment survive? Is a lifelong commitment,
our being together for sixty years and more, possible or even de-

sirable? And what is our marriage for? Are we together for each other or for our children? As a family are we meant just for each other or for something more? How can our togetherness lead to something beyond ourselves?

Finally, what does it mean for us to be together, as married and Christian? As Catholic? Does (or should) our religious life change our marriage? These questions anticipate the second concern common to these portraits.

"What is the Church for?" Molly and Doug, the young couple of our first portrait, asked the question: "Why marry in the Church?" The other couples wondered about the role of the Church in their lives. Is the Church more than a place of rules and laws, especially about sex and marriage? Surely, it is meant to be more than a social organization, a "Sunday club" in which social respectability demands membership. How can it be a place that invigorates both those marrying and those long married with values and hopes ordinarily lost in a busy, distracting world? How can the Church show the life of the unmarried man Jesus Christ to be relevant, as a challenge and a hope, for married Christians today?

Molly asks the question bluntly. This Church—so repressive about sexuality, so hostile toward women, so frequently bogged down in its abstract rhetoric about love and service to the world —how can it be expected to help us make our marriage work? Doug is less angry, but his question is similar. Can the Catholic Church speak to the needs and hopes of marriage today? Can the vision of Christianity touch the "real world" of love and sex and career and family? Or do the Church's past biases block the renewal needed for a more fruitful ministry to marriage?

Doug and Steve and Martina are all impressed with changes in their parishes. A less rhetorical and more practical ministry is being developed. Will this ministry revitalize the Church and provide hope for the future of Christian marriage?

"Can we trust ourselves?" A less obvious question within the common concerns of these three couples, and many others, is that of psychological and religious maturity. Many Catholics feel they have grown up as both children of God and children of the clergy. Fully dependent in questions of personal morality, they

learned to trust the external authority of the teaching Church to
the neglect of the growing authority of their own adult experience. Many of these Catholics today feel the need and challenge
to come to a greater trust of their own judgment. Is this possible
only at the expense of trust in the Church? Are these opposing
authorities, so that we must be faithful either to the Church or
to ourselves? How do Christians come to trust God's guiding
presence both in their own lives and in the Church? In marriage,
this means coming to trust our own awareness—an awareness
shaped by years and even decades of Christian living—concerning sexual sharing, concerning the size of our family, concerning
how our family will contribute to the larger community. This
complex question of mature fidelity, to our religious heritage
and to ourselves, will be a central concern of this book.

The Shape of Christian Marriage

In Chapters 2 and 3 we will explore the psychological and social dimensions of marriage today. Here we will present a
religious perspective on the enduring elements of Christian marriage.

What, then, is "Christian marriage"? Do Christians marry and
live marriage differently than others? Do married Christians
make love in ways that are different or better? The meaning of
Christian marriage hinges on our understanding of Christian
faith and its influence in our lives. At its core Christian faith entails two elements—seeing and responding. Christians see with
an energy and a vision not shared by everyone; they also try to
shape their lives according to this vision.

Seeing. Christians are people who see a certain way. What
does this mean? As Christians we see that life, despite much evidence to the contrary, has a meaning and a direction. Life is not a
random or pointless venture. We recognize (at least on our better days) that our own life is not absurd and empty. This peculiar, individual life that I lead, which seems so strange compared
to the seemingly stable and normal lives of others around me,
has—perhaps to my surprise—purpose and meaning. Seeing a

point and direction to life is personalized for Christians; we come to recognize that we have been invited in a certain direction, toward a specific calling. We sense this personal call as an invitation rooted in our own best hopes. Our abilities and dreams point us toward a certain way to live—this career, marriage to this person, these children. Christians are those who experience this "seeing" of direction in their life, however obscure and partial it is, as a gift. They are surprised and grateful for this recognition of purpose in their life and they look for someone to thank. This Someone was named, in our earliest tradition, Yahweh. Jesus told us to call our God Father, though today we acknowledge our God as also mother, friend, enduring lover and much more.

This seeing is the beginning of religious faith. It reveals to us who we are and might be, and imparts a special vision of our social world. Christians are people who begin to see, influenced by the stories and images of the Judeo-Christian Scriptures, that "others" are not aliens or strangers but brothers and sisters. The "others" who make up our world, whether these are women or blacks or gay people, are more like us than different. In privileged moments we are given insight into the meaning of human community. Putting aside the defenses which protect us from those of a different gender, or color, or custom, we see their similarity to us. Such a peculiar and surprising insight, which flies in the face of much of our socialization, invites us to care for those others in justice and love.

Spending time with the Christian gospels, we begin to appreciate the special life of Jesus Christ. His life argues that personal commitment and vulnerability are worth the risk. He challenges the cultural vision that self-preservation and "getting my fair share" are the central goals of human life. Committing myself to another person—even for life—and learning to forgive and be forgiven begin to be seen as possible and worthy goals.

This vision, which is the beginning of faith, sometimes seems evanescent. Its insights come and go; nor do they always seem defensible. On certain days the evidence against them overwhelms us: we lose the point of our own life, or we are confused by those "others," or we are injured by a loved one. We sense the vision is not totally under our control. It comes instead as gift. We find that we do not invent or manufacture it. Often we are not sure whence it comes, but when it arrives, we find ourselves living differently. Christians have traditionally called this vision-as-gift by the name of faith. Faith is a vision "with strings attached"—we must do something about it.

Before turning to this second aspect of Christian life, our response to the vision of faith, it is important to recall why we call this vision "Christian." This rather uncommon, relatively indefensible vision—that life has purpose, that "others" are more like us than different, that personal commitment and fidelity are possible—has illumined several religious traditions. These are *Christian* insights for us because our God has revealed these possibilities to us through the life of Jesus Christ. We name ourselves Christian because our vision of meaning and justice and love has appeared in the life and witness of Jesus Christ. His way of seeing has altered us and we find ourselves believing, seeing differently.

Practically and immediately, we come to this particular vision through the important people in our lives—parents, friends, teachers. We see these people living, or trying to live, according to some rather special values, and we begin to learn the practical shape of Christian life. We find around us others living marriages shaped by Christian faith: generosity, forgiveness and a sense of purpose gradually form such relationships into recognizably Christian marriages. Such marriages—when they are available to us—tell us two things: they announce that a lifetime of committed Christian love is possible, and they provide us with images of what it looks like.

Responding. Christian living begins in vision; we start by seeing differently. But this sight is not speculative or theoretical. It invites us to act, to change our lives to fit these insights. We are not only surprised but often made uncomfortable in this new vision. How shall we respond to it? What must I change if my life is to reflect this beautiful but challenging understanding of the world?

Christian faith becomes practical in the effort to live, in a daily and concrete fashion, what we have received. This challenge brings us to two realities central to our religious heritage: grace and virtue.

All of us hope for a graceful marriage. What is the religious meaning of such a hope? Grace is at the heart of Christian life because it is how God penetrates and shapes our behavior. Grace, in the Christian tradition, is that gift of God which allows us to act with a certain ease and effectiveness. Very early in Luke's gospel we read of Jesus' maturing in these terms: "The child grew in maturity, and he was filled with wisdom; and God's grace was with him." The basic notion of gracefulness as an ability to act well, as a "gifted performance," has frequently been lost in Christian history. In its place an abstract notion of grace emerged: grace became an imperceptible benefit received from God. Such an understanding, which often accompanied a rather magical view of sacraments, tended to neglect the connection between God's grace and human dispositions and maturity.

The graces of a Christian marriage will be explored here in a very different fashion. We will detail the different psychological and religious elements of a graceful marriage, as a couple grow gradually into making their relationship a "gifted performance." Such an exploration will necessarily include the demythologizing of gracefulness. The skilled linguist or the graceful dancer appears to perform effortlessly and with an almost magical ease. Behind such a performance, however, lie years of training and effort: repeated practice at specific behaviors, innumerable mistakes, and a very gradual development of dependable patterns of action. Such is the stuff of gracefulness in marriage as well.

The specific graces of marriage—the ability to entrust myself to another, to forgive and be forgiven, to communicate and confront effectively, to let go of my children as they mature—are indeed gifts of God. Yet they include much personal effort. This book will trace the expectable efforts that contribute to a psychologically and religiously graceful marriage.

Complementing the notion of grace in Christian history is that of virtue. Virtue, a word which unfortunately still carries for many people the puritan nuances of "abstaining" (whether from alcohol or sex or anger), originally meant power. Virtue is the personal power or ability to act in an effective fashion. Christian virtue has a special paradoxical feature: it is a personal ability that we recognize simultaneously as a gift of God. Whether the virtue is the capacity to hope or the ability to ask forgiveness, it is a power that belongs genuinely to the person whose efforts contribute to its development. Yet we experience this ability as a gift. And seeing someone who is unable to hope or incapable of asking forgiveness, we recognize that we are not the sole authors of this strength.

A challenging lifelong relationship like marriage requires a variety of strengths and virtues. Unfortunately, the traditional Christian virtues of marriage—love, fidelity, endurance—have often been obscured by rhetoric and abstractness. Christians, exhorted to these virtues, were frequently left unsure how, practically, to exercise themselves in these necessary strengths. We will try, by relating Christian virtues to the psychological strengths which describe human maturing, to give contemporary and practical shape to the virtues of marriage. Finally, we will attempt to rescue virtue from rhetoric alone by rooting it in specific interpersonal skills of behavior. These skills, whether of self-disclosure or empathy or confrontation, are a practical exercise of Christian virtue. All of this will suggest one way of understanding contemporary Christian marriage as both graceful and virtuous.

A Spirituality of Marriage

The traditional name for the Christian combination of seeing and responding, and the effort to grow in gracefulness and virtue, is spirituality. Admittedly, this a word that is almost bankrupt from misuse. For many Christians today, spirituality refers to what "specialists" in Christianity do—monks, vowed religious, priests. Further, the word suggests to many the private pursuit of holiness, a lifestyle which necessitates stepping aside from the messy, interfering details of a secular career, a mate, and managing a family.

The word can also suggest a split between the worlds of spirit and flesh—the spirit which is suspiciously invisible and other-worldly, and the flesh which is all too visible and most unruly. When this split is in force, spirituality most often has to do with abstaining from making love, rather than becoming good at it.

Finally, spirituality may seem to be limited to ways of feeling —a question of inner attitudes and private emotions, discon-nected from social life. Again, spirituality comes to indicate a specialized path rather than the practical pattern of living out our vision.

It is uncertain that this word "spirituality" can survive. Per-haps these limiting historical connotations so strangle it that it should be allowed to perish. If we are to rescue this term and make it vital again we will have to link Christian vision with practical, effective performance of this vision. A contemporary spirituality of Christian marriage will explore the different ways that Christians have envisioned married life, sexuality and religious fruitfulness. It will "re-vise," or look again at, these in-sights as they have changed in response to different needs and possibilities in late-twentieth-century American life. It will also be concerned with how we are to live out this vision of married life. Thus a contemporary spirituality will address questions of personal maturity, values and lifestyle.

Such a spirituality addresses practical aspects of life—how we spend our time, how much we work, how and when we worship and play and make love. A spirituality of marriage, as we will pursue it in this book, concerns not only praying together but also developing the skills (or better, the virtues) which make our marriage and family life fruitful.

Such a spirituality is, at heart, a discipline. This word "disci-pline," a bit forbidding in tone, recalls another word from tradi-tional Christian vocabulary which is more forbidding yet: ascet-icism. This word conjures up images of emaciated monks fasting, scourging themselves and praying through the night in their esoteric pursuit of holiness. Historically, the word does refer to specialists in the Christian life. In this book we will try to expand the notion of asceticism beyond this highly specialized

meaning and define it, instead, as the "expectable discipline of a
Christian life." The conviction behind this is that Christian living—and so, Christian marriage—requires a sustained commitment and a daily discipline.

Many Catholics, because of their recent past, are ambivalent
about religious discipline. Casting off earlier forms of Catholic
practice (Friday abstinence from meat, Lenten observances and
even an obligatory Sunday Eucharist), many of us entered the
1970s happily free from discipline. We looked forward to letting
our lives and our religious growth happen more naturally and
spontaneously. Those of us who survived the seventies found
that this attitude—at the opposite extreme from an earlier, more
impersonal and rigid approach to discipline—was itself neither
satisfying nor fruitful.

Many Catholics and other Christians are today much more interested in discipline and in systematic ways to improve their
personal and marital lives. We have discovered that life and
marriage, allowed to unfold "naturally," do not always mature of
their own accord. This renewed interest in discipline in the
Christian community is not surprising. Asceticism is, in fact,
much in vogue in American culture today. Careful dieters, daily
joggers, patient practitioners of yoga and meditation abound.
People are intent on assertively structuring their eating, exercise
and interpersonal habits not only for their own private profit but
to benefit their spouses and families as well.

Such a "secular asceticism" can, of course, be motivated by
selfish and narcissistic goals—just as more classical forms of asceticism such as prayer and fasting may be guided by less than
pure motives. But this secular asceticism regarding diet, exercise and the use of one's time can remind us that marriage, too,
requires discipline. Maturing in marriage, for example, demands
an ascetical development of skills and virtues of communication
—in conversation, in lovemaking and in confrontation. Such virtues shape a lifestyle and give our religious hopes for our marriage a better chance to be realized. In an effort to describe a
religious discipline that will make our marriages more graceful,

we will attempt in the chapters ahead to outline a contemporary asceticism of Christian marriage.

The Method of Reflection

In pursuit of a spirituality at once Christian and contemporary we will attend to three sources of insight, even revelation. We will turn frequently to the images and convictions from our religious heritage to discover what they tell us about the shapes and hopes of marriage among Christians. This source of reflection, which includes Scripture and our long history as a religious people, is a most complex one. The Christian tradition is not simply a sacred and unchanging reservoir of revelation about marriage. Along with its rich inheritance of God's revelation are included all the misuses of this history to which our fears and neglect have led. Thus our religious tradition is at once holy and unholy, grace-filled and desperately in need of reform. The task, then, as it has always been, is to discern amid this marvelous and confusing history the insights and revelations which speak to the experience of marriage today. We will be searching not for Scriptural passages which justify our own resistance to change, but for the images and values and convictions which excite us to more generous love.

As we listen to the many voices of our Christian heritage on marriage, we will set this witness in dialogue with another powerful influence in our lives—the culture in which we live. Being an American in the 1980s puts special pressures and affords certain advantages for a married Christian. But if our religious tradition is a complex source of information, our cultural life is even more so. Pornography, the pill and no-fault divorce powerfully influence Americans' attitudes toward interpersonal commitment and marriage. But from this culture also come the findings of research in psychology and sociology, as these disciplines continue to clarify both the pressures and possibilities of marriage today. In this book we will attend carefully to information from the social sciences on such issues as the changing shape of family life, the shifting expectations of women and men in marriage and the role of conflict in love.

A third important partner in this dialogue of the Christian tradition and the social sciences is the reader's own experience. We trust this book will be read by those who have, whether for a few years or for many decades, lived Christian marriage—not some "ideal" version of marriage but a personal and shared effort to let Christian faith shape marriage and family life. In a time of extraordinary societal change, this fund of lived Christian experience takes on special significance. Readers will be invited, at different points in the book, to reflect on their own experience of marriage—to savor the specific strengths and frailties, the wounds and graces and frustrations of their own marriages. It is, after all, in these concrete experiences that religious faith is tested and refined. It is here that we find, or fail to find, the presence of God.

Christians living marriage today and struggling to be faithful and fruitful in genuinely religious ways teach the Church about Christian marriage. And in this instruction they forecast the future shape of this commitment. A traditional theological category for this witness of "ordinary" Christians is *the sense of the faithful*. A maturing Christian community—and its families—can be expected to possess a "sense" or instinct of what Christian faith requires today. Included in this larger "sense of the faithful" are its understandings of human sexuality, of marriage, of fidelity, of commitment. A dialogue on marriage between the Christian tradition and the social sciences will be sterile if not joined by this testimony of married Christians. By encouraging these Christians—engaged, married and divorced—to reflect, carefully and confidently, on their lives with God, the Church will tap an important source of ongoing revelation.

Such a dialogue of our religious tradition, cultural information and personal experience has as its goal the development of a spirituality of marriage that is genuinely Christian, contemporary and practical. Such a dialogue, with its careful attention to our own lived experience of marriage, also contributes to a larger goal of Christian maturity—that we come into the authority of our own lives.

Religious maturing is more than a question of faithful obedience to the Church's rules. Maturity demands the personalizing of this external authority; a mature Christian is someone whose instincts—about God's presence in life, about sex and friendship, about generosity and compromise—have been shaped by our Christian heritage. But these instincts are neither those of a child nor those of a robot. As Christian conviction matures it becomes personalized. Shaped by both our religious history and our individual experience, our mature instincts become trustworthy. We attain, in Erik Erikson's phrase, that independence that makes us dependable. This ideal of psychological and religious maturity is, of course, the challenge of a lifetime, but it stands as an expectable goal for the Christian adult.

Reflective Exercise

At the end of each of the following chapters we will offer a reflective exercise. In these, readers are invited to spend some time recalling their own experiences concerning an issue or topic under consideration. The goal of these exercises is self-exploration—to come to a clear and more confident awareness of what marriage means to me. This personal awareness of marriage is a special resource that each reader, whether married or not, brings to the book's ongoing conversation concerning Christian marriage now and in the future.

Several suggestions may help make these reflections more useful for you. The first concerns atmosphere. For most of us, personal reflection is difficult in the midst of the pressing activities of our normal schedule. If we are to look within, we need a quiet environment—one with fewer distractions and a less hurried pace. These experiences are likely to be more fruitful if you can turn to them at a time when you are not too tired and are not likely to be interrupted.

A second suggestion is that the exercises be shared in some way. This does not mean that they must be done in a group setting. A group discussion is often valuable but often it is not possible. Sometimes it is not even desirable. But most of us find it helpful to be able to talk about the convictions and questions that can arise in our reflection, especially in the supportive context of persons who care. This may mean that my spouse and I do the reflections together. It may mean that I do the reflection on my own and later share my comments with a friend. The goal of the sharing is twofold: to deepen my own realizations by disclosing them to another and to explore these realizations further in an atmosphere that can provide both support and responsible challenge.

The third suggestion is that the reflection be as concrete as possible. Both the reflection and the sharing that follows can be enlivened by my being able to focus on actual events and feelings and convictions. This concreteness can rescue my reflection from vague generalities. The goal of these reflective exercises is to understand and appreciate the particular experience of marriage that is my own. (And, again, whether I am married or not I do have experience of marriage.) My own experience is not all there is but it is a significant starting point for understanding marriage as it exists today.

REFLECTION: What Makes Up Marriage for Me

Take time at this early point in our consideration of marriage to look at what marriage means to you. The goal of this reflection is to assist you to become more aware of your own insights and convictions about marriage. The reflection has four movements.

What is a "good marriage"? Write down the words or phrases or sentences that express your own sense of what makes up a good marriage. Try to be as concrete as possible: include attitudes and feelings, values and behaviors.

As another way to get at some of the same information, ask yourself what signs you use to judge that a particular marriage is successful—your own or someone else's. Again, list the indications that are significant to you: the ways people act, the things people do and say.

From these two listings of elements that you see as important in marriage, select three or four items that strike you now as most significant. Spend some time with each of these items of significance, taking note of why each seems important to you.

An important next step can be the discussion of your own responses with others—your spouse, a close friend, members of a discussion group. This step can be especially valuable when it begins in an attitude of exploration rather than debate. There may, of course, be important differences that come to light in this process of sharing views. But the examination of these differences is often more productive in an atmosphere of trust than in a stance of self-defense.

Additional Resources

John Shea explores an approach to Christian spirituality similar to that discussed in this book. In *Stories of God* (Thomas More Press, 1978) he examines several different contexts in which Christians today can recognize God in their lives and begin the lifelong process of responding to this presence. For a further discussion of adult maturity which relates Christian virtue to psychological strength, see our *Christian Life Patterns: The Psychological Challenges and Religious Invitations of Adult Life* (Doubleday, 1979).

In *Living Happily Ever After: Toward a Theology of Christian Marriage* (Paulist Press, 1979) Thomas Hart offers a simple and excellent discussion of spirituality in Christian marriage. For further exploration of the dialogue between personal experience and the Christian tradition, see John Shea's *Stories of Faith* (Thomas More Press, 1980) and our *Method in Ministry: Theological Reflection and Christian Ministry* (Seabury, 1980).

2

THE MEANING OF MARRIAGE

The word "marriage" refers to many things. We can use the word to mean our own experience of the day-to-day relationship we share. The word can also mean the social institution of matrimony, which has legal definition and rights and duties that are regulated by the state and sanctioned in many religious traditions through special rites and ceremonies. Between these two senses of the word—marriage as my experience and marriage as a social institution—there are other meanings as well. Marriage is a relationship; marriage is a commitment; marriage is a lifestyle.

When we speak of marriage as a *relationship* we focus on the quality of the bond that exists between us, our mutual love. The *commitment* of marriage refers to the promises we make to do "whatever is necessary" to deepen and develop this love and, in this love, to move beyond ourselves in creativity and care. The *lifestyle* of marriage describes the patterns that we develop as we attempt to live out these promises—our choices among values and activities, the organization of our daily life, our patterns in the use of time and money and the other resources we have. These three facets of marriage are overlapping and interrelated. Each contributes richly to the complexity of our life together and to the satisfaction we experience in marriage. And, as we are becoming more aware, none of these aspects of our marriage is ever finished or static. Each is in movement, in an ongoing process of realization and development—or decline.

The Relationship of Marriage—Mutual Love

Mutual love is the heart of the process of marriage as we envision it today. This has not always been the case. In patriarchal understandings of marriage the wife is more property than partner. Vestiges of this "wife as possession" are still to be found (often embodied in laws and customs surrounding sexuality in marriage) but the movement toward mutuality continues in the way many married people choose to live and, gradually, in the larger social definitions of marriage as well.

The expectations for love in marriage today are high. The "ideal" of married love for most people includes romance, sex, friendship and devotion. Romance: We want the emotional and physical attraction that we experienced early in our relationship to continue through our married years. Sex: We want our lovemaking to be lively and mutually satisfying, enhanced by a deepening responsiveness to each other's preferences and needs. Friendship: We want to continue to like each other, to enjoy each other's company, to find in each other the sources of comfort and challenge, of solace and stimulation that we need for continuing growth. Devotion: We want to be able to "count on" one another, to give our trust in the deep conviction that it shall not be betrayed, to experience the awesome responsibility and transforming power of holding someone else's well-being as important to us as our own and to know that we, too, are held in such care.

These are not easy accomplishments. With these high expectations come equally high demands. In a relationship that is mutual, I must be ready to give these benefits as well as to receive them. And for many of us these emotional benefits are sought and expected only in marriage. We have no other so serious or so sustained an adult relationship.

Marriage did not always carry such high emotional demands. Wives and husbands did not generally expect to be one another's

chief companion or best friend. Each could be expected to
develop a range of social relationships—in the extended family,
in the neighborhood, in the workplace, in clubs and churches
and associations—that provided support and a sense of belonging to complement the marriage relationship. Today our involvement in these wider circles seems to have slipped. Economic and
geographic mobility can cut into, even cut off, ties with family
and neighborhood. The workplace is increasingly competitive;
our relationships there seem of necessity to remain superficial.
No one wants to take the risk of deeper friendship with a potential rival. And here, too, mobility plays a part in keeping these
relationships light. We know it is likely that one or both of us
may move to another job. Many associations—political parties,
civic groups, churches—seem to have lost the consensus they
formerly enjoyed. In these groupings today we are likely to experience polarization rather than a sense of belonging. Now it is
often only from my spouse and, perhaps, my children that I expect any deep or continuing emotional response. This expectation has enriched the experience of mutuality in marriage, but it
has also added to its strains. There are few of us today who
would choose a style of marriage that did not include friendship
and mutuality among its chief goals. But we have not given
much attention to pressures that are inevitable in the com-
panionate marriage or to the resources that may be required for
us to live well this style of mutual love.

Marriage brings us in touch with our incompatible hopes for
human life. It is useful to look at some of these incompatibles—
the tensions and ambiguities that are inevitable as we attempt to
live as complex a relationship as marriage. These tensions exist
not simply because I am "selfish" or my spouse is "unreasonable"
or "immature." These tensions are built into the experience of
relationship—most relationships, but especially relationships as
encompassing as marriage.

Security and adventure are both significant goals in adult life.
We seek the stability of established patterns, and yet we are attracted by the new and the unknown. Often we sense these goals
in opposition; life seems to force our choice of one over the
other. To seek adventure means to risk some of the security I

have known; to be secure means to turn away from some of life's invitations to novelty and change. Most of us learn to make these choices, but an ambivalence remains. At times, when the pull of security is strong, change may be seen as uninviting or even dangerous. A preference for stability is then easy to sustain. But at other times the appeal of change will be compelling and stability will seem a synonym for boredom and stagnation.

One of the ongoing tensions of marriage concerns this conflict between freedom and security, adventure and stability. I want to deepen the love and life we share, and I want to be able to pursue other possibilities that are open to me, unencumbered by the limits that come with my commitment to you. I need change and novelty and challenge; I need what is predictable and familiar and sure. I want to be close to you in a way that lets me share my weaknesses as well as my strengths, and I want to be strong enough to stand apart from you and from the relationship we share. Again, the presence of these incompatibles is not, of itself, cause for concern. These are normal, expectable, inevitable. But, then, neither is it surprising that the process of mediating among these needs generates considerable stress.

The commitment of marriage takes us to the heart of this ambivalence between stability and change. In marriage we say both "yes" and "no"—"yes" to each other and to the known and unknown possibilities that will be a part of our life together as it unfolds, "no" to the known and unknown possibilities that our life together will exclude. Marriage for a lifetime demands both stability (that we hold ourselves faithful to the promises we have made) and change (that we recognize the changing context in which our promises remain alive). We can anticipate that at different points in our marriage we will experience this ambivalence—sometimes celebrating the new developments in our life together, sometimes resisting these changes; sometimes grateful for the stability of our love, sometimes resenting its "sameness."

Marriage invites me to recognize these ambiguities of my own heart as I attempt to choose a style of life and love in which both to express myself and to hold myself accountable. Without

commitment and choices, I know I remain a child, but that realization seldom makes the process of choice any easier.

The Commitments of Marriage—Priority and Permanence

The commitments of marriage are the promises we make. In
many ways it is these mutual promises that transform our experience of love into marriage—an enduring relationship of mutual
care and shared life-giving. Both by our choice and by the
momentum of its own dynamics, marriage takes us beyond
where we are now. It projects us into the future. Through the
hopes we hold for our life together we condition the future—we
begin to mold and shape it. We open ourselves to possibilities,
we make demands, we place limits, we hold each other in trust.

Our commitments, of course, do not control the future. We
learn this mighty lesson as we move through adult life, invited
by the events of our days to give up one by one our adolescent
images of omnipotence. An illusory sense of the degree to which
we can control our own destinies may have once served us well,
energizing us to move beyond indecision and enter the complex
world of adult responsibility. But maturity modifies both our
sense of power and our sense of control. We are both stronger
and weaker than we had known. Our promises are fragile, but
they still have force. It is on this vulnerable strength of human
commitment that we base our hope. And it is through our commitments that we engage the future.

The commitments of marriage are the promises we make—to
ourselves, to one another, to the world beyond—to do "whatever
is necessary" so that the love that we experience may endure;
even more, that it may flourish. Our own relationship of love is,
we know, similar to that which other couples share. But it is in
many ways special, unique to who we are, peculiar to the
strengths and needs and history we have. Our commitments,
then, will reflect features in common with most marriages as
well as the demands and possibilities that are particularly our
own.

Two of the commitments that have been seen to be at the core of marriage are sexual exclusivity and permanence. The social meaning of these commitments has fluctuated across time. Stress on the importance of the woman's virginity at marriage and her sexual availability only to her husband after marriage is particularly strong in cultures where property and social status are transferred according to the male line of descent. It is important here that there be no confusion about paternity. And strict regulation of the woman's sexual experience is one way to keep the facts of paternity clear.

There are other instances where the stress on sexual exclusivity is intended to regulate the wife's behavior but not, or not to the same degree, the husband's. This double standard of sexual morality, which looks with some leniency on a married man's "fooling around" while it castigates a married woman as a wanton or an adulteress, has been tied closely with those understandings of marriage that see the wife as, in some ways, the property or possession of her husband.

In many current marriages the commitment to sexual exclusivity has expanded toward an expectation that neither spouse shall have any emotional involvement outside the marriage itself. By conscious decision or simply by circumstances, the couple or the small family unit depend exclusively upon one another for emotional sustenance. They have become an emotional island, apart. Neither wife nor husband has any other substantive adult friendship; their network of social acquaintances is shifting and somewhat superficial. Each may also feel that to need or seek support from someone other than the spouse is itself a kind of "infidelity." Sometimes this caution in exploring wider friendship is rooted in a fear of the "inevitable" sexual overtones of relationships between women and men. "Better not to start anything than to find this friendship slipping into an affair." Sometimes it responds to real insecurity or jealousy in one or both spouses. Sometimes, however, this insistent emotional exclusivity is more an expression of what couples judge to be "expected" of marriage. Emotions and needs, personal values and concerns—these are of the substance of my "private life." Family is the unit of private life in our society. It is to my family, especially to my spouse, that I retreat from the arbitrary and impersonal "public world." Increasingly, colleagues at work, people in the neighborhood, fellow citizens are all seen as part of the "public world." My relations with them are limited, objective and often hostile. There is little opportunity and less ability to share with them any meaningful part of life. It is in marriage that I expect that my subjectivity will be nourished. Here, and possibly here alone, "who I am" is more important than "what I can do." As the polarization of the subjective and the objective worlds, the realms of the private and the public, increases, so do the pressures for emotional exclusivity in marriage.

Many judge that the pressures of the emotionally exclusive marriage ultimately work against its development and permanence. Permanence is the second of the commitments that have generally described marriage. Here, too, the promise has been experienced differently at different times. Seldom has this expectation been absolute. Cultures and legal systems, while stressing the significance of permanence to the interpersonal experience and the legal contract of marriage, have also stipulated a variety of circumstances under which this commitment can be set aside. Sometimes childlessness was justification, frequently adultery has been sufficient cause. Religious conversion, desertion, physical abuse, psychological immaturity, emotional illness—each has been seen as of sufficient weight to justify the dissolution of marriage, whether through annulment or divorce.

The commitment of permanence has also had different psychological meaning. As recently as a century ago "marriage for a lifetime" often did not last very long. The woman's death in childbirth ended many marriages. An average life expectancy of some fifty years meant that many marriages ended in mid-life. In 1870, for example, a married woman could expect that her husband would die before her youngest child would leave home. Today, increasingly, couples can anticipate some twenty or more years together, alone, after the children have left the family household and are on their own. Movement into this time of "post-parental intimacy" is hard on some marriages. Couples may be surprised to find that, without their shared concern for parenting, they have little left of mutuality. They face the challenge of developing anew a life in common, one that is adequate to the reality of each partner now and to the possibilities that are present in their relationship. Other couples have been aware of a deteriorating relationship and yet have chosen to remain together through the years of their most active family responsibilities. These past, they judge there is no further bond to hold them together.

The strains on permanence can be experienced earlier in marriage as well. The accelerated pace of social change today is reflected in the experience of personal change. As we approach marriage we judge—to some degree correctly, to some degree in error—that we "fit" together, that we shall be able to offer each other the resources of love and support and challenge that will enable us to find and to give life. And then we change, sometimes each of us and in ways that enrich our mutual commitment. Sometimes, though, there is not such synchrony. One of us changes in ways that are threatening or seem unfair to the other. Each of us develops—perhaps gradually, perhaps suddenly—in directions that lead us apart and leave us without a clear sense of how we can be together now. Are there ways we might stay better in touch over the course of change so that we are not so taken by surprise? Or must the loss of our relationship be the price we pay for growth?

There are those who suggest that the prevalence of divorce among us today has dissolved our expectations of permanence in marriage. Young people approaching marriage, it seems, do not expect it to last. And, so the argument goes, married people today consider divorce a ready option, one which they anticipate that they, too, will use. There are, obviously, people of whom this characterization is true. But the effect of the increasing incidence of divorce on the expectations of permanence in marriage is more complex than these attitudes suggest. Permanence is no longer a guarantee of marriage even when it is promised. This awareness permeates our consciousness today. This may lead us to question whether, or under what circumstances, permanence is possible. But it seldom leads us, whether we are beginning a relationship of marriage or ending one, to judge that perma-

nence is not to be preferred. Permanence is not to be preferred
to everything, so that under no circumstances will I consider the
end of my own marriage. But permanence is to be preferred as
the goal and intention of our life together. And it is to be preferred, if it is in any way possible, to the pain of divorce.

Most people want marriage to last. It is in the hope of an enduring relationship that we take the emotional and the practical,
legal steps that lead us into marriage. Our standards are high for
what constitutes the kind of relationship that we want to endure,
and sometimes these criteria are not always clear or compatible.
(We may want to be the central figure in each other's life and
also want each to be open to continuing growth in new relationships. We may want to start our family now and yet to have
each of us pursue the development of our own career without
serious interruption.) Each of our goals for marriage, taken
alone, may be worthy. But taken together they may place considerable strain on our resourcefulness. While no one of our
goals may be incompatible with our marriage flourishing over a
lifetime, the combination of goals and priorities that we establish may carry heavy costs. We may find, in living out these patterns that define our marriage, that the strain is taxing. This realization invites us to reconsider—to reexamine what it is we want
together, to reassess the strengths and needs we bring to the
relationship, to recommit ourselves to its development and continuation.

We may find, especially if it is through a period of pain or
deprivation that we come to a sense of the costs of sustaining
this relationship, that the price is too high. Our own goals are no
longer fulfilled, our resources are spent, our trust is broken. The
movement through legal divorce will seem the only reasonable
option to terminate a relationship that has already died.

But for many people the prevalence of divorce set against
their own hope of an enduring relationship in marriage leads not
to taking marriage lightly but to approaching it with greater
seriousness, even caution. The expectation of permanence, sometimes experienced as an all too fragile hope, remains. The concern becomes how we shall safeguard and make robust this fragile conviction of our love.

Each marriage today must come to terms with these two dimensions of commitment: our expectations of exclusivity (What is the meaning of the priority in which we hold each other in love? How is this priority expressed?) and our expectations of permanence (What is the significance of our hope that our love shall flourish for our lifetime? How does this hope influence our lives now?).

The Lifestyle of Marriage

Marriage is love, marriage is commitment, marriage is also a lifestyle—not one lifestyle experienced universally but the many particular lifestyles through which married couples express their love and live out the promises that hold them in mutual care. The lifestyle of marriage is the design or pattern of our life together that emerges in the choices we make. Many people do not experience the patterns of their daily life as open to personal choice. By the time of marriage, and from long before, factors of poverty or class or personality have narrowed the range of those parts of my life over which I have much say. I live out life, but I do not see myself as influencing its design in many important ways. Things happen to me, to my marriage, to my family—and I make the best of them. But I have little conviction that I can initiate changes or take responsibility on my own.

But for most Americans today there is a heightened consciousness of choice. We are aware that there are different ways in which the possibilities of life and of marriage may be lived out. And while our choices are always limited, we are aware that we not only can but must choose among these options for ourselves. The lifestyle of our marriage thus results from both our choices and our circumstances.

The choices that construct the lifestyle of our marriage include the decisions we make about the practical details of living —the routine of our daily activities, how we allocate the recurrent tasks of family and household care. But more basic decisions are involved—the values we hold important, the goals we

have for our life together, the ways we choose to invest ourselves in the world.

At the heart of our decision about lifestyle is the question:
What is our marriage for? Are we married only for ourselves?
Does our life together exist chiefly as a place of personal security
and a source of mutual satisfaction? Or is our marriage also
about more than just the two of us? Is it a way for us to engage
ourselves—together—in a world that is bigger than ourselves?

In previous decades the expectable presence of children in
marriage answered this question in part. One of the things our
marriage is for is our children. A child is so concrete an expression of the love that exists between us and so insistent an invitation that this love now go beyond itself in care. In parenting we
experience the scope of our love widening to include our children. Often this broadening of concern continues, expanding to
include more of the world and even the future, in which "our
children's children" shall have to find their own way. Married
people have always been generously engaged in the world in
ways other than as parents, as well. But the central connection
between being married and having children has been so clear
and so prevalent for centuries that it has been a defining characteristic of the lifestyle of marriage.

Today there is more choice involved in the link between marriage and parenthood. Couples come to the decision to have a
child with more consideration given to how many children there
shall be in the family, how the births of these children shall be
spaced, when in the marriage the commitments of family life
shall begin. Some couples who have been unable to have children of their own seek other ways to expand their life together
as a family—through adoption or foster care or through the assistance of recent developments in the biological sciences and
medical practice. Other couples decide not to have a family and,
instead, to express their love beyond themselves in other forms
of creativity and care.

A comparable challenge accompanies each of these options—
to develop a way of being together in marriage that takes
seriously the demands of mutuality in our own relationship as it
takes seriously the challenge that we look beyond ourselves in

genuine contribution and care. Thus a central choice in marriage concerns our progeny—how shall we give and nurture life beyond ourselves: in our own children? in our friendships and other relationships? in our creative work? in our generous concern for the world? And the decisions that we come to here do much to determine the design of our daily life together.

Beyond this central choice concerning the focus of our creative love, there are other decisions of lifestyle. How shall we use the resources we possess? How, especially, do we allocate our money and our time? Here, again, the questions can be stated simply: What is our money for? What has priority in our time? We can respond to these questions at the practical level, offering the balance sheet of the family budget and our calendar of weekly events. But as an issue in lifestyle the question is more to the core: How are our own deepest values expressed or obscured in how we spend our money and our time?

Most American families today experience both money and time as scarce. There is not enough of either to go around. There seem to be always more possibilities, more demands for each than we feel we can meet. We have little "discretionary" income and even less "free" time. But among the demands that seem both genuine and inevitable there are others that seem to squander us uselessly, leaving us no time to be together or to be at peace and leaving us few resources to use for any purpose beyond ourselves. This sense of overextension characterizes the lifestyle of many marriages. Its prevalence invites us to reflect on our own patterns of money and time, not looking to praise or blame but trying to come to a better sense of the motives and pressures that move us and, in that way, define our lives. How much does our use of money and time revolve around "us," somewhat narrowly conceived—as a couple or a family over against "others"? What are the ways in which our decisions about time and money are more reflective of what our society expects of us than of the values and activities and possessions that make sense to us? Couples and families will differ in their responses to these questions, as they will differ on other issues of value and lifestyle. But the reflective process can lead to a greater congruence between the goals we have for our life together in marriage and the ways that this life is lived on a day-to-day basis.

Establishing our lifestyle in marriage is not done once and for all, but is itself an ongoing process. The lifestyle of our marriage must respond to the movements of development and change in each of us, in our relationship and in our responsibilities.

Marriage for a lifetime, then, is constituted by the interaction of our relationship, our commitments and our lifestyle. Our mutual love is at the core of our marriage. But in marriage we experience our relationship as more than just our love here and now. Marriage is focused by the promises to which we hold ourselves. It is the commitments that we made to one another that ground our love and give it duration. These commitments give us courage to undertake the risks of creative and procreative activity together. It is these commitments that are expressed in the choices and behavior and attitudes that make up the patterns of our lifestyle. And it is, in turn, an important goal of the commitments of our marriage and the lifestyle to which these commitments give shape, to sustain and deepen and mature the relationship of love between us.

It is important to note, as we begin our consideration of marriage for a lifetime, that the relationship and commitment and lifestyle of marriage do not exist in a vacuum. For each of us our experience of marriage is influenced by legal and historical and cultural understandings of what marriage is. In the next chapter we shall examine more closely the ways in which these social understandings of marriage are themselves undergoing change.

Reflective Exercise

These sentence stems may help you to explore your own awareness of the relationship, the commitments and the lifestyle that are marriage today. Complete the sentence begun by each of these phrases. There is no need to force an answer, just respond with what comes to mind at the time. For some phrases you may have several responses; others may call up little for you right now.

The relationship of marriage . . .

For me, mutual love . . .

Romance is a part of marriage . . .

The commitments of married people . . .

Today permanence in marriage . . .

The lifestyle of married people today . . .

Children bring to marriage . . .

Marriage for a lifetime is . . .

After you have completed the sentences, read through your whole list a couple of times to see if there is a dominant theme or tone to your responses.

Additional Resources

Much of the most useful discussion of marriage and family life today takes place in an interdisciplinary context. In *The Family in Crisis or in Transition* (Seabury, 1979) Andrew Greeley has drawn together a series of articles exploring the current reality of family life from both sociological and theological perspectives. In observance of the International Year of the Child in 1979 the American Psychological Association commissioned a special issue of its journal, *American Psychologist*, devoted to "Psychology and Children: Current Research and Practice." The essays here are a rich introduction to the best resources available across the spectrum of psychology, social psychology, family therapy and social intervention. In a more explicitly pastoral vein, the Fall 1979 issue of *Chicago Studies* brings together theologians, ministers, psychologists and social scientists in a series of essays on "Ministry to Marriage." Three of these essays have been reprinted as *Marriage* and are available from *Chicago Studies*.

3

MARRIAGE IN TRANSITION

There is an image of marriage with which most of us are familiar; husband and wife with several young children living in an apartment or home of their own. The husband's principal time commitment is to his job. Through this work he fulfills his primary responsibility as financial provider for his wife and children. The demands of the job can be considerable and he may experience their negative effects. Physical strain, the emotional stress of competition in the workplace, travel and overtime that keep him away from home and limit his availability to his wife and children, little time to pursue other interests in his life— these are seen as necessary sacrifices to his larger commitment to his family: to ensure their economic security and financial advancement. It is to his home and family that the husband returns for the solace and support that enable him to remain responsible to the demands of steady work and the challenges of career advancement. There are joys and consolations that come to him within his family and, as well, pride when he senses that his responsibilities as husband and provider have been well met. But he has little time for himself.

The care of the home and family is entrusted to the wife. The physical and emotional well-being of her husband and children are her primary concern. She discharges this multi-faceted responsibility through her practical daily activities of child care, meal preparation, cleaning, laundry, shopping and other errands that constitute the tasks of housekeeping and homemaking. Her husband and children may assist her in one or more of these areas, but the overseeing, planning and—most often—the execution of these chores remain largely hers. Beyond these practical tasks she sees herself (and is seen by others, as well) as primarily responsible for the emotional needs of her husband and children. It is her job to "be there" for them. To her husband she is to be lover, comforter, companion, helpmate. To her children she is nurturer, teacher, disciplinarian, entertainer. There are joys and consolations that come to her within her family and, as well, pride when she senses that her responsibilities as wife and mother have been well met. But she has little time for herself.

This image of the nuclear family and the distinct responsibilities of wife and husband has been powerful in shaping our understanding of marriage over the recent past. For some of us, this describes the marriage of our parents, the marriage of which —after our own—we have the most immediate experience. For some of us, it describes our own marriage, or how it once was, or how we or others think it ought to be. For several decades this image of marriage has functioned as a cultural norm, expressing both our experience of marriage (what we actually see going on) and our expectations (the way we think things ought to be).

This image of marriage endures today. It expresses one of the ways in which married people choose to live their lives and to express their love. It is a pattern reinforced by many of the expectations each of us carries within concerning what it is to be a woman or a man, to be a husband or a wife, to be a mother or a father. It is an image safeguarded in much of our legal system and sanctioned by many official statements of the churches. And it is an image in serious trouble.

This conventional image is in trouble, first, because it no longer serves as well as it once did to describe the actual experience of marriage. It does not say what is really happening. Increasingly, the distinction between the man's work in marriage (employment in the larger social world) and the woman's (care for family and household in the private sphere) does not hold. In more and more marriages, partners work out new arrangements for sharing the tasks of work and family. Sometimes this merging of roles that were once considered distinct happens by necessity. The husband becomes ill or cannot find work; the family needs more money, so the wife takes a job to supplement her husband's income; death of the spouse or divorce forces the single parent to take on a full range of both work and family responsibilities. But often this sharing of roles happens by preference. Couples approaching marriage and couples already married determine that for them the conventional division of labor does not work. It does not fit their own talents and interests; it does not describe the way they choose to be with each other. These couples devise new ways to be together, new patterns for sharing responsibilities that are more congruent with their own relationship.

Even in many marriages where there is a division of man's role and woman's role along conventional lines (the woman engaged full-time at home in the responsibilities of child rearing and homemaking; her husband's primary commitment to his job as sole breadwinner for the family) there is an accompanying realization that this pattern will not continue unchanged through all their married life. Rather it describes how the couple is together during one significant phase of their marriage—the time of active child rearing. The years during which parents are involved in the day-to-day responsibilities of raising children at home (though while we are in the midst of them they may seem to go on forever) are, in fact, only a portion of the lifetime the couple can expect to share. Before the first child is born and as the children grow into increasing independence through the school years and then leave home, couples today develop ways of being together and of involving themselves beyond the home that deviate from the conventional expectations regarding woman's role and man's role in marriage. A married woman today often continues her job until well into her first pregnancy. Several years later, when her youngest child enters school, she takes on a part-time job or a volunteer commitment that is flexible enough for her to meet what she judges to be her prior commitment to be home when the children return from school. As the children grow older she moves toward a full-time job or community involvement that carries significant responsibility on its own. In this instance, her commitment (and that of her husband) to the conventional roles within the family may be unshaken, but these roles are seen as describing not all of married life but simply the best way to meet the responsibilities of parenthood. (And, as we shall see again in Chapters 16 and 17, not all married people agree that these conventional roles are the best way to meet their responsibilities as parents.)

The conventional image of marriage is in further trouble. If it does not describe the actual *experience* of marriage for many people, it also fails to express their hopes and *expectations*. Persons approaching marriage today as well as those currently married have decided, in large numbers, that they do not want to be married "that way." Most people today want in their marriages both something more and something less than what is expressed in the standard norm. We want more choice in how the goals and roles of marriage shall exist between us, more flexibility to modify these patterns to fit us at different points in our lives and in our developing marriage relationship. We want less rigidity in the social expectations of marriage that have traditionally set off men from women, work from family, public from private, and that isolate the family within itself with little realistic possibility of support from, or contribution to, the larger world.

Many of those who are dissatisfied with the established pattern of marriage do not see themselves as revolutionaries. They are not against conventional marriage for some theoretical reason or because they espouse some ideological conviction. It is simply that the pattern no longer serves as well as it once did. It is no longer the experience of most married people over most of their lives. It is no longer the exclusive ideal, expressing what married people judge to be best for their own marriages.

The Changing Experience of Marriage

Marriage is a committed life together of love for one another and creative involvement in the world that goes beyond the self. Many different elements have been seen as part of this life—

romance, genital love, sexual exclusivity, monogamy, parent-hood, permanence, generosity, self-sacrifice, devotion, companionship, mutual affection, friendship. Not all these elements are present in every definition, still less in every marriage. Some are recent expectations—romantic love, friendship, real mutuality between spouses. For others of these elements the connections with marriage are neither automatic nor assured. Some marriages do, in fact, end in divorce. Permanence is not always guaranteed, in some cases it is not even expected. A number of people in America today do not consider marriage to be the sole context for sexual sharing or even for parenting. Some marriages do not include children, by circumstances or—increasingly—by choice. Monogamy prevails among us, but the necessity of sexual exclusivity is often questioned in theory or in practice.

A marriage that did not involve any of these elements would, to most of us, appear to be empty—at best, a legal fiction. But we probably all know marriages that exist, and even flourish, with only a few of these elements in evidence. And in the marriages we do know we are likely to see these factors in many different and sometimes even unusual combinations.

We are aware, then, that marriage is diverse. And beyond that, we are aware that marriage is changing. Some of the changes have become so commonplace that they no longer strike most of us as unusual. Increasingly, both spouses are employed outside the home during a significant part or most of their marriage. Sometimes it is economic necessity that draws the wife into the workplace, but often it is her decision to be involved in significant work beyond as well as within the family. Changes are happening within the home as well, with both women and men seeking more flexible ways to be responsible and available as parents. Couples are aware of more choices as parents: whether to have a child, how many children, how soon, how to share the tasks of raising a family.

These changes in our experience of how marriage is lived today go against many recent cultural norms of what it means to be married. Norms are the standards of behavior that are shared within a society. These standards express a culture's preferences among the various options that are open to human life. Norms guide our activity by influencing our choices, inclining us to see one way of doing things as acceptable and other ways as deviant or deficient. These shared and sanctioned options develop strong emotional force. Through laws and social pressure we hold ourselves and others accountable to these norms; through education and example we pass on to our children's generation these shared expectations of how life should be lived.

Every culture has norms about marriage, sanctioned preferences among the various options open to women and men in regard to sexuality, parenthood, family life, social participation. The *content* of the norms concerning marriage, we now know, has been different in different cultures and at different times in history—even recent history. Humankind has made many different choices in regard to who shall marry and what it means for them to be together. But in each culture its own norms point out and protect the patterns that have prevailed among its people thus far. At their best these norms distill from the broad historical experience of a people their best wisdom about what works in life. They express the deepest values of the culture. In times of relative stability such norms serve well as guides for present behavior and as standards to be used in educating the next generation for its own future. In times of cultural transition, however, the value of past norms is called into question. To what extent is the wisdom of the past adequate to our present and to our children's future? This is the question that challenges our normative understandings of marriage today.

Both advocates and critics of the conventional image of marriage agree that the experience of marriage today does not fit the established norms. That, the advocates would argue, is precisely the trouble. If married people would bring their experience of marriage more in line with these normative expectations, with what marriage *should be*, many of the contemporary problems regarding marriage would be resolved. Most of those who support the conventional understanding of marriage recognize many factors in contemporary life that make it difficult for couples to shape their marriage to this norm. It is not just personal selfishness or "bad will" that is at fault. Economic insecurity plays a part, especially in a cultural climate of consumerism.

These pressures are compounded by faulty understandings of sexuality and overstress on individual freedom to the detriment of responsible commitment. Often the influence of the women's movement is singled out for special blame.

For critics of the conventional norms this analysis does not go far enough. Factors of consumerism and pornography and personal immaturity do affect the experience of marriage today and, clearly, for the worse. But these influences, of themselves, do not explain why the former ideal of marriage has lost so much of its power. There are larger historical factors that are more to the point.

Marriage in Historical View

There is a greater awareness today of the gradual development and ongoing change of the norms regarding marriage. Across time, even the facts of marriage have changed. In contemporary experience, virtually all adults marry. This has not always been the case. There is historical evidence that in Europe over many centuries marriage occurred relatively late in adult life and a significant proportion of the adult population never married.

Since the nineteenth century, however, marriage has become more and more prevalent. In industrialized societies, a larger proportion of the adult population is married today than almost ever before.

With a heightened sense of history we realize that the forms of marriage have undergone many variations as well. For example, many criteria have been used to determine who shall marry whom: political considerations, issues of dynastic purity, questions of property, the decision of parents, the advice of matchmakers. It is not until quite recently on the historian's scale of time that marriage has become principally a matter of personal choice. Over many centuries marriage was primarily a social and economic contract between families. As a firm social institution, marriage was contracted for purposes of continuity rather than romance. It had a dual function—to contribute to the group's survival through lineage (children) and to the group's stability through inheritance (the orderly transfer of property). Affection and personal love between the individuals who married might be an outgrowth of marriage but these were certainly not prerequisites. In the West it was not until the late Middle Ages that romantic love became an important (though even then not primary) consideration in marriage. Not until this century has self-selection of one's marriage partner become the dominant pattern.

What many people speak of today as "traditional" marriage—the separate household consisting of husband-provider and wife-homemaker living with only their young and adolescent children —has not long been on the scene. It dates from the social and political changes epitomized in the industrial revolution of the late 1700s. The emerging economic system of mass production drew workers out of the family-based livelihoods, such as farming and skilled crafts, into factories. Labor laws and other social reforms gradually succeeded in limiting the factory work force to men, since the health and moral welfare of women (and children) were judged to be in jeopardy under the hazardous conditions that often prevailed. Thus economic involvement in the larger social world came to be seen as man's work and the care for the emotional and practical necessities of daily life, especially in the home, as that of woman. These factors in broader social history, then, contributed to the traditional or, more precisely, the conventional image of marriage and the family. (These social factors, by themselves, do not fully explain the images of women and men dominant today. The ambiguous origins of the divisions between "man's work" and "woman's work" go much deeper into history and psyche.)

This conventional image of marriage was dramatically reinforced in the United States during the years just after World War II. Analysts speak of the period between 1947 and 1957 as the "decade of marital togetherness." The experience of marriage and family life became more central goals of Americans during these few years than ever before or since. The country had survived a depression and a major war. Each of these events, for different reasons, had had a negative effect on marriage and family. Tight money during the 1930s and military conscription in the 1940s led many people to delay marriage. The birth rate fell. The immediate postwar years changed all this. The men were home for good. It was now time to start the long-overdue projects of normal life—taking up a job, getting married, establishing our own home, raising a family. Families grew larger than they had been, not only during the lean years of the depression and the war, but larger than they had been for several generations. The economic affluence of these years enabled couples to support these large families on a single (male) paycheck. More and more women became full-time homemakers. This pattern prevailed throughout most of the 1950s. It thus describes the marriage pattern that is most familiar to us from our immediate past, as individuals and as a society. It is, however, a pattern that has had a relatively brief period of dominance. And today this conventional image of marriage—the nuclear family and its attendant clear and distinct roles for woman and man—is itself in transition.

The Possibilities for Marriage Today

An awareness of this history of marriage can be comforting. Our sense that the reality of marriage is undergoing dramatic change in our time need not alarm us, since the images of marriage and the forms of family life have been in movement from the beginning. But in spite of this assurance many of us are alarmed or at least uneasy over the shifts in marriage today. As the power of the conventional image to help us understand our own marriage diminishes, we are aware that there is nothing of comparable clarity and consensus yet to replace it. We are surer of what we are leaving behind than of what lies ahead. And for most of us we leave the conventional patterns behind with real ambivalence. We have known much there that has been attractive as well as much that is now no longer adequate.

Thus marriage has become a contemporary problematic. Concerning almost every element of marriage today there is more controversy than agreement. Aspects of marriage once seen as determined—the husband's role as economic provider, the wife's role as homemaker, the experience of parenting, the emotional self-sufficiency of the family unit—are now seen as options, as "one way of doing it." There is almost no part of marriage that has not become to some degree a matter of choice.

This new awareness of change and choice leads some couples to approach marriage cautiously. The love they experience between them is rich, holding promise of growth into a strong relationship that can give life to them and beyond. But they have seen many marriages fail—either fail to last, or fail to develop, or fail to give life. And these failures, they know, can occur even in "good" marriages. More and more it does not seem to be on the tragic elements of life that marriage founders; often there is not alcoholism or violence or illness to blame. Rather the relationship just seems to have deteriorated over time. When it does come, divorce may be experienced as a relief, even as the only realistic option available, but it nevertheless is almost universally experienced as painful. The prevalence of divorce has decreased the social stigma attached to it, but it has done little to decrease the sense of failure. This consciousness of divorce can have various effects. For some it results in a reluctance to marry at all. "If it doesn't work for so many people, I'd be foolish to think it could work for me." It can lead to a sense that divorce is inevitable. "We'll be together as long as our marriage works for us, but when it doesn't work any longer we'll get a divorce." With today's awareness of divorce, however, some people are becoming more circumspect as they approach marriage and more deeply committed to the processes and resources that they hope may strengthen their love.

So while this is a problematic time for marriage it is also a time of great possibility. Marriage is the preferred lifestyle of most people and, in spite of its well-acknowledged shortcomings, it continues to be so. Most Americans live in households created by marriage; most of those whose marriages have ended in divorce look forward to and do remarry. Almost all young people indicate that they intend to marry.

Yet there are other movements as well. Aware of the controversy surrounding the norms of marriage and the pain and confusion that most often accompany divorce, couples are exploring with greater care the sometimes fragile but rewarding structures of committed life together. While marriage remains most people's choice there are indications that the choice is less automatic. The decision to marry has become more complex as more elements of marriage are seen to be open to variation. There is growing realization that marriage itself is a choice, not simply whom to marry but whether to marry. The age at marriage is being delayed among some groups. Some couples live together before formal marriage in an attempt to test their relationship. The decision to remain single, while not commonplace, has become more acceptable.

Today a couple must choose, among plural options and even contrary evidence, the images and hopes that shall define their own marriage. The demand that we choose requires us to be more thoughtful about what it means *for us* to be married. The range of alternatives invites us to deeper self-knowledge and a greater awareness of each other, in order that our choice may reflect who we are and express who we wish to become together. The fact of choice can deepen our experience of responsibility and personal agency. The content of our choice will say something important to us about the shape of our future.

Faced with this choice, some couples find earlier definitions of marriage the most satisfying. The pattern of married life they develop corresponds closely to that of their parents' generation. But for many this earlier pattern no longer serves. The image of marriage that it supports is judged to be inadequate, misleading, even harmful. For them this earlier model seems to obscure rather than to manifest the important values of marriage. The norms that surround it no longer safeguard an enduring relationship of mutual and generative love; they stand instead as barriers to its development.

The Experience of Transition

For many of us living marriage today, the audacious hope for a lifetime together requires new images and new norms. Yet the

shape of these new images and norms is still less than clear. We
are keenly aware of being caught in the transition in marriage,
even mired in it. Sometimes the realization of being "in transition" seems to strike the already-married even harder than it
does those who are only now approaching marriage. Those
approaching marriage seem to have a clean slate. They can plan
and decide together now, as they begin their lives together, and
thus start off with a commitment to exploration, evaluation and
ongoing change as they attempt to devise forms of marriage and
family more compatible with their own hopes and needs. The
already-married, on the other hand, have to make their changes
in "midstream." After a common history of doing things in one
pattern they find themselves wanting to, or having to, change.
Often the need for change will be perceived by one of the partners before the other, or the partners will differ in their sense of
what needs to change or in what way. This situation can make
the experience of transition in an already established relationship even more difficult.

But all the advantages are clearly not on the side of the not-
yet-married. Each situation, in fact each couple, will have
different strengths and limitations to bring to this experience of
transition. Many currently married couples bring the depth of
their ongoing commitment to one another, their longstanding
and tested love, and a resiliency of personal maturity and flexibility that is not available to a younger couple at an earlier
stage in their relationship.

The transition is alternately exciting and enervating for everyone. And it is an experience that will be shared by the already-
married and those approaching marriage over the next decades.
By historical circumstance, we will experience marriage during a
time when its forms, its norms, its goals and its structures will be
changing. Some of these changes will be open to our choice and
personal action. Other elements in the transition will seem much
more alien, as though they are happening to us beyond our
choice and even against our will. But the experience of transition will be there.

This period of cultural and personal transition does not call for a repudiation of all that previous decades have known of married life. There are many problematic elements in the conventional marriage and we will consider some of these more fully at later points in the book. But there are also, and obviously, values in the conventional image as well. A social pattern does not become sufficiently widespread to be considered "conventional" if it has nothing to offer the individual or the group.

In the chapters which follow we will explore more fully the contemporary experience of marriage in this time of transition, alert to the diversity that exists in the ways that married people today express their needs and their hopes for a committed life together of mutual love and generative care.

Reflective Exercise

This chapter opens in a description of what we have called the conventional pattern of marriage. To what degree does this description fit the marriages you know best?

Recall for yourself several marriages that you know well— your own or your parents' or those of friends or colleagues or family members. Spend some time letting your memories of these various relationships become clear. Then consider one of these at a time.

How closely does the image of the conventional marriage, as described in this chapter, fit *this* marriage? Where are there differences? How significant are these? What factors seem to be most involved in these differences—personal choices, external circumstances, other forces?

Then turn to the other marriages that you know well. Examine each in relation to the conventional marriage patterns.

After this consideration of several marriages in your own experience, look back over what you have found. How similar, how different, are the marriages that you know best? Do you have a sense of what accounts for these similarities, these differences? How prevalent in these marriages are the conventional patterns? In what areas do they most diverge from the conventional image?

Additional Resources

For those interested in exploring further the changing shape of marriage and family life, there are valuable sources available. A classic of the recent social histories of family life is Philippe Ariès' *Centuries of Childhood* (Vintage Books, 1962). Ariès linked the evolution of the modern understanding of the family to the gradual emergence of childhood as a distinct phase of life.

A dozen years later historian Edward Shorter turned to this theme in *The Making of the Modern Family* (Basic Books, 1975). He understands the movement from the traditional to the modern family to be the result of the growing importance of emotional ties in the relationship between spouses as well as that between parent and child. This "surge of sentiment" marks a change in priorities. As the family becomes less important as a productive and reproductive unit it gains significance as a principal source of affection and emotional support.

This tradition of historical analysis continues in a volume edited by Virginia Tufte and Barbara Myerhoff, *Changing Images of the Family* (Yale University Press, 1979). This compilation of the current work of scholars in several disciplines serves as a good sourcebook. It gives the reader a sense of how much interest there is today in the analysis of changing forms of marriage and family life. It also makes it clear how far these serious students are from consensus concerning marriage's past and its future. In *The Politics of Domesticity* (Wesleyan University Press, 1981) Barbara Leslie Epstein traces the emergence of a popular consciousness among women in the nineteenth century of their special moral role in marriage and family life.

Marriage has been a subject of inquiry for sociologists as well as historians. Jesse Bernard, herself a pioneer in the analysis of marriage and family life, provides a summary of the most significant findings of marriage research through the early 1970s in *The Future of Marriage* (World Books, 1972). It is here that she advances the provocative image of "his and hers" marriage, the structural differences that exist between marriage as experienced by men and marriage as experienced by women.

Carl Degler continues this examination of the ways in which marriage and family have been experienced by women. In *At Odds* (Oxford University Press, 1980) he traces the interaction between the movement for women's emancipation and the emergence of the modern American family, from the time of the American Revolution through the revitalization of the women's movement in the 1970s.

Three recent discussions of the American family that include social commentary along with social analysis are Mary Jo Bane's *Here to Stay: American Families in the Twentieth Century* (Basic Books, 1976), Kenneth Keniston's *All Our Children: The American Family Under Pressure* (Harcourt Brace Jovanovich, 1977) and Christopher Lasch's *Haven in a Heartless World: The Family Besieged* (Basic Books, 1977).

4

CHRISTIAN SEX AND MARRIAGE—
ORIGINS AND IMAGES

Most of us carry our religious heritage as a rich and dense storehouse of values and memories. Powerful hopes and lingering guilts abide there together. Images abound: God as a loving parent, God as an unforgiving judge; our bodies as temples of the Holy Spirit, our bodies as shameful and inherently sinful. Christian maturing in sexuality and in marriage depends on our attending to the full range of values, convictions and images we have inherited from our religious past.

The Christian tradition holds an especially rich set of images and values about sexuality and marriage. Just as marriage is about much more than sexuality, so our reflection on Christian marriage will encompass more than what our tradition has said about sex. But we will begin this reflection in a consideration of the profound and enduring ambivalence toward sexuality to which we Christians are heir. We will then examine marriage as a religious metaphor and review some of the uses of this metaphor in our religious heritage. Finally we will focus on another crucial aspect of marriage—the relationship of woman and man and the different ways this relationship has been understood in Christian history.

The Christian Ambivalence Toward Sexuality

An intriguing parallel exists between the ambiguity about sexuality in the Judeo-Christian Scriptures and in our own lived experience. Most of us are both excited and confused by our bodies and the desires and fears that live here. Many of our best moments in life—and our worst—are touched and colored by our sexuality. Our creativity finds its release and expression in sexuality, as does our destructiveness. Genital arousal turns us outward in love and care; it can also turn us inward in self-absorption.

If we are perplexed by this confusing ambiguity that surrounds our own sexual lives, we find a similar ambiguity in the book of Genesis. Having created sexual, human persons and all other things, God judges that "it is good!" Everything in life, as created by a loving God, is good and holy. The mythic picture of a naked couple enjoying each other can be, even for sophisticated modern readers, more than a fairy tale. It still stands as a promise and a hope—a hope realized in part in those extraordinary moments of uncovering ourselves to one another. In such moments, however rare, we find a more than genital pleasure in the discovery of the goodness of life.

But in this very story of innocent sexual sharing by this first couple, another view of sexuality insinuates itself. The failure of this couple—some terrible, original mistake that seems necessary to account for the deep and continuous ways we fail ourselves and each other—appears to be connected in some manner with sexuality. Though the book of Genesis describes this original sin as disobedience, the woman's involvement with a serpent (and its sexual suggestiveness) hints of sexual misconduct. (In a story from patriarchal times it is not surprising that the woman initiates this sinning, but that it takes man's complicity in this choice to raise it to a world-changing event.) After their sin, the couple's nakedness is suddenly a source of shame. The punishment following on their sin seems to take special force in their sexual lives: they (and we) become prey to unpredictable and sometimes uncontrollable genital urges; the fruit of sexual involvement, children, are now to be born in pain and anguish.

This confusing nexus between an apparently non-sexual sin and our sexual natures was reinforced by St. Augustine in the fourth and fifth centuries of Christianity. Impressed both by the pervasiveness of sexual sin and by the universal sinfulness of humanity, Augustine judged that original sin—that enduring and effective predisposition to failure—must be transmitted in sexual intercourse. This connection explained the universal inheritance of human sinfulness; it also, unfortunately, rooted our sinfulness in our sexuality. From this view it would be a very short step to the interpretation of sexuality as a necessary evil. It should be emphasized that neither Augustine nor the Christian Church (at least not in its orthodox teaching) took that step, though their resistance to it was not always vigorous.

Nor was this connection between our sinfulness and our sexuality merely a belief of early Christianity. In the 1930 encyclical of Pope Pius XI on Christian marriage, a teaching letter which would enjoy enormous influence in Catholic pastoral practice, we read: "The very natural process of generating life has become the way of death by which original sin is passed on to posterity . . ." (※14, p. 81). Such a near equation of sinfulness and sexuality has for many Christians made sexuality a suspect and even unholy part of life.

This ambivalence toward sexuality in our religious history can also be discovered in the New Testament. A central ambiguity about the meaning and value of human sexuality appears in the accounts of the Incarnation itself. God is made flesh, becomes a bodily, sexual and genital person like us. In this event our own bodies are blessed and reaffirmed in their holiness. The Incarnation is good news for the flesh. Yet this enfleshing of God's son is portrayed in Matthew and Luke as occurring asexually. The infancy narratives in these two gospel accounts describe an asexual conception and birth of Jesus Christ. God became human but not in a sexual or genital fashion. For both Matthew and Luke, Mary's virginity stands as a sign of the sacredness of Jesus' birth. Yet it has also signaled to many Christians (the unavoidable ambiguity of symbols!) a necessary distance between holiness and human genital behavior. For many Christians today this is an Incarnation compromised.

It is important to recall that the first generations of Christians lived in a milieu that urged two very different views of sexuality. In places like Corinth (as we learn from Paul) sexual promiscuity was rampant; for many in the Near East at that time sexual activity held no special place in life, possessed no potential holiness to be guarded by care and fidelity in expression. At the same time in Israel and elsewhere a Gnostic bias against the human body and sexuality was urged: the human person was understood as a soul imprisoned in a material, sexual body. Salvation meant escape from this body and its demands. Gnosticism in its Manichaean form had a profound influence on Augustine; in its Docetic form it argued for a Christ who only *appeared* to be an embodied, sexual person. The first generations of Christians struggled against both extremes. For them, sexuality was not an everyday commodity but something holy to be guarded and exercised in care. Nor was it intrisically evil, to be avoided whenever possible. To hold to this middle position proved difficult; that Christian practice often wavered in the direction of Manichaean prejudice against the body and sexuality is a historical fact. More striking, perhaps, is that despite these failings and in the face of innumerable cultural forces, Christianity has preserved the fragile conviction revealed to it that sexuality is good and holy, a part of our godliness and a mode of celebrating our humanness.

It was in this cultural ambiguity that Paul wrote to the first generation of Christians. In his letters a similar ambiguity appears. Paul reminds his readers that their bodies are the temple of the Holy Spirit (I Corinthians 6). These sexual bodies, subject to a variety of needs, are where God lives. The God of Christians inhabits not just our spiritual, intangible souls but these peculiar, sometimes unruly, yet lovely bodies. This conviction has a number of implications: our sexual bodies are not only holy, but also are more than our own. They belong to the loving God who dwells in them; as such, our style of sexual shar-

ing and commitment will necessarily express our reverence for
these holy places.

Elsewhere, Paul's writings exhibit a more suspicious view of
human sexuality. In his first letter to the Corinthians he
discusses some of the sexual difficulties that this community was
experiencing, including incest and promiscuity. Then turning to
their questions about marriage in this troubled time, he responds:

> Yes, it is a good thing for a man not to touch a woman, but since
> sex is always a danger, let each man have his own wife and each
> woman her own husband (7:1–2).

He would prefer that anyone who can might remain unmarried
like himself (7:7), but "if they cannot control their sexual urges,
they should get married, since it is better to be married than to
be tortured" (7:9). These statements, as they have been most
often interpreted in the Catholic historical tradition, seem to
portray marriage as a concession. It is a vocation for the weak,
for those who cannot control their passions. This negative and
condescending interpretation of sexuality and marriage became
institutionalized in the Catholic Church's canon law on marriage. These laws, most fully formulated at the Council of Trent
in the sixteenth century and reiterated at the beginning of this
century (and, as we shall discuss more fully in Chapter 5, currently under revision), defined one of the secondary ends of
marriage as "a remedy for concupiscence" (Canon ⅜1013).

Important as the statement of Paul in I Corinthians is, it is
useful to recall the context in which he was writing. This letter
was written about A.D. 57. In it Paul repeatedly expresses the
apocalyptic awareness of the time: "These present times of stress
. . . our time is growing short . . . the world as we know it is
passing away." This apprehension, so widespread in the first century of the Christian era, is foreign to the religious awareness of
most of us today. Acutely conscious of an impending end to the
world, Paul offers this counsel: In a time of severe crisis, do not
change your state in life.

The second context of the Pauline letters we have already
mentioned—Gnosticism. Gnosticism with its rejection of the

body and sexual activity gains considerable appeal in a time of severe crisis (as does any fundamentalistic or dualistic belief). Paul was aware of the false teachers who argued that marriage should be forbidden (see I Timothy 4:3). Perhaps Paul's remarks to the Corinthians are, in fact, a defense of marriage. Against such Gnostic voices he is asserting—even if with arguments that carry little conviction for the reader today—the goodness of marriage.

Debate will, and should, continue over the meaning of Paul's many judgments about sexuality, marriage and the relationship of women and men. We will return to a number of these statements in the course of our reflection on Christian marriage. Here it may suffice to observe that a profound ambiguity about human sexuality exists in the Pauline letters. More important than the Pauline view of sexuality, however, are the attitudes toward sexuality that have been discerned in the gospel accounts of Jesus' life and teaching.

Jesus and Sex

In the gospels the Christian encounters the Good News of Jesus Christ. This Good News appears not as a biography of Jesus nor as a set of instructions on how we should behave—sexually or otherwise. This Good News is announced in the remembered vignettes recalling the actions and statements of Jesus Christ.

A first fact that impresses the reader of the gospels is the relative absence of talk about sexuality. There is no reference to sexuality in, for example, the Sermon on the Mount, in the stories of Jesus' temptations or in the Lord's Prayer. The gospels do witness to a life that is overwhelmingly concerned with change and healing: Jesus heals the sick and the possessed; he invites sinners to change their lives; he urges others to leave their present lifestyles and to follow a different way of life with him. Personal change, conversion and a life lived with and for others—these, rather than a set of specific instructions about moral behavior, form the core of Jesus' message in the gospels.

Jesus' attitude toward sexuality may be glimpsed indirectly in his associations. He was known and criticized for associating with "tax collectors and sinners" (Matthew 9 and Luke 7). In Luke's gospel this observation is followed by the story of the woman "who had a bad name in the town," who lavishes attention on Jesus during a meal. Jesus' friends are scandalized that he lets a sinful woman touch him. But Jesus recognizes her approach as signaling a desire to change. His response is not one of judgment. Instead he assures her that her sins are forgiven and that she should go in peace. The person's sinfulness (even of a sexual variety) was less significant than a desire to change.

Two other stories, both in the gospel of John, further illustrate Jesus' attitude toward sexuality. (Again, both stories are about women sinners and may lead the contemporary reader to wonder that women seem to be the only sexual sinners in the New Testament. This is an important feature of sex in the Christian Scriptures. We shall explore this later in this chapter when we examine more fully Paul's treatment of sexuality and women.)

The story of Jesus' conversation with the Samaritan woman at the well (John 4) shows a Jesus surprisingly familiar toward a woman, who was also a foreigner. In a dialogue about refreshment—water from this well and water of a more powerful kind —Jesus invites this woman to admit the disarray of her marital life. But again her marital irregularity (five marriages and now living with another man) is not the focus. Instead Jesus invites her to conversion: he offers her a different way to be refreshened and to worship God.

The second story is that of the woman caught in adultery. The context is a familiar one, that of a religious debate. Jesus' adversaries argue that such a person, by law, is to be stoned. When they persist in their suggestion, Jesus replies, "If there is one of you who has not sinned, let him be the first to throw a stone at her" (John 8:7). With her arrogant judges shamed away from the scene, Jesus feels no need to condemn her past, but instead encourages her to a new and different future. Again Jesus displays both a comfort being among those rejected for sexual sins and an interest not in judgment but in personal change.

These are but a few episodes in an extraordinary life about

which we know very little. The history of Christianity is rich with interpretations of what is right and wrong sexually. Theology manuals and catechisms of the past four centuries have sought to clarify the morality of almost every conceivable sexual action. We see an astonishing distance between such explicit (and even compulsive) efforts and the gospel accounts of Jesus' life and teaching.

If the Christian gospels do not provide directives about specific sexual behavior, they do portray a person himself uninvolved in sexual activity. Although the New Testament letter to the Hebrews observed that Jesus was a person "who has been tempted in every way that we are, though he is without sin" (4:15), there is no suggestion in the New Testament of Jesus being sexually tempted or involved in any kind of sexual activity. Jesus' career and mission did not include marriage. This is not so difficult for contemporary Christians to understand, for we see among us dedicated, holy persons absorbed in life efforts that exclude a commitment to a spouse and family. Yet the celibate lifestyle of Jesus Christ has had a profound and fascinating impact on the Christian understanding of sexuality and marriage—in both a positive and a negative fashion. Christians have seen this life as a sign of a radical commitment to the service of God. In his life and lifestyle Jesus speaks to us of the relative unimportance of everything beyond love and justice and the healing that these virtues effect. Our sexuality, holy as it is, is not the most important aspect of who we are or what we are about. For almost all of us, sexuality is a significant part of our growth in love and a central part of our healing. But, Jesus' life witnesses, we are sexual and more. His life thus invites us to take our sexuality both more seriously and less seriously than otherwise we might.

Unfortunately, this is not how Jesus' life has always been interpreted in Christian history. Christianity's victory over Gnosticism was a partial one; Christians continued to distrust the flesh and its exciting and distracting desires. Jesus' life was often seen as suggesting the ideal of love without sex. The *best* way to love is without sex; holiness is a spiritual, unfleshly goal and our sexuality will unerringly deter us from it. Religious goals of purity and "inviolateness" (suggesting that sexual contact equals violation) seem to argue against physical contact and sexual intercourse as ways to love.

The severe historical ambivalence surrounding this figure of the unmarried Jesus is reflected in celibacy in today's Church. Catholics recognize many celibates as living lives of deep love and commitment; these celibates celebrate again today Jesus' witness: we are called, married and unmarried, to a more than genital love, a more than biological family, a fruitfulness that is not equivalent to our genital fecundity. And married Christians are also aware of celibates who use this way of life to hide, to avoid contact and risk of every type. In such persons Christ's witness is cruelly distorted and a Gnostic fear and rejection of the body and sexuality survive. So Jesus' life has been understood in different ways—as an invitation to a more than physical and biological involvement in life in the midst of (for most of us) a fully sexual, genital life; and as a cover for a lifestyle of avoiding the contact through which love, justice and healing take place.

Three Options Today

We have argued here that Christian history and experience is deeply ambivalent about sexuality. The goal has not been to fix blame or find scapegoats but to illumine where we have come from, some of the baggage (*impedimenta,* in Latin) that we bring with us, and where we find ourselves today. In the face of such a mixed and complex inheritance, three general responses seem available. We may choose to interpret the Christian tradition as a single, indistinguishable and absolute Revelation. To do this we need to ignore or deny the seamier side of our inheritance. But in a rapidly changing world we may choose not to involve ourselves in the taxing effort to distinguish more enduring Christian values from the many misinterpretations to which we and earlier generations have contributed. In an effort to remain faithful to Christianity in a time of enormous transition, some of us may feel the need to affirm the tradition as it now stands, arguing for its unchanging stability, clarity and rightness.

A second option pursued by others today is simply to reject the tradition. A body of thought that contains so many negative attitudes about sexuality, a history of pastoral practice that has offered so much harmful counsel to married people, surely it is to be rejected—even denounced! These persons, wounded by biases they feel they learned from the Church, now judge it to be bankrupt. They are no longer able to discern any value in the murky heritage of Christian belief and behavior.

A third response is to acknowledge this complex and long religious tradition as both *mixed* and *mine*. Since Vactican II many Catholics, for instance, have come, through a period of struggle with the Church, to a deeper realization that they *are* Catholics—for better and for worse. The Catholic faith is our heritage and our home. It is not a home that we can leave like angry children, but a home where we belong and to which we must tend. We begin to recognize that the Church, in its history and practice, is not the "unblemished spouse" or the "perfect society." It is, instead, incomplete and wounded, very much like ourselves. The marvel of Christ's promise "to be with you all days, even until the end of the world" is that it is *this* Church, this flawed, often shortsighted and sometimes arrogant group—ourselves—with whom God has promised to stay.

As we are stripped of our childhood fantasy of a perfect and sinless Church, we find that the rhetorical flourish, "we are the Church," takes on a new and powerful meaning. There is better fit between the Christian Church and who we know ourselves to be. We can experience this as an invitation to a new level of participation in our religious tradition. This third response can lead us to a more personal investment in our lovely but scarred heritage. It is we who must participate in Christianity's recognition of its continuing unholy attitudes toward sexuality and in the recovery of its deepest convictions about our sexual selves and the celebration of its hopes for a lifetime of committed and fruitful love.

Such involvement in a sacred tradition is dangerous business.

Mistakes will be made and conflict can be predicted. But these have always been part of the process of interpreting Christian faith in each new historical context. A difference today is that many more people will be involved in this "re-vising" and handing on of a fragile but holy revelation and belief.

Marriage as Metaphor

In the three thousand and more years of our religious heritage Jews and Christians have crafted the values and images that describe marriage for us today. They have done this in response to God's continual self-revelation and God's revelation of us to ourselves. When we reflect on the images of marriage during this long, eventful history, it is useful to recall the cultural meaning of marriage for much of this time. Marriage was essentially a pact between families or clans, an arrangement and agreement whose central concerns were the survival and continuity of the group. This survival and continuity—and purity—would be ensured through offspring, especially males. In this contractual arrangement, it was essential that the woman be fertile and be a virgin, this last requirement ensuring the ethnic purity of this group.

It was this basic human relationship that Jews and Christians would reflect on and gradually transform. One way this transformation occurred was in the recognition of marriage as a symbol and a metaphor—a sign of other relationships and values in life. For the earliest Israelites marriage was not an image of the original wedding of a male and female god. Reacting against the Canaanites, whose lands they had entered, the Israelites worshipped a God who was not a god of nature; good crops and family fecundity did not depend on cultic sexual practices. Sex and marriage were *not sacred* in this way.

Marriage was, for these early Israelites, a rather secular event, since it did not repeat or commemorate the mythic marriage of gods. The holiness of marriage began to be celebrated as the followers of Yahweh began to see parallels between this social institution and the central religious relationship in their life.

The Israelites recognized the profound challenge to fidelity in a marriage: it was a relationship that must have stability and endurance, even through periods of failure and infidelity. In the eighth century B.C. the prophet Hosea first made an explicit connection between marital commitment and Israel's covenant with Yahweh. His beautiful poetry concerning marital failure and recovery, very likely arising from his own experience in marriage, compared Yahweh's resolute love for Israel to a marriage partner's love for an unfaithful spouse. Though Yahweh was not a sexual God, this comparison of a marriage and a faith covenant caught the imagination of the Israelites. Both relationships were commitments of love which strove after a lifelong fidelity. Thus did human marriage become a metaphor for, and a sign of, God's enduring love for this group of people.

The first generations of Christians reinterpreted the relationship of Yahweh and Israel in terms of Christ and the Church. Christ was God's son and this new relationship was likewise pictured in marital imagery: in the Pauline letters to the Romans (Chapter 7) and to the Ephesians (Chapter 5) the fidelity of Christians to Christ was compared to that of a wife to her husband.

Both Jews and Christians have found this metaphor of marriage to be powerful and exciting. The all but universal experience of marriage has been able to suggest to us, to reveal to us, how God is with us through whatever failure or infidelity on our part. Marriage—this common, ordinary experience—has become for us a sign of something more than itself. In this, it has become a sacrament of God's enduring presence in our lives.

Metaphors, however marvelous and exciting, have limits. Suggestive and revelatory as a metaphor may be, it shares the limitations of its cultural origins. This is so with marriage as a metaphor of our faith relationship with God. It is important to note the original direction of this metaphor: the human relationship of marriage describes our faith relationship with God. To reverse this comparison—our faith relationship with God describes the nature of human marriage—is to change the metaphor. Commitment and fidelity between two humans have different limits than a relationship between us and God. God, we believe, cannot fail us; ultimately we have no one else, no other God to whom we belong. Our faith relationship with God knows an absoluteness and impossibility of "divorce" that human relationships cannot enjoy. In Christian marriage God may be present and empowering the partners, but God is not one of these partners. Thus, in a very important way, the faith relationship between us and God is *unlike* a human marriage. Although marriage is a powerful metaphor of our faith relationship with God, we are beginning to see more clearly the distinct limits of this image.

Another limitation of this metaphor concerns the role of the partners in marriage and in a faith relationship. In a patriarchal period, such as the eighth century when Hosea was composing his beautiful portrait of a God who remains faithful to a faithless (idolatrous and adulterous) nation, it was quite natural to depict Israel as the harlot, the adulterous woman. Yahweh, in turn, was identified as a patient and loving husband. In the New Testament this distinction continues in Paul's comparison of Christ to a husband and the Church to a wife. Such a development of this metaphor appears troublesome today when marriage is understood in terms of a greater mutuality of wife and husband. When God and husband are explicitly paralleled in this metaphor, it is suggested that a husband is the stable, faithful and more God-like member of a marriage relationship. The woman, identified with Israel and the Church, is portrayed as the sinful, failing member of the relationship. When such a comparison reinforces (as it also originates in) a cultural bias against women as the weaker sex, those more likely to fail, this marital imagery itself becomes unfaithful. It is untrue to the experience of couples, equally sinful and struggling, equally capable of forgiveness and generous self-disregard.

The identification of God as husband seemed natural, if anthropomorphic, when God was imaged exclusively as male. Today Christians are recovering what we have always believed: our God, unlike the gods of the Canaanites, is not a sexual God and is, therefore, neither male nor female. Though we call God "father" as Jesus has taught us, we acknowledge that God is also mother, leader, friend and much more. Human names and roles suggest aspects of our God, but cannot define this unnameable

Presence. The enduring challenge of every religious community is to image God in exciting and provocative ways without allowing these images to harden into idols. Icon making and icon breaking are both indispensable elements in religious development and purification.

Covenant and Contract: A Changing Tradition

Marriage, which served as a metaphor of Israel's enduring commitment with Yahweh, was itself imaged both as a covenant and a contract. These two kinds of social agreements share many features, and only with time have they inherited very different nuances.

In the Middle East during the first millennium before the time of Christ, the notion of covenant embraced a variety of pacts and agreements—from trade arrangements between clans and nations to marriage pacts between families. A covenant, then, was a reciprocally binding agreement between parties.

A subtle nuance to this idea of covenant was introduced as Israel began to use it to describe the relationship with its God, Yahweh. This faith relationship was understood as an agreement to belong to each other forever. Complementing the legal and binding aspects of this covenant was the notion of a commitment of love and affection. This was more than a legal, business arrangement. Further, the usual conditional nature of a trade pact (an agreement limited by specific terms) was altered by Yahweh's revelation that this faith commitment was meant to survive every change and reversal. The covenant between this group of people and God became an unconditional one.

When the prophets of Israel began to compare this faith commitment to the commitment of a woman and man in marriage, they began the transformation of marriage still continuing in Christian life today. Although marriage was initially used to suggest the nature of a faith commitment, soon this faith relationship with Yahweh began to influence how Israel thought about marriage. The reciprocal agreement between husband and wife, if it is genuinely like the covenant of Yahweh and Israel, must be more than a business arrangement. A wife is more than one's property. The reciprocal rights and obligations of marriage must be infused by the love and affection that God has for Israel. The legal commitment and contract of marriage must be matched by an internal, personal commitment if it is to imitate that covenant that Yahweh established with Israel, "writing it in their hearts" (Jeremiah 31:33). Marriage was not to be only an institutional agreement about the transmission of family name and property, but a personal agreement as well. Finally, the unconditional nature of Israel's faith covenant suggested a new and radical view of marriage: it did not depend just on the husband's good pleasure, or on the wife's fertility or fidelity. This too was to be an unconditional covenant. An inability to bear children did not terminate this agreement and contract. Jews (and later, Christians) learned from their God about their own extraordinary capacity for change and forgiveness.

Unlikely as it seemed, a lifelong commitment of married love was possible. Thus in the history of Israel the cultural notion of a covenant was altered by its use to describe the love relationship of Yahweh with this band of believers. The cultural meaning of marriage was, in turn, altered as this legal institution was interpreted as an unconditional covenant of love and fidelity.

Marriage between Jews and between Christians was understood as both a legal agreement (contract) and a commitment of personal love (covenant). The impressive role of law in Roman society, especially in its ability to order and humanize social life, did not go unnoticed in the early centuries of Christianity. With the conversion of the Emperor Constantine in A.D. 313, Christianity became a state religion and began to organize itself as a social and legal institution. A steadily developing interest in law was crystallized in the Church in the codification of its law. First systematized by Gratian in the twelfth century, this code of law was fully elaborated during the Council of Trent in the sixteenth century.

With the Church's development of an elaborate set of laws on marriage, the image of contract quite naturally, if unfortunately, replaced that of covenant. Christian marriage came to be defined, and taught, in legal and even legalistic terms. A concern for specific rights and obligations and an absorption with the legal consummation of marriage replaced attention to the more personal aspects and inner dimensions of this life commitment. Part of the reform represented by the Second Vatican Council has been the return to the imagery of covenant in understanding Christian marriage. The revision of the Church's laws on marriage includes a redefinition of marriage as a covenant; in many places the Church's ministry today is characterized by a more pastoral and less legalistic approach to marriage.

In American culture today there is an interesting movement in regard to the imagery of marriage. As the Church returns from a contractual to a covenantal view, many Americans are becoming interested in marriage as an explicit contract. As marriage continues to become de-institutionalized—which means there is less stable social agreement on what this commitment entails—people are motivated by a variety of reasons to turn to a contractual approach to marriage.

A first motive for an interest in marriage as a contract is a desire to put conditions on this commitment. If a covenant suggests the unconditional character of marriage, a contract suggests limits and conditions. A written contract of marriage today might specify limits to childbearing, financial responsibility, sexual exclusiveness and even the length of the commitment. Overwhelmed by changes in society and a sense of their own limits, a couple may feel compelled to defend their individual and collective future with predesignated limits and boundaries. In many instances this kind of movement toward a contract in marriage seems not to be influenced by the best wisdom of the Christian heritage.

Another, more Christian motive for turning to a contractual view of marriage can begin as a response to the extraordinary shift in expectations about marriage today. Without the powerful common understandings of marriage, and Christian marriage, that were once available in our culture, a couple may enter this commitment with very different expectations and hopes. If each of us pursues a career, whose career or job comes first? Will we have children, and when? How is our own religious faith similar;

how different? What do we hope to hand on to our children? In the enthusiasm of romance that suffuses the months around our entering marriage, we may assume we agree on these questions. Concrete and specific discussions of these expectations can help a couple clarify and strengthen the particular covenant they are entering. For many the cold and legalistic tone of "a contract" may be offensive, though their prudent discussions intend the same clarity and agreement as a contract.

These two powerful images of marriage—as covenant and as contract—are part of our religious heritage. These are not mutually exclusive notions: both are binding commitments between parties which include reciprocal rights and obligations. A contemporary Christian ministry to marriage will invite couples to explore the nuances of each of these images. With this covenant we commit ourselves to each other unconditionally, believing our love can survive the many changes and even failures that await our common life. In this covenant our own sense of personal love and commitment is enhanced by the recollection that we are strengthened by the enduring love of God. But we also need to continue to clarify our own expectations and hopes for this relationship: a contractlike specifying of these expectations may well assist this covenant to grow and endure.

In the Christian tradition elements of both covenant and contract have been incorporated into the sacrament of Matrimony. The marriage commitment has come to be seen as a special religious event which strengthens the couple and which makes them a sign and a witness to the larger community of God's saving presence in the world. In subsequent chapters we will examine this sacrament as neither an automatic nor a magical event, but part of the journey of Christian marriage—the gradual development of committed Christian love.

The Marriage Relationship: Hierarchy or Mutuality?

A contemporary reflection on marriage must confront the question: how are a woman and a man to be with each other, and for each other? The answer to this question reveals our belief about the difference between men and women and our expectations for marriage.

The covenant between Yahweh and Israel and between Christ and the Church is a relationship of non-equals. God initiates this covenant and we struggle, through multiple failures, to be faithful to it. The Israelites and early Christians likewise understood marriage to be a relationship of non-equals: the man was the head of the house—as he still is in many cultures and houses today. In this understanding the covenants of Christ and the Church, and of man and woman in marriage, were *reciprocal* but not *mutual* in character: the commitment was embraced by both parties, but in a hierarchical (superior/inferior) rather than a mutual fashion. Is this still the Church's understanding of the man/woman relationship in marriage?

One place to begin exploring this question is with the Pauline understanding of women and men. Paul preached the gospel of Jesus Christ in a thoroughly patriarchal society; he gave thanks each morning (as every male Jew was instructed) that he was not born a woman. It was through this extraordinary man and this cultural milieu that an important part of Christian belief about marriage has been transmitted. In examining the Pauline correspondence in the New Testament, two very different views of the marriage relationship emerge. These can be described as relationships of hierarchy and of mutuality.

Toward the end of his first letter to the Corinthians, Paul urges the community to observe the custom of women covering their heads in church. The reason for this custom, Paul argues, is a hierarchical one: "Christ is the head of every man, man is the head of woman and God is the head of Christ" (11:3). At the bottom of this hierarchy of being, woman is to show her deference by covering her hair and head. Paul elaborates this hierarchical relationship: "Man was not created for the sake of woman, but woman was created for the sake of man" (verse 9). In the world view of Paul's time a marriage was naturally a hierarchical relationship. And the inferiority of woman also had its theological justification, as we read in the first letter to

Timothy: "A woman ought not to speak, because Adam was formed first and then Eve, and it was not Adam who was led astray, but the woman who was led astray and fell into sin" (2:12–14). Her role as the *real* original sinner has earned woman her place at the bottom of this hierarchy.

In the letter to the Colossians a similar conviction leads the writer to urge: "Wives, give way to your husbands as you should in the Lord. Husbands, love your wives and treat them with gentleness" (3:18). Children are then told to obey their parents, and slaves their masters. The entire passage about these three relationships is warm with concern: within a cultural context of hierarchy, Paul argues for love and gentleness. These are all personal relationships in the Lord, not property relationships. In this passage Paul does not overturn a cultural hierarchical system but attempts to transform it with Christian love. In retrospect we can see the potency of Christian love. Initially just modifying the hierarchical relationship of husband and wife or master and slave from one of control of property to a reciprocal love of persons, Christian love will come in time to challenge the hierarchy itself. The radical mutuality implied in self-giving Christian love would, after many centuries, contribute to the overthrow of the hierarchy of master and slave. In our own day this challenge of the inequity of every hierarchy continues—both in regard to marriage and in the structure of the Church itself.

In the letter to the Ephesians this hierarchy of husband and wife is once more explained, again with much affection:

> Wives should regard their husbands as they regard the Lord since as Christ is the head of the Church and saves the whole body, so is a husband the head of his wife; and as the Church submits to Christ, so should wives to their husbands, in everything (5:22–24).

As we saw above, here Christian love is combined with a hierarchical view of marriage. In the mid-first century the amount of affection called for here must have been striking: a man is expected to love his wife like Christ loves the Church. Such love and fidelity would make Christian marriage a very special relationship. In the late twentieth century, however, the hierarchical orientation in the Pauline letters distracts from the lesson of love. To many readers today this view of marriage encourages the husband to an improperly God-like and even paternalistic love of his spouse. While paternal love can be profound, it is nonetheless the love of a father, not a husband.

In these three passages we find Paul trying to alter the cultural relationship of marriage for Christians, not by changing its hierarchical orientation, but by transforming this superior/inferior relationship with Christian care and gentleness. Impressive as this is, we find him in three other passages hinting of a radical mutuality among Christians that may shatter every cultural hierarchy—even marriage.

In the same chapter of his first letter to the Corinthians where Paul urges the hierarchical view of man's natural precedence over woman, there appears a sentence which gives a quite different picture:

> However, though woman cannot do without man, neither can man do without woman, *in the Lord*. Woman may come from man, but man is born of woman—both come from God (11:11–12).

This passage suggests an unheard-of mutuality between women and men—a mutuality grounded not in social custom or cultural understandings of male and female, but "in the Lord." If the creation story in the book of Genesis tells us that woman came from man's rib, ordinary birth has every man come from a woman; the mutuality and interdependence suggested here are rooted in their both coming from and belonging to God. This peculiar passage in Paul might be discounted if this notion of a radical mutuality of sexes did not appear again.

But in the letter to the Colossians the writer exhorts his readers to live out the radically new life they have as Christians: "You have stripped off your old behavior with your old self and you have put on a new self which will progress toward true knowledge the more it is renewed in the image of its creator" (3:9–10). And this image is again described as entailing a radical equality:

In that image there is no room for distinction between Greek and Jew, between the circumcised or the uncircumcised, or between barbarian and Scythian, slave or free man. There is only Christ; he is everything and he is in everything (3:11–12).

This passage describes a new order, a different way of being with each other that is an expectable part of Christian life. Belonging to Christ makes us equal; we are together in a way that transcends all the cultural demands for dominance, control and superiority. That Christians have so consistently fallen short of this ideal is perhaps less significant than that we continue to aspire to such mutuality.

This radical and improbable vision of Christian life is repeated in Paul's letter to the Galatians. Here Paul reminds his readers how Baptism has altered their lives: no longer living according to the Jewish law, Christians are called to a profoundly different way of being with one another.

All baptized in Chirst, you have all clothed yourselves in Christ, and there are no more distinctions between Jew and Greek, slave and free, male and female, but all of you are one in Christ Jesus (3:27–28).

Some commentators on this extraordinary passage, impressed with the divergence between this picture of unity and contemporary Christian life, have urged that this is a statement of an ideal, of what Christian life together will look like in heaven. Yet even as an ideal, it invites those who would be Christians to set aside distinctions, privileges and cultural expectations in pursuit of a radical mutuality. A Christian theology of marriage today might aspire to such a mutuality in the marriage relationship. This would entail abandoning many cultural roles expected of husband and wife, and learning a different way of being together.

As these passages in the New Testament strike us as marvelous, if idealistic, statements of communal life, it is also important to keep them joined to Paul's other statements about women and marriage. We see in Paul's letters a tension that is still very much alive today: the struggle between a cultural world view (with its expectations for a marriage relationship) and a radical religious vision of life together.

The ambivalence we have seen in Paul—between a hierarchical view of marriage and a vision of radical mutuality in Christ —continues in Augustine. In his treatise on the Trinity Augustine struggled to harmonize the radical and original mutuality suggested in Genesis 1:27 ("in the image of God he created him; male and female he created them") with the view of Paul that women are to keep their heads covered since it is men who are first created in the image of God. Augustine recognized that our being renewed in Christ (and he quotes Ephesians 4:23) and being called to take up a radically new life (and he quotes Colossians 3:9) makes us, women and men, equal disciples: "Who is it, then, that would exclude women from this fellowship, since they are with us co-heirs of grace . . ." Augustine's conclusion is an uneasy compromise: women and men enjoy a religious mutuality as images of God and disciples of Christ, but women, in their role as wives, are subordinate to men.

This ambivalence about the relationship of men and women endures in the Church today. We have come to believe—at least in our best moments—that in Baptism we become one in Christ, whatever our nationality, color or gender. The documents of Vatican II emphasize the equality and mutuality of all the people of God. Yet many Catholics are still sensitive to Pope Pius XI's warning, a half century ago in his letter on Christian marriage, against movements which attribute to a wife "a false liberty and unnatural equality with the husband" (⌗75, p. 98). These Catholics still understand marriage as a hierarchical relationship which, in Pius XI's words, "includes the primacy of the husband with regard to the wife and children, the ready subjection of the wife and her willing obedience" (⌗26, p. 84). Other Catholics see marriage as a commitment of radical mutuality where hierarchical distinctions of primacy and unequal obedience are improper. A continued focus throughout this book will be the relationship of woman and man in Christian marriage and the challenges which test it. Today the Christian vision of a radical mutuality in marriage and elsewhere survives in a social

structure which continually threatens it. It survives in a Church
still hierarchical in structure. This hierarchy, inherited from an
earlier cultural milieu rather than the New Testament, distinguishes a group of male leaders from a "wifely" laity from whom
submission and obedience are expected. This hierarchy controls
service in the community by restricting access to sacramental
ministry. If this, and more, is a scandal, it is not novel. We
Christians are always a scandal to ourselves as we struggle to let
go of "old ways of life"—whether compulsions of control and
conformity or other learned expectations—and live a new challenging life in Christ. This has been true in Christian history; it
is true in our private lives; we can expect it to be true in our
marriages.

The 1980s

Catholic ambivalence about sexuality, marriage and the relationship between women and men continues into the 1980s. During October of 1980 an international synod of Catholic bishops
was held in Rome on "The Role of the Christian Family in the
Modern World." During this meeting—still an exclusive gathering of the hierarchy, with only a small number of married people present as non-voting observers—participants made a number of striking interventions. African bishops called for changes
in the Catholic approach to marriage preparation and celebration which would better harmonize Christian and African views
of marriage. Bishops from England, Canada and the United
States made bold speeches in favor of a more positive attitude
toward sexuality, marriage and women. Archbishop Bernadin of
Cincinnati, at the beginning of the synod, issued a stirring call
for a more positive theology of the body and of human sexuality.
Archbishop Legare of Alberta, Canada urged the synod to examine more carefully the comparison of Christ and the Church
with husband and wife. This brief but bold speech also argued
for a reexamination of the linking of the sacrament of Matrimony with the civil wedding ceremony. Cardinal Hume of
Westminster, England suggested that the lived experience of

married persons must provide a more powerful source for theological reflection on marriage.

An intervention offered at the synod by the National Council of Catholic Bishops of the United States emphasized the changing roles of women and men and how these changes are influencing family life. Bishop Lebel of Quebec, Canada spoke on the oppression of women in the Church as a sinful situation demanding healing.

There was, of course, disagreement about these positions. Despite, for example, the several speeches that stressed a new equality between women and men, Pope John Paul II urged, in his closing homily, a much more traditional view: human society must be so constituted that women not feel the need to leave home, "but rather so that the family might be able to live rightly, that the mother might devote herself fully to the family."

As Francis X. Murphy observed in his review of the synod, disagreements continue among Catholic leaders about, for example, the relative importance of law and compassion in Church legislation about marriage and divorce. Ambivalence, debate and even conflict have been a part of the Christian heritage from its inception regarding sexuality and marriage. As witnessed at the 1980 synod, this debate and conflict will also be an important part of our future.

Reflective Exercise

In this chapter we have suggested there is an ambivalence at the heart of Christianity's understanding of human sexuality. It may be useful to test this out in your own experience, consulting the images of sexuality that are a part of your own religious awareness.

In a time of quiet reflection, turn your memory back over the many images and convictions concerning sexuality that have come to you from the Christian tradition. These may include passages from Scripture or other religious reading, memories of prayer or religious instruction, the words and attitudes of significant persons. Take time to let the memories come.

After a while, select one of these images that speaks to you positively about sexuality. What is the source of the image: does it come to you from Scripture or from personal testimony or from seeing how religious persons have behaved? What is the most important information this image has given you about sex? What are the feelings that are associated with this image for you?

Then turn to a memory or an image that is more negative in its view of sexuality. Again, what is the source of this image? What information has it given you about sex? What are the feelings that accompany this image for you?

As you reflect on these images today, which of the two seems to come closer to representing Christianity's contribution to your own current appreciation of sexuality? Why do you think that this is the case?

Additional Resources

The ambivalence toward sexuality in our religious heritage is emphatically shown in Denis Doherty's discussion of "The Tradition in History" in *Dimensions of Human Sexuality* (Doubleday, 1979). The collection of essays in this volume, which Doherty edited, is a response to the much debated report *Human Sexuality: New Directions in American Catholic Thought* (Paulist Press, 1977), undertaken by Anthony Kosnik and his associates for the Catholic Theological Society of America. A useful discussion of sexuality from a Protestant perspective can be found in James B. Nelson's *Embodiment: An Approach to Sexuality and Christian Theology* (Augsburg, 1978).

In his brief paper "The History of Christian Marriage," which appeared in the Fall 1979 issue of *Chicago Studies*, Michael Place gives an excellent overview of marriage in the Christian, and especially Catholic, tradition. The German Catholic theologian Walter Kasper reviews the changing understandings of marriage and divorce in his *Theology of Christian Marriage* (Seabury, 1980). The more ambitious reader might consult Edward Schillebeeckx's *Marriage: Secular Reality and Saving Mystery* (Sheed and Ward, 1965) and Bernard Häring's *Marriage in the Modern World* (Newman Press, 1965). These two volumes were written at the time of Vatican II by theologians whose work was influential in the Council's reformulation of Catholic thought on marriage. If somewhat dated now, these books stand in Catholic thought at the watershed between a more dogmatic and a more experience-based approach to Christian marriage.

In a challenging but important article, on "Marriage as a Sacrament," in Volume 10 of his *Theological Investigations* (Seabury, 1973), Karl Rahner discusses the relationship of marriage to the Church. Rahner explores the ways in which both marriage and the Church are signs, pointing to more than themselves, and also examines some of the complexity involved in the comparison of the relationship of husband and wife to that of Christ and the Church.

Scripture scholar Pierre Benoit discusses the context and meaning of Paul's judgments about marriage in "Christian Marriage According to St. Paul," which appeared in 1980 in *Clergy Review*. Augustine explores the relationship of men and women in Book Twelve of his treatise "On the Trinity." The text is available in Latin in Volume 42 of *Patrologia Latina* (Paris, 1841), edited by J. P. Minge, and in English in *The Fathers of the Church* (New York, 1955). Augustine undertakes a more detailed examination of marriage in his letter "On the Good of Marriage," which will be discussed further in the next chapter.

The first part of the "Secretariat's Working Paper" that was used at the 1980 synod of bishops on "The Role of the Christian Family in the Modern World" appeared in *Origins* (National Catholic Documentary Service), September 25, 1980. The speeches at the synod that are referred to in this chapter are reprinted in the weekly issues of *Origins* between October 9 and November 20, 1980. Francis X. Murphy's reflection on the synod appeared in his article "Of Sex and the Catholic Church," in the February 1981 issue of *The Atlantic Monthly*.

5

CHRISTIAN MARRIAGE—FUTURE TENSE

The past two decades have witnessed a revolution in Christian, and especially Catholic, thinking about marriage. When the Second Vatican Council opened in 1962 there existed among Catholics a rather stable consensus on the meaning and purpose of marriage. This consensus had been most profoundly influenced by two documents: the code of canon law published in 1917 and Pope Pius XI's encyclical letter of 1930 on Christian marriage.

Law and Order

The canon law of the Church, whose very recent and significant revisions we will examine shortly, reached an early formulation in the sixteenth century, after the Council of Trent. At the beginning of the twentieth century this set of laws was revised and again promulgated to the entire Church. In terms of the present and future of Christian marriage, two features of this legal document are most important. First, the Church's legal teaching here on the meaning and purpose of marriage was not complemented by a vibrant spirituality of marriage. As a legal document, the code defined marriage as a contract with specific rights and duties. No well-developed theology of the personal relationship of marriage accompanied this view of marriage as a contract. The central legal element of a Christian marriage defined in this document was the right of each partner to the other's body (Canon 1081: "a perpetual and exclusive right over the body for acts which are of themselves suitable for the generation of children"). As a contract, marriage was a legal agreement sealed in the first act of sexual intercourse, regardless of the accompanying emotional or religious maturity.

Another aspect of the code which would eventually require reformulation was its understanding of the purpose of marriage. The fruitfulness of marriage, its primary purpose, was interpreted rather exclusively in terms of biological progeny; the secondary purposes of marriage were defined as "mutual help and the remedying of concupiscence" (Canon 1013). This statute would be altered after Vatican II, as Catholic thinking returned to interpersonal love rather than concupiscence as a more crucial focus in Christian marriage.

What is the importance of this document of the early twentieth century, now under such considerable revision? Its significance lies in its use for a half century as a major text in the instruction of seminarians and priests in the Catholic Church. Its suspicious attitude toward sexuality and its legalistic understanding of marriage as a contract with specific, corporal rights shaped several generations of Catholic priests and, through them, the consciences of married Catholics. Although recent revisions in canon law and a renewed theology of marriage have radically altered our orientation to marriage today, older Catholics often carry this legalistic and suspicious heritage—a legacy that may still require healing as we move together toward the future of Christian marriage.

The second document which had a profound impact on pre-Vatican II attitudes about Christian marriage was Pope Pius XI's teaching letter on Christian marriage published in 1930. This letter would be widely used through the middle third of this century in marriage preparation and enrichment programs. The letter, which presents marriage as a stable, unchanging phenomenon instituted by God, is often aggressively apologetic in tone—at least to a contemporary reader. Christian beliefs about marriage are urged against what is perceived as a pervasive cultural surrender to lust, concupiscence and selfishness. The letter is, to many readers today, an uneasy combination of a suspicion of sexuality and a celebration of the best Christian hopes for marriage.

The papal letter consistently and emphatically teaches that procreation of children is the primary goal of marriage. Yet in elaborating the relationship of the spouses, the letter offers a surprising reflection on the broader goal of marriage:

> This mutual inward moulding of husband and wife, this determined effort to perfect each other, can in a very real sense, as the Roman Catechism teaches, be said to be the chief reason and purpose of matrimony . . . (※24, p. 84).

This sentence concludes with a distinction between a restricted and a broader view of marriage:

> . . . provided matrimony be looked at not in the restricted sense as instituted for the proper conception and education of the child, but more widely as the blending of life as a whole and the mutual interchange and sharing thereof.

This distinction of a restricted and a broader view departs from a customary stress on procreation as the primary goal of marriage. Yet this statement of Pius XI is not a simple departure from the Church's tradition. To justify his statement here Pius XI refers to a catechism issued from the Council of Trent four hundred years earlier. The Roman Catechism, a sixteenth-century document intended for parish priests, began its consideration of the motives and ends of marriage not with procreation but with companionship. The first motive is a lifelong relationship which "is further encouraged by the hope of mutual support in bearing more easily the difficulties of life and the diminishments of aging." (Drawing from contemporary gerontology, we have used the phrase "the diminishments of aging" to translate the more poignant Latin phrase "senectutis imbecillitatem.") This emphasis on the interpersonal society of the couple and the lifelong mutuality of the marriage relationship stands in striking contrast to the more common Catholic focus on child-bearing as marriage's primary goal.

Unfortunately, neither this sixteenth-century statement nor its 1930 counterpart received much elaboration in Catholic thinking before Vatican II. The orientation toward marriage expressed in the rest of Pius XI's letter on Christian marriage and in the code of canon law continued to dominate Catholic reflection on marriage. In 1942, however, there appeared in English a slim volume (64 pages) which foreshadowed the significant changes about to happen in Catholic thinking about marriage. This was Dietrich von Hildebrand's *Marriage*.

The first striking feature of this book is its author: a married lay person. Nearly all theological thinking and legislating about marriage in the Catholic tradition has been by unmarried clergy. It would be two decades and more after the appearance of Hildebrand's work before married Catholics in America would begin to discuss and write, with some authority, about Christian marriage. A second notable feature of this brief text of Hildebrand is its tone. A more positive and optimistic attitude about marriage replaces the traditional cautious tone, with its fascination for lust and concupiscence. Apart from the tone of this volume and the status of its author, two points of Hildebrand's presentation illustrate the prophetic character of this book.

Hildebrand repeatedly and surprisingly stressed the interpersonal relationship of the couple as the core of marriage. If procreation is the goal of marriage, love is its inspiration and meaning. To emphasize that interpersonal love and commitment stand as the ground of a marriage, Hildebrand takes what was, in context, a rather daring tack: even if children are not or cannot be part of a marriage, "the physical union between man and wife still retains its subjective significance and its intrinsic beauty" (p. 23). He elaborates this sensitive point:

> Is not the ideal of marriage to an even higher degree when both partners, even though childless, belong to each other in the most perfect conjugal love, in unchangeable loyalty to one another, in imitation of the union of the soul with God, than in the case of a marriage with perhaps many children, where the partners are unfaithful to each other and desecrate the sacred tie by a lack of love and loyalty? (p. 24).

Hildebrand's stress on the relationship itself, in an effort to counterbalance the traditional emphasis on procreation as the sole legitimizing reason for sexual union, is grounded in an understanding of psychological and spiritual fruitfulness.

> We must not forget that every true love possesses an intrinsic spiritual fruitfulness and that conjugal love harbours this spiritual fruitfulness of love quite independently of procreation (p. 25).

Hildebrand, himself a parent, is not here denying the importance of children but is trying to recapture the holiness of the interpersonal relationship of marriage which is celebrated in sexual intercourse. Likewise, he is arguing for a psychological and spiritual fruitfulness in the relationship which will undergird and guide the biological fecundity of most couples.

In the last part of his essay, Hildebrand recalls an aspect of the sacramental theology of marriage. According to this theology —traditional, if neglected—the couple are the ministers of the sacrament of marriage. That is, they are not married "by the priest," nor are they the passive recipients of this sacrament. The couple themselves administer the sacrament. In a Church still all too clearly separated into the clergy who provide sacramental ministry and the laity who have come to see themselves as the passive recipients of ministry, this is a powerful notion. The lay couple administer the sacrament of Matrimony. They are the religious agents of their marriage. The religious implications of this traditional but still radical realization are only now becoming clear. The couple must have the ability to perform their marriage—the psychological and religious maturity to effect such a challenging and enduring relationship. In the chapters ahead, we will return frequently to this and other implications of this emerging view of the sacrament of marriage.

Hildebrand also recalls that, according to traditional theology, the sacrament is effected in the mutual consent to this union. This consent happens both in the acceptance of each other in the liturgical celebration and in the sexual acceptance of each other in marriage. This explicit connection of the sacrament with sexual sharing is important for two reasons: it points to the sacramental holiness of sexuality and it rescues sexual intercourse from its legalistic status as the consummation of a contract, no matter the psychological or religious maturity of the partners. Hildebrand's argument, subtly pursued, is impressive forty years later because it predicts the direction of much contemporary theological thought concerning Christian marriage. Graceful love-making is meant not just to generate children or allay concupiscence; it celebrates marital love and—like a sacrament—effects what it signifies.

Vatican II: Recovered Values and New Directions

The *aggiornamento*—bringing up to date—that Pope John XXIII initiated in the Second Vatican Council was especially needed in the Church's understanding of marriage. And in its document, *The Church in the Modern World*, the Council set out on its marriage *aggiornamento*.

Significant shifts here in vocabulary and imagery signal a more positive and less legalistic orientation to Christian marriage. The central image, repeated frequently in this text, is that of covenant: the explicitly religious nuances of this image and its focus on a commitment of mutual love turn our attention away from the earlier concentration on marriage as a contract.

The truculent terminology of lust and concupiscence, traditional in Church documents on marriage, is replaced by a more optimistic and positive vocabulary. The secondary end of marriage as "the allaying of concupiscence" is abandoned; the dangers of sexual selfishness in marriage are alluded to, more gently, in such phrases as "mere erotic inclination."

But perhaps most compelling is the document's emphasis on the relationship itself of the couple. Though repeatedly affirming the centrality of children to a marriage, the document gives new and elaborate attention to the psychological and sexual sharing on which a marriage is founded:

> The actions within marriage by which the couple are united intimately and chastely are noble and worthy ones. Expressed in a manner which is truly human, these actions signify and promote that mutual self-giving by which spouses enrich each other with a joyful and thankful will (#49).

Not only is the importance of sexual expressiveness in marriage stressed, but the traditional limitation of sexual sharing to "those acts ordained to procreation" is modified, leaving room for a recognition of the variety of sexual expressions by which a married couple care for each other's body and "enrich each other with a joyful and a thankful will."

This new enthusiasm of the Church for the importance of the relationship itself continues in the document's explicit affirmation of the religious value of marriage even when there are no children. "Marriage persists as a whole manner and communion of life, and maintains its value and indissolubility, even when offspring are lacking—despite, often, the very intense desire of the couple" (※50).

As with similar statements of Pius XI and Hildebrand, the intent here is not to lessen the importance of children in marriage, but to distinguish more clearly the fruitfulness *for the couple* of their committed love and the fruitfulness of procreation. Avoiding the traditional ordering of the ends of marriage (procreation as the primary end of marriage; mutual love and help as the secondary end), this document speaks instead of children as "the supreme gift of marriage." This not only reminds us that biological fecundity is a gift for which to be grateful, but reunderstands children as the gift of marital love, rather than its duty. Although this text's discussion of childless marriage seems to assume the inability rather than the choice not to have children, it does allow room for the contemporary experience in which some married couples choose not to have children, but to contribute to their social and religious communities in other ways.

When it turns to questions about the family, the text's theological rather than legalistic orientation is again evident. The family that the couple is called to care for is not simply and narrowly their own nuclear family. Christian parenting is a more than private endeavor:

> The couple [should] be ready with stout hearts to cooperate with the love of the creator and the savior, who through them will enlarge and enrich *his own family* day by day (※50; our emphasis).

Married Christians are not called to put all their energy into the development of individual, private families. Christians belong, by profession, to a larger family and community. Married couples are called, just as clergy and celibate religious are called, to the enlarging and enriching of this family day by day. This statement also reveals a theological conviction about stewardship. Our own children and our own family are not simply "ours"; the members of our immediate family for which we care belong to a larger family. Christian generating is more than biological, as Christian family is more than nuclear. All of us, married or not, with or without children, gay or straight, belong to "his own family" and are called, in whatever way our vocation leads us, to be fruitful and to contribute to the enlarging and enrichment of this family.

A most significant portion of this section in *The Church and the Modern World* does not concern sexuality or the marital relationship as such. It has to do with the couple's responsibility and freedom to decide themselves about the shape and size of their family.

> They will thoughtfully take into account both their own welfare and that of their children, those already born and those who may be foreseen. For this accounting they will reckon with both the material and the spiritual conditions of the times as well as those of their state in life (✳50).

The suggestion, new at this point in Vatican documents, is that Christian couples are not simply to accept the ways of nature and whatever size family their own fertility generates. Rather they are called to serious reflection and personal decision about this family. "The parents themselves should ultimately make the judgment, in the sight of God" (✳50). Christian adults are seen here as the responsible agents of their own sexual and family lives. As the Christian couple is called to listen to the wisdom of the Church in questions of sexuality and family life, this attentiveness is to be complemented by a careful and faithful listening to their own life experience, "the conditions of the times" and "their state in life."

This emphasis on the religious responsibility of adult Catho-

lics and the importance of developing and *following* a mature
Christian conscience opens a new era in Catholic thinking about
sexuality and marriage. It furthers the move away from a
Church dichotomized between a teaching clergy and a submissive, childlike laity. It recalls to prominence not only the individual Christian conscience—and the dual challenge of forming it
and trusting it—but also the theological notion of a "sense of the
faithful" in sexual and marital matters. This theological category
which refers to a community's "sense" or instinct of faith, of
what it means to believe as a Catholic, is now being applied to
sexual and marriage practice. (For example, three of the first
four resolutions of the 1980 synod on the Christian family address this "sense of the faithful.") As families and communities
mature in the faith, they develop a sense of what is Christian
and Catholic. Married Catholics, encouraged by Vatican II's insistence on their own responsibility and choice in marriage, are
learning to witness to Church authorities about the meaning of
Christian sex and marriage. When Pope Paul VI's decree against
the use of contraceptives in marriage appeared in 1968 something quite novel occurred: it was rejected by a great portion of
mature, believing Catholics. Trusting their own lived experience
in a new way, Catholics dissented from the teaching Church on
this question, without feeling it necessary to leave the Church.
As sociologist Andrew Greeley and others have noted, the crisis
which ensued from this decree was more one of authority than
sexuality. This crisis of authority concerned the right and obligation of married Catholics to follow their own mature consciences
as well as the teachings of the Church. Troublesome as this crisis has been, it marked—along with Vatican II—the beginning
of a new era in Catholic marriage.

The Revision of the Church's Laws on Marriage

When Pope John XXIII announced in 1959 his plans for a Second Vatican Council, he also called for a revision of the laws of
the Catholic Church. Because so many Catholics have been trou-

bled by this legalistic side of the Church, it will be useful to review some of the significant and healing changes in these laws.

The goal of the commissions working on this revision of Church law on marriage has been to move beyond the narrow legalism of the earlier code and to take advantage of a more sophisticated understanding of both sexuality and human development. By so doing, they have hoped to close the considerable gap between the Church's legal orientation to marriage and its more caring pastoral practice.

In 1975 and again in 1978 a set of revised laws on marriage (and other aspects of Church life) was presented to the Church. These laws, after discussion and revision, are expected to be promulgated to the entire Church very soon. Two parts of these revised laws will illustrate the promising new orientation to marriage in the Catholic Church.

Perhaps the most significant change appears at the very beginning. The revised definition of marriage reads:

> . . . the matrimonial covenant, by which a man and a woman constitute between themselves a communion of the whole of life, which by its nature is ordered to the good of children, has been raised by Christ the Lord to the dignity of a Sacrament (*Origins*, p. 211).

Following the lead of Vatican II, this statement presents marriage as a covenant rather than a contract. More than a contractual arrangement for the mutual right to each other's body, marriage is "a communion of the whole of life." The traditional ranking of the ends of marriage—the procreation of children as primary and mutual help as the secondary end—is omitted. In fact, the ends of marriage are here reversed: marriage is defined, first, as the lifelong communion of two persons and, second, as a relationship "ordered to the good of children." The important redefinition of marriage as "a communion of life" points to the more than genital relationship that must exist in a Christian marriage. No longer seen as a contract that is consummated in the physical union of sexual intercourse, marriage is understood much more broadly, and properly, as a relationship and commitment which include the communion of "the whole of life"—a union which involves each other's affection and lifestyle, hopes and ambitions, fears and doubts. Within this orientation, both the entry into marriage and its fruitfulness can find their fully human and more than genital significance. In this book we aim to explore more fully the meaning of marriage as "a communion of the whole of life."

A second feature of the revised code is its greater sophistication concerning the maturity required for Christian marriage. Psychological incapacities for marriage, resulting from illness or immaturity, receive serious attention in the revised code, as they do in the pastoral practice of the Church today. And if marriage demands considerable psychological maturity, Christian marriage requires the religious maturity of a "living faith." What does this mean? The sacrament of Matrimony is more than a question of two legitimately baptized persons signing the necessary documents and going through a religious ceremony. This sacrament must be an exercise of faith, just as a person's Baptism must be exercised to have any real meaning. If one or both of the marrying couple have no practical "living faith" there can be no *Christian* marriage.

This question of the faith required for the sacrament of Matrimony is a difficult but important one. (Regrettably, the revised code still sees the Baptism of both partners as sufficient indication of the faith that is necessary for marriage to be a sacrament.) The couple must possess some active faith if this marriage is to be a genuine Christian commitment. But who is to decide whether a couple have such living faith? The question is most easily answered in the negative. The couple themselves cannot be the sole judge, since this sacrament is, importantly, the celebration of a faith community. Nor can the parents of the couple decide on their own—whether these parents understand the rich meaning of the sacrament or are insisting on a "Church wedding" for social and cosmetic reasons. Nor can the pastor be the sole judge or authority here. The answer, still to be grasped and exercised, lies in some communal response. Christian Matrimony is a celebration of a community. It bears crucially on the preservation and continuity of the believing community. Faith communities—parishes and dioceses—must develop a more lively sense of Christian marriage and, with this, better criteria for the visible commitment to Christian faith and community life that is required to initiate this covenant in the community of belief. Without making the sacrament simply an elitist event, we may come to distinguish marriage from Christian Matrimony. Those who are very young but insistent on marrying might do so, even with the Church's blessing, but not as a sacrament. Christians with little more than a cultural interest in their Church might marry, but not as a sacrament. The challenge of such a strategy is not to turn the sacrament of Matrimony into a reward for a life well lived; the goal is to make of it the celebration of a commitment that is mature—psychologically and religiously—and that significantly affects the future of the Church as community. If the celebration of Christian sacraments does not depend solely on the personal faith of the celebrants, without such faith the full meaning and force of a sacrament is lost.

A Translation for the Future

The future of Christian marriage depends on our ability, as Christians in the late twentieth century, to translate the wisdom of our past in a way that excites and challenges the next generation. This is the activity of "traditioning," our efforts as a believing community to reinterpret Christian insights about marriage in a way that is faithful both to our heritage and to our present experience. We offer an example here.

Traditional reflection on Christian marriage has often focused on the "three goods of marriage." Augustine, in his letter "On the Good of Marriage," written at the beginning of the fifth century, introduced this approach into the Christian discussion of marriage. In the thirteenth century Thomas Aquinas reinterpreted these goods or benefits of marriage to fit the Church and human experience of his day. Another reinterpretation today may clarify our own experience of marriage and alert us to how God is at work in this complex human relationship.

In his reflection Augustine pointed to the purposes and fruits of marriage. These goods are what marriage is about, how it

contributes to and shapes human life. For Augustine the three
goods or chief benefits of marriage are descendants, mutual love
and fidelity, and the witness marriage offers of God's love for
humankind.

For Augustine descendants were the first benefit. In an era
when marriage was understood predominantly as a social institution, children—and through them the survival and continuity of
the human family—were seen as marriage's first concern and
major effect. Marriage is the context or milieu in which children
are born and raised. In marriage sexual desire and genital expression are brought into the service of the human community.
In marriage, sexuality finds its home. Sexual intercourse is no
longer only for individual delight and expression; this powerful
part of life is made to serve our continuity as a people.

This good of marriage, the essential fruit of marriage as an institution, can of course be realized without personal love. Traditionally, arranged marriages between families have sought the
good of descendants (and the orderly survival of the family
name and transmission of its property) without a necessary concern for personal compatibility and love between the partners.
It is this more personal side of marriage that is addressed in
Augustine's second good of marriage.

This second good is mutual love and fidelity. If in the first
good of marriage human sexuality is socialized, in this second
good it is personalized. Personal commitment and faithfulness,
as a goal of marriage, balances the institutional side of this relationship. Just as marriage is not only to produce offspring, the
marriage partner is not merely the vehicle of sexual release or
progeny. This second goal of marriage points to the humanizing
of sexuality. Within this good arise the many questions of mutuality and fidelity. How are a woman and man to be together?
How much exclusiveness does marital fidelity entail? As we shall
discuss shortly, the contemporary emphasis on this second good
of marriage—as an interpersonal relationship—challenges the
understanding of marriage as an institution. The demise of the
institutional understanding can lead to either a personalizing or
a privatizing of marriage.

A third good of marriage for Augustine was marriage as a

sacramentum. For Augustine this word did not mean "sacrament" in its modern sense, but rather "a mystery." Augustine is referring to St. Paul's statement in his letter to the Ephesians that marriage is a mystery (5:32) and a sign of Christ's love for the Church. The extraordinary commitment of a marriage, expressed in the vow of fidelity and capable of surviving a variety of weaknesses and failures, can be a sign to us of God's enduring love. In this good of marriage, human sexuality is further sanctified. We say "further" because we believe as Christians that our sexuality is already holy. But when sexual love matures in marriage over a lifetime, Christians see here an image of God's tested fidelity to the human community and to the Church.

This summary of Augustine's teaching on marriage has stressed the most positive side of his approach. Another analysis might stress Augustine's repeated urgings that continence and virginity were to be preferred to marriage and sexual intercourse. It is also in Augustine's writings that the Church's historical understanding of marriage as a remedy for concupiscence is rooted: "The concupiscence of the flesh, which parental affection tempers, is repressed and becomes inflamed more modestly (in marriage)." In his analysis of the goods of marriage, Thomas Aquinas opposed these goods of marriage to the loss of reason in sexual intercourse. These goods balance that loss and, in so doing, "excuse marriage and make it right (*matrimonium excusant et honestum reddunt*)."

Little profit results from either exalting these two Christian predecessors or celebrating their limitations. Their efforts to understand Christian marriage for their time provide us not with finished answers, but with the encouragement to do likewise. How might we interpret these goods of Christian marriage in the United States in the 1980s? Taking our direction from the statements of Vatican II on marriage, we might translate these goods in terms of a marriage's fruitfulness in the task of communicating life.

Vatican II focused on Christian marriage as a "communion of life" and as a relationship which intends, in a variety of ways, the communication of life. The three goods of marriage appear

to concern three different modes of fruitfulness in such communication.

The first good of marriage—children—can be understood in
terms of *external fruitfulness*. A marriage is more than a relationship of two persons. It is meant to go beyond itself, to generate new life. Children are an important source and sign of this
fruitfulness. But the traditional concern for the survival of the
species and the continuity of "our group" can today be translated more as the challenge to contribute to the maturing of the
human community. With vastly improved hygiene and nutrition
and a reduced infant mortality rate, issues of survival are less
compelling than they once were. Today as a society we are more
concerned with enhancing the quality of human life. Our question is: how can marriage, as an institution, be fruitful in this
contribution to a more graceful human future?

The second good of marriage, mutual love and fidelity, can be
translated in terms of *internal fruitfulness*. The commitment of
marriage is meant to nourish and transform the two partners.
Their growth beyond the initial excitement of romance and their
adjustment to each other's rhythms and needs is a specific good:
this maturing as a couple is a fruitfulness which is the foundation of all other fruitfulness in marriage.

The reordering of these two benefits, placing the internal
fruitfulness of mutual love before the external fruitfulness of
having children, is a reevaluation being performed both by our
culture and by the Church. The revised definition of Christian
marriage in canon law, which we noted earlier in this chapter,
follows Vatican II in reordering the goals of the covenant. In
this reordering of the first two goods of marriage the Church is
influenced by the contemporary deemphasis on marriage as an
institution (with its preeminent goal of human continuity) and a
greater appreciation of how the maturity of a couple's love for
each other contributes to their own and their children's growth.

As mutual love replaces children as the primary good and goal
of marriage, the result can be either the personalizing or the
privatizing of the relationship. The personalizing of marriage occurs when we marry not because we "should" (our parents or
culture telling us it is time and suggesting whom to marry), but

because we choose. I marry this person, at this point in my life,
with a sense that this contributes to the movement I choose for
my life. The personalizing of a family continues as a couple bear
children by personal choice and later as they attempt to share
rather than enforce their own values with their "descendants."

But as marriage and the family are de-institutionalized, a
process of privatizing can also occur. Separating themselves
from the families of origin (a natural and necessary process), a
couple today may also turn away from any involvement in the
community. "Our marriage is just for ourselves." The internal
fruitfulness of mutual love is pursued to the exclusion of any
concern for external fruitfulness—whether this be children or
other contributions to the human community. The privatizing of
a family develops as the couple turn all their attention and resources to their own children. Disconnected from the larger
community, such a family can become "us against the world."
Although "private" may at first have a refreshing nuance—
suggesting that we are protected from the intrusions of an extended family and the nagging rules of the Church—the word is,
at root, a negative one. As social analyst Hannah Arendt has
shown, privacy also suggests "de-privation," a lack of the privileges and advantages of society and the larger human community.

The personalizing of marriage, as we understand it, refers to
the deepening of love between two people, an enrichment that is
generative. This enrichment is fruitful in two directions: it leads
the couple into a closer relationship with each other and leads
them to an expression of this love beyond themselves. Such a
personalizing of married love is guided by the strengths of intimacy and generativity which will be explored in Part Three of
this book.

The third good of marriage we may call *transcendent fruitfulness*. Admittedly, the word "transcendent" is obscure and,
perhaps, too weighty as well. But we use it here to show that the
fruitfulness of a marriage may also include a most extraordinary
aspect: *our lasting love* can make visible the enduring, faithful
presence of God in our lives. Augustine described marriage as a
mystery and a sacrament: its vowed commitment and tested

fidelity witness to God's marriagelike relationship with us. This
sacramental fruitfulness is properly considered the third good of
marriage, since it depends on the presence of the other two. Not
every marriage affords such an extraordinary witness. Only as a
marriage matures in its internal fruitfulness (mutual love and
fidelity) and in its external fruitfulness (children and the other
gifts that are generated for the community) does it come to
stand as a sign and sacrament to the world. A marriage *becomes*
a sacrament as it matures and begins to generate such a witness.
In Part Two we will examine in more detail the ways in which
this sense of marriage as a sacrament differs from more traditional notions of the sacrament of Matrimony.

Reflective Exercise

In a discussion of changes in the Christian understanding of
marriage, it is important to reflect on our own experience of
change. Do you think differently about marriage than you did
ten years ago? How, specifically, have your own attitudes
changed? What most influenced those changes? New attitudes
in the Church? Your personal experience? A combination of
these?

Reflect for a moment on a Christian marriage that means very
much to you. It may be your own, that of your parents or of
close friends. What makes this marriage Christian, for you?
What is its best feature, its greatest value from your point of
view? Since this marriage is important to you, it is probably a
fruitful relationship. In what specific ways does it give life? What
is the particular shape of this marriage's fruitfulness?

Additional Resources

For a glimpse at the evolution of Catholic legal teaching on
marriage it is instructive to compare the text which served as a
basic educational resource for priests over several decades,
Canon Law: A Text and Commentary edited by T. Bouscaren

and A. Ellis (Bruce, 1946), with Francis Morrissey's recent report, "Revising Church Legislation on Marriage," found in the September 20, 1979, issue of *Origins*. Thomas Green reviews these changes in a more exhaustive fashion in "The Revision of Canon Law: Theological Implications," which appeared in *Theological Studies* (December 1979). Canon lawyer Ladislas Orsy provides an excellent discussion of the context of the revisions of the Church's laws on marriage in "Christian Marriage: Doctrine and Law *Glossae* on Canons 1012–1015," which appeared in *Jurist* in 1980.

Pope Pius XI's encyclical letter on Christian marriage, traditionally entitled by its opening words in Latin—*Casti Conubii*, is available in *Seven Great Encyclicals* (Paulist Press, 1963). Dietrich von Hildebrand's *Marriage* was published in English by Longmans, Green in 1942. The initial chapters of Part Two of the document from Vatican II, "Pastoral Constitution on the Church in the Modern World" (*Gaudium et Spes*), are devoted to marriage and the family. This text is available in *The Documents of Vatican II* (America Press, 1966), edited by Walter Abbott.

The Catholic theological debate over the past decade concerning marriage and divorce can be reviewed by following Richard McCormick's "Notes on Moral Theology," which appear in the March issues of *Theological Studies* in 1971, 1975 and 1980. For a fine theological reflection on marriages without children, see Denis Doherty's "Childfree Marriage—A Theological View" in the Summer 1979 issue of *Chicago Studies*.

Since Vatican II there has emerged a more frank and forceful discussion of marriage by married Catholics. Representative of this refreshing movement are Joseph and Lois Bird's *The Freedom of Sexual Love* (Doubleday Image Books, 1970) and their *Marriage Is for Grownups* (Doubleday Image Books, 1971). For a more theological consideration, see Rosemary Haughton's *The Theology of Marriage* (Fides, 1971).

Augustine discusses the three goods of marriage (*proles, fides, sacramentum*) in his treatise "On the Good of Marriage," written in A.D. 401. This text is available in Volume 27 of *The Fathers of the Church* (Fathers of the Church, Inc.: 1955). Augustine's lifelong struggle to allow his Christian conviction concerning the Incarnation to heal his suspicious view of the body (and so of sexuality and marriage) is discussed by Margaret Miles in *Augustine on the Body* (Scholars Press, 1979). Thomas Aquinas takes up the three goods of marriage in the Supplement to his *Summa Theologica* (Benziger, 1948), Question 49. For a useful brief reflection on Augustine's and Thomas' approaches to the goods of marriage, see Chapter One of Walter Kasper's *Theology of Christian Marriage* (Seabury, 1980).

Part Two:

MARRIAGE— PSYCHOLOGICAL AND RELIGIOUS PASSAGES

Marriage today is less a social institution and more a life-long journey. In Part Two we explore the transitions that describe this complex journey: the movement of two individuals into a shared identity; the development of romance into committed love; the maturing transition from "we are" to "we care." The many transitions—both *into* marriage and those demanded as this relationship matures—of this life-long journey are examined in the light of the religious image of passage. A religious passage threatens loss and makes us vulnerable, but it is our route to greater maturity and fruit-fulness. The religious passage into marriage is explored in three stages: engagement, the wedding ceremony and the birth of the first child. In this interpretation, the sacrament of Matrimony becomes a lengthy process rather than a sudden transformation. The subsequent stages of the maturing of a marriage are examined in discussions of the family years and the mature years.

6

MARRIAGE BECOMES A JOURNEY

From Institution to Journey

This book, as we have said, is about the dissolution of marriage as a state in life and its survival as a journey. More precisely it is about the growing awareness of the fluidity and movement that mark marriage today. The changes and transitions which are a necessary part of a maturing marriage give it less the appearance of a stable institution than of a complicated journey. Pope Paul VI turned, in a speech in 1970, to this metaphor of movement:

> The journey of married people, like that of all human lives, has its stages; difficult and sorrowful moments have their place in it, as you know from your experience through the years.

But the Pope then suggested that, though such a journey includes difficulty and sorrow, it ought not to entail anxiety or fear: "But it must be stated clearly that anxiety and fear should never be found in souls of good will." In our discussion of marriage as a journey in the following chapters, we will understand anxiety and fear, not as indicators of a failure of good will, but as expectable perils on the way.

An institution can be imagined as a building that one enters. It is a solid, fixed place. Most everyone is expected to enter this institution and to remain in it. Once inside, a person receives the traditional privileges and obligations that come with residence.

The rules that apply here are well known and constant; everyone inside this institution is expected to follow them.

Understood as an institution, marriage has been a state that one either did or did not inhabit. Legally, a person is either married or not married; there is no in-between. The Christian Church, influenced by this legal orientation toward marriage, came to view matrimony as an either/or situation. Christian ambivalence about sexuality found a clear resolution in this institutional view of marriage. Outside this well-defined state no sexual sharing was permitted; once inside this institution, one could even demand one's sexual rights. There seemed no gradualness or development in this commitment; one was either in or out. The periods of engagement and of marriage preparation were anomalies; little effective attention and ministry could be given to these "borderline" events.

The shift in the image of marriage from that of an institution to that of a journey is in line with our experience of marriage today. The commitment of marriage is increasingly seen not as a contract between families but as a personal covenant between individuals. The *necessary instability* of marriage—the changes required as a person approaches it (and when a person must exit from it) and the transitions demanded within such a complex relationship—gives it less and less an institutional appearance.

The continuing shifts and challenges of a maturing marriage give it the appearance of a journey. Marriage as a journey suggests that this relationship is not a location in life but a pattern of movement. Marriage is not a place where we live but a way that we travel through life. The image of journey responds to our sense of the precariousness of marriage. Even after this trek is well begun, we continue to learn new things about ourself and our partner. These are often subtle and confusing things, not covered under the contract or the institutional warranty.

The change in our image of marriage reminds us that new skills and virtues will be needed: different strengths are required to live in an institution and to survive on a journey. More adaptable and even wily skills are called for on a trip that is only partly charted beforehand. The shift in our understanding of the virtues of marriage, once marriage becomes a journey, will be one of our concerns in Part Three of this book.

A second concern will be the patterns of movement discernible in this journey of marriage. Are we married people enough alike so that we can expect our marriages to be more than "private trips"? If so, what are the expectable turns, and detours, of this journey? What is the terrain of contemporary marriage? Is it similar enough that we can learn from one another how to become skillful travelers? In this section of the book we will examine the patterns of change in marriage today, especially under the rubric of marriage as a passage. But before turning to the transitions which bring us into marriage and would mature us there, let us recall that the images of institution and journey are both influential in our religious history.

Marriage was seen as an institution during the centuries when the Church itself was becoming a powerful social institution. Especially from the fourth century the Christian Church, originating as scattered groups of believers in Jesus Christ, increasingly pictured itself as an institution. At the beginning of the fifth century St. Augustine captured this self-understanding in the attractive image of the City of God. A city is a sort of institution: a stable, legal entity, it enjoys clear and certain boundaries. The citizens of the City of God were recognizable by their credential of Baptism. These citizens were expected to stay in the institution—to marry other Christians, their own kind. (This would get more complicated after the Reformation when Catholics would banish Protestants from their city, making them religiously "uncivilized" and therefore unmarriable.)

This institutionalizing of religious faith gave great clarity and stability to Christianity. Stability, unfortunately, is sometimes but a few steps from rigidity. The image of the City of God further solidified in the sixteenth-century hymn "A Mighty Fortress Is Our God." This hymn, still popular today, suggests a well-defended, institutional view of God and Christian faith. It also suggests, at least to many Christians today, that we know for certain where God is—with *us*. An institutional view of God tends to locate and even localize God in a definite, defended space. God is enshrined and "tabernacled" as ours. The legalistic management of this institution—be it the Church or marriage—naturally ensues.

Parallel to our recognition of marriage as a journey is our return to this primordial image as a description of our common religious faith. It was in the circuitous trek through the Sinai Desert that our religious ancestors came to their earliest encounters and covenant with God. Journey, then, should be an especially sacred image for us, whether describing our fragile and changing relationship with God or with our marriage partner. The metaphor of journey includes discovery and doubt, detours and new beginnings. It suggests the special set of virtues required for religious faith and for marriage—virtues which help us decide when to settle down and when to keep moving, which way to turn at a fork in the road, how to read the signs that tell us where we are.

The image of faith and of marriage as a journey also suggests a different understanding of our God. Not institutionalized in a shrine or other stable location, God is a presence sensed on the trip. God is a presence that visits our life in strange and unpredictable ways to give it meaning and direction. Religious faith and a Christian marriage require our attentiveness to this subtle and graceful presence.

Attractive as this image of the journey is, marriage today remains an institution as well. Marriage is too important for all of us for it to be reduced to a private affair. Every community has a stake in its marriages and so this commitment must remain public as a legal, social and religious institution. Yet today we are more conscious of marriage as a process, a path pursued, a journey which includes both expected and unexpected events.

Three Psychological Transitions in Marriage

Of the many transitions which describe the journey of a growing marriage, three merit special attention here. The first of these is the gradual movement from "I" to "we," the transition into married mutuality.

A couple may bring to marriage very different histories and identities. You are Italian, from a large and demonstrative family; I am English, an only child and unaccustomed to emotional displays. Each of us has lived apart from our families for a few years, establishing our independent ways of work and recreation. Now we would bring together these very separate "I's" into the "we" of marriage. The commonness of this "we" involves more than having the same address and sharing bed and board. It involves the merging of our separate patterns of living into a shared life. The stakes here are high; the risks can be considerable. A life-in-common will involve practical questions of how we use time and money and how we shall establish together the rhythms that make up a lifestyle. And deeper issues are concerned—our priorities and values, our energies and enthusiasms, our patterns of emotional responsiveness and sexual expression. The establishment of such a new life together includes the lengthy process of mutual knowledge and mutual influence. The challenge here is to create a "we" that is an expression of both "I's," where the identity of each is tested and expanded, probably even changed, but not destroyed.

This movement from two separate "I's" toward a shared life as "we" has long been seen as essential to the relationship of marriage. The Bible speaks of this common life in powerful images of union: "bone from my bones and flesh from my flesh" (Genesis 2:23) and "a man leaves his father and mother and joins himself to his wife, and they become one body" (Genesis 2:24). This close union is stressed in English common law statements, an important part of our own legal heritage, that in marriage "the two shall become one."

But what does it mean, that we two shall become one? At one level this image captures a psychological experience that is strong in romantic love—the desire to be together, to share everything, to overcome whatever separates us and to merge ourselves as fully as we can. And this image of union is not limited to early romance. For many who are married, "two becoming one" describes their experience of love growing and tested over time. "And they become one body" may not say all we know about marriage but it expresses both a reality and a hope in which our love is grounded.

Psychologically, then, these images of union ring true, even where they express only part of the larger reality of married love. But marriage is more than a psychological reality; it takes on social forms as well. And these social forms both reflect and influence how we understand the union of woman and man in marriage. In a society in which patriarchy is strong the union of marriage will be understood in terms of the legal preeminence of the husband. Thus an early formulation of English common law states bluntly that "the husband and wife are as one and that one is the husband."

In earlier generations in our own country this union of two-in-one has often been achieved by incorporating the wife—her ambitions, her energies, her values and opinions, often her material resources as well—into the plan and plot of her husband's life. And many women have found personal meaning and genuine fulfillment in this experience of marriage: giving themselves—even somewhat exclusively—to tasks and roles that have served, and often been subservient to, their husbands. But today there are new expectations of mutuality in the "we" of marriage. It is less and less acceptable among women (and, to be sure, among many men) that the "we" of marriage be achieved primarily through the absorption of the wife into her husband's identity and life ambition. So today the process of marriage involves the more difficult—and more rewarding—effort to create a "we" that bears the stamp of both spouses, a "we" that moves beyond each into a larger reality of a common life.

To create a life in common in which both of us survive and continue to grow, together—it is in this hope that couples approach marriage today. To achieve this we must each bring to marriage some beginning sense of confidence and comfort in "who I am." Neither a defended nor an unclear identity can easily move toward mutuality. If I am largely unsure of who I am, I am not able easily to sustain a relationship. If I must defend a fragile sense of self against the demands of change, then flexibility and compromise will be hard. In either case, it will be difficult for me to come close to you without the fear that I will lose myself. And it is this fear, that "we" must mean a loss of "I," that complicates the transition into a common life in marriage.

Complementarity, Equality, Mutuality

The mutuality that is a goal in marriage today takes us beyond the understanding of women and men as "complementary." Many couples experience themselves as complementing one another. We "fit" together well. Your dynamism enlivens me; my patience is a useful balance to your enthusiasm. Or, more pragmatically, I like to cook and you like to clean house. But as a cultural image "complementarity" does not celebrate these individual differences. Instead it reinforces the notion of the "innate" differences between all women and all men. In this understanding our complementarity in marriage is not something that we discover between us; it is rather a *given.* "After all, he's a man and she's a woman. It should be clear how their marriage should work." In this view it is not as two particular persons that we complement each other in our marriage; it is rather because each of us falls into one of the two "complementary" categories —male or female. Very often, then, as the image of complementarity actually functions, its appealing nuances of interdependence and exploration are lost. It becomes instead a restatement of a conventional notion of what marriage should be. Many critics judge that the impulse to understand women as "complementary" to men in marriage is similar to that which sees blacks as "separate but equal" in society. Both find their roots in a conviction of "the way things are" that owes more to ideology than to the evidence available.

If mutuality takes us beyond "complementarity" it takes us beyond "equality" as well. "Equality of opportunity" and "equality under the law" are appropriate statements of societal goals. But equality is a tricky objective in close relationships. This is not to say that intimacy always works itself out into some uneven dichotomy—leader-led or dominant-submissive. It suggests rather that quantitative images,. such as equality, are not always useful in personal relations. It is difficult to determine "equality" in emotion or concern or generosity. It is hard to measure what is "enough" for each of us to give in order that our love might develop or survive. We must each nurture our own integrity in our marriage, but this will go beyond keeping count of who "gives in" the most. For many of us, these core issues of mutuality—the tension between integrity and interdependence, between autonomy and compromise—are not adequately covered by the term "equality."

Mutuality implies real engagement between people. I am open enough in this engagement to meet *you*, not just my stereotypes of you or my prejudices about *your kind*. In mutuality both of us experience ourselves giving and receiving. We can acknowledge our dependence on one another without guilt or shame; we can celebrate the ways we empower each other, without resentment or control. We each sense that our greatest strength is born of our being together. It is truly my strength, but I owe it to our love. And together *we* are more than either of us is alone.

Establishing this kind of mutuality in our marriage involves the ongoing process of learning more about each other and ourselves and of influencing each other as we develop toward a life together. It is not just a process of the first years of marriage but a continuing dynamic of growth and change over a lifetime. So the "we" of our marriage is to be celebrated now, but we know also that it is still becoming.

From Romance to Committed Love

A second transition in marriage today is from romance to committed love. The dominant norm of marriage in America today is self-selection based on the criteria of romantic love. *I* choose whom I shall marry, and I choose to marry someone with whom I have fallen in love. The choice of romantic love is a complicated one, since romance often includes some element of projection. Part of what I see in you is my ideal of "man" or "woman," especially of the woman or man I shall marry. This ideal, itself partly a statement of my values and partly an expression of my needs, may correspond more or less closely to who you really are. So while romance may appear to be a highly personalized love, in many ways it is not. Romance often involves "falling in love with love." In the romantic stimulation of our discovery of love, we are likely to sense that we are perfectly suited to each other: we like the same things, we never argue, we share the same values of marriage and family life. As we live together in our marriage we will each have the chance to examine more closely this ideal. I will learn more about what I really want; I will learn more about who you really are.

The impact of romance in love may be described by the term "enchantment." I am enchanted by the one I love, enthralled by each detail and every mannerism. I am swept off my feet. *This* person, I am convinced, can rescue me at last—from my parents, from my dull job, even from myself. This marvelous power of romance appears in life as a most useful illusion. This larger-than-life, idealized view of the other energizes me to take on the commitments of married life. As an adult career often begins in larger-than-life ambitions of what I will be able to achieve, so romance leads me into marriage with powerful hopes of what our life together will be.

The route from romantic love toward a maturing marriage often goes by way of disenchantment. This is not to suggest that our prince (or princess) must always turn into a frog. It does mean that the enchanted, idealized view of my spouse will likely change as I come to know this person better. Practical decisions we must make about our children, our careers, even our house-cleaning, can reveal unknown parts of who we are, to ourselves and to each other. As our life together matures, I am invited to love not just my ideal spouse, but the simultaneously lovely and limited person whom I have married.

"Disenchantment" is an ambiguous term, to be sure. While for many of us it is a necessary stage between romance and a matured love, it is for some an experience simply of falling out of love. Unable to tolerate a non-ideal lover or a growing realization that the person I married is not the person I dated, I may find that for me disenchantment leads to divorce. Or it may lead to my beginning the cycle of romance again, this time in an extramarital affair with a more exciting (because still unknown) partner. Here disenchantment is not part of the maturing of our love into a resilient and personalized commitment but an experience that sets off a cycle of immaturity: needing the enchantment of romance, I seek "someone new," leaving behind the demands and invitations that arise in the familiarity of my experience of my spouse.

The process of maturing in marriage thus requires a movement beyond the exhilarating but largely passive experience of falling in love, to the experience of love as a chosen and cultivated commitment. It is the added element of commitment that transforms romantic love into the love that is able to sustain marriage for a lifetime. Committed love grows as I am able to know and cherish my spouse "as is," beyond the idealized images that may have been a part of our early experience of romance. I come to know you more completely and more clearly, as perhaps more gifted than I had dreamed but also as more flawed than I had hoped. This is a maturing love of choice. In the light of this deepening awareness of who you are and who I really am, I choose anew to love you. I reaffirm the commitment to do "whatever is necessary" so that this relationship in which we hold each other may live and grow.

This is the movement from romantic love to the love of mutual devotion, strong enough to sustain us in the moments of strain and confusion that are inevitably associated with our continuing close contact. Such devotion is possible only if each of us is capable of generous self-disregard.

This dynamic of mutual devotion is one of the most profound movements in marriage. In it the "active" and "passive" sides of love seem to merge in an experience of both caring and being cared for. We are together deeply and we each feel this as a strength. You know me so well . . . and still you love me. You care for me in ways that go beyond what I could ask for. You call me out to what is best in myself. I know you hold my life as important to you as your own. And all these gifts I give to you as well.

Most of us are not capable of this quality of love in adolescence or even in young adulthood. In our twenties few of us have the resources of self-possession and self-transcendence that are needed. Mature inner commitment is the fruit of our married love, not its initial seed. Romance gives us the hope of mutual love, but only the test of time together can bring its realization.

For some this test is too difficult. Romance does not mature into commitment but simply fades, leaving us dissatisfied and disillusioned. The movement beyond romance is expectable—even inevitable—in marriage. But the loss of love is not. The expectation that the quality of our commitment to one another will change does not mean that we must fall out of love. It means rather that we must move into a love that is larger than romance.

The Process of Sexual Maturing

While the commitment of marriage matures into a love that is larger than romance, it remains a love in which sexuality and affection are central. We approach sexual maturity in our marriage as we develop our capacity for sharing physical affection and genital pleasure. This sexual maturity, too, is more a process than a state. We learn to be good lovers and, for most of us, it takes time.

To give ourselves to this process of sexual maturing we must each be able to move beyond the experience of love play and intercourse as chiefly competitive—an experience of proving myself as a "real" woman or man or "winning out" over my partner. These interpretations of sex keep the focus on "me," making mutuality difficult. And without mutuality, sex is more often a barrier to, than a part of, the larger psychological experience of intimacy.

In contrast with many marriages of a generation ago, couples today generally approach marriage with greater awareness of their own bodies and with more information about genital sex. This intellectual sophistication is a boon to marriage, but it is, again, more a starting point of a satisfying sex life than its guarantee. Married sex is a process through which we both learn to contribute to what is, for us, mutually satisfying shared sexual experience. We learn the physical and emotional nuances that make lovemaking special for us. We develop the patterns of expression that fit us—patterns of frequency, of time and place, of initiation and response. We discover the ways in which passion and affection, humor and intensity, are a part of our own love life.

The exhilaration of sexual discovery is usually strong early in marriage, at least if we are able to move beyond an initial embarrassment. For most of us, it is our spouse who gives us the gift of knowing our sexuality to be beautiful. Loving me in my body, you invite me beyond the shame and guilt I carry still. With you, I am free to explore my passion and to expose my vulnerability and self-doubt. Having risked the self-revelation of sex —and survived—we can approach with greater confidence the other, even more threatening, processes of self-disclosure upon which the quality of our life together will depend.

After this early period of exploration, our sexual life may begin to level off. We have found a pattern that works for us and, especially in the press of the other responsibilities of our lives, this pattern can become routine.

It may be only gradually that we realize in our marriage that, though our love is strong, our lovemaking somehow falls short. Our early sexual sharing was surrounded with an aura of romance. Frequently, this romantic aura made our experiences of sex more satisfying than our lovemaking skills would otherwise justify! Now sex seems to have lost this savor. We know that the substance of our love is more important than our sexual style, but the questions of sexual style and satisfaction may begin to become more important than they were for us earlier in our marriage.

American culture's current interest in sexual techniques reinforces this concern over our own sex life. We are more aware of the richness of human sexuality and of the diversity of sexual expression. This new awareness can work destructively, setting up yet another standard of "success" against which to evaluate our own intimacy. But it need not have this negative effect. Instead it can remind us that the patterns of mutually satisfying sexual experience can be expected to differ from couple to couple. And that it is *we* who can best discover what these patterns are for us. In sex, as in most other aspects of our marriage, to be "mature" does not mean to fit some general criterion of performance but to have a developing (and, perhaps, changing) sense of what is appropriate *for us,* what works *for us.*

Sex research shows the contribution that diversity and surprise make to long-term sexual satisfaction. This realization can be liberating, inviting us to expand the ways in which we celebrate the sexuality of our marriage. This sense of exploration helps us move beyond a point of sexual boredom or routine, stimulating our own creativity in lovemaking. The expanding literature of sexual functioning can assist this process of sexual maturity in marriage, not by giving us a norm of what is "best" but by providing information that can enrich our own experimentation and choice.

The Movement from "We Are" to "We Care"

A third significant transition in the process of marriage is the movement from "we are" to "we care." Here we are involved in balancing the tensions between our own intimacy and the larger responsibilities of our lives. There is the challenge to move beyond our love as a couple in order that we may contribute to, and care for, a larger world. We can experience some strain as we try to learn ways to move beyond ourselves that do not destroy the experience and commitments of mutuality between us. The birth of the first child can be an early experience of this challenge. How shall we be for each other when we now must also be for our child? Job responsibilities and career choices also raise the challenge. Does marriage mean that only one of us may pursue a career? How do I, how do we, manage the multiple demands of being responsible citizen, financial provider, parent and spouse? The question can surface as an issue of social concern. How do we balance our commitments to each other and to our children alongside our responsibility to the needs of the world beyond ourselves?

The dilemma may be posed this way: What is our marriage for? Do we exist as a couple only for ourselves? Or does our being together go beyond ourselves? Are the resources of support and challenge that we generate in our family to be spent solely within our family? Or is there "enough" of us so that we can take the risk of sharing some of our resources (of love or concern or time or goods) with the world beyond? Is the love we share simply "a haven in a hostile world" or is it also a force that frees us to "love our neighbor as ourselves"?

Love is creative beyond itself and it must be so if it is to endure. A love that does not give life beyond itself risks becoming a caricature of intimacy. It is true that there is often a stage of mutual absorption in love, especially in the early experience of romance. The lovers are enthralled with each other. Everything about the other person is engrossing—and there is little beyond this relationship itself that seems worthy of attention. Job responsibilities, school activities, other friends and family—all pale to insignificance. In this timeless present of romance, "you and I" is all there is.

The world tends to be tolerant of this attitude in lovers—at least for a while. Recalling our own experience with romance we overlook much of the bizarre behavior of new love and excuse the rest. We know this shared obsession is but a phase of romance; soon it passes. The romance may mature into a deeper love or it may die from lack of any further substance. But in either case the charmed circle of exclusive fascination will be broken. Soon the lovers shall rejoin us—better, we trust, for the experience.

This early exclusivity in love is normal, an important dynamic of the process of exploration and self-disclosure that contributes to the possibility of commitment. But maturing love moderates this exclusivity. Being *for* one another does not require that each of us must be against everyone else. Indeed, the enrichment we experience in being for one another leads us to be for more than "just us." Our love for one another gives us more of what is best in each of us. We feel the impetus to move beyond ourselves, to share this wealth, to bring others into the power of what our love has given us. This movement of expansion is itself an expectable dynamic of love as it matures. Psychologists are aware of the importance to our love of this impulse beyond ourselves.

They warn that the absence of any movement beyond "just us" imperils a love relationship. A "pseudo-intimacy" can result, turning the partners in upon themselves in a way that gradually impoverishes the relationship. What results from this failure to expand our concern is not an intimacy more protected and complete, but stagnation. Having failed to share our love beyond ourselves we soon find that we have little left to give each other.

This truth about love, of concern in current psychology, does not come as news to our religious tradition. Love that does not give life beyond itself will die—Christian wisdom has long proclaimed this sometimes fleeting insight of our own experience. There is an essential connection between loving and giving life. It is, in part, this abiding truth that the Church has tried to share in its celebration of the fruitfulness of marriage.

In our history there has been a tendency to understand this connection in an almost exclusively biological sense—that every act of genital love must be open to the creation of a child, that bearing children is the most important goal of marriage and married love. Many Catholics today, especially married lay persons, find these statements of the connection between marriage and generative love to be at odds with their own experience. But the larger truth, that a maturing love in marriage both wants to and needs to go beyond itself, is reinforced by our experience and our religious heritage.

Reflective Exercise

Spend some time in reflection on the movement of your own marriage. (An unmarried person may find it useful to reflect here on a marriage that he or she knows well.)

Recall the events and directions, the changes and reverses, the choices and surprises that have been part of it. Take time with this recollective phase. Be aware of your sense of the movement of the months and years, your awareness of your own marriage in process.

Then consider in turn each of the three transitions discussed in this chapter.

The movement from "I" to "we." How has this been a part of your marriage? What times or events seem especially significant here? Has the transition been gradual or has it been marked by particular challenges or struggles?

The movement from romance to committed love. Do you sense that your marriage has moved beyond romance? In what ways has this been an experience of loss? In what ways, an experience of gain? What transitions have you known in your sexual life together? How would you describe your commitment to one another at this time in your marriage?

The movement from "we are" to "we care." Can you trace the ways in which your love for one another has moved beyond yourselves over the years of your marriage thus far? How has this expansion of your care contributed to your marriage? How has it challenged your marriage? What is it that you care for together now?

Additional Resources

Gerald Joyce and James Zullo give a concise overview of the research information available concerning the expectable issues that may arise in a marriage over the course of its development in "Ministry to Marital Growth: A Developmental Perspective," which appeared originally in the Fall 1979 issue of *Chicago Studies* and is reprinted in the *Chicago Studies* collection on *Marriage*. Joan Meyer Anzia and Mary G. Durkin, drawing on the discussions of an interdisciplinary colloquium on human intimacy, explore the key moments in the marriage journey in terms of the cycles of marital intimacy in *Marital Intimacy: A Catholic Perspective* (Andrews and McMeel, 1980). The text of Pope Paul VI's discussion of marriage as a journey may be found in the May 4, 1970, issue of *The Pope Speaks*.

Social scientists have taken up the examination of romantic love and its place in the larger experience of love, sexuality and devotion. Two recent examples are Kenneth Pope and associates, *On Love and Loving* (Jossey-Bass, 1980), a consideration of romantic love as a psychological experience, and John Money's

Love and Love Sickness (Johns Hopkins University Press, 1980), in which he examines issues of sex and gender difference in love relationships and beyond. In *Sexpression* (Prentice-Hall, 1980) Janice Wilson focuses on improving sexual communication in love relationships.

7

PASSAGE AND RELIGIOUS CHANGE

If marrying is a lifelong journey, how shall we map its maturing? Does marriage, which today encompasses so many different ways of being together, have a common terrain? Are there some movements which are to be expected in most marriages? We will draw on the anthropological category of *passage* to help us understand these expectable movements of marriage. The notion of passage, recently popularized in Gail Sheehy's book by this title, has deeply religious roots. Unfortunately, though, the word has become a part of the jargon of the day, thus losing much of its clarifying force. Any confusing time in our own or someone else's life is now called a passage. This ready explanation can distract us from the deeper learning that may be available to us in the complex transitions of our lives. But if we follow the term beyond its superficial meaning it can alert us to the specific elements and inner dynamic of significant life changes. Marriage as a passage will be our central concern here, though the term can refer to other significant transitions as well, such as a career change or the loss of a spouse. The goal of this examination is to clarify the psychological transition into marriage and to highlight the religious nature of this passage. As we proceed we will also gain some clues to how a community might more effectively care for its members as they enter this challenging passage.

The Stages of a Passage

A life passage such as marriage can be expected to have three stages. An initial stage of *separation* is followed by a middle period of some duration, called the stage of *marginality*. A passage is successfully completed as a person moves into a third stage of *reintegration* in the community in a new and different way of living.

Separation. A passage is begun as a person realizes that she or he is being separated from a former way of living or of understanding self. This change may happen abruptly or gradually. A passage involving a career change may begin in my growing dissatisfaction with my present job. This vague sense of discomfort or stagnation may develop into a clear need to find another kind of career. But this same kind of passage can also be initiated by my being fired. Very suddenly I am separated from my work and the important information it gives me about who I am and what I am worth. A passage begins in this being separated from familiar and secure ways of acting and of thinking about myself. Sometimes we are forcibly pulled away from this familiarity and security; other times we choose gladly to leave a security that has become restricting and stagnant.

This stage of separation in the passage into marriage is often obscured by the fascination of meeting another person and falling in love. However conscious we are of it, we are invited here to begin to separate ourselves from former ways of doing things. My dependence on my parents or my independent manner of making decisions, my daily habits of work and play, these will be altered as I move toward a life with someone else. The romance and excitement which accompany this time can disguise the necessary ambiguity of this separation. Moved by the prospect of a new life with you, I am glad to leave behind old ways of doing things, old ways of deciding and acting. I enthusiastically separate myself from my former lifestyle and independence to pursue this new, common life. Bachelor parties and bridal showers are customs that contribute to this separation. In the bachelor party the bridegroom both celebrates and takes his leave from his former way of life. Showers for the bride, with their focus on gifts and the preparation for marriage, may disguise the separation of the woman from her former way of being with her friends, but these, too, celebrate a coming change.

But I can also expect to experience—especially as I take the time to reflect and make this transition more consciously—some threat in this separation. I am losing parts of my life that had been very familiar and important to me. My identity, my sense of who I am and what I am for, was tied to these customary ways of thinking and acting. I can expect some anxiety in this separation. It is even useful for me to be aware of the separation that is happening. The later distress of a marriage is, at times, related to a delayed discovery of what has been lost in this transition into a communal life. Part of the concern that interested outsiders often experience over a marriage which follows a very brief courtship is that there may not have been sufficient opportunity to allow this separation to happen. We fear that the man may find himself married but still not having left his parents or that the woman may have married without separating from some of her former independence in the pursuit of her career.

A Period of Marginality. After an introductory stage of separation, persons moving toward marriage can expect a period of marginality, or "in-betweenness." This period of ambiguity often parallels the time between a couple's decision to marry and the marriage itself. With this decision a person leaves behind, in part, a former way of living; yet the person has not fully begun the new way of life which is marriage. Old ways of thinking and acting, though familiar, no longer quite fit; but new, communal ways of acting are neither familiar nor fully in place.

Parallels with the passage into a new career may be helpful. A person decides to leave the old job or career, but has not quite effected the change yet. The person is in between the old and the new; this period may last several months or a year. During this time of in-betweenness, of being on the margin, we can expect considerable anxiety. What if I let go my former job and the new one falls through? What if I leave behind the familiar, secure career and fail at the new one? Thus with the passage into marriage: what if I give up my single life and this marriage venture fails? During the period of a couple's engagement (and beyond) we can expect these "second thoughts." They are a healthy part of the assessment and reassessment that make up the passage into marriage.

This period of the passage is a time of risk and vulnerability. The person is *in the middle* of a transition, without the protection and security of familiar habits. It is a time for deepening the risky process of intimate sharing and self-disclosure that will allow the marriage to grow. We sense that this process makes us vulnerable, but most of us take the chance of being hurt because we sense the risk is worth it. With some hesitance, we move further on the continuing journey into a deep and complex personal intimacy.

Those who write about passages, such as anthropologists Mary Douglas and Victor Turner, note the extraordinary opportunity of this period. Mary Douglas terms this "the potency of disorder." During a time when customary and familiar ways are being set aside we can become very disoriented; our life is disordered. But this disorientation and loss make room for reorientation and great gain. If I do not lose my orientation as a single person, I remain single in my heart—even though I go through a marriage ceremony. Disorientation—and the distress that accompanies it—is expectable and necessary if I am to be reoriented, changed by the demands and invitations of my new life with another person. The challenge of this middle period can be complicated by cultural expectations that, as "grown-ups," we be mature, stable, unconfused and decisive. If we have learned well such expectations for ourselves, we may be embarrassed by the confusion, ambivalence and even distress of a passage. But such distress and anxiety are normal: we are trying to let go a familiar, secure way of life and are not yet at ease with our new, hoped-for way of being. We resist letting go the familiar, even when we know it is the only way to grow.

The duration of this central part of a passage is important. The wisdom of an engagement period before marriage responds to the need for time to separate from old ways, tentatively practice new ways and deal with the anxieties that will accompany these tasks. When a couple weds very quickly we wonder if the work of this passage has been accomplished, or whether it will add a burden to the marriage in later months and years. Likewise, when we see a person marry on the rebound after a divorce, we ask: has the work of mourning the loss of the other relationship been completed? Has the person fully let go that relationship, facing its failure and the accompanying movements of anger, guilt and blame? Or is the new marriage less a passage into a new life than a means of blocking or distracting the person from the pain and loneliness of the present?

Finally, as we better recognize the enormous potential of this time—the peculiar openness to learning and the opportunity for reorientation and personal change—we can ask how a community, especially a Christian community, can more effectively care for its members during this time. We will explore this question of ministry later in this chapter.

Reincorporation: Exit from the Passage. After some time in this "in-between" stage, a person finds that he or she has "come through," is emerging from the passage. The letting go the old and putting on the new is (to some extent) accomplished. This marks the exit from the passage and the entry again into a more stable way of life, at least for the present. One's movement into this stage is often signaled by the feeling that it is now time to get on with life. A clear example of this occurs in the passage brought about by the death of a spouse or a child. Abruptly or gradually separated from this loved one, a person is plunged into a transition that leads toward life without that person. During the in-between, the marginal state, mourning may occupy much energy and attention: regret, anger, guilt, sorrow flow through me as I try both to let go my loved one who has died and to find a new way of being, now alone. This mourning will take months, even several years. In the successful negotiation of such a painful passage, I finally come to a realization that it is over: the mourning, I find (maybe to my surprise), is finished; it is time to go on.

We all feel the need to acknowledge this completion. We want to say publicly: "it is accomplished." We want to give thanks, to acknowledge a work finished, a new stage of life begun. Religious or not, we turn to ritual to help us here—to say in a more formal, emphatic way what has happened to us and where we are. It is important to note that the timing of these social rituals does not always coincide with our own movement through the phases of a passage. For example, a funeral ceremony rarely marks the end of a passage; this ritual of formal mourning usually precedes the longer passage of personal mourning. This is also the case with the passage into marriage: a formal engagement does not necessarily mark the entry into the crucial "in-between" stage of this passage and the marriage ceremony does not necessarily celebrate the completion of the transition. As adults, we mature on different schedules. The challenge to each of us is to become aware of our own schedule; the challenge to the Christian community is to effect a better fit between ritual celebrations of marriage and the schedules of maturing for particular Christian couples.

When a Passage Fails

When we talk about marriage and other adult events as passages, we may give the impression that these transitions are automatic, that a person always "gets through" them. But this is not so. We can, in various ways, fail to negotiate the important transitions of adult life. Or having begun, we can become enmeshed and fail to get through to the other side. Again, a clear example is the loss of a loved one. A parent who loses a child is invited into a process of mourning, letting go and coming to a new relationship with the child who has died. But such a complex and painful passage sometimes breaks down; the parent can be overcome by sorrow and regret and can refuse to admit this death and its changes. Chronic grief ensues and the parent is unable to get through the passage.

A less dramatic but similar response can happen with a person approaching marriage. In the midst of increasing intimacy, a person can become very apprehensive about a marriage commitment. Is this the right thing for me, or not? The person goes back and forth—but cannot decide. The engagement or the marriage is postponed, replanned, postponed again. One way to describe this situation is to see the person caught in the middle of a passage. This is not to say that a person in this dilemma should always go ahead with the marriage; but it does remind us that passages are not for "settling in," but for "going through."

To turn back from a life transition is another way we can fail to complete a passage. As the transition begins I may be overwhelmed by its danger and confusion. If it appears too dangerous, I will turn back. If it seems to me that I will lose too much of myself in this transition, I must choose not to continue through it. As I approach marriage I may sense that I will lose too much of what I cherish. I fear being absorbed into the other person or brought into a way of life that is simply not tolerable for me. So I choose not to go ahead with such a transition. It is important to add that this is not necessarily done out of fear or cowardice; it may be mature insight into myself that leads me not to undertake the passage.

The psychological and religious transitions of marriage are not always identical with the public, social act of marrying. I can choose not to pass through this profound passage, with its required losses and new demands, even though I am married in public. I appear to enter marriage—appear so even to my spouse or to myself—but interiorly I refuse the changes, the transitions required for this entry into a fully common life. In fact, I remain single. In such a marriage it becomes clear over time that the ceremony did not, in reality, celebrate a passage from two independent "I's" into a communal "we."

Passage as a Religious Event

We humans have always recognized some of the transitions in life to be extraordinarily important. The passages of birth and death demand special attention: with various rituals we try to slow down enough to pay attention to these important transitions at the boundaries of human life. The two other most impressive transitions are the movement from adolescence into adulthood and the movement into marriage. These extraordinary transitions have always invited us out of our busy, distracted routines of daily life into reflection on our deeper values, often obscured by these routines.

Religious people—those of us who envision, at least at times, a special purpose to and a special presence in life—find these passages to be times of religious opportunity. We recognize these transitions as times of special grace, times of personal growth that hold opportunities for recommitment to our sometimes fragile religious beliefs.

To suggest that passages are religious events is not to "baptize" a basically secular concept. Deep in our history stands a passage that both began our religious history and still describes our own lives. This is the passage of the Exodus. This very long journey, recalled in Chapter 6, shows the specific structure of a passage. In this archetypal passage a group of people separated themselves from a familiar if restrictive life, went through a long period "in-between" in the Sinai Desert and finally found their way to a new life in a new land. Israel and the Judeo-Christian tradition were born in that passage. Christians, in times of personal transition and confusion (as in the experience of the post-Vatican II Church), have always identified with this originating passage. Enduring ambiguity and the loss of what is familiar, we trek toward a place promised to us.

The Exodus and, especially, the passage that Jesus went through in his death and resurrection alert Christians to the potential holiness of their own life passages. Here we will examine the religious character of life passages in three aspects: the central dynamic of loss and gain, the discipline or asceticism of letting go and the response of a community in rites of passages.

The Dynamic of Loss and Gain

The central dynamic of a passage is that of loss and discovery. In a passage we come to recognize that we must give something up. In marriage, for example, we become aware that we are being deprived of some previous part of ourselves—perhaps a cherished and important part. Yet we sense that only by each of us surrendering some part of our identity and self-sufficiency will we able to grow into a new interdependence. The loss leaves room for gain; emptying makes space for the new.

The exuberance which naturally accompanies the transition into marriage may easily obscure the loss we are being invited to undergo. The Christian community, in education and ritual, will try to assist its members concretely to identify that loss and celebrate it as part of the religious growth into the new life of marriage.

This mystery, that in dying we find life, is both a psychological paradox and a Christian mystery. It is a truth of everyday life, but a truth obscured. Jesus' life stands for us as the central instance of this mystery: in his premature death he generated a new way of living for those who would believe. In calling his friends to this mature insight Jesus turned to the example of agricultural fertility: "Unless a grain of wheat falls on the ground and dies, it remains only a single grain; but if it dies, it yields a rich harvest" (John 12:24). Christ's life and our own transitions invite us, repeatedly, to rediscover and embrace this extraordinary truth.

The Discipline of Letting Go

This religious dynamic of loss and gain calls a person in passage to the discipline of letting go. Again, this is both a natural and a religious discipline. We cling to our possessions and the gains that come to us in life. They signal our value and worth; they tell us and others who we are and how important we are. Yet in every significant transition of life we are asked to let go of something important: to put away the carefreeness and relative lack of responsibility of youth in becoming an adult; to let go of the social identity tied to our job in the passage into retirement. The person who hoards things is one who cannot let go, who needs it all. If we are all shaped by the cultural values of gain and accumulation, Christianity stands as a counterculture, urging another attitude toward accumulation and loss. And passages teach us all that hoarding is not a proper response to life;

passages teach us to let go. The *repeated* passages of life begin to teach us a discipline, a way of being virtuous. Virtue and maturity in this sense mean becoming skilled at letting go—knowing what and when to give up. The Christian tradition teaches us this discipline preeminently in the life of Jesus Christ. Christian concern for detachment, indifference and even self-abnegation point to this same insight: to hoard—not only physical possessions but even past parts of myself—is to encumber myself on the journey. This letting go, learned with special force in the transitions of our life, is a discipline or asceticism for maturing in holiness. And at the heart of this discipline is the virtue of faith: as we let go some part of the self there is a period when we have not entered into a firm possession of our gain. During this interval we must believe. The person who cannot believe cannot afford the risk of letting go. For the person unable to let go, transitions through the passages of life will be very harrowing.

As we approach and enter marriage we exercise this discipline in clarifying, for ourselves and one another, what each of us must let go if we are to grow into a life together.

Rites of Passage

Human communities have always structured rites of passage to assist their members through these life transitions. In times of change or of danger and confusion—as in birth, or death, or coming to adulthood—a community was called to one of its essential roles: to make sense of what confuses the individual and to support the person through this vulnerable time.

Passages are not to be navigated alone. The experience and wisdom of a community are needed to help tame the distress and even terror of these times. In its rites of passage a community acts to protect and to predict: it protects the individual from the danger and disorientation of this life transition; it also predicts—in story, symbol and ritual—that the person will come through successfully.

The Christian community devises rites that allow us to recognize the religious opportunity of these dangerous times. With ritual and sacramental celebration the community acknowledges these moments as filled with grace and as holding special religious invitations. The challenging and potentially graceful passage into marriage has been celebrated by Catholics in the sacrament of Matrimony.

Marriage as a Sacramental Passage

We have been discussing marriage as a complex passage of some duration. In the sacramental theology of our recent past, however, Matrimony was understood as a more abrupt entry into a state in life. A different theology of sacraments will be necessary to support the view of marriage as both a sacrament and a passage.

Catholic liturgists and theologians have been reluctant to compare Christian sacraments and life passages. There are important differences between the two symbol systems: Baptism does not belong to biological infancy, but to a person's entry into Christian faith and community, *whenever* it occurs; Confirmation is not a religious puberty rite. Yet despite these and many other differences, marriage does appear as both a life passage and Christian sacrament. A reflection on marriage as a passage may help us recognize the ongoing quality of this and other sacraments.

Such a reflection begins with the now common insight that marriage is not a state that we suddenly enter on our wedding day. The sacrament of marriage cannot be understood in terms of a single ritual which magically transforms us from two into one forever. The sacramental celebration of marriage in the rites and ceremonies of the Christian Church must be the celebration of a process already well under way and of a process which has still some considerable way to go. We will try, then, to rescue the meaning of sacrament from a narrow "rite only" interpretation and explore how the *process* of approaching and beginning marriage is part of the sacrament of Matrimony.

This effort to understand a sacrament as more than a ritual—

as, in fact, a combination of ritual celebration and gradual in-
duction ("leading into")—is not restricted to the transition of
marriage. The sacrament of Baptism clearly includes this combination of ritual and process. In the sacramental ritual of Baptism, Christians celebrate the entry of (most often) a child into
the Christian community. In this sacramental celebration the
Church and the family welcome the child into Christian life: we
invoke God's blessing on the long journey just beginning; we
hope for the child all the goodness and holiness that such a life
can mean; and we ritually celebrate the child's passage from an
unnamed infant to a named member of this faith community.
But this celebration, effected in a brief ritual on a single day,
must be complemented by the process, years long, of actually
bringing the child into Christian living. The ritual celebration of
Baptism depends on this process of love and care and example
which will show this child what Christian living means in practice. The importance of this *process* of being practically introduced into Christian life is such that we may think of it as part
of the sacrament.

Changing practices in Christian missions today point to this
broader understanding of the sacrament. Missionaries no longer
baptize every child possible, believing that this ritual *of itself*
will transform the child into a Christian. Without the support of
a believing community—a group that can show the child what
Christian loving, trusting and caring actually look like—a child
is not properly baptized. A fascination with the sacramental ritual itself has in the past distracted us from the importance of the
process of the sacraments. To baptize a child and not provide a
community which, over time, can practically effect this introduction into Christian life, is a magical and false application of
the sacrament.

The parallels between the sacraments of Baptism and Matrimony are easy to see. The sacrament of Matrimony combines a
ritual celebration and a process or passage. In the ritual celebration the couple publicly express their life commitment and formally begin their life together. In this public and Christian commitment, the couple are empowered (receive the grace of this
sacrament) to pursue the fidelity and fruitfulness of a Christian

marriage. But the celebration of a single *ritual* must be complemented by a Christian sacramental *process*. This process, like that of Baptism, can be expected to have a significant duration. As with Baptism, we often do see the sacrament of Matrimony celebrated without any supporting process. A couple who have little or no practical commitment to Christian living are married in the Church. (The parents may insist on it, or the couple think it is more appealing than a ceremony before the justice of the peace.) A narrow focus on the sacrament as effected in a single ritual leads to the impression that this is Matrimony—the beginning of an explicitly Christian marriage. But, as in Baptism, this ritual celebration does not enjoy the magical power to effect a way of life to which the couple are not otherwise practically committed.

The narrow focus on Matrimony as a single ritual celebration has been aided by a restricted view of Christian responsibility and ministry. As ministry in the Catholic tradition became increasingly understood as the exclusive domain of the clergy, the laity became more and more passive. The sacraments were administered by the clergy; the laity received the sacraments; the faith community became the almost neutral site where this ministry transpired.

Today we are recovering a view of Christian ministry that more powerfully involves all adult believers. Regarding Matrimony, we are recalling that the couple are themselves the celebrants of their marriage; the priest does not marry them but witnesses in the name of the Church their performing of this sacrament. And our recovery of marriage as an ongoing passage further reminds us of the active role of the believing community. Just as the individuals marrying do not passively receive this sacrament, the faith community has an active contribution to make to this and every sacrament. Our changed vocabulary signals this shift: the priest does not "say Mass"; the faith community "celebrates the Eucharist."

If the priest is not the minister of Matrimony, neither can the couple be its sole and independent celebrants. The community's support, expressed in wedding gifts and congratulations, must also find a more sustained and explicitly religious expression.

Sacramental theology since Vatican II has stressed again the role of the Church as itself a sacrament. Practically, this means that a particular Christian community is called to witness, to couples approaching and those already living marriage, to what Christian marriage really looks like. Further, this sacramental role of the community necessitates more than a general witness. A faith community concretely participates in the ongoing celebration of Christian marriage by structuring educational opportunities for those approaching and living marriage. These will include specific programs—in the parish or elsewhere—that allow a couple, engaged or married, to explore their relationship and deal with its questions and challenges. These opportunities should not be understood as merely psychological or secular events, however helpful. When structured skillfully and with a specifically religious intent, these programs are an integral part of the sacrament of Matrimony. In this assistance a community itself becomes a sacrament in more than rhetoric and gracefully contributes to the sacramental passage of its members into Christian marriage.

This sacramental response of a community to couples entering and pursuing married life can more broadly be understood in terms of rites of passage. In a variety of ways, over an extended period, we are called to provide practical means of caring for those entering marriage. This is a challenge not just for a pastor but for the community itself. And the community will structure effective means of support and challenge as it better understands the different stages of this transition into marriage. In the next chapter we will examine the complex passage *into* marriage. In the two chapters that follow we will explore the movements of a marriage as it matures.

Reflective Exercise

In this exercise you are invited to revisit the past five years of your life. Take some time to let the events of these years—your work, friendships, changes—return to you. Where have you been and what have you been doing during these years?

As these years become more present to you, select a significant change or transition that stands out in this period. Inquire whether this transition has some of the signs of a passage: Did this change entail losing or letting go of something? Was there a period of "in-betweenness" when you were unsure where this change was leading? How long did it last? Who helped you through this passage and how was it finally concluded?

As you look back on this important transition, can you sense God at work in it? Was there some force outside yourself leading you to change and grow? What was the grace of this passage —the surprising ability to let go of some part of yourself? The courage to face a new stage in your life?

Finally you might ask: Does this passage feel fully completed? Is it still so recent or painful to recall that you sense it needs more attention? Does it yet require some mourning and letting go?

Additional Resources

The work of anthropologist Victor Turner provides excellent descriptions and analyses of human passages; see especially his *The Ritual Process* (Cornell University Press, 1969) and "Passages, Margins, and Poverty: Religious Symbols of Communitas," which appeared in two parts in the August and October 1972 issues of *Worship*. We consider the relation of adult crises to religious passages in Chapter 2 of our *Christian Life Patterns* (Doubleday, 1979).

In *Liturgy and Human Passage* (Seabury, 1978), edited by David Powers and Luis Maldonado, Aidan Kavanaugh and David Powers each urge the careful distinction of life passages from the Christian sacraments. All the contributors to this volume seem to sense, though with much caution, the fruitfulness of comparing these two symbol systems.

With our colleague Gordon Myers we discuss the process or passage aspects of traditional Christian sacraments in our paper "The Parish and Sacraments of Adulthood: Accesses to an

Educational Future," in the Spring 1977 issue of *Listening: Journal of Religion and Culture.*

Karl Rahner's theological reflection on "Considerations of the Active Role of the Person in the Sacramental Event," found in Volume 14 of his *Theological Investigations* (Seabury, 1976), is difficult reading but rewards the effort with important insight into a central question in sacramental theology today. For a collection of brief and clear essays on Christian sacraments, see *The Sacraments* (Alba House, 1981), edited by Michael J. Taylor.

8

THE PASSAGE INTO MARRIAGE

To recognize marriage as a passage is to see it as a transition that takes time, one composed of different stages, each with its own tasks and challenges. In this chapter we will examine three stages within the complex passage *into* marriage. These stages, in turn, can teach us how a community might more effectively care for its members who are making this passage.

Engagement

The first stage of marriage begins in the decision to marry. With or without a formal engagement ceremony, a couple at some point come to a decision to marry. With this decision they enter the process and begin the passage of marriage. Historically, a couple were "betrothed." An agreement—usually between the families of the couple—initiated this first, ambiguous stage of commitment.

This first stage is ambiguous because the couple are committed *to* marry, but are not yet committed *in* marriage. Exactly how "engaged" are we or should we be? Typical of a passage, this stage begins the process of separation from our former life and introduces us to an "in-betweenness." We enter into a serious but partial commitment. Religious people, sometimes apprehensive that such a partial commitment will involve sexual and genital engagement, have often argued against the seriousness of this stage of the relationship. The question of sexual expression is important here and must be considered in the context of a deepening psychological intimacy and commitment.

The peculiarity and ambiguity of this in-between stage of engagement beg for some comparisons. Similar experiences of serious but partial commitment occur for persons in seminaries and religious novitiates (preparing to enter a religious order or congregation). These men and women, often of comparable age to those entering marriage, begin to live a lifestyle and vocation to which they have yet to fully commit themselves. They live in an in-between stage—acting much like vowed religious or priests but not yet formally or finally committed to such a vocation. This comparison will be odious for some, since it seems to raise the specter of "trial marriage." Yet it remains intriguing for us to consider that we have young persons move gradually and carefully into certain vocations, but rather abruptly and often without preparation into others. Quite apart from questions of sexual expression between an engaged couple, we can ask how the passage into marriage might be structured with some of the care that goes into the vocations of the priest and vowed religious.

During this ambiguous time of engagement, what are the specific tasks for the couple? An obvious task, though it is not always attended to, is that of mutual sharing and self-disclosure. Who are we? What do we hope for in this relationship? What apprehensions arise as we spend time together? The *duration* of this stage becomes important in regard to these apprehensions: only with time can I become aware of my deepest hopes and fears about a lifetime together. Whether these fears concern sexuality, control or career, it is most valuable that they can be heard and shared now. Our ability to attend to these parts of ourselves now will be an indication of our ability to confront and resolve other difficulties and fears which will arise later in our marriage.

In this early stage of the passage into marriage, a couple might inquire: From what is each of us separating? What must we let go as we move into this new relationship? What, for instance, are our expectations about closeness to our parents and family? Do we have significantly different notions about our independence from, or continuing relation with, these families? It can be very useful to examine these questions for a first time now rather than two years after we are married.

Expectably, an engaged couple's attention is focused on the future. There are questions here, too, that can help them explore the similarities and differences that exist in their visions of life together. How do we think we should make our decisions after we are married? What size family do we hope for? Whatever the content of the reflection, these questions invite the couple beyond the glow of romantic excitement which convinces them that "we like all the same things." Without suggesting that an engaged couple become calculating and overly methodical, we can hope that they use this time well to deepen their intimacy through a continuing and concrete sharing of hopes.

The discussion of intimacy and self-disclosure returns us to the question of sexual sharing. What is appropriate and what is permitted? The notion of marriage as a passage with stages of deepening intimacy and commitment threatens the conventional Christian understanding that all genital expression is forbidden before marriage. In the past, Christians have been concerned that the growing intimacy between the engaged couple not reach genital expression. A more contemporary concern of Christians might be that this intimacy not be limited to genital expression. Many young adults today find sexual sharing easier than psychological and religious self-disclosure. Christians hope for a growing intimacy which is more than improved sexual compatibility: an increase in intimacy which includes a greater openness not only to each other's bodies but also to each other's dreams and faith.

Rites of Passage: Ministering to Engaged Couples

In this important stage of the passage into marriage a variety of secular rites of passage have evolved to signal and assist the transition. As we noted in Chapter 7, a wedding shower celebrates the new relationship and attempts to equip the couple (with gifts) for this new life. A bachelor party confronts the separation of the man from his former relationship with his men friends. Though such a rite need not be effective (his relationship with "the boys" may not change at all), *as a rite* it does acknowledge separation, loss and the beginning of a new relationship.

The Christian community has always been aware that it is called to assist couples in this period of transition. For Catholics, "pre-Cana" programs have traditionally sought to contribute to this passage. The challenge today is how to make this tradition of care, of ministering to marriage, more than merely exhortative. Most married people and ministers today agree that two or three evening discussions with the pastor do not suffice as an educational rite for this stage of the passage into marriage. Many creative efforts are being undertaken to improve and strengthen the Church's desire to minister to this stage of Christian maturing.

The revitalization of this ministry to engaged couples has begun with the recognition that the community of faith, and especially its married members, has an important role to play. The Church's ministry to the engaged cannot be the sole responsibility of the pastor. The community of faith, from its accumulated experience and its lived hope for marriage, has a contribution to make. We must do more than admonish the couple to abstain from genital sharing before the marriage ceremony. We must develop means of assisting couples to explore their own hopes and expectations, to recognize areas of potential difficulty and conflict, to acknowledge the fears and apprehensions that arise during this time. However life-giving we know the Christian vision of married love to be, this vision risks remaining rhetorical and vaguely unconvincing if not made available in ways that are attractive and effective.

One of the results of current efforts in the Church to devise effective means to prepare for Christian marriage has been to reinforce the expectation that engagement takes time. A number of Catholic dioceses now require a six-month engagement period before marriage. If such a requirement is merely one more "marriage law," if it is not supported by compelling opportunities to use this time well, it will necessarily fail in its intent. But in many areas the effectiveness of Engagement Encounter and other programs of marriage preparation developed at the diocesan or parish level are signs that this time is being well spent.

What might the educational rites of passage into marriage include? One appropriate component is education in the skills of communication that are crucial to a lasting relationship. We will examine the skillful behavior of communication and conflict resolution in marriage in further detail in Chapter 18. Here we may just note that it is fitting that the Christian community take advantage of information the psychological disciplines provide concerning successful interpersonal communication. The skills of listening, empathy and self-disclosure are neither mysteries nor gimmicks. They are behaviors that can be learned and that assist the development of open and direct communication. We can learn to identify our own feelings more accurately and to share these with others in ways that are appropriate. We can learn more effective ways to support and to challenge the people we love. Communication skills in themselves are morally neutral; they can be used to pursue a variety of goals—expressing love, selling products, manipulating other people to my way of doing things. But mutual manipulation is not the usual or necessary result of improved communication. And in the context of the Christian vision of married love, these skills can become virtues —part of our habitual way of loving one another well. The skills of communication do not magically abolish conflict or do away with all difficulties between us, but they help us deal gracefully with these problems when they do arise.

To some, these skills still seem to be secular techniques, not quite fitting for the Church to include in its ministry. In such an understanding the faith community is left to exhort and encourage but has few practical ways to equip its marrying members for the challenging journey ahead. When we can envision the skills of listening, empathy and assertion as Christian virtues we will begin to develop ways to include these practical and powerful tools in our marriage preparation programs. Part of the weakness that some sense in Christian life today is that our highest values and hopes have been disengaged from the practical means of pursuing these ideals; we have the goals and ambitions without the virtues to pursue them. Regarding marriage, for example, the Church exhorts fidelity, trust, endurance in love; but *how* are we to achieve these? How—practically—are we to deal with our anger, or shame, or frustration, or inability to share ourselves? These are all questions of virtue; they point to the skills of effective living and loving. Without these, our values and ambitions for Christian marriage may too easily become unattainable ideals.

Marriage is for the virtuous. Our living of marriage will make us stronger, more virtuous, but some strengths are required even to begin the journey. A contemporary rite of passage at this early stage of engagement will include educational programs which provide the skills and virtues that will allow our intimacy to grow and to flourish.

The Wedding Celebration

The ceremony and celebration of marriage—"marrying" in the usual if limited sense—is both a brief stage in the marriage passage and a ritual transition between stages. If a wedding is seen as including the various events that immediately surround a marriage ceremony, it can be understood as having some duration. Being more than the magical transition from unmarried to married "in the twinkling of an eye," this brief stage merits special attention here. Its position between the other two stages of the passage into marriage is significant. Our attitude toward the marriage ceremony reveals our understanding of the larger process of marrying. The ritual celebration of a marriage neither *begins* the passage into marriage nor *concludes* it. This public ritual event, occurring in a single day, ideally celebrates a relationship well begun; it celebrates the conclusion of the work and exploration of a courtship and engagement. Such a ritual should *testify* to the success of the engaging: this is a relationship with recognized potential. Both the couple and the believing community to which they belong should be able to acknowledge this potential—a potential concretely based in

increased awareness of who each of these persons is and what
their hopes are, as well as in the evidence that they possess the
virtues necessary to sustain this relationship. The wedding ceremony is thus both a recognition (of a process well begun) and a
promise. It initiates the next stage of marriage and promises that
this commitment will endure.

Perhaps most impressive today is our awareness of the frailty
of this ritual celebration. From a secular point of view, we recognize that our deepest good will and intentions cannot effect an
enduring marriage commitment. We cannot simply *will* our marriage; no matter how loud or emphatic our "I do!" at the wedding ceremony, other forces at work within us and beyond us
profoundly influence our survival as a married couple. From a
religious viewpoint, we recognize that our firm consent does not
guarantee a lasting marriage; seeing marriage as a complex
religious passage, we acknowledge that God cannot miraculously
bring about in this ritual the strengths of an enduring commitment if these are lacking in what we bring to the relationship.

Christian theologians in the past have focused considerable attention on this ritual and sacramental celebration. Theological
convictions about the force of the ritual found expression in such
pieties as "God will provide." Indeed, as Christians, we believe
that God does and will provide; but today we demand less of this
single ritual moment. The grace of marriage—God's intervention
into our life, empowering us to love well and enduringly—is not
concentrated in a single ritual. This grace is encountered and re-
sponded to in the discussions, sharings and conflicts through
which engagement grows; this grace also strengthens us as we
build our marriage during its first months and years. If we are
oblivious to these graces and to God's active presence in the
other phases of this passage, it is religious romanticism to search
for this grace and presence in the wedding ceremony.

In religious reflection on the sacrament of Matrimony today,
as we have noted, there is renewed interest in the role of the
couple. As the Church assumed, over the centuries, more and
more control over the civic as well as the sacramental reality of
marriage, the priest or minister became increasingly central to
the celebration. Today sacramental theology is struggling to re-

call the more ancient Christian realization that it is the woman and man who marry each other. Theologically speaking, the couple perform the sacrament: they are the celebrants and agents of this religious ceremony. Today many priests and ministers—and couples—are striving to recover the proper agency of the marrying couple. Rather than simply being led through a service, couples today often participate in the design of the ceremony and even the formulation of the vows. In this and other ways we are attempting to overcome the caricature of ministry to marriage in our recent past: ministerial neglect during engagement and the first years of marriage, accompanied by a formal control of the sacrament of Matrimony itself.

The intent of these reflections has not been to deny the importance of the wedding ceremony and the sacramental celebration of marriage. Rather we have intended to locate this celebration more firmly in its context—the several-year-long passage into marriage.

Completing the Passage into Marriage

With our wedding vows and ceremony our journey is not completed; it moves into another stage. There is widespread recognition that the first months of a marriage are especially crucial to the relationship. What occurs in this period will powerfully influence the later shape of the marriage and its viability. We would like to explore this period—the first year or two of marriage—as a stage in the passage into marriage. This approach reminds us that the couple are still in the process of marrying. This analysis will help clarify the agenda that is special to this time and show how this stage of the passage into marriage is itself concluded.

This stage likely begins with the honeymoon—a brief period of privacy and intimacy as the couple are dramatically separated from their former ties. The commitment of exclusive intimacy that was promised is now ritualized in this special time together which, fittingly, we take apart from the distractions of jobs and everyday life. The honeymoon is preeminently a time for the couple alone: a time to celebrate and build their intimacy, between the past demands and distractions of their former families and the coming demands and distractions of their future family.

Many couples today are choosing to lengthen, if not the honeymoon, at least the initial phase of their marriage, in which they give special attention to their relationship itself and its patterns of intimacy. Two factors contribute to this. First, we are more impressed today with the need to understand each other's patterns of work and play, of value and stress. In the first year or so of marriage a couple can expect to learn many new things about themselves and each other. We may find that it is necessary for us to reflect together on the importance of a career: What priority does work have in our marriage? What will we sacrifice for your career, for my job? How will work fit in with the demands of raising a family? This kind of decision making may be impossible to accomplish fully before we are married and share the everyday experiences and stress of life together. We recognize the need to clarify some of these questions before we begin our family.

There is another, related factor. Couples today are impressed with the important differences between being a spouse and being a parent. As obvious as this may be, historical assumptions about marriage and family have clouded the practical distinction between these two roles and vocations. When "wife" and "mother" merged as a single expectation of marriage, the important difference between these two roles was obscured. Likewise with the man: "husband" and "parent" both awaited him, but how, precisely and practically, would these roles and tasks differ? Today many couples judge that they need time to learn what it is to be spouse before taking on the responsibilities of being parent as well.

The delay in beginning a family often comes not from an unwillingness to have children, but from a realization that we had best give careful attention to our intimacy—who we are together and how we can support and challenge each other —before beginning our family. In the first few years of marriage such careful attention to the relationship, assisted by the skills learned during the stage of engagement, can build a strong foundation for our future family. Less optimistically, such attention will, in some instances, help a couple to recognize a deep and unforeseen incompatibility. As tragic as this may be, it is less tragic than discovering this after, and perhaps by means of, the birth of children.

The passage into marriage is completed in this mutual exploration of our priorities about work, our styles of lovemaking and our methods for handling everyday decisions. Such a passage cannot happen on a honeymoon. Yet we can hope that in a year or two of careful attention to our mutual love we can build a relationship that is able to support new life. For an effective ministry to marriage, it is important to highlight this period, its expectable duration (certainly different for different couples) and its specific tasks. Such attention will take us beyond exhortation and toward structuring opportunities in the parish and elsewhere for couples to reflect together, concretely and skillfully, on the tasks of intimacy they are confronting in these early years.

This important stage of the passage into marriage is emerging today with greater clarity. As it does, we also see more clearly how this stage is most often concluded. The several-year-long transition, with its focus on the couple and their growing mutuality, often comes to its fruition in the arrival of the first child. Of course, a married couple's intimacy continues to grow and change throughout their life. And, as we shall discuss below, not every couple can or chooses to have children. Yet the usual, expectable conclusion of the initial passage *into* a life of married intimacy occurs in the birth of the first child.

Most couples testify to the radical change in their marriage that accompanies the arrival of this first child. Some experience an abrupt shift in their sexual relations. Their pattern of sexual sharing, already adjusted during the last months of pregnancy, changes further with the presence of a new person in the family. Attention to this new life is fatiguing; sexual interest changes for one or both of us; or our pattern of frequency or timing has to be altered. Other physical or psychological aspects of our life together enter in here: my increased weight makes me feel less lovely and lovable; our exhaustion with nighttime feeding may arouse anger and blame. Along with the joy and excitement of childbearing, a couple can expect also to feel new and considerable strain in their own relationship.

Our understanding of marriage as a passage suggests that one part of this lifelong journey, the *entry* into mutual love, is concluding as the couple's love is turning in a new, outward direction. As the relationship turns in this unfamiliar (though familial) direction, conflict and strain are expectable. An effective Christian ministry to marriage will help couples anticipate this significant change. It will allow couples to recognize this transition as not only a confusing time but one with great potential. By so doing, Christian ministers and communities can lead new parents beyond embarrassment into a recognition that they are in a new place in their marriage. Such ministry, again, is best understood not in terms of exhortation, but as facilitating the sharing of feelings and the effective communication of needs in this time of stress and transition.

The recognition of the birth of the first child as the conclusion of the passage into marriage and the beginning of the family stage alerts us to a merging of ministries at this time. With the arrival of the baby most Christian couples begin to plan for bringing this child into the believing community in Baptism. The parents' interest in Baptism may arise from any number of sources, ranging from social pressure and guilt to a much more mature ambition for their child's religious formation. Whatever the motivation, Christian ministers are recognizing the time of Baptism as a special opportunity not only for the child but for the parents as well.

As Christian ministry itself moves beyond the image of the clergy ministering to a passive laity, parents are being brought into the ministry to the newborn child. And this does not mean only that the parents take a greater part in the baptismal liturgy. In many communities ministers to Baptism invite the parents of the child to reflect on and share their reasons for bringing this child forward for Baptism. Why are we doing this? What do we hope will happen with this ritual and beyond? What of our own faith do we have to share with this child?

Such an exploration, facilitated in a non-threatening and skillful fashion, is not only a ministry to the child; it is also a direct and effective ministry to the couple. The birth of their child is an extraordinary opportunity for them to inquire into what they hold sacred, what they would have their child share and continue. It is a special opportunity for them to say aloud—to each other and even to their community—what they believe. Such explicit faith sharing, for which there is little opportunity in a busy, workaday life, will include belief and unbelief, deep hopes that surprise us and doubts that frighten us. To share these deepest parts of oneself is itself an exceptional act of intimacy—religious intimacy. We are often either too distracted or too embarrassed to share in this way. The birth of a child may be the best opportunity we ever have. This is a part of the sacredness of this special time. The ministry of Baptism is also a ministry to the family: the child's chances of growing up in a vital Christian family are greatly enhanced by the religious sharing the parents are brought to at this time. The paradox of this opportunity and this transition from *marriage-as-couple* to *marriage-as-family* is that as we minister to our child in Baptism, this child ministers to us, inviting us to a deeper and more explicit experience of our faith.

To return to this event as the conclusion of the passage into marriage: with the birth of the child the focus of our marriage is shifted away from us toward this new life. We now become less exclusively *for ourselves,* concluding an important but limited stage in our marriage. Our attention now begins to turn outward, more emphatically beyond ourselves. This shift in focus is crucial for every marriage. The deepest sense of the fruitfulness of a marriage is related to this impulse to make more life, to create and go beyond ourselves. A marriage which fails to develop this external impulse we call selfish: with or without children, a couple can live a selfish, unfruitful life together. This notion of the fruitfulness of a marriage (to be discussed more extensively in Chapter 14) and the transition from marriage to family raises the question of a childless marriage. The phrase itself may frighten us, with its connotations of frustration and emptiness. We are reminded in these connotations that marriage is meant to go beyond itself; lovemaking is to make more life. But we also recognize that every adult life, whether one is married or not, must necessarily be fruitful. Married and unmarried can remain barren—with no generating of new life, no caring for the next generation and no moving beyond their own immediacy. And we know, too, that the biological generation of children does not guarantee human fruitfulness.

A number of marriages will be childless. Some couples unable to bear their own children will adopt children as a means of moving beyond themselves and becoming fruitful. Other couples will choose not to have children. Some, to be sure, may choose this future out of selfish reasons, just as some will give birth to children from self-centered or irresponsible motives. Still other couples will seek other routes to fruitfulness, to having their mutual love go beyond themselves in creative care for the next generation. The selfishness or maturity of a couple cannot be immediately identified in their decision to have few, none or many children. Their maturity or selfishness becomes clear only in what they do during the decades which follow this decision.

In a discussion of rites of passage, it may be important to inquire how a couple who do not have children can signal this transition from an inner focus in their marriage to an outer focus and fruitfulness. What kind of rites might assist them to celebrate this turning of their attention and other resources beyond themselves? Will it be a shift in career, or perhaps a broader involvement in the civic community, or a more visible commitment to some aspect of social justice that will indicate to them, and their closest friends, that this transition is taking place? It is clear that we have much left to learn about the rituals that serve us effectively in adult life.

With the conclusion of the passage into marriage, attention turns more definitely outward. Roles are multiplied as "parent" combines with "spouse." Marriage, well begun and now maturing, turns to new challenges.

Reflective Exercise

Select a marriage with which you are very familiar, whether this is your own or that of close friends.

Recall how the relationship began. What were its first stages of growth? How and when did the couple become "engaged"? Specifically, how long were they committed to marrying before they were actually wed? How did their sexual sharing change and mature during this period? Was there a significant contribution of the Church or of friends to their life at this time?

To whom did the wedding planning and ceremony belong—to themselves, or their parents, or the officiating minister? How different did they feel or act after formally beginning their life together?

How long were they married when their first child was born? Do they now feel that this happened too soon, was too delayed, or happened right on time? What was the chief challenge i· their marriage at that time? Of the many changes introduced into their marriage by their children, what change was most difficult for them? What change has been most gratifying?

Additional Resources

The 1980 synod of Catholic bishops, devoted to "The Role of the Christian Family in the World Today," addressed a number of the concerns which we discuss in this chapter. Among the resolutions presented to Pope John Paul II by the bishops at the end of the sessions, for example, are those stressing the importance of ascertaining the faith maturity of the couple desiring Christian marriage (※12) and urging each diocese to develop betrothal or engagement rites to help the couple better recognize the religious tasks of this important period in their relationship (※13). The December 12, 1980, issue of *National Catholic Reporter* included the texts of these resolutions and others offered by the convening bishops.

Many Catholic dioceses have developed quite practical and effective guidelines for marriage preparation. An example is the publication of the Archdiocese of Chicago, *Beginning Your Marriage* (Buckley Publications, 1980) by John L. Thomas, and the accompanying guide for those ministering to the engaged couple, *A Special Kind of Marrying* (Buckley Publications, 1980).

Carl Arico reviews the Catholic effort in marriage preparation in his "Ministry to the Engaged" in the Fall 1979 issue of *Chicago Studies*.

Marjorie Fiske Lowenthal and her colleagues include a group of newlywed couples in their developmental analysis, *Four Stages of Life: A Comparative Study of Women and Men Facing Transitions* (Jossey-Bass, 1976). Drawing on a growing body of research now available, Frances Kaplan Grossman and her associates discuss the adaptations that are required of new parents in *Pregnancy, Birth, and Parenthood* (Jossey-Bass, 1980).

9

THE FAMILY YEARS

The journey becomes more complex as a marriage matures into a family. With more travelers in the caravan, movement becomes both more exciting and more confusing. Unanticipated challenges arise as different lives merge in a shared adventure.

To understand what it means for us to be parents—this is the first challenge we face during the family years. To understand what being parents means for our marriage—this is the next. In our children our love moves beyond ourselves. Our sense of who and how we are together broadens to include what we have created together—our child. But what we have created together we must now care for. We are bound to our children not only by birth but by continuing responsibility. And these responsibilities will, in turn, influence our love. In this chapter we will examine several of the relationships that contribute significantly to the experience of marriage during these years of our most active responsibility as parents—our relations with our children, with each other and with the larger family network. Here we will consider principally some of the psychological and social dynamics involved. The religious dimensions of these relationships we explore more fully in Part Three.

Let us begin by noting that the family years are only part of the experience of marriage. And then let us add immediately that they are crucial. The experience of marriage both precedes and continues beyond the experience of active parenting, the "family" years. With increasing life expectancy, couples can anticipate that they will live in a household with their children for less than half the years of their marriage. For some, the family years begin quickly with the birth of a child in the first year of marriage. Increasingly, however, couples delay the birth of the first child and thus have a period of some years to establish a pattern together in marriage before they experience themselves as a family. And for a small but significant number of couples, those without children, the experience of marriage does not include the family years at all. Couples with children today can expect that their life together after their children have left home will extend another twenty years or more. And while their adult children will remain an important part of their life, their marriage in these years after active parenting is of a different quality than is marriage in the family years.

So the family years are only one of the important phases of the experience of marriage for a lifetime, but they are centrally significant. Most couples not only expect that there will be children in their marriage but actively choose to become parents. This choice and its consequences create the most influential context within which their marriage relationship will develop.

For many couples today the decision to start a family is made with the realization that for the next twenty years or so what their marriage *is* will depend on how they deal with the possibilities and problems that come with being parents. For most couples during these family years children are not a sideline. They are of the substance of the marriage relationship itself. Who we are to each other—and how—is strongly influenced by the psychological and practical responsibilities of being parents.

Relationships with Our Children

Over the twenty years or so that our children are with us in our home our relations with them are multiple and complex. The issues that are central in these relationships themselves shift and change over the years. Here we will look at three of the central issues: dependence, discipline and sexuality.

Dependence

As parents we have to learn to deal respectfully with dependence. We must first be willing to accept the radical dependence of the infant and the young child, not shying away from the weight of the demands their dependence brings. We must learn to respond to our children's needs in ways that neither betray nor exploit their vulnerability. And, all the while, we must nurture their movement away from dependence on us into more autonomous adulthood. We must be able, finally, to accept as a sign of our success as parents that point when our children move away from us, when they do not "need" us anymore.

To nurture the growing independence of our children we must be aware of their individuality. "How *different* our children are —from us, to be sure, but also from each other!" This sense of the uniqueness of each child is especially helpful when it leads us to approach our children with greater sensitivity to the special needs or possibilities that exist for each. We want to be fair and consistent in the ways we deal with them, but we sense that this does not mean treating each child exactly the same. One of our children is easygoing, the other more anxious and concerned. Or one responds enthusiastically to challenge while another is shy and easily defeated. Our nurturing of these children will necessarily be different, especially in regard to their growing sense of competence in the world beyond our home.

For each of our children we want our family to be a resource of security and strength, a place they know they belong and are safe. But as they grow through the school years we know that the world in which they belong and feel safe must expand beyond our household. Their attachment to us and to our home life begins to be modified by a growing autonomy. Personal decision becomes increasingly a more important part of their experience. The early choices of friends and interests in the grammar-school

years are followed in adolescence by the weightier options concerning values and vocation. It is in these choices that our children begin to develop a sense of their own adequacy to the decisions that adult life holds. And we know that the way we
respond to their choices influences their confidence and their
comfort with independence. We can help them see alternatives,
we can urge them to consider consequences, but we cannot protect them from making mistakes, at least not for long. We may
be able to help them realize that mistakes are not so bad, that in
fact these are an inevitable and even useful part of life. If we
can do this, we have given them a boost toward a satisfying
style of adult independence.

Discipline

Discipline is a central concern in the family years. The way
we discipline the children has a significant effect on our household. Patterns of authority and permission, styles of dealing with
conflict, even our expectations regarding etiquette and courtesy
—these influence everything from our family's sense of well-
being to the noise level in our home! And most of us today are
even more sensitive to the formative effects of discipline on our
children themselves. We know that the way *we* deal with their
movements of affection and anger and autonomy will have much
impact on the attitudes that they develop toward self-expression
and self-control. We also know that there is some considerable
diversity among the experts—whether parents or educators or
psychologists—concerning which patterns of discipline are to be
preferred. Even within this diversity, however, some common
themes emerge. Discipline provides structure: it helps a child interpret her or his experience ("These impulses and actions are
acceptable, these others are not"); it helps the child make sense
of the world by establishing some reasonably predictable patterns ("When I behave this way, this is how my parents are
likely to respond").

There is much direct control in the way we structure the experience of an infant and toddler. We physically place our baby in the environment we think is best—the playpen, the stroller, the baby bed—and we control who comes into this environment; we watch over the child's activities; we take away objects that we think are dangerous. As our children grow into the school years we have less physical control over their experience. We are not always with them; we cannot give them directives for each situation they will face on their own. The patterns of discipline that we establish are increasingly important now. Limit setting becomes a way in which we continue to influence our children's experience. We put limits on their time ("You can play after school but you must be home for supper"), on their movement ("Don't cross the thoroughfare unless your older sister is with you"), on their activities ("No television until homework is done"), on their associates ("I want to check who else is going on the camping trip before I agree that you can go"). We know the children will test these limits to see how serious we are. We also know that there will be occasions when we will want to modify the rules we have made. But the presence of boundaries that are clear and consistently maintained is an important part of the contribution we make to our children's sense of security in the expanding world of their own experience.

As our children move into adolescence the dynamic of discipline is seriously challenged. The structure that discipline provides remains important, perhaps especially important in the midst of the momentous physical and psychological changes of the early teen years. But the focus of this structure changes from the limits that *we* have established "for their own good" to a process of dialogue and discussion (often, to be sure, in the form of argument!). Disciplining teenagers is tricky business, as all those who have tried can attest. But the chances of success are improved by our recognition of the expanding capacity of *this* young person to understand the issues and evaluate the options. Effective discipline will seldom mean leaving early teens on their own, but it is likely to involve much compromise, with their preferences taken more and more into account and their own efforts at problem solving increasingly respected.

It is as our children reach adolescence that many of us first realize—and seldom without pain—that we have to establish a new kind of relationship with them, one based much more centrally on their growing independence than on the significant bonds of need and care that have held them close until now. We sense in these years the inevitability of the separation ahead. Most parents approach this separation with both gratitude and regret. We are often weary of the turmoil of their adolescence; we know, perhaps only vaguely, that our children's movement beyond this turmoil is in part a movement beyond us. It will be good to see the kids move out on their own—but how we will miss them! And we will probably worry as well: Are they ready? Have we done enough? Will they be able to make their way? This ambivalence we feel about our adolescent children growing up and leaving home can complicate our efforts at discipline during the teen years.

Sexuality

Questions of sexuality are an especially important part of the responsibility that parents feel toward their children today. "We don't want our children to grow up with the strange ideas about sex that we had as youngsters." This is a strong conviction among many of us. We want our children to be comfortable with their bodies. We want them to be comfortable with us, to come to us with their questions and concerns about sex. In the face of the lopsided cultural messages about beauty and pleasure and romance that they will receive, we want to be sure they hear the fuller story of intimacy and commitment and trust. We want to help them appreciate the important connections between sex and love, and also the important differences. Especially, we want to help them to learn to love well.

So sex education has become, increasingly, an explicit part of the relationship between parent and child. Since many of us who are now parents judge that the way we learned about our own sexuality and about sexual behavior was at least inadequate and often even worse, there is considerable reliance today on what experts have to tell us about proper timing and successful strategies to assist our children in their exploration and understanding of sex. And there are many excellent resources available—from pediatricians, psychologists, ministers, educators and others—to support parents in this ongoing conversation with their children.

For a growing number of parents, gender education is as significant an issue as sex education. We are more aware today of the ways in which children learn early on what is expected of them as "girls" and "boys." Many parents find these cultural definitions of masculine and feminine to be restrictive. We do not want to set such rigid and even arbitrary boundaries for our own children. Instead we set out consciously to work against many of the obvious and subtle patterns of child rearing that treat boys and girls differently—different kinds of toys, different expectations in behavior, differing participation in family chores. We see this as a part of our larger attempt to respond to the particular interests and needs of each child and to open a fuller range of experiences to both our male and female children.

Our efforts here may be on a modest scale. We support our daughter's interest in sports; we encourage our son to learn to cook; we hold them both accountable for baby-sitting responsibilities with the younger children. But on occasion these efforts may involve us in a more dramatic challenge to the patterns of socialization, as in a confrontation with a school system that excludes our daughter from a "boys only" program for which she is otherwise qualified. Increasingly these questions of "gender expectations" are issues on which parents—and children, too—are taking a stand.

While these questions of gender and sexuality are significant from the early years, they become especially volatile in most families as the children move into adolescence. Puberty is a confusing, sometimes even frightening, experience for teenagers. It is equally challenging for most parents. The physical changes remind us all—parents and teenager alike—that this child is no longer a child. The more explicit sexuality of our daughter or son may surprise us or worry us or, scarier still, arouse us. As our children move toward making their own choices about sexuality

—in the way they dress, in their preferences in films and music and reading, in dating and other social activities—we can experience their behavior as a challenge to our values, even as a threat to our lifestyle. If sex has become troublesome between us we may find our son's heightened sexual curiosity somewhat disturbing. If we have tried to set sex aside in our relationship because we have found it unsatisfying, our daughter's lively preoccupation with dating and romance may provoke these unsettling issues for us again. And if we feel that our sex life together is good we may still feel somewhat awkward as we sense ourselves under the scrutiny of our teenager's new and more sexually sophisticated gaze. We find ourselves in agreement with family therapist Sonya Rhodes's observation that "sexually interested and active teenagers expose the sexual maturity of the marriage."

The Family Is the Arena of Dreams

As our children grow, they begin to dream their future. Adult careers and vocational choices begin in childhood, in those first tentative announcements of "what I want to be when I grow up." If we can understand these early dreams as the first important movements of a life ambition, that deepest hope of "what I might do with my life," we can sense the importance of the family years in giving shape to the life dream.

Parenthood is largely about the fostering of dreams. In our relationship with each other, in our selection of our children's toys and their school and even their clothes, in our own activities and conversations, we influence the possibility of our children's dreams. It is from us that our children first learn about the future: Is it friendly? Can one shape it? Are there choices in life? Parenthood matures in the careful fostering of dreams as we listen for, encourage, question and support our child's early hopes.

If our discipline within the family sets the boundaries for dreaming, our children's growing independence contributes significantly to the maturing of their dreams. It is as our children

mature that we come to the clearest realization of how different
from us they are; we have not, after all, simply reproduced ourselves! This recognition may be especially strong as we learn of
their own hopes for the future. Their dreams are not ours; in
fact they leave us wondering wherever did they get *that* idea.
We may sense in this that some of our concern for our children,
some of our conviction that they should have benefits in life
that we feel we ourselves were denied, may be in part an effort
to have them live out *our* dreams. But to impose our dreams on
our children, especially during the vulnerable time of their adolescence, may distract them from the fragile hopes only gradually becoming clear within them.

Parenting is, for the Christian, the most basic example of stewardship. We learn that our children ultimately are not "ours."
As we acknowledge that they belong to themselves and to God
more than to us, we must also recognize that their dreams in life
may be different from those we cherish for them. Fostering our
child's dream and life ambition demands that we distinguish
hers or his from our own. We are called to foster something that
we do not control, to care intensely for something over which we
do not have final say. This is the heart of stewardship . . . and
of parenting.

The growing dream of our child is also the beginning of a vocation. Here vocation goes beyond the narrow sense in which
the term has until recently been used among Catholics, to refer
to the call to the priesthood or the life of a vowed religious. All
Christians have a calling, a vocation in which they will try to realize their best hopes for love and justice in the world. And this
Christian vocation begins in the dream, the child's tentative
hopes for the future.

It is in childhood that dreams begin, in adolescence that they
are fostered or defeated. Thus the family years can be understood as the arena of dreams. Here our children come upon the
earliest intimations of what they might do with their lives. It is
here that this fragile dream is fostered, clarified and first tested
against external reality. It is in the family years, too, that our
children's dreams are gradually disengaged from our own.
Strengthened by our care and rooted in the values they have

learned from us, our maturing children can dare to try their
dream in the adult world. We will return to a consideration of
this maturing dream in Chapter 12.

The Challenge of the Family Years

During these family years, especially, our responsibilities as
parents and our relationships with our children significantly
affect our marriage. Being parents together can call out in each
of us qualities of generosity and inventiveness that make us even
more lovable to one another. I learn there is a playfulness in you
that I have not seen so well before; you come to cherish the
breadth of my care. Our commitment to each other is
strengthened as our lives are woven together in patterns of concern and joy and responsibility for our children. But being parents can also "use us up," leaving us with a sense that we have
little left to give one another. Our resources of energy and emotion can seem strained to their limit, with nothing left over. We
have little time to spend alone together. When we are together
we are often both very tired or distracted by other concerns.
Our essential family expenses leave us very little money to spend
for extras—so an evening out together, a weekend away without
the children, a special trip or a concert or a study course—these
seem beyond our reach. We sense our perspective shrinking as
the practical tasks of daily life and the job seem to be all there is
for us.

A central challenge in the movement through the family years
is to understand and to deal with the inevitable strains of parenthood in ways that contribute to, rather than detract from, the
marriage relationship. Parents know that children bring happiness and satisfaction to their lives. But they also know that it is
not easy to raise a family. It is hard to take responsibility for
the continuing tasks of child care, value formation, discipline
and development. It is hard to spend so many of my resources
beyond myself, often with no apparent effect. It is hard to face
the emotional shocks and the sometimes embarrassing lessons of
self-knowledge that being a parent brings. How can such a little

baby make me so angry? How can I be jealous of my own child? What kind of an ogre am I that I can hit my child like that? And today, when the criteria of what constitutes a good parent are so much in flux, it is hard even to judge whether one is doing an acceptable job.

The evidence we have from marriage research reinforces this sober picture. Parenthood is a strain on marriage. The demands on each of us are heightened. Both as workers and as parents, spouses are stretched during the family years beyond the demands they experienced together earlier in their relationship. The presence of children makes financial demands that we did not have before, demands reinforced by the powerful middle-class norm that we provide our children as high a standard of living as possible. There is pressure to make more money. Among professionals and others whose work has a career line, this pressure is translated as the necessity to do whatever possible to advance into a position that offers better salary and greater prestige, usually along with increased work responsibilities. For other workers these same pressures can translate into moonlighting, taking on additional part-time employment to supplement one's regular wage. Our growing children also make direct demands on our time and attention, demands that can often seem endless. There are small triumphs to share, fears to quiet, quarrels to mediate, school activities to attend, homework projects to help with, family trips to plan and the never-ending need to drive the children to the next event!

Roles in Tension—How Do We Respond?

For many couples these added responsibilities at work and as parents are met at the expense of the marriage. The extra time and energy that must be spent at work or with the children are siphoned away from the resources we have formerly devoted to maintaining and maturing our own relationship. Our roles as parents overshadow our relationship and the roles we share there as friend, companion, spouse. This is a part of the decreasing satisfaction in marriage that many couples report over the family years, a dissatisfaction that reaches its lowest ebb when the children at home come into their teen years.

Through the family years the quality of our relationship is likely to change as the focus of who we are together enlarges to include our children and their lives. The "we" of our marriage begins to be experienced less exclusively in terms of our mutual relationship and increasingly in terms of our shared responsibilities as parents. The success of our marriage now involves more than our mutual satisfaction. It includes our ability to care for our children and to provide for their future. This shift in priorities is a significant psychological experience, a part of the deeper movement from "we are" to "we care." But this shift in priorities can be experienced as a loss in our relationship rather than its enlargement. The romance is gone and in its place we have only role expectations—to be a good "provider" or "care giver" or "disciplinarian."

Thus the requirements of being a parent can seem to, and can in fact, encroach on the special relationship we have shared before the children came. The first experience of this intrusion can come early. The time just after the birth of a child, especially the first child, is a period of great physical and emotional demands for both wife and husband. In some cases the new mother experiences keenly the loss of the special attentiveness that her husband showed her during pregnancy, as now both of them are caught up in establishing a household regime that meets the needs of the new infant in the home. A first-time father can experience a comparable loss. His wife is less available to him as she focuses much of her time and energy on the new child. The shape of the demands that children make on their parents will change as the children grow, but their urgency does not. And these urgent demands take a toll.

For both men and women the family years add stress to the marriage relationship. And the strain associated with being a parent is especially felt by women, who in most marriages today still carry the principal burden of the day-to-day responsibilities for child care, often at the expense of their other goals of personal creativity or wider social participation. For some women the tasks of parenthood are not felt as a burden. In fact, a significant number of women report greater satisfaction in their roles as mother than in their roles as wife. But even among women who choose the role of full-time homemaker the family years are reported as a time of heightened anxiety and low morale.

Most marriages, then, are problematically affected by the presence of children in the household. This finding, which is not news to parents, does not say all there is to say about the family years but it does say something that is important. It suggests, first, that the experience of marital strain at this time is normal. And when we experience this strain in our own lives, it can help for us to recognize the strain for what it is—an expectable effect of the "life cycle squeeze" in which we find ourselves. It is a time when our resources are taxed to overload, when the responsibilities of marriage and parenthood can be felt to outweigh the rewards. This period in a marriage does not last forever, but we can experience it—perhaps off and on—over a decade or more. And when we are in the midst of it, it can seem interminable.

The challenge of this time in our marriage is to be able to meet our many responsibilities as parents in ways that enrich rather than erode our experience of mutual love. This does not often seem easy to do. Our children's needs are insistent; our concerns for them are myriad; we have such high expectations ourselves of what is required of us as parents. But to give ourselves over to the multiple tasks of "being good parents," without comparable care for the special experience of love that is between us, is risky. The joys and burdens of raising our children can overwhelm us. Gradually our shared commitment as parents can come to substitute for, rather than to strengthen, our maturing commitment to each other.

Our Own Relationship in Focus

Most couples find they must pay special attention to their own relationship during these years, or there will be bad effects. This can require scheduling some special time every day or two for us just to be together to talk about more than work and family demands. Or doing something together that we both especially enjoy—a hobby or a project or a visit with some friends. We may arrange for time away from the children—a weekend vacation or a romantic evening at home when our lovemaking will not be interrupted. It is not unusual for a couple to find that the hectic pace of life in the family years threatens to leave their lovemaking in neglect. Our time is seldom our own. We no longer have the leisure or the privacy that nurtures romance. If our life together these days is to include a satisfying experience of sexual love we are likely to have to plan for it. This does not mean that our sex life must lose all spontaneity or that the passion and surprise that enriched our early lovemaking must forever be set aside. To plan for sex need not mean to routinize it. It is more likely to ensure that we have time to be lovers—time to prepare for making love, so that we can be really present to each other; time to love each other well, responsive to the rhythms of our own and each other's pleasure; time to share the special sense of security and well-being that lingers after lovemaking.

So while the additional demands of the family years can draw us closer together, strengthening our mutual love and our commitment to each other, this seldom happens automatically. Left to their own dynamics, these multiple demands can draw us apart. We may be led to "explain" the very real stress we experience by blaming each other or by finding fault with our marriage. "Life is so hard for us right now. Surely something is wrong. Someone must be to blame."

The move to fix blame, as understandable as it is, is not likely to be of much help here because in most cases whatever "fault" there is lies more in the situation than in bad will. This does not mean that there is nothing we can do, that we must just suffer passively through these years until they pass. But it does mean that our attempts to change things should begin in an awareness of how ambitious is the undertaking in which we are involved: we are attempting in the midst of today's complex world to nurture well the children born of our love. This awareness can help us toward an acceptance of this season in our life. The pressures we experience now are real and they are normal. We need not blame ourselves or each other. We need not judge our relationship to be dangerously deficient. These negative evaluations may, in a particular case, be accurate but there are other possibilities as well to explain the malaise we experience and to guide our attempts to change things for the better.

We are at a point, each of us and as a couple, when our own resourcefulness is taxed in the face of many responsibilities. Some of the strain we can moderate—we can talk things out more often, we can reexamine the way we use our time and money and energy, we can try to be clearer about our real priorities as a family, we can change some of the patterns that do not work very well for us. But many of our responsibilities remain, and there may not be a lot we can do right now to change things. So while passivity is not likely to serve us, there is a special wisdom to the counsel of patience at this time. As those who have been parents before us attest, many of the problems of raising children are not so much "solved" as they are "outlasted." As our children grow, our experience in the family keeps changing. Often we find that we have left behind some of the problems that bedeviled us earlier. We have moved beyond them, not into a trouble-free time as a family but into a time with different concerns and possibilities. This experience can give us hope and help us, in the midst of the family years, to come to a sense of the larger movement of our marriage. A sense of humor, too, will help.

The Larger Family Network

We have been using the word "family" here to refer to the household—parents and their young children living together at home. And the establishment and nurturance of one's own family, in the home-and-household sense, is at the heart of marriage during these years. But there is another experience of family that is important for marriage. This is the larger network of persons—grandparents, in-laws, adult sisters and brothers and their families—related by birth and emotional ties. This larger network, with its bonds of affection and concern, is an important part of marriage for most Americans. It is true that our current value system stresses the importance of each married couple's economic independence and emotional self-sufficiency. It is true that most married couples live in nuclear households, that is, separate living units composed of only wife and husband and, over the middle years of the marriage, their pre-adult children. But it can be misleading to consider this nuclear household an isolated family unit. The sense of family for most Americans, even today, goes well beyond "our household." There are generally expected ties of support and communication across generations. While job demands and personal preferences result in much geographic mobility for Americans, a good number of married people (almost one couple in four, according to some studies) live within ten miles of a close relative. And even for households that live at a distance there is generally a pattern of letters, long-distance telephone calls and regular family visits that reinforce a sense of involvement in each other's lives.

In addition to the emotional ties of familiarity (which in most families include both affection and antagonism) there are patterns of mutual assistance as well. Family members expect to be able to turn to one another in need. In an important sense, to be "family" means to be able to make demands on one another. As American adults, most of us hold self-sufficiency as a primary value. But when our own resources are not enough—in cases of illness, emotional trouble, financial difficulty—it is most often to family members that we turn first. And it is not only tragedy that draws out this pattern of mutual assistance. Family members give one another time, advice and practical assistance. Grandparents take the children for a weekend so that parents may have some time alone; a daughter-in-law who is an accountant assists family members with their tax returns; the adult children share the cost of a party and a vacation trip for their parents' golden wedding anniversary.

The larger family network can also be a source of some strain within marriage. By the fact of my marriage to you, I am expected to be able to establish—quickly—an emotional relationship of some intimacy with members of your family. The same demands for rapid intimacy are made on them; they have to establish a close relationship with me. This is not always easily done. And the demands go in several directions: your relationship with my parents and with others in my family, their response to you and to me-as-now-married-to-you, the relationship that exists between our two larger family networks.

There is truth as well as prejudice in the myths about "trouble with the in-laws." There is no evidence to substantiate the sense that most wives (or most husbands) have a particularly stormy relationship with their spouse's mother. The image of the "mother-in-law as shrew" seems to reflect our culture's more generally negative evaluation of women (especially older women) than it does the experience that married people report. But couples do experience strain with their own parents over questions of having and raising children. Both values and emotions are deeply involved in decisions about child rearing. And often both parents and grandparents judge that they have a stake in these decisions. Each generation feels that it has a special wisdom to bring to bear. Parents rely on their day-to-day experience with the children and their own best image of how they want their children to "turn out." Grandparents claim the benefit of their longer experience and the clearer vision which their distance from the day-to-day pressures of parenting brings them. Expectably, then (even if not inevitably), our children can become a focus of strain not only in our own household but in our relations with the larger family as well.

One of the challenges, then, in our marriage at this time may be to develop a sense of our relationship, as a couple and as a family, to the larger family network. This will require ongoing communication and clarity between us, with an awareness of the special sensitivity that one or both of us may feel. Family relationships hold hidden hurts. These wounds may stand behind the difficulty I experience with your family or the special vulnerability I feel in regard to my own. There is evidence that when marriage quarrels expand to include references to "your parents" or "your family," they often escalate into more serious conflicts. Couples learn that such family references are "off limits," especially when emotions are running high. Problems that arise be-

tween us over each other's family demand an even greater deli-
cacy than usual in the way we deal with each other.

As our marriage matures we can become better aware of the
areas of possible strain in the way our household interacts with
the larger family network. Differences between us in our sense
of involvement with and obligation to our family of origin, their
concerns over the way we are raising our children, dissatisfaction over how much time we spend with each set of parents
—these or other issues may surface as troublesome. Anticipating
these areas of tension, we can be better prepared to acknowledge what is going on and to resolve the issues before they take
on additional emotional weight.

Reflective Exercise

The family years—what have these been in your own marriage? Spend some time first in quiet reflection. Recall the years
of your marriage since the birth of your first child. Let the memories come as they will, marking the events of your lives together
as a family. Note the way, perhaps, that some months or years
fall together in your memory and the way that other times stand
apart. Note, especially, the feelings that mark different times in
the family years.

After you have given time for the memories to return, consider
these questions:

What are the special joys you have known as a parent? (Recall the events and instances that express for you the gifts you
have received from your children.)

What are the particular concerns and problems that you have
known as a parent? (Again, recall the events and examples in
your own life.)

Are there ways in which your responsibilities as a parent have
caused strain or tension in your marriage? How has your relationship with your spouse been strengthened by your being parents together?

Additional Resources

In his analysis of research data in *The Young Catholic Family* (Thomas More Press, 1980) Andrew Greeley calls into question much of the conventional wisdom about the family years. Sonya Rhodes traces the movement of the relationship between parents and children over the family years in her article "A Developmental Approach to the Life Cycle of the Family" in the May 1977 issue of *Social Casework*.

St. Meinrads Press publishes the monthly *Marriage and Family Living,* a practical resource dealing with questions of family life and the spirituality of marriage. The Sex Information and Education Council of the United States (SIECUS) is a valuable resource for parents, educators and others who minister to young people. Their monthly *SIECUS Report* provides articles and reviews of books and other materials that are available for children of different ages. The founder and long-time director of SIECUS, physician Mary S. Calderone, joins her colleague Eric W. Johnson in a discussion of the family's role in sex education in *The Family Book About Sexuality* (Harper & Row, 1981).

Thomas Gordon's work in *Parent Effectiveness Training* (NAL, 1975) has been helpful for many parents, as has Carrie Carmichael's discussion of *Non-Sexist Childraising* (Beacon Press, 1978). Susan A. Basow presents an overview of current research concerning the origins and effects of gender socialization in *Sex-Role Stereotypes: Traditions and Alternatives* (Brooks/Cole, 1981).

Mary Good examines, from both the psychological and the religious perspective, the development of the family system as a network of relationships in her audio-tape cassette "Stages of Family Development," available from NCR Cassettes, Kansas City, Missouri. Some of the issues of parenthood and the larger family network are explored by Bertram Cohler and Henry Grunebaum in *Mothers, Grandmothers and Daughters* (Wiley, 1980)

"Paths of Life," the Family Life Series available through

Paulist Press, includes four small volumes entitled *Christian Parenting*. Three of these focus on particular phases of child development ("The Young Child," "The Grammar School Child," "The Adolescent") and the fourth takes up a range of larger questions of marriage and family life.

10

THE MATURE YEARS OF MARRIAGE

Over the last fifty years a new phase of marriage has begun to unfold—the post-parental years. Most marriages include children. In these marriages the rewards and demands of child rearing can be expected to exert major influence on the relationship of the couple and on their lifestyle over a period of some twenty years or more. But, as we have noted earlier, for more and more couples these years of active child rearing describe only half of their life together. Couples today can look forward, whether in anticipation or in dread, to the possibility of a "post-parental" marriage of some two decades or more.

The post-parental years can be an experience of rich fulfillment in marriage. We are proud of our children and of our role, now reaching a new stage, as parents. Many of the tensions that accompany a household with growing children have eased. We are free of some of the financial strain that may have haunted us earlier. With a smaller household now that the children are gone, some of our expenses have lessened. It is also probable that both of us are employed. In a marriage in which the wife has been a full-time homemaker during the family years it is likely that she will return to work now, at least on a part-time basis. And in many marriages the wife has been employed all along. With the children gone, we each have more time for ourselves and more energy to devote to long-delayed projects or to enlarging our network of friends. We can begin to define in-

terests that will be important to us in the lifestyle we choose
after retirement. And we have quality time to spend with each
other.

Our daily household again becomes "the two of us." This new
intimacy in our lifestyle may be a delight ("At last we have
some time for each other!") but there may be complications as
well. The identities (who we are to one another) and roles
(what each of us does in our relationship) that seemed to fit the
requirements of the family years may no longer work as well. As
a wife, with the homebound tasks of motherhood behind me, I
may look forward to involving myself in a job or a volunteer role
that carries with it requirements for scheduling my time and
being available to outside demands. My husband, however, is
grateful that the financial pressures of raising and educating our
family have been lifted from his shoulders. He is hoping for us
to establish a more leisurely schedule with more time at home
together, longer vacations, no more evening meetings and freer
weekends. Or he may feel that his own career has leveled off.
Now he faces twenty or more years of routine and boring work
just as I am beginning to move into a time of growth and excitement in my life.

As we begin to recover from the hectic pace of our past
twenty years as parents and providers, we may realize that we
have each changed in important ways over this time and yet
have had little opportunity to share these changes with each
other. We are different people, maybe even strangers. We must
meet each other again and explore together the new and possibly changing shape of our relationship.

Or we may have, for some time, realized that the quality of
love between us has deteriorated. A sense of responsibility for
our growing children has held us together but now, as they become more independent and move out on their own, we must
face more directly the issue of our troubled relationship.

Each of these instances is a test of intimacy. We are required
to look more closely at how we have been together, to determine
if these understandings and patterns are adequate to who we are
now and to the years that lie ahead. This may mean rein-
forcement of the patterns we have shared "all these years." We

know these patterns work for us. We are comfortable and creative together now and as we look toward the future we sense that we shall continue to be so.

But we may well find that the questions that are raised in this reevaluation of our marriage are not so easily resolved. Hurts from the past may surface, accompanied by bitterness and blame. To continue as we are now may seem to me to close off the future or to hold me back from my "last chance"—to experience love, to succeed, to find meaning, to be what I have always wanted to be. There is not time enough or forgiveness enough or flexibility enough for us to start over, together.

The invitation to reexamine our relationship is an expectable part of the movement into mature marriage. For some couples this movement is marked by a mellow sense of the fruition of their love. Our commitment to one another, well begun in our early years and tested and deepened as we faced our responsibilities together as parents, is strong and secure. It is an abiding source of peace and purpose in our life. Others will find this transition more troublesome. The difficulty of this time will lead some marriages toward divorce and others into stalemate or stagnation. But most couples move through the challenge of this post-parental transition into a period of their marriage marked by a matured relationship and a more satisfying lifestyle.

Changes in the Family Network

An important movement in this process of mature marriage is a shift in relationships within the larger family network, the several generations that are related by birth and marriage. Early in the post-parental phase we rework our relationship with our children as they leave home to establish themselves "on their own." The responsibilities of child rearing are replaced by concerns of child launching—our efforts to contribute, in ways acceptable both to us and to our young adult offspring, to the young person's movement into the adult world. These concerns touch especially on decisions about work and marriage. Most middle-aged parents recognize that there is a delicate balance to be maintained between concern and intrusion. Their children are now adults and must make their own way. This will include their making their own mistakes, even mistakes as costly as a poor marriage or a false start in a career. But even in the face of the ambivalence which may continue at this time (parents alternate between care and control; young adults waver between independence and dependence), many young adults see their parents as resources in their own decisions regarding marriage and work. Parents want to, and do, offer advice, provide contacts, make suggestions. Young adults seek out and are often influenced by their parents' judgments on job possibilities, financial decisions and, especially, whom they shall marry. To be successful these interactions between parents and their adult children must take on a different tone than that which marked their earlier relationships, no matter how satisfying these were to both. Working to establish this new relationship with our now adult children is one of the family dynamics in mature marriage.

Becoming Grandparents

A second family dynamic is initiated with the birth of grandchildren. Our children themselves becoming parents marks a time of family celebration. The event also has repercussions in terms of relationships among the generations. For the grandparents it can reinforce a sense of continuity and connection with the future. Or it may be a presage of aging—"Being a 'grandparent' sounds so old!" It may signal to us in some way that our children—now themselves parents—are really adults. They have moved beyond us. They are not beyond our love but they are well beyond the scope of our protective control.

On the other hand, the birth of grandchildren can strengthen family ties. For many young adults, becoming parents reestablishes a sense of belonging to the larger family. Faced with the delights and dilemmas of raising my own children, I gain new appreciation for my parents, a new sympathy for what the tasks of parenting must have been like for them and a new respect for how well they did the job. But often, as we noted in Chapter

9, there are strains between the generations as well, especially over how the grandchildren shall be raised.

Becoming grandparents, then, can test and redefine our relationship within the family generations. Students of family life discuss being a grandparent as a "roleless role." First, it is one of the adult roles over which we have little personal control. "Becoming grandparents" happens to us. Second, there is little agreement on what it involves. Generally, grandparents are seen positively in our society. (Consider, for example, the different feelings associated with the words "grandparents" and "in-laws.") But there are few generalized expectations of "grandparenthood," in the sense of clear rights and obligations that come automatically with being a grandparent or certain behaviors that all grandparents are expected to display. Some grandparents are actively and regularly involved in the ongoing care of their grandchildren, but most are not. Some grandparents make significant financial contributions to their grandchildren's upkeep or education, but most do not. "Grandparenting" is more an emotional relationship than a social role. And the way that this relationship is expressed is worked out not "in general" but "in particular." We develop our own understanding of what it means for us to be grandparents, possibly different understandings for each of our grandchildren.

Many couples find their relationship with their grandchildren one of the delights of the mature years of their marriage. Grandparents and grandchildren are free to experience each other; often they enjoy each other as well. Their relationship is usually unclouded by the kinds of emotional strains that can continue between the grandparents and their adult children. In addition, there are not many demands built into the relationship. "We love them but we are not responsible for them. We like being with the grandchildren and we especially like being able to return to our own home after a visit." Increasingly, contact between grandparents and grandchildren is voluntary. We choose when to see the children, how frequently, for how long. Grandparents can leave when the children become tiresome; parents cannot. This fact alone can contribute mightily to the continuing

good will experienced between grandparents and their grandchildren.

Our Aging Parents

The reassessment of our place in the family is also affected by
a changing relationship with the senior generation. The emergence of a new sense of responsibility to my aging parents is
often taken as an indication of the move, psychologically, into
middle age. Earlier in this century the period of active concern
for my aging parents might overlap the years of my heaviest responsibility for adolescent children in my own household. But
now the senior generation "ages" more slowly. Changes in vitality and expected longevity mean that many of us will be in our
fifties and sixties, perhaps even approaching our own retirement,
before our parents experience failing health or other debilitating
effects of advanced age.

The larger social changes involved in increased life expectancy will affect the relationship between these two "mature"
generations. "Parent care" may become an increasing concern of
married couples in their post-parental years. Most often this will
not mean assuming the day-to-day responsibilities of care in our
home for a bedridden or seriously incapacitated elder (though
some couples or widowed spouses will provide this kind of care
for an aged parent). Parent care is more likely to be experienced
as an increased sense of our responsibility to contribute to the
well-being of our parents as they move into advanced age. Many
times our active contribution is chiefly in terms of emotional
support—more frequent visits, letters to keep in touch, telephone calls to ensure that all is well with them (or her, since
current statistics indicate that the parent of advanced years is
more likely to be a widowed mother).

But there is an accompanying awareness that over the next
years our responsibility may expand to include much more—
financial assistance, actual physical care, decisions about living
arrangements and medical costs. These responsibilities are often
difficult in themselves. They can be experienced as more burden-

some when they seem to come just as our previous responsibilities (for raising and educating our own children, for responding to the demands of our work) are lessening, just as we are beginning to have time and other resources for ourselves and each other. The evidence is that most married people not only feel responsible for the well-being of their aging parents but meet these responsibilities competently and with care. This challenge of reassessing our relationship with the generation ahead of us is one of the expectable processes of marriage in the mature years.

Retirement

Another experience that is a part of the expectable process of the mature years of marriage concerns the transition of retirement. Americans have mixed feelings about retirement. Public sentiment is hostile toward many of the elements that are a part of retirement today—the inflexibility of a mandatory retirement age; the difficulty of living on a reduced and often fixed income, in a time of economic inflation. But it is primarily toward the involuntary aspects of retirement that this resentment is focused. Through mid-life most of us look forward to the prospect of moderating our involvement in the demanding world of employment, of bringing our work more under our direct control and lessening its pervasive and all-consuming place in our lives. There is evidence today that, increasingly, Americans do look forward to retirement, especially if they judge they will have the financial resources to maintain an acceptable lifestyle.

The transition through retirement into the next stage of life and of marriage is, again, a time of both possibility and challenge. The dynamic processes of our knowing one another and accommodating to each other's hopes and needs continue. Now these processes of maturity are focused on the tasks of mature age. For most of us retirement introduces significant changes in lifestyle. After retirement, we use our time differently. Whether in part-time employment, as committed volunteers or as leisured senior citizens, we are likely to spend more time together as a

couple. We will probably change our living arrangement—
selling our home of many years and moving to a smaller apartment, even moving across country to a more congenial climate
or to be nearer (or away from) our adult children and their
families. This change will influence our friendships and other social contacts.

But retirement may be more than a social transition. For
Christians it is likely to take the form of a religious passage.
Whether we look forward to and choose our retirement, or have
it suddenly thrust on us, this transition has many of the characteristics of a passage. As we discussed in Chapter 7, a passage entails three stages: separation, an in-betweenness and a
resolution. In examining these aspects of retirement we may
glimpse something of the difficulty that many retiring persons
experience and also the religious potential of this time in life.

Retirement removes from us our former, long familiar social
identity. For decades I have been known—and have known
myself—as a teacher, or salesperson, or engineer. Now this
identity and its accompanying social roles are gone. Whether by
my choice or not, I no longer *am* who I have been for many
years. With such an important separation, it is expectable that
I experience a period of "in-betweenness": I still wake up expecting to go to work; other daily habits return my attention to
the job that is no longer part of who I am. This can be a time
of much confusion and distress. I have lost something very
important to me; deprived of my social identity (even if I have
chosen this), I may wonder: what am I good for now? No longer
doing anything worthwhile, what am I worth? For many of
us this uneasiness is gradually resolved as we become more comfortable with our new life and develop new habits of recreation
and social involvement. The specifically religious nature of this
passage, hinted at in the questions that arise about our self-
worth, is more clearly revealed in analyzing the special threat of
this time and its peculiar grace.

The transition of retirement gains some of its special vulnerability from its place in the life-span: it is likely the penultimate
passage of my life. I may sense that the changes and loss experienced in retirement forecast another loss, my own death. If
death is an especially frightening part of my future, then retire-

ment may inherit some of its terror. And here too we recall the asceticism built into human life: in each passage—whether from adolescence to adult life, or from a single life into marriage, or any other—I am invited to learn how to let go of some cherished parts of myself. In these passages we learn the rhythm of life itself: outgrowing our past, we let go of it with some hesitance; mourning this loss through a period of confusion and even disorientation, we come into a new stage in life. As Christians we celebrate these changes, grateful for the surprising new life that emerges from loss and confusion. And in each passage we get better, more virtuous, at letting go and at trusting this natural and more than natural process of life through death. And as we learn, we rehearse: we ready ourselves for future challenges and passages. Retirement, then, may be such a rehearsal for the ultimate passage of our life. If we have learned that the passage through death to life is more than pale religious rhetoric—that is, that this process describes what we have known in our own life—we will more heartily embrace retirement and even the future passage it foretells.

The Experience of Aging

The experience of growing older and being old is itself in transition in America. Students of the aging process note the emergence of a new social category—the "young-old." These are people in their sixties and seventies who are relatively healthy and financially independent, who are free of earlier responsibilities of work and family, who are engaged in active lifestyles of leisure and civic involvement, and who remain interested in the political processes of the nation and in its future. These young-old experience few of the problems (serious illness, poverty, loneliness) associated with the culture's negative stereotypes of "being old." And in studies of marriage and life satisfaction, young-old persons tend to offer a gratifying report of their own experiences of marriage in the mature years.

This is not to deny that diminishment and loss are a part of aging. It is rather to restore the full ambiguity of this univer-

sal and inevitable human experience. The years of late adulthood, as every other phase of life, have both possibilities and
problems that are unique to this time. But in a society such as
ours, which tends to focus on only the burdens of age, it can be
useful to recall that most people experience these burdens as
part of a larger human process. To grow older and to be old also
include experiences of satisfaction, fulfillment and joy.

To many persons moving through their senior years, their
own continuing and changing marriage is a central instance of
life's fulfillment. Formal research into long-term successful marriages is still at an early stage, but we do have clues concerning
what makes such marriages work. One group of couples married
more than fifty years came up with their own list of factors that
go into a happy marriage: love, commitment, "give and take,"
understanding, patience, communication. There are no real surprises here, but rather an "expert's" confirmation of the hints we
have in our own marriages.

One of the most common misperceptions about the mature
years has been that sexual interest and capacity diminish dramatically as one ages. In this view mature marriages have been
understood to be sexless, either because the partners were no
longer interested in genital sex or, more likely, because one or
both were no longer capable of sexual arousal, intercourse and
orgasm. We know now that this is not the case. The hormonal
and other physiological changes that accompany aging can
influence sexual arousal and modify the pace of sexual activity,
but only in rare instances does genital activity become impossible. In the older years as earlier in life, problems in sexuality
more often stem from psychological factors than physical inca-
pacity. An instance in which an older couple no longer share a
sex life is more likely to be related to their attitudes about sex
and to the quality of their relationship than to physiological
changes.

Most older couples report continuing sexual interest and sexual satisfaction in their marriage. In some marriages sex becomes
a new source of satisfaction in middle age and beyond. We are
no longer concerned about pregnancy, we know better how to

please one another in lovemaking, we are often more at ease. These benefits of age and experience can make us better lovers than we have been before. Couples often experience a broadening of the affectionate side of their sex life—lying together, holding one another, affectionate kisses and touches become a more significant part of their physical love.

Emotional closeness, a part of the early romantic ideal of most marriages, can assume a new importance at this time. As newlyweds, couples tend to evaluate the success of their marriage in terms of the quality of their emotional relationship. Over the next two or three decades the criteria of a "successful marriage" shift. During the family years most couples emphasize the role responsibilities of marriage. Our success has more to do now with how well we are able together to meet the demands of being parents and providers. As our marriage moves into its mature years, emotional closeness again becomes an important part of our shared satisfaction. With the children gone and retirement approaching or now already past, we can give more time to our relationship. And, once again, the quality of this relationship becomes significant in a judgment of whether ours is a "successful" marriage.

Change and Loss

Another critical aspect of the success of marriage in the mature years concerns how well we deal with change and, especially, loss. Loss is as much a part of life as is growth and fulfillment. We come to know diminishment and limitation as inevitably bound up with life's movement, whether in my own life or in others'. There are experiences of loss that are particular to the movement of the mature years—some gradual diminishment of my physical vigor, the loss of my job in retirement and a possible loss in income as well, the loss of cherished friends through death. We can delay some of these (a regime of good diet and exercise can offset many of the negative physical effects of aging) and compensate for others (financial planning can bring

us to retirement with an assured and more adequate income)—
but the experience of loss is expectable and inevitable. And the
ways in which we deal with these experiences will say much
about our marriage in its mature years.

Marriage in the mature years carries us, eventually, into the
profound experience of aging and death. Growing old together
is among the maturest joys of marriage for a lifetime. The death
of my spouse is one of its deepest pains. Some older couples are
able to prepare together for death. They take the practical steps
of making a will and securing a burial plot in advance. More
poignantly, they confront the expectation that they shall be separated by death. We know it is most likely one of us shall die
before the other; one of us shall be left behind, alone. For many
older couples, a life without the spouse is harder to face than is
one's own death. Together we share with one another not only
our life now, but the richness of our memories, our common
past. Without you, I am deprived of all of this. Without you, I
am not wholly me.

It is women, more than men, who experience the challenge of
living beyond the death of the spouse. Most married women live
longer than their husbands. There are several factors involved:
in most marriages the man is older than his wife; in America
today men tend to die at earlier ages than do women. The
result is a much larger number of widows than widowers. Aware
of this, many married women in their fifties (and often much
earlier) begin to anticipate what it will mean for them to be
alone. "Many of my friends are widows. Their husbands were
younger than mine, and yet they are now gone. What will it
be like for me when my husband dies?" These musings may be
disconcerting as they arise or may even seem disloyal. But they
can serve as a kind of emotional preparation or, as psychologists describe it, a "rehearsal" for widowhood, helping the woman
to recognize in advance many issues that will arise for her when
her husband dies. Recognizing these, she may be in a better position to prepare for widowhood or, at least, to deal with the
emotional and practical challenges that the bereavement period
will bring.

To prepare for our own and each other's death may not be

easy, but not to do so is harder still. Looking together toward our deaths can be a profound experience. It may bring sadness and fear and uncertainty. It can also bring us to gratitude—a wonder at the goodness with which our life together has been graced. To reaffirm our love in the face of the reality that we each shall die—this is the rich fruit of a love that has lasted a lifetime.

There are many ways to grow old, together, well. One response to the changes of mature age is disengagement, a gradual process of withdrawing from many former activities and relationships in favor of a simpler and possibly more reflective lifestyle. This movement is preferred and richly satisfying for some older couples. But most older people do not choose to disengage. Their response to the losses and diminishments of aging is reengagement. Their lives and marriages display patterns of creative reinvestment in roles and relationships that suit them now. New roles are taken up as earlier ones are set aside, by choice or necessity. A second career, a part-time job, a schedule of volunteer responsibilities, a new pattern of leisure activities—any of these may replace the earlier work and household commitments from which we are now retired. New relationships can develop—in friendships for which one did not have time during the height of one's mid-life responsibilities, in a new relationship with one's adult children and grandchildren, and for a number of older people, in remarriage after the death of the spouse.

Remarriage in middle and later life is on the increase in America. More and more adults who are left alone by divorce or death choose to marry again. This means that for a significant number of people the marriage they share in their mature years is a second marriage. Senior adults sometimes report resistance from their adult children to the notion of their marrying again. And there are adjustments required as two, and sometimes three, generations of family on both sides become accustomed to the reality of the "new couple." But these marriages among widowed older people are on the increase now and are likely to be an increasingly important part of the experience of marriage in the mature years.

Reflective Exercise

Recall a marriage, your own or another that you know well, that has moved into its mature years. Consider what this relationship tells you about the opportunities and challenges of marriage for a lifetime.

How would you describe the relationship now between the spouses? Select three or four words or phrases that best capture this marriage now.

In what ways do they connect with the larger family network —their now adult children? their grandchildren? their own aging parents? other members of the extended family?

How would you characterize their attitude toward the past? the present? the future? Give examples, if you can, of these attitudes.

What do you see as the greatest strength of this maturing marriage? What is its most troublesome concern?

Additional Resources

Several of the articles in *Transitions of Aging* (Academic Press, 1980), edited by Nancy Datan and Nancy Lohmann, are helpful for an understanding of the questions we have addressed in this chapter. See, for example, Lillian Troll's discussion of "Intergenerational Relations in Later Life" from a family systems point of view and Helena Lopata's consideration of "The Widowed Family Member."

The Family Coordinator, the journal of the National Council of Family Relations, devoted its October 1978 issue to *Aging in a Changing Family Context*. Available in reprint, this issue includes a range of articles that touch on the experience of marriage in the mature years. Among these is "Prescriptions for Happy Marriage: Adjustments and Satisfactions of Couples Married for 50 or More Years," by M. J. Sporakowski and G. A. Hughston. Sociologist Ethel Shanas, a leading investigator of both aging and the family, offers an overview of current research along with her own valuable comments in "Older People and Their Families: The New Pioneers" in the February 1980 issue of *Journal of Marriage and the Family*. Ruth Harriet Jacobs and Barbara H. Vinick explore an increasingly important experience in *Re-Engagement in Later Life: Re-Employment and Remarriage* (Greylock Publishers, 1979).

Bernice Neugarten, a pioneer in the psychology of aging, was among the first to call attention to the emergence of the "young-old." She discusses "The Future of the Young-Old" in *Aging in the Year 2000: A Look at the Future*, which appeared in February 1975 as a special issue of *The Gerontologist*.

In *The Reality of Retirement* (Wm. Morrow, 1981), Jules Z. Willing explores "the inner experience of becoming a retired person," including the ways that retirement can affect both the marriage partners and their relationship. We explore more fully "Retirement as a Religious Passage" in our chapter in William Clements' book *Ministry with the Aging* (Harper & Row, 1981).

In *Good Sex After 50* (Regency Press, 1980), Ruth Witkin and Robert Nissen give a positive and realistic appraisal of sexual experience and sexual expression in the mature years. Pastoral counselors Andrew and Judith Lester examine the special relationship between middle-aged adults and their aging parents in *Understanding Aging Parents* (Westminster, 1980).

Part Three:

THE VIRTUES OF MARRIAGE

Two features of Christian spirituality—presence and power —are the background of Part Three. In marriage we come into one another's presence and are challenged to grow strong. Marriage both demands and builds personal strengths—in Christian vocabulary, virtues. The virtue that grounds a marriage commitment is the strength of knowing who we are and what we are for. This virtue combines a sense of personal identity and Christian vocation. A developing sense of identity strengthens us for the challenge of intimacy: in marriage we are tested and matured by the many and different embraces of intimacy. As this virtue grows, we are invited to be fruitful and generative. Again, we are tested and strengthened in ways of making our love go beyond ourselves. In our mature years especially we are called to another virtue—that of wisdom or integrity. A marriage may fail for the lack of these virtues; our marriage will grow as we come gradually and more powerfully into the presence of each other, our God and ourselves.

Part Three

THE WRECKS OF MARRIAGE

II

THE VIRTUES OF MARRIAGE—
PATTERNS AND POWERS

Habits—Powerful Patterns

We are creatures of habit. These habits can be our best friends, for they can rescue us from devoting each day to thousands of minor decisions—when to get up, what route to take to work, which words to choose in a conversation. Habits provide patterns for our life: we establish familiar routes and routines in our work, our leisure, even our lovemaking.

But, as we well know, habits can also make our routines dull and deadly. Routes become ruts; we find ourselves eating the same meals, playing the same games, having the same arguments. Sometimes habits simply reinforce boredom, making it easy for us to repeat ourselves again and again. At other times habits can turn destructive. Sarcasm or silence becomes the mode of communication between us. We seem to be stuck in a pattern of action. Even though we hate this way of behaving, we fall into it again and again. This is the meaning—and the curse —of a habit: we act repeatedly and easily in the same way.

The blessing of habits is that they can turn particular actions that are loving and effective into patterns of action that are readily available to us. Once in the habit of complimenting my children for their accomplishments, I am able to repeat this supportive action easily and naturally. As I develop the ability to assert myself—the capacity to express my needs and desires in different situations, while respecting the needs and desires of other people—this pattern of action begins to shape and improve all my relationships.

Habits are "natural virtues." They are patterns of action that make us graceful. The cultivated habits of a juggler or a linguist, for example, make them adept at difficult actions. They do not even have to think about what they are doing; they perform these complicated actions easily and gracefully. What looks to the outsider like magic—keeping all those balls in the air or reeling off those foreign sounds—is, in fact, the result of many hours of practice. This effort and discipline culminate in well-developed habits and a learned gracefulness.

Marriage is not so unlike juggling or speaking a foreign language. To do it well requires a variety of skills and abilities. And sustained discipline is required if one is to learn to live this complex and enduring relationship gracefully. Marriage itself may not be a habit, but its survival and growth will depend on the development of specific habits of communication and patterns of generous care.

There is a widespread sense today that many of the traditional virtues of marriage have been altered or overthrown. In the "once upon a time" stability of Christian life we imagine our grandparents to have known, habits and virtues were more clear and stable. A wife and mother knew what was expected of her; lay persons knew the patterns of church participation proper for them; Catholics "habituated themselves" to the Church's clear instructions about sexual conduct in and out of marriage. Little wonder if we sometimes feel nostalgia for this time of stable habits and virtues.

The recent, almost revolutionary, developments in marriage and in Christian life have broken down these habits. If we have not lost our way, we have lost many of our virtues. To some of us this loss has been invigorating: freed from more rigid patterns of behaving, we find both our marriage and our Christian life enlivened by the search for new virtues and more responsible patterns of love and justice. For others of us this loss has been more confusing: deprived of routines that once seemed to us both sensible and holy, life becomes increasingly incoherent and unreliable. So the 1980s find many Christians searching for contemporary patterns of love and work and prayer that will strengthen their marriage and mature them as Christians.

In the several chapters of Part Three we will explore the powerful patterns of action that assist the maturing of marriage. For Christians, such patterns are not only habits but virtues—ways we are graced by the Lord and challenged to further growth. This exploration of the virtues of Christian marriage is central to the larger goal of this book, the development of a spirituality of marriage that is at once Christian and contemporary.

A Christian Spirituality of Marriage: Presence and Power

Presence

In Chapter 1 we described Christian faith as beginning in an awareness of a presence. Christians are those who perceive the presence in their lives of a caring God. A believer is someone who envisions God's presence—a presence which is sometimes consoling, sometimes challenging, sometimes troublesome. Just as the Israelites detected a guiding presence in their journey through the desert, and just as Jesus lived in the presence of his loving Father, we Christians believe in a presence which gives purpose and challenge to our lives.

Our awareness of this presence may assume different forms. For one person it may grow into the tyrannical image of a God who commands and punishes; for another, this awareness can serve as an escapist consolation in the midst of a confusing or disappointing life. Yet in its most authentic form our awareness of God's presence becomes a continuing invitation to move beyond a self-sufficient and well-defended life in order to care for others. However God's presence is interpreted (or misinterpreted), however it is shaped by, or gives shape to, our lives, religious living *begins* in the recognition of this presence.

Presence also stands at the beginning and at the core of every marriage. Many of us recall our first exciting encounters with the person we would eventually marry; we sensed here a different and especially attractive presence. As we fell in love, we entered more deeply into this presence and its power. Even when we were apart, our lover was present to us. This absorbing presence distracted us from our work and other involvements.

Our experience of the uniqueness of our lover and the force of her or his presence in our life bears some resemblance to God's presence in the life of a believer. A Christian experiences a presence in life that other people do not see. Looking at the same facts of life, a religious person sees them differently. As the non-believer wonders where we find evidence of God's guiding presence, our friends may wonder what we see in the person whom we love. Shaking their heads, they reaffirm that "love is blind." A person without the gift of religious faith, who can find no special caring presence in life, similarly must judge that Christians are misguided. To the outsider and the non-participant, both religious faith and human love can appear blind. But to the insider —the believer and the lover—faith and love are wonderfully sighted. We see something we may have never seen before and something that many others do not see. And this sight, this presence, begins to change our life.

As both religious faith and marriage begin in an experience of another's presence, they both mature in the development of our relationship and commitment to this presence. Living in the presence of God, we quickly find, has both its delights and its demands. This presence gives our life meaning and direction; it convinces us of the ultimate benevolence of existence, giving our fragile hopes an advantage over our enduring misgivings about life. But as we are enlivened by the delights of this presence we are also challenged and at times distressed by its demands. This presence invites us to see life in unaccustomed and uncomfortable ways—recognizing others, for instance, as our sisters and brothers, as persons who have a claim on our time and possessions.

The presence of the one I love also has its delights and demands. When we marry and begin a life of committed love, our mutual presence becomes unlike the togetherness we had known before with roommates or family or friends. Marriage quickly draws us into a daily intimacy that teaches us new and unexpected things about ourselves and each other.

The maturing of religious faith and of a marriage occurs in relation to the delights and demands of these special resources in my life. If I allow myself to become distracted by the busyness of life or disturbed by the demands of God's presence, I may experience this presence slipping from my life. This is the process of "losing my faith." I may still attend church and call myself a Christian, but once this presence and its invitations are lost, I am in no real sense a believer. We are all aware of the parallel event in marriage. An absorbing career or the distractions of raising children and running a household can begin to work against our presence to each other. Either distracted from or distressed with one another, we become less and less present to each other. We may find we have little to talk about; it becomes easier and even preferable to spend less time together. This demise of our relationship is a fading of presence. As with the dying of the presence that is the core of religious faith, we may continue to share the same house and name, but with no real sharing of each other's presence we are already in the process that leads many to divorce.

Christian spirituality can be described as our consistent efforts to respond to the delights and demands of God's presence in our life. This spirituality does not mean simply our private attempt to protect and savor the comforting feelings that may be part of this presence. It rather concerns the practical choices we make—about lifestyle, career, relationships, the use of our resources—as these foster the powerful but easily lost awareness of our God. Again the parallels between a Christian spirituality and the religious discipline of marriage are clear. A marriage matures as a direct result of these same choices about lifestyle, career, relationships and resources. These choices influence our presence to one another and concretize the commitments that ground our love.

Power

The presence of God and the presence of our marriage partner are *powerful* presences. God's presence is neither a static nor a romantic event; rather it transforms me. It calls me to live differently—to love more completely and to care for others more effectively. This presence empowers me: it excites me with a new vision of life and energizes me to begin to live according to this vision. The new presence in my life of a deeply loved person has a similar kind of power. Not only am I excited by this love and its possibilities for our future, but the presence of this loved one begins to effect changes in my life. I think differently about myself now that I am loved; I may even begin to dress differently. Friends tell me I smile more often these days and walk with a lighter step. More profoundly, I have new hopes and dreams for my life.

But power is a volatile and ambivalent aspect of life. The power of another's presence in my life can move me in different ways. Both in religious faith and in married love this power can develop strength and beauty; it can also simply wither, or destroy.

We have already described the withering of the power of a marriage. The excitement and energy with which a marriage begins can, if left unattended, dissipate. Unable to grow spontaneously, this energy gradually subsides. We no longer excite each other, sexually or otherwise, and we have less and less reason to stay in each other's presence. Something similar may happen to the Christian who is no longer moved by God's powerful presence. Having paid too little attention to this sometimes fragile awareness, a person no longer experiences it in any practical way. Though this person may continue to be called a Christian, there is little sense of God's power active in his or her life.

It is important to note that a failed marriage does not necessarily point to a loss of religious faith. But despite this and many other important differences between the loss of faith's power and the loss of love's power, there are some intriguing parallels. Inattention and distraction, a narrowing focus on myself and a defended attitude toward the other—these lead to the loss of married love and to the failure of religious faith. We are at first empowered, moved by faith and love; but the survival and development of these extraordinary gifts are intimately related to ways in which we respond to their power in our life.

If the power, excitement and energy of a marriage relationship and of a faith relationship can wither and die, they can also develop a destructive force. As I become aware of the enormous power of God's presence, it can be warped into a compulsive force in my life. Instead of freeing me, this power can take the shape of obsession—the rigid "shoulds" of a tyrannical God. Religion becomes law with the deity as its enforcer. That in this instance religious power has been perverted is clear in the lack of freedom that results. Driven by this power, the religious compulsive or bigot or zealot responds to the force of a tyrannical presence.

Unfortunately, a parallel transformation of power can occur in a marriage relationship. The original excitement and energy that brought the couple together can be shaped into a destructive force. Whatever the mode of abuse, the power of the relationship no longer serves to excite and deepen intimacy, but to constrain and compel. The energy of the embrace of such a marriage is expressed not in caresses which enliven love but in blows—whether physical or psychological—which injure and punish. Research in family therapy suggests that this is rarely a question of one partner's destructiveness and the other partner's innocent suffering. Marriage patterns are more generally jointly developed and jointly sustained. But wherever the guilt or failure, the original power and energy of the relationship can become twisted into a destructive and harmful power. Such a marriage may survive, but its hostility, anger and destructiveness witness to the perversion of the power of married love.

The power that brings two people together in marriage can wither and be lost and it can be twisted into a destructive dance. But this power can also be tended by the couple so that it flourishes in a strong and resilient relationship able to endure both the delights and the demands of married love. Such maturing of power is described by Christians in the language of virtue. We will turn now to an exploration of the virtues or personal strengths which assist the maturing of a marriage. But before doing this it may be necessary to try to recover some of the original vitality of the word itself.

Virtues: Strengths That Make Us Graceful

If the word "spirituality" has lost much of its force for Christians today, the idea of virtue has also become anemic. "Virtue" may conjure up notions of stoicism or vague images of half-hearted efforts to be kind or temperate or thrifty. The recovery of a vital and exciting meaning for virtue, a recovery crucial for a contemporary spirituality, begins in a consideration of the root meaning of the word: strength. Drawn from the Latin word for man, *vir*, this term originally referred to the stuff that it took "to be a man"—human strength, *vir*ility. In this root sense a virtuous individual is a strong person, one able to do the things required of a mature adult. Virtue quickly translates into specific skills, as suggested in the term "virtuoso"—one who is adept at some art or task. Virtue, then, refers not to a general attitude but to the specific strengths or abilities that make us effective as adults.

Christians have given the word "virtue" some special meanings. As we reflect on these meanings we will begin to recognize the specific strengths required in a Christian marriage today. Virtue, for Christians, has four aspects: it is a personal strength; it is a strength experienced as a gift; it is a strength for others, that is, it is to be exercised in actions of love and justice; it is a strength that needs continuing development.

A virtue is, first, a particular way in which we are powerful and effective in life. You have a special ability to listen to people in distress; I have a skill for planning and organizing events in the community; she is able to challenge the "haves" to consider the rights of the "have nots"; he is gifted at helping a group celebrate important events. Virtue refers to a specific ability, a way of acting or performing that is especially effective.

Christians have always acknowledged a special feature of these abilities: they are experienced as gifts. We sense that we do not simply make ourselves good at what we do. We find ourselves gifted with an aptitude for such behavior. Finding ourselves so disposed, we are surprised—and grateful. We know that we are not the only source of our own abilities. Our talent for planning or teaching, our skill at listening or resolving conflict—these surprise us; they appear to us as gifts. In ordinary language we describe someone who is especially adroit in some behavior as "graceful." Such a person is both able to do something and able to do it well. We Christians describe ourselves similarly: we find ourselves, in some specific ways, gifted and graced. Our ability to love and care for others does not appear to us to be rooted solely in ourselves; these strengths and capabilities come from God. They come as gifts, allowing us to act and live gracefully.

Virtues are how we are powerful. They are the stuff that helps us pursue our lives and careers with some effectiveness. But they are also how God is present in us. Thus virtues, for Christians, are about power and also about presence. God's presence in us is not just a nebulous feeling; it is not simply an awareness which can console us in the midst of otherwise futile lives. As Christians we believe that our God dwells in us in ways that shape our behavior, that bring us to love better, care more effectively and act more justly. God's presence—the beginning of a spirituality—is not just a general or undefined presence. God enters and shapes our life in specific ways that profoundly influence our behavior and its gracefulness. God abides in us in virtues.

We have suggested that Christian spirituality is concerned with presence and power. In virtues, God's presence is experienced in our own powers and abilities. In this practical presence of God we find ourselves empowered to act, effectively, in certain specific ways. Our ability to transcend our self-concern in empathy for others, or to envision the future and plan for its challenges and possibilities—these are personal powers, and also Christian virtues. They are ways of acting that make us stronger and more effective contributors to our common life.

A third aspect of these graceful abilities, for Christians, is their purpose: they are meant for others. Virtues are the means by which we spend our power beyond ourselves—in married love, in service to the community, in care for those who suffer. And in this invitation of virtue to move beyond ourselves we find, paradoxically, that we are not emptied but strengthened.

There is another paradox in our experience of virtue. The

source of virtue is beyond us; the goal of virtue is also beyond ourselves; and yet these strengths that are virtues are genuinely ours. The conviction that these virtues are *us* brings recognition of the fourth aspect of Christian virtue. These are not miraculous or finished powers but fragile, growing abilities that call for daily care and nurturing. Virtues do not appear in us magically nor do they develop automatically. They are gifts that grow in response to effort and attention. In exploring the virtues of marriage we will examine those particular abilities that we need as we pursue a graceful marriage and the ways in which these strengths are tested and developed during our years together.

One final characteristic of Christian virtues deserves mention. Christian virtues are not spur-of-the-moment strengths; they are not abilities that we exercise only in moments of high inspiration or peak performance. Virtue describes a specific strength that is maturing into a *constant and consistent* ability. This is a strength that is regularly available to me. Precisely because I have been working at it for some time, it becomes my habitual way of acting. I can rely on it regularly, repeatedly, confidently. The importance of such virtues for the complex life of marriage is clear. In marriage we cannot depend on inspiration or peak moments to sustain our relationship and commitment. We need specific strengths which are regularly available. A Christian spirituality of marriage will be concerned with the daily efforts we make to respond to the presence of our partner, and of God, in our marriage. It will find its shape in the patterns of action which make our marriage graceful.

In the next chapters we will examine four virtues which are crucial for the health and growth of marriage. The first virtue (though it is rarely so named) is that of our vocation. This is the ability to know who I am and who I am called to be. Rooted in the psychological strength of identity, this is the virtue of self-knowledge. Becoming gradually stronger in a sense of who I am, I am more able to make life choices—such as those touching marriage and career—that fit me and my vocation. This personal strength, as we shall see, is also the foundation of the virtue of fidelity: faithful to a clear yet flexible sense of myself, I am more able to be faithful to my spouse and to the commitments we share.

A second virtue required in marriage we shall name intimacy. This is the ability to risk myself in commitment to an enduring personal relationship. This virtue, whose traditional name is charity, draws strength from those personal resources which enable us to tolerate the exhilaration and strain of being "up close" to other people—whether in sexual love, in friendship, in competition or in conflict.

A third virtue crucial to marriage is fruitfulness. Rooted in the human desire to generate and nurture new life, this virtue is expressed not only in our care for our children but also in our efforts to hand on to the future the values of our faith. We will explore the many expressions of this engaging virture, which leads us to establish our own families and also to care for the world beyond the limits of "our own."

The fourth and culminating virtue of married life we shall call wisdom. Growing out of the other three, and experienced most surely in our maturest years, this virtue empowers us to give witness to the presence and power of God in our own lives. Savoring our own matured identity and celebrating the intimacy and fruitfulness we have known, we are able to share with the next generations the values that we have found realized in the particularity of "this marriage" and "this life."

In these discussions of the virtues of marriage over a lifetime we begin to outline a contemporary spirituality of married love.

Reflective Exercise

For this part of the book to be as useful as possible, it will help to reflect for a moment on some of the habits you live with. Apart from all questions of marriage, how are you a person of habits, for better and for worse?

Select one habit that you have—a usual, repeated way of acting—that is very helpful in your life now. This may be a skill you exercise in your work, or a way of responding to friends, or a daily practice of prayer or reflection. How is this habit a virtue, making you more effective and even graceful in your life?

Then reflect on another kind of habit in your life, one that is troublesome or even harmful. Notice its similarities to the more

positive habit: you act this way naturally and easily, almost
without thinking. Then note its difference—how it easily leads
you into actions or attitudes that do not contribute to what you
want most for your life.

Additional Resources

The Christians spirituality of presence is rooted in the Israelites' experience of "a presence" (*Shekinah*) in their midst during the Exodus. This experience was especially remembered in
association with Mount Sinai (Exodus 19) and the tent of visita-
tion (Exodus 33, 34). Contemporary Christian spirituality,
influenced by Eastern religions, is returning to an interest in
methods of centering and concentration which assist us in being
present to God and to ourselves. See, for example, M. Basil Pennington's *Centering Prayer* (Doubleday, 1980).

The intimate connections between power and religious experience are again being explored in Christian theology. On the understandings of power in the Christian Scriptures, see Cyril Powell's *The Biblical Concept of Power* (Epworth, 1963) and
Martin Hengel's *Christ and Power* (Fortress, 1977). In *Power:
The Inner Experience* (Irvington, 1975), social scientist David
McClelland relates the experience of power to different stages of
psychological maturity. Richard Niebuhr presents religious faith
as a relationship to power in *Experiential Religion* (Harper &
Row, 1972).

An important part of Thomas Aquinas' theology of the human
person was his understanding of virtues as habits. How these
repeated behaviors make a person both capable and consistent is
explored in his *Summa Theologica*, I–II, Questions 49 and following; see Anton Pegis' edition of the *Basic Writings of St.
Thomas Aquinas* (Random House, 1945). Erik Erikson relates
virtues to different stages of psychosocial development in "A
Schedule of Virtues" in *Insight and Responsibility* (Norton,
1964).

12

IDENTITY:
VOCATION AND MARRIAGE

In marriage I choose to share myself with another person for a lifetime. Who is this "self" that I want to share and how is this self-giving a part of my larger sense of what my life is about? Success in sharing myself in marriage depends on my growing awareness of, and confidence in, who this self is. The maturity that comes from such clarity and flexibility about myself is rooted in the psychological strength of identity and in the religious sense of a vocation.

Identity and Vocation

In our late teens and early twenties we are especially busy exploring who we are. Information about who I am comes to me from many sources during this time: my own ambitions, the dreams and hopes that arise from within, the expectations of my parents and others who are important to me. We learn much about ourself from other people's responses to us. Am I competent or clumsy? Am I lovable or unattractive? Can I trust myself or not? It is from what other people say to me and how they behave toward me that I develop my first (and often, enduring) sense of these "truths" about myself. The process of maturing involves my coming to a sense of balance between inner and outer information about who I am and who I should become. What can emerge in this process is the psychological strength of identity, a personal resource that will contribute to, and be further tested in, my marriage.

Clarity about who I am can be expected to grow only gradually as I mature. My sense of myself in adolescence is marked by the perplexities of puberty, the expectations of my parents and peers, the identifications I establish with my heroes, whether teachers, athletes or celebrities. Some of this confusion is likely to continue into early adulthood. Daniel Levinson's research, reported in *The Seasons of a Man's Life,* points to the years of one's twenties as an extended period of testing, exploring and clarifying both "who I am" and "what I can do." It may be that as life expectancy lengthens, with more and more of us living into our seventies and beyond, more time is needed at the beginning of adult life to deal with these questions of identity.

A young person today may need considerable time and a range of experience to come to a sense of personal identity and vocation. It is only as such confidence develops that I can determine how, and if, marriage is to be a part of my life. Yet expectations to marry earlier may abound. My parents want me to "get married and settle down"; my friends are marrying; other pressures on the inside and on the outside push me into this important commitment. This is not to suggest that early marriages are doomed; many, we know, flourish. But when marriage (at whatever age) begins more as an effort to prove myself than to give myself, it can be considered "premature."

Falling in love in adolescence and early adult life is often part of an attempt to have another person help me discover my own identity. In the mirror of the person brought close in affection I hope to have revealed to me a clearer sense of who I am. Marriage in adolescence often has more to do with these issues of identity than with questions of intimacy. If I marry with little sense of who I am or what I *am for,* I may bring to our relationship the additional demand that *you* supply these answers for me. In every marriage, of course, the partners continue to learn from each other about their own identities and potential. But a marriage entered when the partners have little clarity about themselves is a marriage in which personal identity is not a resource to rely on but a task yet to be achieved. The many challenges of an intimately shared life are better met when each person has attained some clarity and confidence about "who I am."

This identity question—"who am I?"—is also intimately related to the question "what am I worth?" Confused about my identity and unsure of my worth, I may be attracted to the "worthy" roles of marriage. To be a wife or a husband, to be a parent—people see these as important. Married persons are treated as adults; parents are seen as responsible agents. I may want to marry hoping that these roles will signal to me and to others that I have achieved independent adulthood, that I am of value. But marrying to prove who I am or what I am worth adds considerable burdens to an already challenging enterprise.

Elements of Identity

The strength of personal identity is not a rigidly clear and non-negotiable picture of who I am. Rather it is a matter of consistency—between my present and my past, and between my inner experience of myself and the expectations that others have of me. As a psychological resource, identity refers to my ability to maintain this consistent sense of myself. The strength of identity, which guides and supports all my adult choices, includes continuity, congruence and self-esteem.

Continuity. As I mature into a clearer sense of my identity I come to feel more connected with my past. I am aware of ways in which my past, with all its peculiarity, is a part of who I am today. Who I was in junior high school and who I was when I graduated—these "selves" survive and contribute to who I am now. I do not need to deny or apologize for my past—its ethnic peculiarities or personal limitations or whatever. My past and my present form an increasingly satisfying continuity.

Congruence. As I mature there develops in me a better "fit" between what I know about myself and how I am known by others, especially people who are important to me. It may be easier to recognize this aspect of identity by focusing on its absence, those times when I am aware of a discrepancy between how I see myself and how I am seen by others. My parents urge me to join the family business while my own dream is to be a journalist. My spouse sees me as a full-time homemaker while I am interested in going back to school now and getting a job in a year or so. There can even be a discomforting discrepancy in regard to my expectations of myself. I have always thought of myself as emotionally strong and unaffected by personal doubts; I am embarrassed as I find myself wishing there were someone to whom I could turn now for acceptance and support. It is upon my resources of identity that I draw as I attempt to evaluate the expectations that are placed on me by myself and others. Some of these I sense as appropriate for me, confirming who I am or calling me forth toward the best of what I can be. Others I experience as inappropriate: they are not congruent with what I know about myself; they do not fit my own best hopes or dreams.

Self-esteem. Maturing in my sense of personal identity also includes a greater tolerance for, and love of, who I am. I come to recognize and appreciate the strengths and limits that are really me; I can tolerate the ambiguity that remains as my sense of who I am develops and undergoes change.

As a psychological resource, then, identity is a gradually developing sense of the abilities and limits, the ambitions and apprehensions that make up my uniqueness. These strengths and ambitions describe me to myself and suggest ways I might live my life. The psychological strength of identity develops in a growing awareness that gives me some clarity about who I am and some enthusiasm for sharing myself with others. Clarity evolves as I can better recognize my own talents and limits, and can distinguish these from what others expect of me. If the expectations of others overwhelm me, if my fears about my own uniqueness are too great, I may not be able to come to a sense of clarity about myself and my vocation. I am also likely to be unsure of what I am bringing to my marriage.

But identity needs not only clarity; it requires flexibility as well. Marriage requires that I be able to risk myself in close contact with another—in love, in sex, in cooperation, in conflict. For most of us it takes time to learn how to be "up close." In friendships, in collaboration at work, in taking responsibility for my life, I learn important lessons about myself and about how I am tested and changed in contact with others. These experiences in young adulthood can contribute to the flexibility that I will need in marriage.

It is this flexibility in my sense of who I am that saves my growing self-knowledge from becoming rigid and brittle. Being strong in my identity does not mean being well defended and unchangeable. It means I am confident that being close to others will not destroy me. The development of such a clear and yet flexible sense of self is, of course, a lifelong project. But the initial movements of this strength in early adult life are the foundation upon which my capacity for commitment depends.

Vocation—Who Am I Called to Be?

For Christians, this process of growing into a confident knowledge of who I am is personalized in a vocation. We are not just evolving into our own identities; we are called, each of us, by a loving God to be someone and to do something of significance. The psychological strength of identity can thus develop into the religious strength of a personal vocation. A vocation is both an invitation from God and our response to this call. It is an invitation to live a certain kind of life, one shaped by two powerful influences: the values of Christian faith and the gifts that we find in ourselves. The Christian story, as told in the gospel and retold in our communal history, suggests directions for our life. And when we examine carefully the shape of our own abilities and limits, our hopes and fears, we begin to clarify who we are and what we might do. A vocation is, then, an invitation into my own identity as a Christian. It is an invitation that takes shape both in my deepest hopes and dreams and in the challenges offered me by the significant people in my life. It is the particular way I find myself called to love, to care for the world and to witness to Christian faith. A vocation is not an authoritative decree visited upon me from the outside. It is rather *who I am,* trying to happen.

In recent Catholic history an unfortunately narrow translation of vocation has caused some confusion. In Catholic piety a "vocation" came to refer to the special calling of the vowed religious or priest. On Vocation Sunday, for example, Catholics were urged to pray "for vocations." A proper inference from this practice was that only sisters or brothers or priests had genuine religious vocations. The rest of us, and so all married persons, had to muddle along with no special religious identity or sense of calling. A more adequate theology of Baptism today insists that every adult Christian has a vocation—a personal invitation to live one's life transformed by grace. Grounded in the gifts and inclinations that I find in myself, my vocation calls me to spend myself in a particular way. As I mature in this sense of who I am called to be, this clarity and confidence become resources I can depend on; my vocation becomes a virtue—a resident religious strength that helps me live gracefully. Such a vocation, like a personal identity, often seems hidden to us in our youth. It can be buried beneath the expectations we inherit from our family or our society. It can be obscured by our fears or concealed by the sheer complexity of our inner lives. But its shape is suggested to us in our deepest ambitions and the personal strengths that emerge to give these hopes practical expression.

An attitude of listening is crucial to the maturing of both my identity and my vocation. I must listen to, and sort out, my dreams, apprehensions and expectations, attentive to the information these provide about who I am, how I am gifted, how I might express myself in the world. This discovery of my vocation is not achieved once and for all. It is what I continue to be about—in my marriage and in my work and leisure. A Christian vocation is a lifelong revelation of me to myself. Yet my vocation, as that initial sense of what I am called to be to which I know I must respond, has special importance in young adulthood. It is at the foundation of the critical choices I make at this time, choices that begin to define me as an adult. As this psychological strength and Christian virtue grow in me, I come to a more confident sense of how I might commit myself in personal relationships and in a career. To marry before I have come into some initial strength of my own vocation, to marry when I have little confidence in who I am or awareness of what I am to do with my life, is to marry prematurely.

Christian Vocation and Our Dream

Our identities and vocations, the first inklings of our careers and life work, take shape as dreams. These are not (usually) sleeping dreams; they are pictures or images or hints that emerge in us of what we might do with our life. A dream, as explored by Daniel Levinson in *The Seasons of a Man's Life* and in our *Christian Life Patterns,* is a life ambition. It is my best hopes and deepest ambition for my life. It is what I most want to be "when I grow up."

A dream is thus an image, vague or clear, both of who I am and of what I might do. The first hints of a dream appear in childhood: in our toys and games and coloring books we begin to devise and explore our own dreams. In these early experiences the very possibility of our dreaming begins to be shaped: our parents and others surround us with their dreams (thinly disguised in toys, clothes and manners), suggesting avenues for our own dreaming. The richness or poverty of these inherited dreams profoundly influences our ability to imagine our own futures.

In late adolescence ambitions and dreams emerge with great vigor. As we leave the dependency of adolescence, we are excited by the possibilities of adult life; with enthusiasm and optimism we begin to try out our powers in this exciting world. From the outside our parents are expecting us to find a job or select a career; school counselors talk about "majors," often an early test of a future direction for our dream. In or out of school we sense it is time to decide, to choose what to do with our life.

In very early adulthood we may find ourself with a dream that is quite general. I may have a powerful but indistinct dream of helping others: I want to give my energy to caring for the poor and disadvantaged—but how to do this? Should I become a social worker, a doctor, a minister? Given such a dream, my challenge is to test it out both against the world and against my own developing abilities. How will society support or foster such an ambition? Is there any encouragement out there for this fragile dream? And how does this dream correspond to the abilities emerging in me? Do I have the stuff to realize such an ambition?

Other young adults may have quite specific dreams: to be a biology teacher, a lawyer, a carpenter. With such a specific dream, they still must explore how their abilities fit these dreams —am I, as a matter of fact, very promising as a worker with wood? The necessarily gradual exploring of a specific dream might include reflection on the motivation for such a career: to what extent do I hope to please my father by becoming a lawyer, or win the respect of others by becoming a teacher? How are these motivations balanced by a conviction that such a dream is genuinely *mine*—expressing my own best hopes for my life? Levinson's observation that a dream always represents *one part* of myself is important here. As I begin to pursue a dream in earnest it is helpful to be aware of those parts of myself that will be lost or sacrificed in this pursuit. Unable to be "all things," I benefit by knowing what I am choosing and what I am putting aside. Such knowledge includes both an awareness that this dream is mine and some realization of its cost.

There are two important characteristics of the dream as it unfolds in early adult life: it is necessarily idealistic and its development takes considerable time. Dreams are by nature idealistic; they are properly bigger than life, beyond our talents. This "bigness" of a dream contributes to the optimism of youth. All things are possible; many paths lie open to us. The idealistic character of the dream (the fantasy of myself as a famous novelist, benevolent millionaire or dramatically successful nurse) gives us energy; this energy propels us into adult life, launches us boldly into a very complex world. An asceticism built into adult life and vocation will hone this bigger-than-life dream until it fits us better, expressing our identity in more limited but personalized ways.

The dream, then, is how our adult identity begins to seek expression in a career and lifestyle. For Christians the dream is not just a psychological concept that must be "baptized." Our own religious heritage is rich in dreams; Jews and Christians have traditionally met their God in dreams. Sometimes in sleeping dreams, sometimes in waking insights, they have envisioned God's invitations and commands. Abraham's ambition to journey to a new land and begin a new people was a dream and a vocation—the first of all Jewish and Christian dreams. Israel itself began as a dream: a vision of a promised land to be pursued. This dream, begun in individuals, grew into a collective vocation —an invitation from God to a whole nation to be a special people and to live according to special values and beliefs. This collective dream, inherited from Israel, was reshaped by Jesus Christ into the Christian dream of the Kingdom of God: an energizing vision of a world community where justice and love shape life and action, a place where the blind see and the lame walk and the poor hear the good news of their salvation. This dream can be twisted, as every dream can be, into an escapist fantasy of another world, an illusion used for consolation in the midst of a confusing and futile life. But the Christian dream, like an individual dream, is meant to energize and move us to action. It invites us to become just and loving persons and to transform our community and society in the direction of such an unlikely but compelling vision.

A Christian vocation is a personal dream, an invitation we find developing in ourselves. Although it is an invitation *to me* personally, it is always linked to the collective dream of the Kingdom. It is the way in which I hope to live out my Christian values and convictions through my own particular self-invest-ment in the world.

A vocation is like a dream in a number of ways. Both a dream and a vocation *appear* within us. We are often surprised to see them and wonder about their source; they seem to come from someone or something beyond ourselves. Both are also, by nature, ambiguous. These images of exciting possibilities are rarely resolved into clear or unambiguous goals. Our dream, our voca-tion, can bring us into conflict with other plans, other invitations and responsibilities. Most often we follow a dream or vocation in the hope that we are doing the right thing; we find ourself unsure, yet trusting our instincts concerning this ambiguous call. Adult maturity can be described by the confidence, growing within and confirmed by others who are significant to me, that "I am doing what I should be doing."

The Failure of a Dream and a Vocation

A dream and a vocation have been described in the ideal: arising with much excitement, these impel me to give myself to a certain career and lifestyle. But such a development can, of course, fail. The failure of a dream is the frustration of a vocation.

The first way a vocation may be frustrated is in a dream's failure to be born. Children and adolescents may be barred from dreaming. Taught to think little of themselves, they do not expect dreams; they have no ambitions. As they move into adult life, they may join themselves to other persons—a parent or spouse, usually—and take on that person's dream. Sometimes personal choice is involved in the frustration of a dream. A young person aborts a dream that is trying to be born because it is too confusing or frightening. The heroine of Mary Gordon's novel *Final Payments*, traumatized by an event at nineteen, buries her personal dreams and ambitions in favor of the safety, the "sanctuary" of caring for her father.

> I had won sanctuary by giving up my portion, by accepting as my share far less than my share. I had bought sanctuary by giving up youth and freedom, sex and life (p. 239).

> Here I had built myself a sanctuary, covered over with approval, safe from chance (p. 272).

Whatever the choice or guilt involved, a dream and a Christian vocation can fail by never being born.

A second way a dream fails is in never being tested. A young adult may harbor the exciting dream of being a musician or scientist but never allow this dream to be tested in the external world. Perhaps feeling the dream to be too fragile, the person fosters this possibility within but cannot expose it to the tests and potential rejection of others. Such a dream and possible vocation, kept inside me, turns gradually to illusion and fantasy. In the privacy of my mind I am very good at this career; I savor my imagined success while refusing to let the world shape and tarnish this dream. Distance increases between how I see myself (in fantasy and daydream) and who others know me to be (in the everyday interaction of life). When such a Walter Mitty approach to adult life and vocation becomes predominant, the dream and vocation are frustrated.

A third way a dream fails is by becoming tyrannical. A life ambition can attract us with compulsive force: "I'm going to succeed at this no matter what it takes!" When we give our dream this power over us we may achieve it but at a very high price. My dream is an expression of only part of me, the realization of some particular aspect of myself. In the pursuit of my dream the challenge remains to find its place in the whole of my life. How does my marriage, for instance, fit in with my dream? Has our love flourished along with my ambition or has it been sacrificed to my dream? A tyrannical dream will likely lead to the neglect of my marriage and it may be only at mid-life that I realize this tyranny. At that point survival of my marriage may well require overcoming this tyranny and exploring other, neglected parts of my life and vocation.

The Dream and Marriage

The dream responds most directly to the questions of who I am and what I might do. But these questions necessarily include the question of how I will be with others. Marriage and our choices about it are profoundly intertwined with the pursuit of our dream.

Marrying can be a means of avoiding a dream. Marriage can represent a haven where I belong to others. It may appear, at least as I approach it, to be a stable place with clear roles and rewards. In such a milieu who needs dreams? Supporting my spouse's and fostering my children's dreams should be enough. Only, of course, with any luck we learn it is not.

Marriage is, as well, the milieu in which dreams are fostered. The love we receive in marriage can turn us into more confident dreamers. Marriage is a place of multiple dreams. This can present a challenge that is both exciting and complex. We are invited to support our partner's dreaming while continuing to dream ourselves. As our children begin to dream we need the discipline to distinguish our dreams from theirs. It is most often in the context of marriage that we may discover a dream too long deferred or confront the tyranny of a dream we have pursued compulsively. If these cannot be healed, the anger and guilt released here can destroy a marriage. The reconciliation demanded at such a time begins in the recognition of what is really happening. Because we continue to grow throughout adult life, continue to be revealed to ourselves, our dreams necessarily grow and change. This can be unsettling for us personally and disruptive for our marriage. It can also induce significant change, conversion and forgiveness—of myself and of my partner. The shape of these challenges to the dream and marriage at mid-life is examined in more detail in Chapter 22.

Marriage is not only the milieu of dreams. We bring to it a dream *of* marriage—a hope and ambition for what our marriage might be. This dream, idealistic as all dreams, is refined and purified in the living. Sometimes our experience of marriage breaks this dream. Marriage turns out to be very different from what I had hoped; my hope seems illusory and unrealizable. But when our dream of marriage survives, despite all the changes and compromises, something of significance has happened. It is this lived dream of marriage among Christians that can be transmitted to the next generation of believers.

This transmission of the dream of Christian marriage bears some reflection. We begin as inheritors of dreams, especially the dreams of our parents. Among these received dreams is our parents' lived dream of Christian marriage. If we are fortunate we approach Christian marriage with a sense of what it is about because we have seen it lived in our own families and communities.

As we struggle to live our own dream of marriage we likely experience, as our parents and others before us have done, how inadequate to it we are. This is, in part, because this dream is bigger than life and we are not. As we, despite our limits and failings, mature in our marriage and our Christian faith, we begin to hand on the dream of Christian marriage. We give this ideal, now in lived form, to the next generation. It is, in fact, only through us and our generation of believers that this dream can reach the future. Although it is remembered in the gospel and Christian history, it is in our own lives that the dream of Christian marriage is, practically, handed on. When no one believes in Christian marriage—no longer is excited by the dream of marriage according to the hopes of our religious tradition— Christian marriage dies. Conversely, it lives and survives in our lives. Married Christians not only bear new Christians; they cause the vision of Christian marriage to be reborn again. This may be as holy a gift to the community as their children.

Careers, Identity and Marriage

How does marriage as a life choice relate to a person's vocation? Is there such a thing as a specific calling *to* marriage? Is not marriage just the normal context of adult life? If almost everyone marries, how can it be a specific calling or vocation?

A vocation develops in response to my awareness of who I am and what I can do. The complementary awareness—how I will be with others—has, perhaps, been too little considered in discussions of vocation and identity.

Who I am is expressed not only in what I shall do but also in whom I am with. A vocation to the life of a vowed religious (as, for example, a Dominican brother or a Franciscan sister) is a calling that includes a style of intimacy and community; though it excludes marriage it includes a commitment to a certain style of life together. Such a lifestyle commitment must fit a person's sense of self and her or his capacity for relationships.

Other Christians find themselves called to careers (foreign service, research, social advocacy) that, *for them,* exclude marriage. As their own identity seeks expression in a certain work, they find marriage does not fit this particular life and vocation.

Fidelity to their own vocation excludes, they find, the enduring relationship and commitment of marriage. The conscious choice of such a future requires a strong sense of identity since there is so much social pressure for every adult to marry.

Such variation in adult choice and vocation reminds us that marriage is to be a *chosen* way of life. It should match both who I find myself to be and what I feel called to do with my life. Marriage is not just "what everyone does when they grow up," nor is it a way to prove myself. It is not the best or only place to find myself, nor a means to escape loneliness. Marriage is a complex way of living that should fit, not substitute for, my identity. It is a demanding commitment that should be compatible with the career I am pursuing. As marriage becomes less a biological demand for the survival of the race, the Church might be expected to assist its members to more consciously decide if this lifestyle and commitment really fit their identity and vocation.

If marriage is a most significant aspect of a personal vocation, it is less and less an *exclusive* vocation for anyone. The historical factors which led many women to give their full energy over a lifetime to child rearing and family have changed. With a smaller portion of their lives taken up with the active tasks of raising small children, many women today judge that marriage and family are not their total vocation. Other parts of themselves, a wider range of their abilities, call for expression. The change in consciousness signals an important vocational shift. Increasingly, women recognize that child rearing and a family, an important part of the vocation of most women, is just that—a part. As a result of this realization, the questions of identity, vocation and marriage may be especially important for women today.

Woman's Identity and Marriage

The question "who am I?" is asked by both women and men. But often they look in different places for the evidence that moves them toward an answer. Men, in adult life, have characteristically understood themselves in terms of occupational roles and accomplishments, as worker or warrior or leader. Traditionally, women have answered this question—who am I?—in terms of their interpersonal relationships: I am daughter, wife, mother. Thus the interpersonal relationship of marriage came to figure very prominently in the identity of women. Marriage and especially motherhood were, it seemed, what women *were for*. To have children, to nurture life, to care for others—this is what it has meant to be a woman. These have been her highest privileges and weightiest responsibilities. Not to be married, not to have children has been to be "unfulfilled." Some spinsters or "barren" women (and note the negative feel of these words) might sublimate this frustration of their nature through roles of "spiritual motherhood"—as teachers or nurses or advocates of the needy. But not to be "mother" was, so it seemed, at the deepest level not to be fully woman.

This personal identity as "mother" has been accompanied by a social identity centered in the private sphere. "A woman's place is in the home." A man's involvement in the public world is direct, as wage earner and citizen and decision maker. A woman acts directly in the world of "private life." She supports her husband's goals, she guides her son's ambition, she prepares her daughters to be, in their turn, supportive wives and mothers. Woman participates in the public world only indirectly—as consumer, homemaker, hostess, companion. Woman's absence from the world of paid employment and career has reinforced her lack of a public or social identity.

Work in the world is one of the characteristic ways in which the adolescent-becoming-an-adult begins to establish a social identity. This vehicle of identity formation is often lacking for young women. In past decades many women married just after completing their education (in high school or college) and thus had no young adult involvement in the world of work or career. Many of those women who did work in their late teens or twenties saw this as a period of "waiting to be married" more than as a period of investment of self in a project that had a meaning of its own. Thus work was not a part of "who I am" but rather what I do until I find "who I am" in a relationship with a man in marriage.

Today there are both pragmatic and psychological reasons that urge young women to delay marriage until they have tested themselves in the world of work. The pragmatic reasons are visible in a look at the current scene, the contemporary experience of women. In 1980 over half the adult women in the United States were working. In almost half of American families both wife and husband work outside the home. In most of these families, especially in the face of rising inflation, these two paychecks are needed to maintain the standard of living. Every year thousands of women who are divorced or widowed find themselves suddenly responsible for their own economic well-being and, often, that of their children as well. Of the nearly five million single-parent families in our country, 90 percent are headed by women. Pragmatically then, it seems useful for a young woman today to obtain not only the education but the subsequent work experience that will enable her to support herself and, quite possibly, others as well.

But an even deeper reason moves many young women to engage in work. Work in the world is a vehicle of self-expression and self-transcendence. It is one of the central ways I find out who I am. An experience of financial independence and work autonomy before marriage can be crucial to the psychological development of young women, many of whom are still socialized to evaluate themselves primarily in terms of their relationships— who they are with and who wants to be with them. For both men and women work involvement through the twenties is likely to bring them to the marriage commitment with greater self-awareness and self-assurance. And perhaps especially for women, facing the multiple demands of the changing roles of women in marriage and beyond, this critical experience of self-exploration and growing self-confidence needs to be safe-guarded.

Fidelity—To Marriage and Vocation

When we think of the virtues of marriage, the first to come to mind is likely that of fidelity. Marriage is a commitment of fidelity, of faithfulness to each other. The importance of fidelity is seen in the destructiveness of its opposite, infidelity. Sexual infidelity is for most of us the most dramatic instance of a failed commitment, but our faithfulness to each other is likely to be tested in our marriage in many other ways.

How do we develop the strength and virtue of fidelity? Why do some people seem able to be faithful while for others it is such a struggle? Where is this strength of fidelity rooted in us? In *Insight and Responsibility*, Erik Erikson suggests that fidelity arises out of our sense of identity: "Fidelity is the ability to sustain loyalties freely pledged. . . . It is the cornerstone of identity" (p. 125). My ability to be faithful to my commitments in life depends on a clear and resilient sense of who I am. Faithfulness does not begin in marriage—though it is for most of us thoroughly tested and developed here—but in fidelity to who I am called to be, in faithfulness to my vocation.

For the Christian this is a faithfulness not just to my own desires and goals; it is fidelity to what God would have me become. Beneath and beyond all my social roles and identities—as spouse, as parent, as worker—I am invited into a unique and God-given identity. Although I learn about this identity and personal vocation in relationships and in my work, it is ultimately *my* identity—that particular and peculiar path that I am to follow in life. Such a vocation demands fidelity, a faithfulness to the continuing invitation of God in my life.

Without the strength of a (somewhat) clear sense of who I am, my choices and commitments in life will be responses to external pressures. My actions leading to marriage and a career will be efforts of conformity rather than of fidelity. I will be trying to match others' expectations and ideals because I lack a stable, enduring sense of who God would have me be. Fidelity to another person is grounded in the ability to be faithful to myself. Often we speak of this as integrity or authenticity, but we may also use the word fidelity to describe this faithfulness to my vocation that, in turn, prepares me to be faithful to a marriage commitment.

Fidelity, as a virtue of relationships, includes congruence, confidence and conscience. Fidelity is—like identity—a question of congruence, of "fit" between who I am and what I do. It depends on my knowing and trusting myself sufficiently to be able to commit this self to certain actions and life choices. A vocation refers both to an identity (who I am) and to an expression of this (what I am to do). Acting in a way that is faithful to who I am is an act of fidelity; with this virtue we become able to *do* who we *are*.

Fidelity is also related to confidence—having faith in myself. As I arrive gradually at a clearer sense of myself and my vocation, what I can and should do with my life, I learn to trust myself. This confidence and trust in myself allow me to trust myself with someone else. Entrusting myself to my marriage partner, I give a self that I am familiar with and know I can trust. Trusting myself and believing in the direction of my life, I gain the confidence to meet the surprises and changes that marriage has in store for me.

Self-confidence, as an important part of the strength of identity and the virtue of fidelity, is also related to conscience. Conscience—the ability to discern and decide what is right for me to do—is grounded in my sense of who I am and what I am for. My youthful identity matures as I select and internalize values from my religious faith and culture. As these values become personally mine, adult conscience and responsibility become fully possible. Conscience, then, is the strength and virtue of being able to rely on inner criteria for my actions. A well-developed conscience allows me to trust myself and my decisions; I know my actions and commitments are right and good because they fit, they are faithful to who I am as *this Christian* adult.

Conscience allows me to choose what I should do, not out of a compulsive "should," nor mainly to please others, but because this action is faithful to who I am as *this* Christian, with this set of commitments and gifts. Individual conscience has always been a frightening concept for religious institutions because it can suggest a self-reliance and independence which threaten control and conformity. In fact, as we have noted before, Erik Erikson defines conscience as that independence that makes a person dependable. Both religious and psychological maturity demand this movement beyond conformity to external norms and rules into a confident trust in oneself. As Christians we believe it is God who invites each of us into our particular vocations. And these invitations lead, we believe, not to individualistic self-expression and self-defense, but to a common pursuit of gospel ideals: we are all called to follow the same Lord and to live the same values of love and justice. But we may each do this differently. Christian maturity includes the ability to trust both our own vocation and those of other Christians.

That fidelity is both a virtue necessary for marriage and more generally a virtue required of every adult can be seen in two important examples. A Christian who divorces must survive a failure of faithfulness. Whatever its causes, a divorce acknowledges a break in the fidelity of a relationship and commitment. If a person's identity and fidelity are understood almost exclusively in terms of *this* relationship, how can the person survive divorce? Indeed, the horror of divorce is that it suggests the inability to be faithful; if this relationship fails, what does not? How can I trust myself or someone else again? Surviving a divorce begins when people are invited, in this strange silence which follows years of a marriage relationship, to reinvestigate their own personal identity and vocation. With the fidelity of this marriage ended, how am I now called to be faithful to who I am? How shall I be faithful to a personal vocation and relationship with God that continues through this break? If my vocation has been exclusively identified with my marriage, survival will be most difficult: nothing of worth seems to remain. A central challenge in marriage is fidelity to our mutual commitment. A central challenge in divorce is fidelity to my own vocation. (This will include my fidelity, as a parent, to the children who themselves must be helped to survive this break.) When a divorce is unavoidable I must find how my vocation and identity continue and how I am to be faithful to these. The movement toward divorce can be precipitated by the realization that our marriage is irreparably broken and that fidelity to myself—to my sense of self-worth, to my own religious beliefs—demands a formal end to this relationship. Fidelity, then, is a virtue that belongs to marriage, but a virtue grounded more radically in a recognition of who I am and a commitment to, and trust in, this vocation.

A second instance in which fidelity is seen as a virtue apart from marriage concerns the person whose vocation does not point to marriage. In a culture which celebrates marriage as *the* way to live, some Christians will find that fidelity to their own vocation, to who they are finding themselves to be, does not include marriage. Thus a young woman in her late twenties begins to suspect that marriage will not be a part of her life. This can be disappointing and confusing: I may be tempted to marry anyway, going against my best judgment. Motivations are scrutinized minutely: Am I just selfish? Am I afraid of others, of such a commitment? The challenge here is to discern and then to trust this developing sense of who I am and what I should do with my life. This is essentially a challenge of fidelity: to be faithful to *my* calling as best I see it. Such a decision not to marry, out of fidelity to my vocation, may accompany the move into a formally celibate lifestyle or, less formally, to the Christian vocation of a single adult. It may also be an important part of the maturing of a gay Christian. Pressures from within and without may push a gay Christian to enter a heterosexual marriage. Against such pressures, the gay Christian tries to discern his or her own vocation and identity: what kind of intimacy and lifestyle fit who I am and how God has gifted me? For the gay as for the straight Christian, the challenge of fidelity begins in the invitation to come to know, and then to love and trust, who I am. My ability to be faithful to who I am (as this identity continues to be revealed to me all my life) grounds my fidelity to others and to my work.

Two final observations about the virtue of fidelity and marriage may be useful. The experience and exploration required for the development of this virtue means it will rarely be fully available to seventeen-year-olds; it is much more likely to be a strength of the twenty-seven-year-old. This is not to suggest that we should legislate an older minimum age for marriage. It simply reminds us that just as marriage makes demands that mature us further, it also requires considerable maturity to undertake. Fidelity, as we have defined it here, is a strength best brought to marriage rather than sought only within marriage. Put another way, it is healthier to find out who we are (and come to trust this) before marriage rather than by means of marriage. However we are to deal with the desire of very young Christians to marry, if we believe that Christian marriage is for a lifetime, we had best delay this commitment to interpersonal fidelity until fidelity to one's own vocation has begun to develop.

Secondly, the virtue of fidelity—whether to myself or to my marriage—is a faithfulness not to a finished but to a moving reality. Just as a person's adult identity does not crystallize clearly and finally at age twenty-one, neither is a Christian vocation revealed to us in so finished a fashion. A vocation is a lifelong conversation (rather than a single cosmic command) in which we may expect to hear new invitations throughout our life. This means my fidelity must be to this growing and changing sense of myself. Fidelity is possible because in the midst of significant change my identity—my vocation—endures. Were my identity totally changeable, there would be no enduring person (myself or my marriage partner) to whom to be faithful. Because we are neither totally changeable nor totally finished, we must learn the difficult virtue of fidelity to growing and changing persons—ourselves and others. In marriage I am called to be faithful not only to the person I married but to the person I am now married to. As I change and grow, my partner can be expected to do the same. Fidelity is not a virtue which allows me to hold doggedly to a remembered commitment; it is a virtue which provides resilience in responding to a continuing commitment. This strength allows me to be faithful both to my commitments and to where these commitments lead me. Without a confident sense of who I am and what I am for, I cannot be faithful to this self; in turn, it will be most difficult to sustain fidelity to another person in marriage.

Reflective Exercise

Often a sense of identity and of vocation begins in a dream This dream—my life ambition, the best and deepest hope I have for my life—is an exciting and fragile part of myself that merits some special attention.

In the first part of this reflection you are invited to return, in your imagination, to the outset of your adult life. Pick the age—whether seventeen or twenty-one or twenty-eight—that suits your experience of the beginning of adulthood for you. Picture yourself as you were then: what you looked like, the clothes you wore, what you were doing. Then recall the ambition or dream that occupied you then. What did you most want to do and become? What most excited you about the future? Spend some time with this early dream.

Next, you are invited to explore the dream as it fits in your life now. How has it survived and grown? What parts of it have been lost or been let go? What new and even surprising parts have appeared? What is the strongest feeling you have right now about your dream—gratitude, confusion, contentment, sorrow?

Finally, how is your dream (your identity and vocation) related to marriage? Does your life dream include marriage? Or is marriage not explicitly a part of your dream? Or, perhaps, do other values or goals exclude marriage for you? If you are married, how does your own dream relate to the dream of your spouse? How has your marriage influenced your dreams?

Additional Resources

The work of Erik Erikson underscores the central importance of the psychological strength of identity to adult maturity. In *Identity: Youth and Crisis* (Norton, 1968) he discusses issues of identity in the transition from adolescence into young adulthood; in *Dimensions of a New Identity* (Norton, 1974) he explores some of the broader cultural and social aspects of personal identity. Theodore Lidz provides a useful overview of much that is available in current research on identity and other psychological issues in *The Person: His and Her Development Throughout the Life Cycle* (Basic Books, 1976).

Daniel Levinson uses the notion of the dream as life ambition to chart the development of forty men in his *The Seasons of a Man's Life* (Knopf, 1978). In Chapter 5 of *Christian Life Patterns* (Doubleday, 1979) we relate the notion of dream to religious maturing in adult life.

In *Moving into Adulthood* (Brooks/Cole, 1980) Gerard Egan and Michael Cowan examine several themes of personal identity, in a format that engages the reader in a process of ongoing reflection on the issues under discussion. Questions related to woman's identity in marriage are the focus of *Women into Wives* (Sage Publications, 1977), edited by J. Chapman. Maggie Scarf presents moving examples of ways in which issues of personal identity can arise at "pressure points in the lives of women" in *Unfinished Business* (Doubleday, 1980).

13

INTIMACY—
THE VIRTUE AT THE HEART OF MARRIAGE

Christians and the Language of Love

The ability and the grace to love well has always been described by Christians in terms of charity. Loving, in marriage and in other relationships, is the beginning and end of our religious tradition. "God loved the world so much that he gave his only Son." "This is how you will know them, by their love for one another."

Contemporary Christians are not unaware of the centrality of the love that is charity. But several things have happened to rob this word of much of its forcefulness and depth. Charity has often been understood in a narrow and individualistic fashion; it has been taken to mean thinking and speaking kindly of "my own kind." It has become for some a bland virtue exercised in a too ready smile or the facile enjoinder to "have a nice day." The broader challenges of charity—extending this virtue to effective action in social and political areas and compelling us to love strangers and enemies as well as "our own"—have not received their full due. Beyond this, charity has often remained bound in religious rhetoric. Christians are urged and exhorted to love one another. Homilies, catechisms and pastoral counseling unite in preaching this Christian imperative. But a practical question remains: How? How, practically, can we learn to love well? How are we to deal with anger and conflict when these seem to imperil our married love? Charity as a virtue of contemporary Christian life must include the practical means of expressing this ideal of love. It must include not only the good will and sincere feelings we have for our closest friends but the practical and skillful means we have for loving many different people and giving this love endurance.

In our search for a hardier understanding of the virtue of charity, it may be useful to recall two other words in Christian "love talk." These are the words *eros* and *agape*. *Eros* refers to the human stirrings of love: often explicitly sexual, *eros* includes the various strong feelings of attraction and affection we feel for one another. *Agape* is the unexpected, unaccountable love we receive from God, experienced whenever love comes to us as gift and grace. If its most exalted expression is our being loved by God, its human foundation is the surprise we feel when we are graced by another person's love, beyond all our expectations and merit.

Eros begins in physical, erotic attractiveness. Powerful as this is, its danger is the possible illusion that the body is *eros'* only abode. We may come to believe that we are lovable simply because of our physical appearance or performance. Yet *eros* originates *properly* in the physical aspects of interpersonal love; it is only when it *equates* loveliness with youth or physical beauty or agile performance that *eros* fails us. Change then becomes an enemy and *eros* is unable to probe new channels of mutual love.

The maturing of *eros* leads into a more profound and enduring love, less dependent on immediate sensation and peak feelings. *Eros* matures from romance to committed love; it grows from a love that is more genitally focused to a love that also thrives on a broader sexual expression—in the kinds of verbal and non-verbal strokes that only time together can teach us. It can also develop in ways that appear as non-erotic; the maturing of human love that allows a person to love a marriage partner through a long period of illness. Here a strong affective bond survives and flourishes despite a deprivation of genital expression and even a lack of an accustomed mutuality. All of these developments can be called the natural transformation of *eros*. Begun in genital arousal and exciting sexual expression, *eros* develops—not away from erotic love but into more varied and enduring expressions.

Agape, as God's love for us, is love as gift and grace. This is love in its most unanticipated and unprovoked dimension. *Agape* is at work and recognizable in human interpersonal love in the surprise and unaccountability of our being loved. It appears in the realization that human love itself is beyond calculation and merit; it lies, ultimately, beyond our best planning and our most careful control. *Agape* as God's love is also at work and evidenced beyond *eros:* we experience the invitation to love the unfamiliar face of the stranger and the unlovely body of the wounded. This love, neither rooted in sexual arousal nor fulfilled in genital sharing, is both natural and more than natural: to love these others as our sisters and brothers is to be truly human, and yet the ability to do so makes us most exceptional.

Christian love is not a wholly different love: we are not called to love in a wholly unique fashion, but are called to exercise the extraordinary capacity for love that we find within ourselves. What stamps this maturation as Christian are the values and images that excite us to such love. Our tradition is filled with stories and images and models of extraordinary love, within marriage and without. The Christian tradition celebrates this loving, telling us it is possible and showing us what it looks like. It also alerts us to expect the unexpected: our own lovableness and our surprising capacity for faithfulness to the loves and commitments of our life.

Christian charity has always been seen as a synthesis of *eros* and *agape.* As David Tracy has shown in his essay in *The Family in Crisis or in Transition,* Christians have argued for three different syntheses. In the first, *agape* as God's love overwhelms and replaces all human love or *eros.* Such a view understands erotic love as suspect, limited and even intrinsically turned in on itself. Our fall from grace in the garden of Eden has perverted our inclinations of love. An ideal of Christian love as a love above human feeling and erotic expression lies but a short step from this orientation. A second effort to relate *eros* and *agape* proposes an immediate compatibility between the two. This optimistic and even simplistic trust in the movements of *eros* leads to a near identification of *eros* and *agape.* Such a humanism tends to neglect the ambiguities and frequent tragedies that accompany our efforts to mature in love.

A third effort to synthesize *eros* and *agape* attempts to celebrate the power and holiness of both erotic love and the larger love that seems not rooted in us, but instead surprises us in our extraordinary experiences of intimacy. God, as creator of our bodies and feelings, has made *eros* a beautiful and graceful love: in our sexuality we can be surprised by love and invited beyond selfishness to enduring care. Yet Christians also believe in a God who challenges us to other kinds of love: *agape* can be experienced at the heart of erotic love, but it also leads us into extra-erotic love—for the stranger, for the needy and for our marriage partner in the difficult periods of our life together.

Christian charity must be grounded in a love of the body: the erotic love which draws most Christians to marriage is itself good and holy. Christian charity is also rooted in the experience of *agape*—God's love penetrating our human love both to fulfill it and to transform it. A Christian virtue of intimacy, then, will necessarily be constituted by a celebration of sexual love and the anticipation of another love. This "other love" is sometimes experienced within erotic love, as we thank God for the love received in our marriage and for the fruitfulness of that love in our children. This love is sometimes experienced in extra-erotic ways, in continuing to love a partner who has acted unfaithfully, or in loving others beyond our own immediate family. Charity, combining erotic and agapic love, describes an *enduring* ability that sees our love through both its exciting and non-exciting times. As a virtue, charity describes a habit, a resident strength which gives my love effective and consistent expression. This virtue is an ability to be up close, erotically and otherwise, and to sustain such intimacy despite its strains and difficulties.

Can the word "charity" bear this load? For some Christians the word has been emptied of most of its force and any resurrection of its deepest meaning will be difficult. A contemporary translation of this virtue may profit by an association with the term "intimacy." Intimacy has connotations of sexual closeness but, in fact, refers to a much broader psychological resource. Charity and intimacy both have to do with an enduring personal strength of "being with" others effectively. Charity and intimacy both include the ability to love erotically and more than erotically. The word "charity" will survive if we can rescue it from its narrow meaning of "feeling kindly toward others" and ground it in both the psychological strength of intimacy and the compelling force of God's love for us.

The Embrace of Intimacy

In our efforts to find and develop this virtue of intimacy, to get better at loving, we Christians turn repeatedly to the Scriptures. We search among the many stories of our ancestors' relationship with each other and with God for models of how to love well, of how to meet the challenge of an enduring intimacy.

In recent years Christians have rediscovered a book of the Old Testament that had previously been avoided out of embarrassment. In the Song of Songs it is sexual, erotic love that is celebrated. Having for some time interpreted these poems antiseptically as allegories of God's love for the human soul, biblical scholarship is returning today to a more straightforward interpretation. Lovely and attractive as this book of poetry is, its romanticism celebrates only one part of human love and intimacy. Intimacy as a Christian virtue is a much broader ability, one that can help mature romance into an enduring commitment.

At another point in the Old Testament we do come across a story about intimacy which describes the testing of the strength required in a serious love relationship. This is the story of Jacob wrestling with Yahweh. The very ancientness of this story allows it to capture the full ambiguity of genuine intimacy, both its excitement and its threat.

> And there was one that wrestled with him until daybreak who, seeing that he could not master him, struck him in the socket of his hip, and Jacob's hip was dislocated as he wrestled with him. He said, "Let me go, for day is breaking." But Jacob answered, "I will not let you go unless you bless me." He then asked, "What is your name?" "Jacob," he replied. He said, "Your name shall no longer be Jacob, but Israel, because you have been strong against God, you shall prevail against men." Jacob then made this

request, "I beg you, tell me your name," but he replied, "Why do you ask my name?" And he blessed him there. Jacob named the place Peniel, "Because I have seen God face to face," he said, "and I have survived." The sun rose as he left Peniel, limping because of his hip (Genesis 32:24–31).

This is a story about wrestling and conflict and also about intimacy. God comes close to Jacob and embraces him—an act of intimacy. But the ambiguity of Jacob's experience, 'and of many of our own experiences of intimacy, is captured in the metaphor of wrestling. Wrestling is an especially invigorating and ambiguous kind of intimacy. We are in each other's arms: we are both holding each other and testing each other. In such a powerful embrace there is much ambiguity: Jacob no doubt feels this nocturnal assailant is trying to hurt him; in the different embraces of marriage I may also fear that I am going to be hurt.

The wrestling embrace is suggestive of the sexual embrace: "And they will cleave to one another." Both embraces are ambiguous, they are at once exciting and threatening. Will I be taken advantage of? Will I be injured? Is such a close encounter too threatening for me? As we struggle with these questions and others that arise in the embraces of marriage, we are tested and can grow in intimacy, the virtue that stands at the heart of marriage.

This story of Jacob describes a struggle of intimacy and Jacob's growth in this virtue. The encounter begins in threat and risk. Jacob is unsure about the other person; he is in the dark. He does not know what this person wants of him. Whether at the beginning of a relationship or well into marriage we may find ourself in a similar situation: unexpected demands, unknown facets of my partner (or of myself) suddenly appear.

The central threat of any close intimacy encounter—whether in married love or in the cooperative work of our careers—is the threat of injury and loss. Intense closeness invites me to risk myself, to expose part of myself to another. This places me in a highly vulnerable position. I may be taken advantage of, may be laughed at or hurt. But I must take this risk if I would participate in love and work, for these are both "contact sports."

Vulnerability has become a cherished attribute today. We

would all like to be sensitive and vulnerable. Unfortunately, as
we learn, vulnerability often leads to injury; if I am vulnerable I
am likely to be hurt. And Jacob is injured, seriously. This encounter left him wounded for life. One of the confusing elements of this ancient story is that God wounds Jacob. It is our
loving God, whom centuries of catechetical refinement have interpreted as almost solely a benign and protective figure, who
injures Jacob. This is clearly a story of intimacy rather than romance.

This story points to what we risk in intimacy: our own identity. Jacob is asked his name, asked to disclose himself. In this
encounter Jacob's identity is not only tested but altered. This
change in Jacob, wrought by his struggle of intimacy, is signaled
in his new name, Israel.

It is precisely in such challenges to identity that the virtue of
intimacy develops. Early in adult life I struggle to come to some
clarity about who I am. As the strength of knowing and believing in myself grows, I come up close to someone who may
threaten this newly formed identity. This threat occurs not because the other person is bad or aggressive; it happens because
this is how I am invited to expand and develop an adult identity. In the close encounter and wrestling of intimacy I should
expect to be changed and even to lose some part of myself. As
Jacob was wounded and had his name changed, my identity
must necessarily be altered as I move into the profound intimacy
of marriage. The "we" of committed intimacy is not the juxtapo-
sition of two "I's" but their transformation into something new. I
can afford to give up part of myself only if I know I will survive.
The virtue of intimacy relies on the prior strengths of identity
and vocation. A clear and flexible sense of myself allows me to
risk part of this self as I move into a life of committed intimacy.

The *mutual* change which occurs in a sustained intimacy embrace is also expressed in the Jacob story. Not only is Jacob
changed—an injury and a new name—but Yahweh is also
changed: "'I will not let you go unless you bless me.' . . . And
he blessed him there." Yahweh is forced to surrender a blessing.
Both partners of this intimacy struggle lose something of themselves and are thus changed. This significant change of identity

that accompanies marriage has been expressed for women in their assumption of their husband's name. A deception can occur for the man, who retains his exact name in marriage. Does it not signify that he has not changed and does not need to change? The practice of women retaining their "maiden names" and of couples joining their family names today responds to the realization that this intimacy has, and will, require significant changes in each of their identities.

This story of religious intimacy concludes with Jacob limping away from this encounter, having prevailed. The Scripture tells us he was victorious, successful at this test of intimacy with God. Does not his success suggest to us a way to "win" at intimacy? Jacob's prevailing was not a conquest: he did not overcome or bring under control his partner in intimacy. He gave up something of himself and gained something (a blessing) from his opponent/partner. Both members of this ambiguous struggle were changed as they came into a more intimate knowledge of each other. Neither fled from the embrace nor achieved total control. Their intimacy, this wrestling, both exhausted and invigorated them. Jacob outlasted the night with its confusion and fear and it was a deeper intimacy with his God that dawned on him. This story from the earliest period of our religious Scripture may give insight to us, three thousand years later, concerning the challenges and possibilities of married intimacy today.

Intimacy in Our Marriage

Intimacy is the psychological strength that grounds my capacity to love. Intimacy here means more than sexuality or romance; it is not just a polite synonym for genital play. My strengths for intimacy help me to be "up close" to people; help me to tolerate both the exhilaration and the strain of coming close enough to others that my own life can be affected. Intimacy is tested in friendship, with its invitation to let myself be known and influenced by someone I love. But intimacy in adult life goes beyond experiences of attraction and love. I come up close to other people in teamwork and collaboration, in conflict and competition, in planning and negotiation. Marriage involves us at all these levels. We come close as lovers, as friends, as partners in the enterprise of daily life. We also experience each other "up close" in the situations of conflict and disagreement that arise between us. And these more negative experiences of being close are as much a part of our intimacy in marriage as are our more idyllic moments of communion and joy.

Sex is not all of intimacy but for many of us it has been central to our maturing in this virtue. We have experienced the power of sexual sharing to open us to a larger communion. Risking closeness in sex play, I have learned to let down my defenses with you in other ways as well. We have been naked together; I know that I can show you who I really am and you will not go away. In orgasm we have shared a mutuality that overcomes our separateness but does not destroy either of us. Our own lovemaking has shown us that "mutual regulation of complicated patterns" that psychologists know is part of any successful adult intimacy, whatever its form. And in our lovemaking we have known the power of intimacy to appease the hostilities that arise —inevitably and expectably—between people who are in continuing close contact.

Each of the intimacy events of marriage, whether lovemaking or argument or compromise, tests my sense of myself. Each raises issues between us of influence and autonomy. Am I sure enough of myself that I can risk getting close to you? Or am I afraid that your power will be too much for me? Am I comfortable enough with what I know about me that I can afford to let you get close? Or must I keep you at a distance, to hide the inadequacy or confusion that I feel inside? Can I face the new information about myself that may arise as we come together? Or must I resist any new information, since it may force me to change? And for most of us this is what frightens us most about intimacy—not what I will learn about you as we come together, but what I may learn about myself. Intimacy, then, is an invitation to self-exploration. Its challenge is that I may have to change.

The movement into marriage involves the risks of intimacy. In

marriage I must be able to come close to you in a way that lets
you know and influence me. I must face the risk of being
changed, of coming to a different awareness of who I am, as a
result of our life together. I must accept the responsibility of my
own influence in your life as well. Intimacy involves an overlapping of space, a willingness to be influenced, an openness to the
possibility of change. It invites me beyond myself. But only with
a strong and flexible sense of self can I accept the invitation. If
my sense of myself is not strong, it may not survive the intimacy
encounter. I fear that if I come close to you, I will be overwhelmed. There will be nothing of me left. Or, without a clear
sense of who I am, I have little to bring to our relationship.
There is no "me" to give to the process of mutual confirmation
and growth. Instead, I try to become what you want me to be,
or what I *think* you want me to be. But, as we have seen in
Chapter 12, intimacy depends on identity; it cannot substitute
for it. My capacity for closeness must be rooted in some sense of
myself as adequate on my own. If it is not, the intimacy which
results will not lead to mutuality but to symbiosis. Mature intimacy is more than an impulse for merger. It includes a sense of
autonomy and an awareness of my continuing responsibility for
myself.

A definition of myself that is too rigid makes mutuality
equally difficult. There is too little flexibility in my sense of who
I am, too little openness to learn something new about myself or
to change. Personal rigidity leaves little room for self-exploration
or self-disclosure. And without self-exploration and self-
disclosure I cannot move beyond myself toward you.

Intimacy invites us beyond individualism but not beyond integrity. And this is the central challenge in marriage, one which
we can experience at several levels. In our relationship we struggle to resolve the tension between dependence and independence. I feel I am becoming too passive in our relationship,
leaving all the family decisions for you to make. I want to
change that way of acting but I sense that you resist my efforts
to make decisions. We don't want to be just each "on our own"—
surely marriage must mean more than that. But it is not clear to

either of us how much independence it is safe to give up. We try
—sometimes systematically, sometimes by trial and error—to determine the balance of interdependence that enhances both of us
and our love.

Or we can experience the tension at the level of lifestyle—how
much time do we need together and apart? We have to learn the
patterns of privacy and participation that suit us both and then
build these into our lifestyle. One couple may prefer to spend
most of their free time together; another couple may have
different leisure interests and prefer to take separate vacations
from time to time. Some couples like to work closely on joint
projects at home or in the community; others know that working
too closely puts added strain on their relationship, so they divide
responsibilities and each works alone.

Or the tension between merger and isolation may be more internal as we each try to understand our own, sometimes conflicting, feelings about how we are together. Sometimes I want to be
with you more deeply, sometimes I am afraid of the price I will
have to pay. I am drawn to give myself more completely to you
and to what we can be together. At the same time I want to
hold some part of myself aloof from you, as a sign of my own
sufficiency or as a safeguard against the time that you may desert me. These are the ambivalences of intimacy—the struggle
between union and separation; between freedom and security.
Maturity does not do away with the struggle, but it gives us the
resources to handle the strain.

To respond successfully to these challenges of intimacy does
not mean that I will experience no fear as we move toward a life
in common; it means rather that I will be able to confront this
fear. Maturity does not eliminate the impulse toward isolation; it
puts it in the service of the self. The ability to set myself off
from you, to be selective in my response to your wishes or needs,
to seek and savor periods of solitude—these are resources important to our marriage. As movements of my integrity, they contribute to our intimacy as well as test its strength. Intimacy and
isolation may be seen as poles of a continuum along which rela-

tionships fall. Our marriage, too, will range along this continuum —sometimes marked by the experience of deep union, sometimes challenged by needs or events that hold us apart.

Intimacy and Commitment

It is intimacy that makes a *particular* commitment possible. I am not married to "most men" or to "most women" but to *this* person. And over the course of marriage I may come to recognize ways in which this person who is my spouse is limited and even flawed—just as I am. If our marriage is to survive this realization, I must be able to commit myself to *this* person in *our* marriage—aware of the limitation and incompleteness that are involved. I draw on intimacy resources to make this commitment and, again, to live it out.

Relationships are not static. People change, and relationships develop over time. Some of the developments in our marriage will bring the fulfillment of promises and the realization of our hopes. Others will make demands for accommodation, for understanding, for tolerance, for forgiveness. A well-developed capacity for intimacy enables us to honor the promises and demands of commitment and to sustain with integrity the adjustments and compromises required in living with one another. It is only with these flexible strengths of intimacy that we can make the open-ended commitment of loyalty, to do whatever is required to enrich our relationship. Without the resiliency of intimacy, the impulse toward union will be overcome by a fear of what these commitments may demand over the long run.

A flexible identity, an empathic awareness of others, an openness to continued development in myself and in you, a sense of the core of my own integrity that cannot be transgressed—these strengths make creative commitment possible. For it is in my commitments that my identity finds its final form. And, as Jesse Bernard notes, it is only through commitment that our relationship of love becomes a marriage.

Married Intimacy and "Lovemaking"

In our current cultural milieu, where blunt words are used to describe sexual intercourse in and out of marriage, the phrase "making love" has a quaint and even Victorian sound. Yet in a discussion of the virtue of intimacy it may be useful to reflect on how we come together, in a variety of "couplings," to express our love and make more of it.

"Lovemaking" suggests that sexual intercourse is about more than the discharge of energy or reduction of tension. When we make love we not only release sexual tension, we express our affection for each other; we also make more love. Lovemaking is, by nature, generative: sometimes this is the generation of children; always it can be the generation of love.

Such lovemaking is the human foundation of marriage as a sacrament. A sacrament is a sign of something. Before our married life can be a sign to others of God's love for all of us, our own lovemaking, genital and otherwise, must be a sign to us of our growing love. When lovemaking is performed as a regrettable duty or we are constrained to it, it is less likely to "make love." It will also less likely serve as a sign; it becomes "insignificant." A sacrament is a sign that brings about what it stands for. Our lovemaking is meant not only to signify our love for each other, but to generate more of it.

Most married people find that their lovemaking changes significantly as they mature. The highly excited and exciting sex play and intercourse that marked the beginning of their love may well grow into a less frequent and more reflective experience. Biological maturing affects some of this change in the style and mood of lovemaking. And the advent of children almost always alters the schedule of love.

Couples can be confused or distressed by this shift in the ways of lovemaking. Has something gone out of our marriage? Are we falling "out of love"? These doubts may be compounded by the vague but insistent expectations of sexual performance that seem to abound in our culture. We are convinced that "other couples" (whoever these are) probably still have sexual intercourse weekly . . . or daily . . . or more!

Several significant shifts in lovemaking may characterize a maturing marriage. To mature, as we have seen, means to come to a clearer sense of, and confidence in, the rhythms and styles of lovemaking that fit us. We are becoming less dependent on the cultural stereotypes of sexual performance. Intriguingly, this liberation from others' expectations for our lovemaking can free us not only from cultural imperatives but also from religious prescriptions we may have inherited in our youth. As we come into a greater trust of our own body and our partner's, we become freer to explore ways of pleasuring each other which make our love grow. Such explorations both add breadth to our lovemaking and assist the maturing of our love into its own uniqueness and authority. As we come to a finer sense of our mutual likes and needs, we can develop a style of sexual intimacy that, in the midst of busy careers and our active responsibilities as parents, will express our love and make more of it.

These shifts in the frequency and style of our lovemaking are more likely to be part of the maturing of our marriage if we can learn how to talk about these changes. The sacredness of sexual sharing has, in our past, often been guarded in darkness and silence. Yet we need not keep each other in the dark about our sexual preferences, or even our disinclinations or doubts. Is the frequency of our lovemaking satisfying for us both? Does a change in frequency signal new difficulties in our relationship? Even though we have intercourse regularly, has our marriage begun to make less and less love? Beyond sexual intercourse, how does each of us like to be touched and held and cared for? Our discussion of these concerns is likely to enhance not only our sex life but our larger love life as well.

Some couples find their lovemaking develops from a more frequent, passion-filled and impetuous style toward a more measured and reflective experience. Movements of personal maturing may combine with the demands of career and family to produce sexual lovemaking of a quieter, more scheduled and, sometimes, more profound quality. As we noted in Chapter 9, couples may find that they need to plan their sexual sharing. As unappealing

as it may sound to the newlywed couple, a wife and husband
may set aside a future Saturday afternoon or weekday evening
for special lovemaking. This planning not only protects their
lovemaking from the incessant demands of married life, but can
help focus and give special attention to this act of love. Rather
than regimenting their sex life, these decisions can be a part of a
couple's cultivated spirituality of marriage.

For most of us, the beginning of married love is fueled and
guided by strong physical attraction. As our lives mature together, other forces and attractions may compete with and, at
times, even mute this originating sexual attraction. The discipline of married love refers not only to refraining from sexual intercourse when health or choice or commitment makes this necessary but also to the careful guarding of space—in the midst of
our crowded lives—for our love to grow. Both in intercourse and
well beyond it, our marriage demands that we make love. The
virtue of intimacy includes a growing skill and adeptness at this
lovemaking. Attention to each other over the years of our marriage can teach us the many ways, genital and otherwise, in
which we can please each other and make more of our love.

Reflective Exercise

Who are the people whom you could call your "intimates,"
those whom you let in close in love or work or friendship? Who
are the persons who really know you—your strengths and limits,
your dreams and apprehensions? Take time to consider who are
these significant persons in your life.

What is your sense of the intimacy that you share with your
spouse? What are the areas in which you find it easiest to share
deeply with one another? Are there areas where it is difficult to
be open? Do you find there are times when you are reluctant to
be too close? Or issues that you do not wish to discuss intimately? How would you assess the quality of intimacy between
you now? It may be important to take time with your spouse to
look together at this experience of intimacy in your life now,
both to recognize any concerns and to celebrate its success.

To approach the experience of intimacy from another side, select a question or an issue over which you have been wrestling with your spouse, with someone else, or even within yourself. Recall the details of this struggle—the issue at stake, the confusion and indecision, the threat that seemed to be involved. As you think back over it now, can you see this wrestling as having something to do with intimacy? Was some significant part of yourself or another person revealed in this struggle? As you look back, did this testing and confrontation lead to a deeper intimacy—a greater familiarity with or acceptance of yourself or the other person?

Additional Resources

The broader view of intimacy as a virtue and as part of an asceticism of marriage was pursued by Archbishop Joseph Bernadin in "Toward a Spirituality of Marital Intimacy," which he delivered before the 1980 synod of Catholic bishops during its deliberations on marriage and family life. The text of his remarks appears in the October 16, 1980, issue of *Origins*. Theologian David Tracy relates *eros* and *agape* to the Christian virtue of charity in his paper "The Catholic Model of Caritas: Self-Transcendence and Transformation" in *The Family in Crisis or in Transition* (Seabury, 1979), edited by Andrew Greeley.

Among the best reflections on the story of Jacob's wrestling with Yahweh are those found in Gerhard von Rad's *Genesis, A Commentary* (Westminster, 1961) and Rollo May's *Love and Will* (Delta, 1973).

Erik Erikson discusses intimacy as a strength of adult maturity in Chapter 7 of his *Childhood and Society* (Norton, 1963) and Chapter 4 in *Insight and Responsibility* (Norton, 1964). We explore the psychological and religious dimensions of intimacy in Chapters 3 and 4 of *Christian Life Patterns* (Doubleday, 1979) and in the audio-tape series "Sexuality and Christian Intimacy," available from NCR Cassettes, Kansas City, Missouri.

14

FRUITFULNESS IN MARRIAGE

The challenge of marriage, as we have seen, is first to be able to share myself with you, to move with integrity from "I" to "we." Marriage matures as we learn the ways in which we shall be creative together. The creative result of our life together may be our children; it may be a shared purpose or a life project. What we have created in our love—a child, a life work, a plan—stands in the world in its own right. It has a life that has come from us but is more than us. But this new life, the product of our shared power, may well die unless we are able to nurture it well. The maturing of our marriage charts this expansion of our intimate life, as we learn to create and care together. The "we" of our mutual love is not left behind; it enlarges as "we care." Psychologically, this is the invitation to fruitfulness.

Christianity has long called us to this truth: Marriage must be about more than itself because love that does not serve life will die. Psychology reinforces this wisdom. Real mutuality is fruitful. The ability to be intimate—whether in genital love or in collaborative work—has productive results. The impulse to act together to create something from our mutual love is a natural part of the psychological experience of intimacy. A marriage in which this impulse is not nurtured, in which creativity beyond ourselves has no part, risks stagnation.

Fruitfulness in marriage has, for millennia, been understood as the ability to generate offspring. It is that basic fecundity on which our survival as a species depends. But fruitfulness is called for in every relationship. We ask: Is this committee creative? Is this business productive? Is this family fruitful? A group that is not generative has no future. A marriage that is not fruitful will not thrive.

Fruitfulness: A Complex Virtue

Fruitfulness as a virtue of marriage is a many-sided strength. Having long identified this capacity quite simply with our children, we have come more recently to appreciate its fuller complexity. If the human family is to survive, biological fecundity must necessarily be complemented by an ability to nurture and care for fragile human life. Procreation, the generation of our own children, is for most of us a profound experience of fruitfulness. But it is only the beginning. Producing a child may demonstrate my biological potency but it does not yet indicate my capacity to care for life. The virtue of fruitfulness, which may begin in the loving and responsible generation of our children, gradually matures in our continuing efforts to nurture this life toward its own independence and growth.

The virtue of fruitfulness has this dual aspect then: it is a capacity to generate life and to nurture it. In marriage this fruitfulness finds its first expression in the relationship itself. Our married love enlivens *us*. Our mutual care, the joy we give one another, the concerns we can share—these gifts are part of our strengths as parents, but they give our life in common a vitality that is independent of and often prior to the fruitfulness of our childbearing. This interpersonal fruitfulness in marriage, of such concern today, was less emphasized during those centuries when marriage was seen more as an institution than a personal relationship. The absence of this fruitfulness is acknowledged in the not-so-rare remark "I have a wonderful family but a terrible marriage."

The capacity to be fruitful together, which begins in our commitment to each other and is expressed in our care for our children, is further extended in the challenge to be fruitful beyond the boundaries of our own family. Fruitfulness is not only more than biological; it is more than familial. As individuals are not meant to be only for themselves (lest they wither in narcissistic self-concern), marriages and families are not meant to be only for themselves (the temptation of the contemporary nuclear family to "group narcissism"). At issue here is how we shall, as individuals and as a family, contribute to the world beyond ourselves. Our contribution to the civic community and to the community of faith is as much a part of the challenge of human fruitfulness as is procreation.

Christians have recognized yet another level of fruitfulness in marriage. This is the power of a loving marriage to witness to the possibility of committed and faithful love. A fruitful marriage is never of value only to itself. Its fruitfulness serves as a sign and a witness: commitment is possible; love can last a lifetime and beyond. Christians have seized on this special witness to argue that marriage is a sacrament—a sign of God's enduring commitment and fidelity to humankind. Seeing a marriage that not only endures but is enriching and enriched, we take hope that our own life with God will be characterized by such faithfulness and fruitfulness.

Fruitfulness in our marriage is both a personal strength and a Christian virtue. As we move toward a reflection on the virtue, let us examine the psychological resource at its core. This is, in the vocabulary of Erik Erikson, the strength of generativity.

Generativity and Parenthood

Generativity is the mature awareness of personal power that grounds my capacity to care. It is a willingness to use my power responsibly to serve life that goes beyond myself. Many of us are led toward this level of maturity through our children. Being a parent reminds me that to be generative goes beyond the ability simply to produce new life. For most of us, to learn to care for the new life we have brought into the world is a much greater challenge than it was to create it! Many impulses come into play in the decision to have a child. Early in our marriage we may sense that our parents expect us to have a baby soon. But to have a child simply because it is the "expected" thing to do can be fraught with problems. To have a child simply to express myself is likewise problematic. All too soon I realize that this child is not "me." There is new life here, with an integrity of its own. Responding to this new life, nurturing its growth, celebrating its own unique direction—this is the generative movement of parenthood.

And we experience this challenge not only in parenthood but in our other adult responsibilities as well. Much of what I do as a responsible adult—in our family, in my work—is influenced by social expectations, the desire to prove myself. In some areas of my life I move beyond this need simply to meet expectations. My efforts here can be more creative. I want to give personal shape and definition to what I do, I want what I do here to say "me." This impulse to be creative has value, but it is not yet generativity. The movement of generativity takes its cue not from my needs (either to prove myself or to express myself) but from the needs of a life that goes beyond myself.

As my capacity for generative care matures, the question of personal power shifts subtly. It is not so much one of adequacy (can I meet the demands of my life?) or even of creativity (can I find a way for my life to say "me" in a special way?). The question of generative power leads beyond myself. Can I nurture life on its own terms? Can I share responsibility for the world?

Learning to be parents together is, as we have said, the context in which many married couples come to sense themselves and their marriage as generative. But having children is no guarantee that our concern will broaden beyond narrow self-interest. The nuclear family is under criticism today in some circles precisely because of a particular kind of "selfishness" it can engender. Often, these critics point out, "our children" become an exclusive focus. There is no involvement in a broader sense of community, no willingness to contribute from our substance to the common good or to the well-being of persons beyond our family. As parents we may sacrifice ourselves for what we per-

ceive to be our children's benefit, but this can become, in the living out, just an expanded circle of narrow self-interest.

For many of us, however, our concern for our children
broadens us into a larger concern for the world. As we mature,
the boundaries of what really matters to us expand to include
more than just those things that touch our family directly. Our
shared responsibility for the well-being of our own children may
then lead to our personal investment in broader social concerns:
not just improving our daughter's classroom, but working for a
better educational system. Not just keeping property values stable in our neighborhood, but supporting a plan for better local
land use and more adequate housing for all. Signs of mature
generativity emerge in my concern for the well-being of a world
that will outlive me. This can, again, be rooted in our concern
for our own children. My care for them includes my effort to
influence the world which shall be their home after I am gone. I
am willing to spend my personal power and social influence in
the purchase of a future that is "better," even though I may not
live to experience these benefits myself. Rather, this future is a
part of the gift I give to my children and to their children's
children—even to the children of the world.

This concern for the future that will outlive me is a movement
of self-transcendence. This impulse to go beyond myself may be
fragile; it may even fail under pressure. But it may also develop
strength, becoming a part of the way in which I understand my
relation to the world. My power, my resources, are for more
than just myself. They are, in fact, for more than that broader
circle of intimates who are my family. In a generative marriage
we sense that the resources of our intimacy are strong enough
that we can take the risk of giving some of these away. We can
even give ourselves to the future, a future we cannot fully control, a future we may not even live long enough to share.

Generativity Beyond Parenthood

If our being parents does not of itself guarantee that we will
develop these resources of self-transcendence, neither does not

having children necessarily mean that our marriage will be focused in upon itself. Parenthood is only one of the ways in which a marriage may be generative. Both couples with children and couples without children face the question of how their love is to be creative in the world beyond themselves. For example, as a couple without children, what we create together in our love may be a lifestyle that enables us to live out our deepest convictions. From the resources of this life we share, we are each stronger in the values that motivate us in our work. And we sense that it is through our work—our two careers—that we can make our own best contribution to the well-being of the world. Or we may devote ourselves to a joint project which becomes the way in which we care for the world beyond ourselves. We have no children, but we are not, for that reason, without a stake in the future. It is through these "works of our hands" that we give ourselves to the world.

Whether with children or without, our marriage is generative to the extent that we are willing to give ourselves to persons and interests that go beyond ourselves. Determining how we can be generative together, how our love will go beyond ourselves, is crucial to our marriage. The decisions we make here, or refuse to make, will influence our own intimacy and shape the way that we are involved in the world.

Our fears can work against this expansion of our marriage. We may be reluctant to disturb the security of our intimate world. We may find it difficult to nurture without control. We may resist the demands of children or the inconveniences of social involvement. But this refusal to go beyond ourselves is not likely to enrich our marriage. It is more likely to lead to boredom and a sense of the impoverishment of our love.

Generativity, as a resource of adult maturity, involves both power and nurturance. For some, the movement into generative maturity involves a struggle to learn how to nurture others. This can be a special concern for men in our society, many of whom have been socialized to see themselves solely as makers and doers in their own right. Learning genuinely to care, to invest myself in persons or projects in such a way that I am guided less by what *I* want and more by what they *need*—this comes as a challenge for many men. For some, this invitation is welcomed. It calls out a part of me that I did not know was there; it makes me more human. For others, nurturance is too difficult or too threatening or just takes too much time. Without the expansion of personality that generativity can bring, this kind of man can approach mid-life with an uneasy sense of stagnation or loss. An aggressive self-starter in his thirties, in his fifties he takes on the defended rigidity of the "self-made man."

For women there can be a different challenge to generativity. Trained since childhood to sense and respond to the needs of others, many women find that nurturing seems to come easy. But personal power is alien. A friend shares her own experience: "I have never really thought of myself as powerful. I don't feel particularly competent or independent or strong. In fact, I feel that I don't have much direct involvement in life. I can care for people—my children, my husband—and I think I do that pretty well. But I have little sense that I make any direct contribution of my own to the world or its future. Sometimes I feel like an empty shell. And now, as my children move into their own independence, I am left wondering how I can engage myself in life, how I can even stand as a person on my own."

For a woman, then, the movement into mature generativity can require the development of her sense of personal power. Her task in mid-life may be to become more aware of, and responsible to, her own needs, rather than to the needs of others. Without this self-awareness, and the self-direction and confidence it can engender, the "nurturing" woman can feel unfocused, insubstantial, "like an empty shell." Without the expansion of personality that generativity brings, her "care" can disintegrate into anxiety or harden to a meddling control. The capacity to care is rooted in an awareness of personal power. It is this power that I use, I spend, I "give away" as I care for others. If I see myself as having no power, I will turn away from the demands that arise in being responsible for other people. If I sense my power to be weak or fleeting, my "need to be needed" may dominate in my care. I will keep others dependent on me, so that I may feel strong.

But this is not generativity. Generativity nurtures life, not continued dependency. To be generative I must have sufficient power to create something beyond myself. But to be generative I must also be strong enough to "let go," gradually to release into its own autonomy the new life I have created and nurtured.

To be truly able to care is to be conscious, as well, of the limits of my power. And one of the ambiguous fruits of the movement into middle age is an awareness of these limits. Gone is the illusion that I can control my world; I am less susceptible to the self-deception that I can "save" myself or those whom I love. Life remains a mystery: I am not privy to its secrets, I have not mastered its design. "What is best" does not reside solely within my view. I am humbled by this realization, but I am also relieved. I learn how to be responsible as an adult; how, in the words of social psychologist Richard Sennett, "to champion a person or a thing without feeling responsible for its destiny."

For most of us, it is not until we have accumulated the psychological resources and social experience that comes with age that such genuinely unself-centered devotion to the well-being of others can be sustained with consistency. This mature capacity to care for my children and the works of my hands includes an ability to make an emotional investment in what I have created, not just as an extension of myself but according to its own requirements. Not until I experience this demand for the unselfish support of a life or work that has an impetus of its own is the core issue of generativity faced. This is the invitation to foster life on its own terms. I am able to resist the impulse to repudiate the work of my hands as it begins to assert its independence. Rather I struggle to learn how to "hold on" appropriately as long as needed and how to "let go" appropriately as soon as needed. This tension, as we shall see, can be experienced in the family as we release our children into independent adulthood; it can be experienced at work, as both projects and junior colleagues move out on their own.

The Movement of Fruitfulness in Marriage

The virtue of fruitfulness draws strength from these resources of generativity. The fruitfulness of our love is deepened and

tested over the decades as our marriage matures. The unfolding
of this virtue encompasses three central challenges—learning to
create, learning to care, learning how and when to let go.

Learning to Create

In the first years of marriage we are invited to generate new
life. We are each called to abandon some part of ourselves, some
degree of our autonomy and control, in making a new life of
married mutuality. If we fail at this we may live together but we
have not created the true life-in-common that is Christian marriage. We are also called to move beyond ourselves as we give
life to and foster the next generation, in our own children and
beyond them. This first stage of our fruitfulness invokes our
power—psychological and religious as well as biological. The
failure of the virtue of fruitfulness at this stage is impotence, not
merely physiological impotence but the deeper inability to
create. Such impotence can be manifest in a failure to give life
to one another in a vital relationship of mutual love or the failure to move beyond this intimacy in creating a larger focus for
our care.

The dynamism of sexual love draws us into this initial stage of
fruitfulness. Our love is already holy as we create life together
and as we begin our family. The virtue of fruitfulness has begun
to take form. But much maturing awaits us as our married love
develops.

Learning to Care

Our fruitfulness in marriage moves to a new stage of maturity
as we learn to care for what we have created. We come to know,
in the words of Bruno Bettelheim, that "love is not enough." We
find our marriage relationship does not develop automatically; it
needs careful and consistent attention. And our children do not
just grow up on their own. Giving them birth is but the first step
in the marvelously complex process of being a parent. We begin

to realize some of the implications of being a creative partici-
pant in the world. There are "strings attached"; we are responsible for other people, accountable for the choices we make both
for ourselves and for them. The new life we have generated
requires of us a new set of resources—abilities to care for, to
watch over, to support development, to foster growth.

We all know of people who, we sense, lack the ability to foster
life. Some of these may be "creative" in that they can generate
ideas and projects, even children. But they seem to lack the
desire or the ability to care for what they have produced. They
leave behind them a trail of creations to which others must tend.
Creative and inventive they may be but they are not, in this
fuller sense of the virtue, fruitful.

The crucial challenge of the virtue in this intermediate stage is
learning to care without control. At many points it is fitting that
our care for new life include high control. A new baby, a project
just beginning, an idea not yet fully formed—in their earliest
stages these new forms of life are totally dependent on us. But
as they grow we become aware, sometimes in ways that are
painful to us, that this new life has a dynamism of its own. As
we realize this, seeing both our children and our projects
develop in unanticipated directions, we may be tempted to re-
strain them or to abandon them in disappointment. Restraining
them, we try to force their growth according to our designs. We
remind them that they are "ours." Our care insists on control and
in this we recognize that our deepest desire is more to reproduce
ourselves than to serve new life on its own terms. Or we abandon them, our children or our projects, bitter that they do not
appreciate "all I have done for you."

We mature, psychologically and religiously, as we acknowledge that our children and our other creations are not our possessions. The asceticism at the heart of parenting (and every
kind of fruitfulness) is to learn to continue the investment of our
care but gradually to diminish our control. When we cannot
"have it our way," when we cannot be guaranteed that the results will be according to our own plan, can we still care? Can
we still give ourselves to the next generation—our own children
and the next generation of the world and the Church—when we

realize that they are not going to be "just like us"? As we mature in our ability to care with less and less control, we are being prepared for the final strength of fruitfulness.

Learning to Let Go

The virtue of fruitfulness meets its most mature test in the challenge to let go what we have generated. We may already have foreseen this challenge in the growing independence of our children. We may dread the time when they must leave us or when the projects we have begun and the works we have undertaken must be turned over to others. We may rebel. We resist these losses, clinging to our children and reinforcing their dependency on us. The invitation to let go seems always to come prematurely. The parent who won't let go is a familiar figure for humor: "Don't leave home yet. You're still young. There's a lot of time. You're only thirty-eight. . . ." But even as we laugh we sense the way this scene captures our own desire to hold on, to our children and the other works of our hands.

We are graced when we recognize that our children's maturing is related to our letting go. In this we touch a larger truth: the continuity of every life project into the future depends on this generation's graciousness in letting go. This can seem to be a cruel irony of maturity and hardly an experience of fruitfulness. This self-denial and abnegation are felt as loss. They foretell not only our loss of control but our own eventual death.

Such letting go is fruitful in that it creates space for the next generation. In the most mature stage of any project—parenthood, a career—we empty ourselves to give room for others to exercise their personal power, for them to begin to assume more of the maturing responsibilities of creativity and care. We can sense the fruitfulness of this letting go by observing its failure. Without this strength we are forced to hold on to center stage: we must dominate our family, control our relationships, make all the decisions on the job. We refuse to "hand over" responsibility to the next generation; we refuse to "hand on" the faith to the next generation of believers. Afraid of loss, we fail the final test of fruitfulness. This can happen in the parent who still seeks to control an adult daughter or son, in the aging pastor's iron control of the parish, in the senior manager's rigid domination of others in the office.

The Paradox of Our Fruitfulness

Fruitfulness, then, is a complex virtue that enables us to foster life. Our fruitfulness begins in creativity, in making new life. It matures in the challenge to care for this life, neither smothering nor neglecting it. Finally, it invites us to let go, to hand on the future to the next generation and to empty ourselves so they have the space to create. In these diverse experiences we touch a lovely paradox. In every act of creativity we are trying to "make something of ourselves." As we act in the world to express ourselves, we expend our energy—physical and otherwise. In that most basic act of genital fruitfulness we "reproduce" ourselves, but at every level of creativity we are trying to make something of ourselves.

At the same time, our most creative (and procreative) moments carry us beyond ourselves. This happens not only in the momentary ecstasy (the word itself signals that we "stand outside" ourselves) that orgasm may produce, but more enduringly in the results of our fruitfulness. Again, this is clear even in regard to our biological fruitfulness. As our children grow, we come to realize that we have *not* reproduced ourselves. We have generated a life that is not us, despite our every effort to name it so. Our fruitfulness has led us beyond ourselves; what we have made is something very different from a "reproduction." Our offspring spring away from us into separate and independent lives. The virtue of fruitfulness may be sorely tested as we attempt to nurture such a life, one that is steadfastly moving away from our control. This challenge of successful parenthood arises in regard to our other "offspring" as well—our work projects, our contributions to the community, our creative ideas. In each of these we have invested ourselves; we have expressed ourselves in the world. As these generated offspring mature and escape us, we realize that we have given ourselves away. We have lost something of ourselves as surely as we have made something of ourselves.

This paradox of human fruitfulness, that in making something of ourselves we also lose something of ourselves, is rooted in its focus. We generate for the future. The survival of our species depends on our creativity and fruitfulness. But the future always escapes us; it is necessarily beyond us and our control. We are invited to pour our creativity and care into the next generation and its future, aware that—ultimately—both are beyond our control. Such an invitation entails considerable risk. To invest myself in a future that I will not live to see, I must believe that my self-giving will bear fruit beyond myself. For Christians this conviction can be deeply grounded in faith, faith that the future belongs to God, that God dwells with the next generation as well as with our own.

Models of Fruitfulness

This movement of fruitfulness in life and the paradox at its heart should be familiar to us. As Christians we have heard the story before. We can recall the story of Moses, an extraordinary man who gave his life to the freedom and future of his people. In his life we can discern the movements of maturing care. His career of leadership began in a highly creative act, the escape from Egypt. His care of his people matured as they wandered through the desert, often unsure that they—that he—had made the right choice. This generation-long effort in the Sinai Desert bore fruit in the realization of a homeland, "a promised land." Yet Moses did not enjoy what he worked for. Looking into this land from across the Jordan River, he gave it as a legacy to the next generation. His efforts had generated something that was beyond himself; he had to let go of what he had brought about. He could forgo the satisfaction of his own entry into this land because he knew this place would belong to future generations; that made it worth his effort. His life illustrates graphically the invitation to every mature Christian: to give oneself away to the future. This challenge begins with our own children but expands to include all the other investments we make in the future that will outlive us. We can do such a "foolish" thing because we believe, like Moses, that it is God who shapes our history and our future.

This movement of maturing fruitfulness is apparent for Christians in the life of Jesus as well. His life is itself a paradox of generativity: childless, he has yet generated all those of us who name ourselves Christian. Calling humankind to a new way of being with God and one another, he gathered around him and cared for a group of followers to whom he would entrust the future of his mission. His prayer over Jerusalem, uttered as his own life was coming—prematurely—to an end, displays the yearning of his generative concern: "How often have I longed to gather your children, as a hen gathers her chicks under her wings, and you refused!" (Matthew 23:37). This prayer signals Jesus' entry into the movement of letting go. The struggle of this stage is seen in his agony in the garden. A creative person in mid-life, Jesus had dreams and ambitions of what he might do in the coming years. In the garden he realized that he was being invited to let go, to follow a more mysterious plan of generativity. He rebelled against this loss, asking for a different future: "'Father,' he said, 'if you are willing, take this cup away from me'" (Luke 22:42). Surely it was too early to let go. His mission was but barely begun, his followers scarcely ready to carry on without him. It was only in great turmoil and the anguish of a bloody sweat that Jesus came to accept this letting go, even letting go his life in death. And yet it is this letting go of his own life that created the space for the disciples to exercise their generative leadership in the infant Church.

Christian theology and piety have often masked the human struggle of Jesus Christ, preferring a God who only "pretended" to be like us. Christ's growth in generativity, especially in the final months of a life cut short, was a growth accompanied with frustration, self-denial and struggle. His life and death reveal to us the way to live—to be creative yet able to let go, to be able to entrust the future to the next generation. The next generation is, almost by definition, never ready. Its members seem to us like the immature disciples asleep in the garden and like our own children who, in our eyes at least, are never quite grown up. But as Christians we are a people who let Christ's life shape our own. So we, following Christ, give ourselves to the future, in faith that God will see it through, blessing and healing what we have begun and must soon let go.

Fruitfulness and an "Afterwards"

Many of our efforts to contribute to our world, in our children and in our work, are efforts to leave a legacy. We want to leave something of ourselves, something good, behind. Mencius, a Chinese sage who lived several hundred years before Christ, provided an intriguing observation about these legacies. Speaking of the importance of being filial, a faithful son or daughter, Mencius noted: "There are three unfilial things, and the greatest of these is to have no posterity." For Mencius, "no posterity" (*wu hou* in Chinese) meant no children, no progeny. Literally, the words mean "no afterwards," reminding us of the broader need to be generative, to make something out of ourselves—for the future.

Extinction is a terror for the human species: progeny ensure our survival. If traditional societies have especially prized offspring as the means of their survival into the future, the Christian tradition has reminded us that "afterwards" of many kinds are necessary. As our legacy for the future we must generate not only children but also religious faith and the values of justice and love. The terror of extinction continues: there is nothing worse than to leave nothing behind us. A life lived only for itself concludes in a most final death. If all my energy goes into my personal defense and satisfaction, if none of it goes beyond me as a gift for the future, then my death is a final and profound ending. The species still shudders at the individual whose selfishness provides for no legacy or progeny or "afterwards."

Leaving an afterwards means making something of our love. We realize that when we "make love" we must *make* love, create more than there was before. Every religious tradition urges this truth: marriage is not a private love affair. It necessarily includes a love for the future. Marriage is for making more of life and of love and of faith. A "contraceptive marriage" frustrates this natural and holy inclination. This may be a marriage whose selfishness frustrates the generation of any kind of new life. It may also be a marriage that has conceived many children but no lasting, mutual love between the partners. Contraception, as non-generative, is best understood in relation to the virtue of generosity. To be generative is to be generous—to give of oneself. Contraceptive, in its profoundest human and religious sense, means ungenerous. As our species senses the destructiveness of such an attitude, the Christian tradition recognizes its deadliness. A marriage whose love does not go beyond itself is not only unfruitful; it foretells the death of Christian faith and virtue. Such a marriage has no afterwards; it has no future.

Mencius' phrase "no afterwards" reminds us of another aspect of our generative marriages: what we generate remains *after* us, it escapes us. Generating—of children and projects and careers —often begins with ambitions of expressing and reproducing ourselves. We seek to extend our own life in our progeny and other creations. The discipline at the heart of a marriage teaches us the deception, even the selfishness, in this. We learn that our children are not us, that they are for more than guaranteeing our survival and importance. We find that to hold too tightly to the projects and careers and works of our adult life is to frustrate their growth: these, too, have to be released into an unforeseeable future.

This consideration of Mencius' "afterwards" brings us back to an image central to the Christian tradition—stewardship. Stewardship requires us to care well for what we do not own. It names what we experience in marriage: our children are not "ours" in a possessive sense. Our offspring and our other creations are, for a time, entrusted to us but must eventually be surrendered. Stewardship describes a style of behavior which combines two potentially conflicting qualities: care and detachment. We are tempted to hold tightly our seeming possessions; what does not seem to belong to us ("other people's children" as well as the world beyond our own concerns) we are tempted to ignore and neglect. Stewardship is a way of being responsible for

what we do not own. We are invited to give ourselves to what
we and others have generated. And even as we invest our energies in this care, we are asked to detach ourselves—to care without control. Such stewardship is an expansion of our fruitfulness,
inviting us beyond self-expression into the deepest maturity of
self-transcendence.

Reflective Exercise

Fruitfulness is a part of successful marriage and successful
maturity. Take some time to reflect on what fruitfulness means
in your own life now. How do you experience this call to contribute to life beyond yourself? In what ways have you realized
some of your earlier dreams and ambitions for a fruitful life?
How has your marriage been part of your experience of fruitfulness? In what ways is your marriage fruitful now? Are there
ways in which you are being called together toward greater
fruitfulness?

To come to a better sense of the movement and maturing of
care, it can help to reflect on your own involvement. Select a recent event or project—your experience with one of your children
or a project that is a part of your job—and recall its different
stages. In what ways were you challenged here to creativity?
When and how did your involvement move more into a second
stage, toward caring and nurturing what had been created and
was now moving into a life or direction of its own? What
changes have you experienced in your sense of control? Have
there been intimations that yet a third stage is approaching, the
time to let go? What are the feelings that accompany this invitation for you to let go? What have you learned in this project
about your own fruitfulness?

Additional Resources

The discussion of the dynamics of generativity in adult maturity has been one of Erik Erikson's most significant contributions

to the psychology of the life cycle. For his most complete treatment of the underlying factors and the ambiguous challenges of this strength, see his *Gandhi's Truth* (Norton, 1969). We take up the exploration of the religious implications of generativity in Chapter 7 of *Christian Life Patterns* (Doubleday, 1979). Madonna Kolbenschlag examines some of the particular challenges of generativity faced by women today in *Kiss Sleeping Beauty Good-bye: Breaking the Spell of Feminine Myths and Models* (Doubleday, 1979).

Walter Kasper discusses the expansion of marital fruitfulness beyond the biological in *Theology of Christian Marriage* (Seabury, 1980), pages 17–21. Dennis Doherty considers the question of fruitfulness in marriages without children in "Childfree Marriage—A Theological View" in the Summer 1979 issue of *Chicago Studies*. An important effort to place the Catholic discussion of contraception in the broader context of fruitfulness and responsible parenthood is seen in Archbishop John Quinn's speech before the 1980 synod of Catholic bishops during their discussions of marriage and family life. The text of his remarks is found in the October 9, 1980, issue of *Origins*.

Richard Sennett's consideration of care is found in *The Uses of Disorder: Personal Identity and City Life* (Vintage, 1970).

15

THE WISDOM OF INTEGRITY

If identity is the strength that prepares us to undertake the journey of marriage for a lifetime, then integrity is the resource that enables us to see it through. Integrity is the strength of identity, tested through the ambiguous experience of my own adulthood, maturing into a mellow realization of what my own life means. And while we may have hints of this resilient strength throughout our life, integrity finds its season in mature age.

The question of personal meaning is a part of marriage today, as more and more couples live to experience their mature years together. And, likewise, their experience of marriage is part of the evidence to which most older persons turn as they examine their own life to trace its purpose. We will begin in a discussion of integrity as a personal strength and then turn to a consideration of its role in a maturing marriage.

What does my life mean?—this is a central question of integrity. The question arises many times over life's course but for most of us it assumes a special salience as we grow older. At this point in my life I can look over the many decades of choice and circumstance that make up my own past. I come to sense, in George Vaillant's phrase, that in my life now I have more yesterdays than tomorrows. I know that my future still holds possibilities, but I realize that most of my life is behind me. Perhaps over the past several years I have become more and more aware of people my own age who have died. This makes the inevitability of my own death much more real for me. I am newly conscious that my life does not simply unfold into a boundless future. My life moves me toward my death. This realization can be frightening—death comes too soon, I have not yet really had a chance to live! Or it can lead to a deeper appreciation of the time that I do have available to me now.

Facing the question of personal meaning as I grow older can be especially challenging for Americans, for it is not easy to grow old in our culture. There seem to be few positive models for us of what a vigorous and meaningful old age might be. Instead, negative stereotypes abound—the bored and useless retired person, the senile resident in a nursing home, the lonely widow who lives in poverty, the "dirty old man." The fact that these negative images do not fit the actual experience of most older persons does not lessen their impact on us. In general we remain anxious about growing old ourselves and uneasy about the place of the aged in our society.

But "the aged" do not exist—only particular persons in a particular phase of their own lives. And, increasingly, both research and the personal testimony of the elders among us are making us aware of the rich diversity that exists among older persons and of the continuing possibilities for personal satisfaction and growth that can characterize the senior years. Most older Americans report themselves as healthy, competent, active and basically satisfied—even happy—with their present lives (see the study by the National Council on Aging, released in 1975). As with the rest of us, their lives are not without problems, but "their problems" are not a special set but rather those that bedevil us all. Poverty, loneliness, the inability to afford the health care we need—these concerns are not the special province of older Americans. They are rather circumstances that make life difficult no matter our age. Inflation, crime, the increasing violence of American life can have a particularly negative effect on some older persons, but again, these are not problems of "being old" but problems of our society in our day.

The image of the "typical older person" as sickly, unhappy and in need of assistance from society is inaccurate. This is not to suggest that the current negative stereotypes of aging should be replaced by equally naïve utopian predictions. It is rather to alert us to both the possibility and the diversity that exist in the mature years of life.

The Social Tasks of Aging

The diversity among older couples is great, but there are some common tasks that most of us face as we move into mature age in our marriage. As we age, we find we have to pay more attention to maintaining our health and to compensating for some loss of physical vigor and stamina. These accommodations begin in middle age and continue as we grow older. In our forties we start to watch our diet more closely; in our fifties we may decide to play more golf than tennis; in our sixties a brisk walk replaces jogging as our usual exercise; in our seventies and eighties we may include an afternoon nap in our daily schedule. There is greater awareness today that aging does not automatically mean sickness or severe physical deterioration. We know that many of the physical changes that are associated with advancing age can be moderated by diet and exercise. But still, as we age our bodies change and gradually these changes influence the way we live.

As we saw in Chapter 10, the social world of older couples undergoes changes as well. Most couples have some experience of retirement, either voluntary or mandatory, and must adjust to the social and financial changes that come with retirement. New roles are adopted (leisured senior citizen, involved civic volunteer) and former roles must be adapted in a flexible way. After retirement, how do we relate to each other? To former colleagues at work? To our adult children and their families? There are often questions of new living arrangements. Should we keep the house or get a smaller apartment? Should we move to a better climate or stay here where we have roots? Do we want to live close to our married children or to strike out on our own?

The death of lifelong friends during our senior years deprives us of persons whose presence cannot easily be replaced, since such an important part of what we shared with them was the richness of our common past. As we grow older we can continue to make new friends but these cannot replace the friends of a lifetime together. The death of friends reminds us, too, that one of us shall likely die before the other, leaving one of us alone. The death of my spouse, as we noted before, may be the most severe loss of my senior years. I experience myself no longer whole. A part of who I am is gone. And beyond my grief there are practical concerns as well. How shall I be able to make it on my own, after all these years together? Will I be able to care for myself as I grow older, or will I have to depend on the children or move to a nursing home? Recognizing and accepting the possibility of an increasing dependence can be the most difficult task of my mature years.

These changes and others that may accompany the movement into my mature years can force me to reexamine the meaning of my life. Through much of my life I have understood myself in terms of the roles and responsibilities I have had. I have been spouse, parent, worker, citizen, householder. Gradually over the course of late adulthood these various roles are either removed (the role of worker is removed at retirement) or significantly changed (our roles as parents are changed as both we and our now adult children continue to age). I must let go some earlier responsibilities and renegotiate my involvement with others. These shifts can change the way I see myself and the way I am seen by others. They open the possibility of a new understanding of myself and of the significance of my life.

The Questions of Personal Meaning

There are, perhaps, questions of meaning that do not arise until the later years. But the most significant issues of meaning in mature age are questions most of us have confronted earlier in life as well. Of what value am I? What does human life mean? How am I to deal with change and loss? Why do those I love suffer? Why must I die? These are central questions of personal meaning. We may distract ourselves from them most of the time, but the questions remain. They inspire us in our moments of solitude, they haunt us in our moments of despair. In my mature years these questions of personal significance arise to prominence. I must now affirm my own meaning against the backdrop of a more immediate realization that "I, too, shall die."

As the question of meaning comes to prominence in my mature years, I can feel a range of responses. I can say "yes" to myself and my present life and reaffirm the past that has brought me here. Or I can resist what I see in my life now and curse the past that has led to this. Impulses toward self-acceptance and a celebration of the wholeness of my life can struggle against a pervading sense of regret and despair. For most of us, each of these judgments is a possible response to the ambiguous evidence that makes up our lives. I sense there is much to celebrate in my own life but there is also much of which I am ashamed. It is not always easy to determine which of these feelings finally wins out.

My resources of integrity are tested as I deal with three questions of personal significance that become central in my mature years. These challenges are: realizing that I am worth more than just what I do; reaching a deeper acceptance of my own life; and facing the reality of my death.

The Basis of Self-Worth

The older person is brought by choices within and by forces without to that point in life where integrity can flourish. Mature age is the season of authenticity. As I grow older, I am challenged to lay aside the illusions that I may have needed in my youth. They have served me once—even well—but they serve me no longer. I am asked to lay aside, as well, many of the fragile advantages that have contributed to my sense of worth.

Now with most of my life behind me I face the question of its significance. This can be an anxious question. As I move into mature age I can feel that many of the answers to which I have customarily turned no longer work as well. Earlier I may have depended on my physical presence to provide some sense of personal significance. Beauty, vigor, strength, stamina—these resources were mine and they told me that I was worthwhile. The physical changes of middle age and aging bring these resources into question. I can, of course, care for my body. Through exercise and diet and reasonable care I can compensate for some of the physical effects of aging and delay others. But there are some physical changes that are inevitably associated with aging. My body will become different as I grow older.

I may have gained much personal meaning from the relationships in my life—those who love me and whom I have loved. As we have noted, there are likely to be significant changes in this network of relationships as I grow older. My adult children need me in different ways now than earlier. My relations with friends may be dramatically altered by retirement or a change in residence. My spouse may die. I sense that I do not have, even here, a firm or unchanging basis for knowing my own worth.

I may turn to my productive involvement in the world for confirmation of my current value and my longer-term significance. But again, changes—both those socially induced and those personally chosen—influence this source of personal meaning. As I grow older I may experience that my productivity decreases or my motivation in my work may shift. I may be required to retire or I may choose to do so. I see myself replaced by others —by persons who are younger than I rather than by persons who are more experienced. Does my accumulated experience, then, that strength that is my particular advantage as I age, now count for nothing? These changes affect the meaning I derive from my being a productive person. And my relationship to what I have produced also changes. The meaning I have achieved in what I can accomplish in the world, while not denied, is nevertheless altered.

Reputation, accomplishment, beauty, power, affection, wealth —these have been important sources of my self-esteem. They have helped me to know myself and to accept myself. In my reflective moments, though, I have been troubled by their power over me. I have sensed how vulnerable I am to their loss. What if I fail? What if I lose? What if they do not like me? . . . Where will I be, who will I be, then? But surely I must be more than just the sum of the circumstances of my life. Surely there must be deeper sources from which I draw my sense of who I truly am.

In our maturest years we are forced to confront what, as Christians, we have always tried to believe: it is not our good works or our accomplishments that make us lovable and worthwhile. Throughout adult life—especially in moments when we have known ourselves to be deeply loved and in periods of illness when we have not been able to "produce" as usual—we have been learning this lesson. But now in our most mature years we are asked to learn it in an even more profound way. Without my former job or the other "works" that have proved my worth, I am invited to celebrate a profound Christian truth, that I am loved apart from my accomplishments. I have been loved by God when, as a child, I had yet no achievements; I am beloved now in my senior years, even as I feel myself stripped of those works that I have mistaken to be the signs of my adult worth.

This religious struggle to see ourselves as more than what we do is a part of the Christian virtue of wisdom with which many Americans are quite uncomfortable. Both childhood and old age may stand for us as experiences of our own uselessness. These are times when we do not earn our way, we do not prove our worth. During the many decades of adult responsibility we have been busily productive. Our children, our jobs, our other projects stand in testimony of our involvement in life. These creations are easily misconstrued as evidence of our value and worth. We point to them with pride! In our maturest years we are invited to return to a childlike truth: we are more than what we do. Lovely and of value before we produced our many good works as adults, we remain lovely and of value when we are too old to be "socially productive" in the ways that our culture generally admires. The uselessness of old age, like that of childhood, reminds us of a more profound uselessness—we do not earn our own salvation. That is the gracious gift of a God who has loved us and loves us still.

But this uselessness is frightening, especially perhaps for Americans. Here we may learn from the wisdom of another religious tradition. In the Taoism of ancient China we find stories which celebrate the value and virtue of uselessness: an ancient gnarled tree is so useless that it is never cut down by the carpenters and so enjoys extraordinary longevity; a crippled man is so useless that he is never drafted for war and thus lives a long life. Chuang Tzu, the storyteller here, concludes, "All people know the use of the useful, but nobody knows the use of the useless." In our own maturest years we may have the wisdom to learn and celebrate "the use of the useless."

Reaching a Deeper Acceptance of Myself

This strength of integrity involves a deep acceptance of myself. It is an appreciation of myself "in particular," with my full range of strengths and limitations. Such an acceptance moves beyond simple acquiescence into a celebration of my unique, even if limited, self. It is likely to result from a profound encounter with my own particularity and even the peculiarity of how my own life has gone. Integrity leads me to be able to say that my own life has been good. The way I have lived my life has contributed to who I am today and to the meaning my life has had over its course. This maturity includes an appreciation of the relativity of my own lifestyle. It is only one of the ways of being human but it is a good way. It has worked for me and can, I believe, work for others, too. In its mature expression, this interest in defending my own lifestyle is part of my effort to pass on to the next generation the "good news" of how to make the perilous but exciting journey of life. My defense of myself may be, in part, an effort at self-verification but it is in good measure disinterested care for the future. In its immature form, it is the need for self-verification that predominates. It is myself whom I am trying to convince as I extol that "I did it my way."

The psychological task of accepting and affirming the whole of my life becomes a religious opportunity when this long life is recognized as a salvation history. The many decades of my life comprise a history that, as always, is a story of both grace and sin. And for most of us adult life goes by so fast and is so dense with the busy activities of our families and careers that only in our later years do we look back to examine more carefully its larger purpose and direction. This effort by which we try to make sense of what we have been and done, which psychologists call the "life review," is also a religious exercise—or can be. When our life is recognized as a salvation history (a recognition that for most of us does not make it any less messy), then this recollection becomes an *anamnesis*, a religious remembering. As Christians we "call to mind" the powerful events of Jesus' life and God's saving action among our earlier ancestors, the Israelites who were called from slavery to be a chosen people. We must also perform a similar recollection of our own saving history. Revisiting the particular turns and detours of this one life journey which is my own, I can recall and celebrate how God has been at work in it. Such a recollection is not an escape from reality (nostalgically remembering only the "good parts," now softly tinted in the distance of time), but a regathering of it all. In such a recollection we can integrate the different parts of our lives—successes, failures, unresolved confusions. The strength of integrity and the virtue of wisdom develop in such recollection. I become better able to celebrate this particular life which has been my own.

But, of course, we can fail at this task. Embittered by the past, I may turn away from it. I may try to forget it, thus denying my own history. Instead of gathering up the past in a religious remembering (*anamnesis*), I move toward *amnesia*—putting it out of mind, its goodness along with its troubles. Unable to integrate the pain and confusion of the past into my present, I am denied the virtue of wisdom and its testimony of how good and holy even this strange life has been. Without this integration I am restless in my mature years and unable to celebrate the history of my own salvation.

Facing the Reality of My Death

We have already noted the repeating dynamic of maturity, that of accepting and then relinquishing, of caring and then letting go. The letting go begun in generativity gains added strength in the virtue of integrity. I become capable of an acceptance of myself and an appreciation of life that transcend the diminishments that are inevitable in advanced age, transcend even the awareness of my own death. In old age I can learn to let go even my life.

In youth, even through middle age, acceptance of death seems an impossible task. And for most of us resistance to the idea of my own death remains through the mature years. My own death is thus the context within which the statement of my integrity is to be heard. My individuality finds its ultimate test as I face personal death; the final acceptance of my own life is the acceptance of my death as its finite boundary. The lack of these resources of integrity can appear in my inability to accept the actual boundaries of my life. I struggle to overcome my past and refuse to acknowledge that death shall come for me. Or I resign myself, in bitterness, to its power. It is integrity that enables me to celebrate the shape that is put on my own life by the reality of my past and the fate of my death.

The fear of death is often one of the faces of despair in old age. This fear is less of annihilation than it is of absurdity. Death comes too soon—it will seal the emptiness of my life before I can make sense of it, before I can complete some last desperate attempt to give it meaning. The resources of spirit that are released in the virtue of integrity can give me strength to affirm a meaning in my life that transcends my own death. This need not mean that I welcome death (though there is evidence that many persons of advanced age do). It need not mean that my final years will hold no doubts or regret or fear. But it means that these are not all there is. With the resources of personal integrity, this virtue of mature life, I can believe that—ultimately —death shall not prevail. I can affirm with Paul the Christian conviction that death has lost its sting. For the sting of death is not the loss of life but the loss of meaning.

Integrity and Wisdom

That my life has a significance that transcends my death, that my value is not limited to my achievements, that some of the experiences which have seemed to me to be "losses" may in fact be "gains"—these are the realizations of integrity. These profound but often fragile intuitions find support in Christianity's vision of human life. Our experience of the Eucharist and our celebration of the Resurrection add depth and conviction to these hopes of human maturity. In the believing community my personal struggle to sense the meaning of my life is strengthened both by the images of our tradition and by the faith of those with whom I live.

Jesus Christ stands for the Christian as the enduring sign of the promise of life through death. My experience of loss and change across the decades of my life finds resonance in the witness of his life. Growth does not always come easily or without distress. At important moments in my life I have experienced the threat of loss, a fear of what lies ahead for me, the temptation to hold on to what I already possess. Yet I know, from my own past and from the life of Jesus, that it is often only through the experiences of confusion and loss that I move toward growth and fulfillment.

It is in the Christian of advancing years that a lifelong experience of faith and the psychological resources of integrity can combine in new possibilities for spiritual awareness. This deepening awareness Christians call wisdom. Wisdom comes in the realization that my life and my own power are bounded by my death, that all life is bounded by death. Yet it is life, not death, that prevails. Death seems to stand as a stubborn impediment to meaning. It destroys plans, it undercuts purpose, it breaks the bonds of love. In the struggle to discern a meaning in life that can stand against the power of death Christians have been among the most audacious. For we know the hope of resurrection. For many of us it does not lessen death's difficulty or lighten its pain. But it rescues death from absurdity.

The virtue of wisdom enables me to affirm the spiritual significance of life "from the inside." I have experienced meaning in my own life; I have known the presence and power of God; it is from these that my conviction that life makes sense gains its force. It is wisdom that shows me, hidden in the dynamic of my own life, this confirmation of Christianity's deepest paradox. I must be willing to lose all in order to find myself. It is in letting go of life that I discover it. And in dying, I believe I shall find life.

The virtue of wisdom develops as I come to savor the *particular* completeness and wholeness of my own life. Through its power I am able to attest to the meaning of life beyond just my own. But this larger witness is rooted in my affirmation of my own life, even in its ambiguities. With this deep acceptance of myself, rooted in the present and going back to include the particularity of my personal past, comes the realization that life has meaning because *my life* does. My life, to be sure, is not the whole of human meaning. But if my life lacks meaning altogether, so does all of human existence. For the meaning of human existence comes down to my personal struggle to affirm the significance of my own life—as partial and limited as it has been—in the face of the realization that I shall soon die.

Acceptance and Forgiveness

The movement of integrity brings me to an appreciation of the "givenness" of my life, both its inevitability and its gift. Because I can accept myself—even love myself—as I am *now*, I can look back to savor the life that has brought me to this point. All the happenings of my life—the expected and the unexpected, those persons whose love nurtured me and those who hurt me, my achievements and my failures—all are vitally a part of who I am now. Therefore I can accept them as they were; I can affirm that it is good that my life has gone as it has. And I can give thanks.

But the movement of affirmation in my mature years can fail. I may be unable to accept who I have become, what my life has been. My response to the givenness of my past is not *yes*, but "if only it had been different." Blame and guilt prevail. This dissatisfaction becomes despair as I realize there is not enough time left. Death will come too soon to permit me one last chance to begin again, to finally make something different—something meaningful—of my life.

Integrity does not eliminate all despair. Guilt and blame can be appropriate responses to some of the limits I have known in my life. I have not realized all the possibilities of my life. Some I have squandered, others have been denied by circumstances beyond my control. I know remorse and regret in the face of what I have done and what I have failed to do. My death will leave problems unresolved, loved ones unattended, possibilities of the future unwitnessed. Only an integrity that can face these realities can bring my life to fruition. Mature integrity remains answerable to despair and regret. Without this tension, my self-acceptance remains naïve and my integrity untested.

This movement of integrity brings both freedom from my past and a deeper respect for its power in my life even to the present. It calls me to both acceptance and forgiveness of those persons who have been so crucial in my past—my parents, my spouse and—ultimately—myself.

Parents are one of the crucial "givens" of any life. Much of psychological growth throughout life is involved in dealing with parents—identifying with them in childhood, struggling to separate myself from them in adolescence, understanding myself apart from them in early adulthood. In this process parents can become scapegoats. "If only my parents had been different . . ." It is true that if my parents had been different I would be different. It may be true that my parents have contributed to difficulties of maturity or personality that assail me even now. But it is not until I can move beyond blaming "them" that I can start to take adult responsibility for myself.

This movement begins in forgiveness, an acceptance of my parents for what they are and for what I have become under their influence. This forgiveness frees me to take responsibility for what I have become on my own. As I am able to free myself from my own ambivalent dependence on my parents, I am able to move toward a more mature love for them—in themselves and for their part in my life. Through the mid-years, aspects of my parents are reassimilated into my adult sense of self. In mature age this acceptance of self can deepen into a profound appreciation of all those persons—parents and others—who have influenced me. Some have touched me benignly, in nurturing care and respect. Others have influenced me, whether through ignorance or malice, in ways I have sensed as negative. But I can come to accept each, even to value each, for a contribution to making me who I am now.

Integrity in Marriage

My love for my spouse matures through a dynamic of acceptance and forgiveness as well. Our marriage moves beyond its first thirty-five or forty years. This marriage has endured—perhaps in triumph, perhaps through troubles—but it has a history, a past that accompanies our present love. As I look back over our past together I see instances of generous love and devotion, of misunderstanding and mutually inflicted pain, of honesty and evasion, of fear and joy. Tracing the path our marriage has taken may bring me to a sense of awe. We have been through so much together; weak as we know ourselves sometimes to be, we have also been courageous and caring—if not always, still with remarkable constancy.

If our marriage has gone well into our mature years, my confrontation with the past will involve a celebration of the continuing commitment of this special relationship, now tested over many decades. If our marriage has been troubled, I may find myself pulled between vindictiveness and guilt, unsure whether to take responsibility for the failure or to blame my spouse.

An important component of integrity is the realization that I have responsibility for my own life. There is evidence that most of us move only gradually into this conviction of personal accountability. Marriage counselors report that most couples who seek help for their marriage present their "problem" in terms of outside causes (often money or some other practical concern; sometimes meddling by parents or in-laws) or at least factors over which they have no real control. My upbringing or your job, my sexual needs or your neurosis—it is these that are at fault. But these factors exist "out there," they are not anything over which either of us senses we have much choice or control. A critical moment in therapy approaches as we begin to assume greater "ownership" for what our marriage is and can be. We have *both* created our marriage as it is today, sometimes by acting, sometimes by failing to act. Each of us can then begin to acknowledge the ways, positive and negative, in which we have shaped our marriage and ourselves. If things are not good between us, I carry some of the responsibility. If change is necessary at this point, I must take some of the initiative. I cannot force you to be different but I also cannot just simply wait for you to change for the better. This clearer awareness of my own responsibility for myself and my real, but limited, responsibility for our relationship takes me beyond the oversimplification of both blame (where the problem is all your fault) and guilt (where it is all mine).

The reflective self-awareness that begins in mid-life and deepens in mature age can bring to light parts of our shared past that are difficult to face—attitudes that have been harmful, actions that seem now to have been malicious or at least ill-advised. I may find myself newly aware of you: things about you that I cherish but also things about which I am angry or bitter, parts of you that I resent. I am likely to be similarly disturbed about parts of myself. This time of critical self-appraisal calls me to reconciliation—with myself, with you, with our marriage. Again, both acceptance and forgiveness are required.

Accepting who we really are, individually and together; standing together, in the power of forgiveness, reconciled to what has been our past and open to our future—this resilient strength is the virtue of integrity, now realized in our marriage. A ministry to such integrity in our marriage will help us celebrate the continuing commitment of our mutual love, now tested by the events of many decades. The celebration may well include a wedding anniversary mass and a reception in the parish hall, but there will be more. Drawing on the resources of integrity which become available at this time, ministry to marriage in the mature years will include opportunities of couples, together and in the larger supportive context of the community of faith, to look at the challenges both of acceptance and of forgiveness that are a part of their spiritual and psychological development now. Our experience of the journey of our marriage has been rich and dense. We have learned much about ourselves, about each other, about God through these years. Now can be an opportunity to explore and savor what we have known along the way: how I have been touched by the presence and power of God in our life together; what I have learned in your love for me, in my own growing capacity for love; the joy of our constancy and the satisfaction of our shared fruitfulness; the poignancy of our failures and the improbable strength of our mutual devotion.

Reflective Exercise

Spend some time in a consideration of the older married couples whom you know. Begin by calling to mind who these persons are—members of your family or your friends, perhaps people you know from work or in the neighborhood.

From these, select one couple who stand for you as an example of persons who have grown old well. Use your own criteria of what it is to "grow old well," whether for you this means "vigorously" or "gracefully" or "wisely." Take time to let your experience of this couple come to mind with some clarity. Then consider these questions.

What does this couple show you about growing older that is attractive for you, that is positive?

Are there, on the other hand, things that you see in their life as they grow older that are negative for you?

What is it about this couple and their marriage that leads you to say that they are growing old well? Be as concrete as you can: give examples, point to instances, try to give names to the strengths you see.

What contribution does the example of this couple make to your own hopes for marriage for a lifetime?

Additional Resources

Erik Erikson's most comprehensive exploration of the resource of integrity in late adult life is found in his evocative essay "Dr.

Borg's Life Cycle" in the collection *Adulthood* (Norton, 1978), which is also edited by Erikson. In *Christian Life Patterns* (Doubleday, 1979) we discuss religious movements of integrity in Chapter 8, "Development in Mature Age," and Chapter 9, "To Grow Old Among Christians." The Swiss physician and Christian writer Paul Tournier draws from the rich experience of his own life for insight into psychological and religious maturity in the senior years in *Learn to Grow Old* (Harper & Row, 1972).

Margaret Huyck and William Hoyer provide a valuable overview of current research in *Adulthood and Aging* (Brooks/Cole, 1981). The findings of the National Council on Aging study of attitudes toward aging in the United States have been published as *The Myth and Reality of Aging* (NCOA, 1975). Henry Maas and Joseph Kuypers discuss issues of marriage, parenthood and aging as these were experienced by a group of men and women over several years in *From Thirty to Seventy* (Jossey-Bass, 1975). Marilyn Block and her associates focus on issues in the lives of aging women in *Women over Forty: Visions and Realities* (Springer, 1980).

James Peterson and Barbara Payne offer an optimistic look at mature marriage in *Love in the Later Years* (Association Press, 1975). Robert N. Butler's discussion, "The Life Review: An Interpretation of Reminiscence in the Aged," is found in *Middle Age and Aging* (University of Chicago Press, 1968), edited by Bernice Neugarten. For the Taoist stories of uselessness see *The Complete Works of Chuang Tzu* (Columbia University Press, 1968), edited by Burton Watson.

Part Four:

MARRIAGE FOR A LIFETIME

The extraordinary ambition to spend a lifetime together in married love meets many challenges in American life today. Chief among these are our own expectations—the inherited understandings of what marriage "is" and "should be" that we use to evaluate our own relationship. Over the next several chapters we will examine changing expectations of marriage in four critical areas—the roles of women and men in marriage, how work and marriage are related, the function of communication and conflict in love, and the emotional self-sufficiency of the married couple. An additional challenge to marriage for a lifetime is our heightened realization that not all marriages survive. In the final chapter here we will explore the psychological and religious dynamics of divorce. The goal will be to develop a more effective Christian response to divorce, by discerning how God may be at work even in the midst of this painful passage.

16

HOW SHALL WE BE TOGETHER? —ROLES IN MARRIAGE

We approach marriage in the hope that it shall endure. It is not simply the institution of marriage we want to survive; it is our own love that we want to flourish over a lifetime. Often today this hope seems audacious. How can any marriage survive the pressures that exist in relationships today? More to the point, how will *we* respond to the movements of our own relationship and the demands that arise from both commitment and change?

Roles in Marriage

There is much discussion today of roles in marriage. The term "role" as it is used in sociology has some relation to the more ordinary understanding of the word—as a part that an actor plays in a theater performance. By knowing what role I have in a particular play (whether, for example, I will play the romantic lead or the villain or the ingénue) you and I both know ahead of time what I can be expected to do in, say, the first scene of the third act. Similarly, by knowing my social role, you and I both know ahead of time what I can be expected to do in a given social situation. A social role, then, refers to what a person actually does but, more importantly, to what a person is expected to do.

The question of roles in marriage—what are the expectations we have of husband and wife—is central in the process of marriage for a lifetime. As we saw in Part One, the conventional image of wife and husband has included role expectations that are both clear and distinct. Each partner has important duties in the relationship; each holds primary responsibility for an important part of their life together, a realm in which the other spouse has little direct concern. In the "husband" role the man is expected to hold an outside job that enables him to support his family financially. This job is his first responsibility; both he and his wife expect his commitment to his work to hold highest priority. In fact, it is in and through his commitment to his work that he fulfills his role as husband and meets his main responsibility to his wife and family. Other responsibilities exist, to be sure, but always subservient to this prior responsibility. So the husband's duty to be a companion to his wife and to spend time with his family is seen as subordinate to his duty to hold a good job and advance as far as possible up the ladder of responsibility and financial success. He sees it this way and so does his wife.

The role of wife is equally clear in the conventional image of marriage. She is expected to work in the home to carry out the many demanding tasks of family life. She holds primary responsibility for raising the children, though her husband may help her in some of these tasks, especially in disciplining them. It is her duty to provide a well-ordered home to which her husband can return from his work site, to meet his practical (meals, clean clothing, rest) and emotional (support, affection, respect) needs —which in turn enables him to be steadfast in his responsibilities as economic provider. Wife and husband may be interested in each other's daily lives; they may "help out" each other in some of their respective tasks. The husband may even have the kind of job that depends on his wife's active collaboration— as hostess, as social companion, as volunteer contributor to particular civic causes. But the spheres of their responsibility are distinct. Husband is responsible for the family's financial well-being; wife is responsible for the family's home life. She sees it that way and so does he.

This conventional understanding of roles in marriage is well summarized in the expression "A woman's place is in the home." Through the nineteenth and much of the twentieth century this was a statement of what most people judged to be both "right" and "good." It was "right" since it expressed the natural order of things. Men and women are different; they have different natures and different purposes in the scheme of things. Equally important, we *know* what these differences are and what they are for. The statement "A woman's place is in the home" enshrines this clear and certain knowledge. Beyond being "right," this statement was "good" because it confirmed a pattern of family life that was thought to benefit all concerned. Children benefit. They receive the undistracted care of a full-time mother, who has their well-being as her principal concern. Husbands benefit. They are freed to concentrate on the arduous but necessary tasks of productive employment, knowing that their own practical and emotional needs, as well as those of their heirs, are being well cared for by a loving wife. Wives benefit. Theirs is a privileged role; they are protected from the physical and moral dangers of the outside world of work and supported financially while they are given nurturing and emotional responsibilities more in line with their natures. And society benefits. This well-ordered family pattern is an effective way of caring for most of the emotional needs and practical needs of the adult work force and for preparing the next generation to assume a productive role in society.

To most of us today, these "benefits" ring a bit false. We sense the accuracy of social critic Judith Lyness' observation: "The stereotype of the traditional marriage has the man achieving satisfaction through his work and the woman finding fulfillment in her maternal activities. But as men and women have been pointing out, men have discovered little in the way of satisfaction, and women have failed to feel fulfilled."

The Conventional Roles Under Question

Many men today are questioning the close identification of the role of husband and father with one's commitment to a job. This identification, as it often works out, results in a diminishment of the father's emotional involvement with his family and reinforces the understanding—which many men today reject or at least question—that a man's chief interest in life is or should be his job. For many men their jobs are not all that satisfying. For some, the job is simply a source of income. Others have a larger interest in the work itself but find that the inefficiency and bureaucracy of the work site erode any sense of personal involvement or accomplishment. And for some men, work is a more unpleasant reality—monotonous activities, in poor working conditions, with little job security, and an impersonal or even hostile atmosphere.

The conventional role of husband tends to identify the man's success in his marriage with his success in his work, at least with his success as a financial provider. And the conventional marriage reinforces the man's investment in his work. With a wife and children counting on me, I am hesitant to break away from a job that is not satisfying. Financial security is more important than my sense of involvement or creativity. Job promotion means more money and more prestige. I "owe it to my family" to go after these benefits, even if there are serious costs—in time and emotional strain—to me, my wife, my children.

The conventional role in marriage takes an even larger toll on many women. Jesse Bernard, a pioneering investigator of marriage patterns in the United States, has documented the "shocks" of marriage for women. For most women, especially among the educated middle class, marriage introduces serious discontinuities into their lives. In the conventional pattern, at marriage the woman ceases to be "catered to," as she was during courtship, and instead becomes responsible for anticipating and serving a wide range of her husband's practical and emotional needs. She may learn through the close contact of married life that her husband does not always fit the dominant stereotype of the "strong, dependable male." She may find, to her surprise, that in many ways she is stronger and more reliable than he. But this realization can be frightening to both of them. Thus in some marriages wives are careful to keep intact the shared fiction of the husband's general superiority. Sometimes a good deal of energy has to be devoted to protecting this conventional image of male dominance. The wife may deeply resent what she comes to see as her husband's "weakness"—that is, the ways in which he does not fit the demands of the conventional role—even as she attempts to hide it, often from herself as well as from others.

In many states women lose legal status when they marry, a factor that can be especially disconcerting to a woman who has been working and living on her own for several years. By the act of getting married her credit rating, her capacity to take out a loan or to enter into a binding contract may all be called into question. But more devastating for many women who attempt to live out the conventional role in marriage is the psychological process of "dwindling into a housewife." This does not describe the experience of all married women, not even all who embrace the conventional image of what it is to be a wife. But it is an experience to which more and more married women attest.

The evidence drawn from many sources—survey research, clinical report, autobiography—is that "being a housewife" affects most women negatively. Married men tend to gain resources of personal and professional maturity as they move from their twenties through their thirties. Most married women who are housewives lose ground over these years. In both self-report and on objective measures they are less confident, less healthy, less spontaneous, less effective than other women or than men. Women receive mixed signals about the role of housewife. Even today the cultural connotations of "wife and mother in the home" are largely positive, while the actual daily tasks of the housewife are seen by most of us—including most housewives—as onerous and of little monetary value. Full-time housewives tend to show symptoms of depression, hypochondria and an unfocused or "non-specific" anxiety more than do working women (whether married or not) or men. After summarizing these somewhat alarming findings of recent research on marriage, Bernard concludes that "it is being relegated to the role of housewife rather than marriage itself which contributes heavily to the poor mental and emotional health of married women" (*The Future of Marriage*, p. 51).

Patterns in Marriage Today

It is an awareness of some of these unsatisfactory effects of the conventional roles on both women and men in marriage that leads many couples to explore alternative ways to be together. Most couples, even today, start out with an implicit commitment to the conventional image of marriage. In trying to live this out they realize that it does not work for them. It is then that they attempt changes, not out of commitment to an ideology but out of direct experience, often negative experience, of being married. We change our expectations of how we will be together in *this* marriage not because we want to be a "liberated" couple but because we realize that things are not going well between us. When we attempt to live out the conventional roles of husband and wife, our relationship does not thrive. But as we open ourselves to change we soon realize that what we have undertaken is not a simple task of substituting a new set of clear expectations for an earlier set that no longer works very well. We have instead begun a process. For most couples the new and more satisfying patterns of being together do not emerge easily or immediately. They result from an ongoing movement of trial and error, one that can often seem to produce as many problems as it resolves. We will look here at some of the patterns that are emerging in this ongoing process and some of the challenges that couples can expect to face along the way.

Many couples today stay close to the conventional roles of wife and husband, at least over the important period of the active family years. A young woman, then, may work for some time immediately after marriage but both she and her husband intend that she shall leave work before their first child is born and shall devote herself full-time as mother and homemaker during the years that their children are at home. Sometimes this pattern is modified to include the possibility that the wife may take a job for a while to earn money for a special family project (a new home or a special vacation or a serious medical expense) or if the family's financial situation becomes shaky. It is also possible that, as the children reach school age, she may take on some part-time work, but her schedule and her responsibilities on the job remain secondary to her responsibilities as wife and mother. Thus even if she works outside the home she is unlikely to consider her job a "career." Her career, in the sense of the involvement that gives direction and meaning to her life, is as wife and mother and homemaker. In this pattern the financial security of the family is the husband's responsibility, although the wife may help out on occasion. Similarly, keeping house and raising the children are the wife's responsibility, though her husband may help out here, especially with some of the less unpleasant or routine family chores. But his job obligations always take precedence over his family and household involvements, just as her family obligations always take precedence over any outside commitments that she develops.

A second pattern that some couples attempt is role reversal or switched roles. Here the boundaries between what each spouse does remain clear and the substance of the roles remains distinct. One person earns a living for the family, the other cares for the home and raises the children. The difference here is that the woman is the worker outside the home and the man is the "househusband." This pattern has received a lot of publicity but it is not widely in effect. Some people find it bizarre or even "unnatural." In any case, it does not suit the talent or interests (or earning power) of most couples. Few men are open to the possibility of not pursuing any employment outside the home; most women want more active involvement in the tasks of parenting than a strict role reversal permits. Many "non-traditional" couples are equally unsatisfied with the switched role pattern. It carries most of the disadvantages that they see in the conventional pattern, the chief difference being in which partner gets to experience the process of "dwindling into a wife." There can be as little flexibility in this pattern as in the conventional. In neither is there much opportunity for our expectations of "who does what" in our marriage to reflect the particular skills or preferences that each of us has. Many couples sense that in both the conventional and the switched role pattern too much is decided "ahead of time," with little respect for the special quality of their own relationship. Both give little room for change; in neither does mutuality have much scope.

It is a pattern of shared, rather than switched, roles that many couples are seeking today. In this pattern, the expectations of what it means to be husband and wife in *this* marriage are worked out between us more than simply taken as "givens." We try to establish patterns that fit us, that reflect the talent and interest and preferences we each have, along with our mutual commitment that we are in this together. There is more choice involved here. This makes the pattern of shared roles both more responsive and more demanding. We have to choose, more often and in more areas of life than if we subscribed to the conventional pattern (or its reverse). In the conventional pattern we know "ahead of time" whose responsibility it is to prepare meals, whose job takes precedence, who stays home from work with a sick child or to meet the repairman. If we share roles, we may have to work out more of these questions as they arise, taking many factors into consideration. Sometimes we will come up with answers that are the same as in the conventional pattern (the husband's job has preference at this point; tonight the wife gets supper), but often we will not (the wife accepts a promotion in her work, even though it means she may have to be away from home some weekends; the husband leaves the office early to attend a parent-teacher conference).

The shared-role pattern doesn't mean that there are no differences between us. It does not mean that we have no established ways of doing things or that we are each equally responsible for every part of our life together. It means rather that the patterns we devise for meeting the responsibilities of our common life are based on wider knowledge of each other than simply that one of us is male and the other female. Which responsibilities we divide and which we share, how we assign tasks in the household and beyond, who is in charge of which areas of family life—we make these decisions based on our skills and interests, along with a generous willingness on the part of both of us to take up our share of the unwanted and unappealing duties that remain. Sometimes tasks may be strictly assigned to either the husband or the wife. But the more general pattern in shared-role marriages is flexibility. I usually keep the family checkbook in order, but if I am out of town or extra busy on a project you can take over that task for me. You usually do the weekly shopping but I can, and will, do it if necessary. We take turns driving the kids to softball practice. Whoever gets home first starts supper. In role sharing there is still differentiation of tasks but according to skill and preference and choice rather than gender. There is also more overlap, with the possibility that each of us can substitute for the other when necessary.

There are many benefits in sharing roles in marriage. Many husbands benefit from knowing that they do not carry alone the heavy responsibility of their family's financial security. A wife who works shares the role of providing financially for the family. Often this frees the husband to enjoy his work more. He can take risks in his career that he would not otherwise. He may be more open to a job change, moving into a work more congruent with his values or more in line with his real interests. Many wives benefit from the sense of competence and confidence that comes from their involvement as workers in the world beyond the household. The responsibilities and rewards that come with having a career contribute to an enhanced sense of self-worth, especially in marriages where the husband supports his wife's accomplishments both emotionally and by sharing in the tasks of home and family life. In general, both husbands and wives judge that everyone benefits, and especially the children, when fathers are more actively engaged in the ordinary tasks of parenting. Fathers and children have more time together. This gives fathers a chance to know and enjoy their children in a way that was not available in the more conventional husband role. This shared-role pattern is often part of a larger mutuality between partners, a mutuality that contributes richly to the emotional texture of the marriage relationship.

The Challenges of Choice

There are benefits that come to a marriage in the process of developing a pattern of shared, rather than segregated, roles.

But there are problems as well. And many of these problems arise from the demands of choice. Once we have determined that the conventional patterns don't work for us, for whatever reason, then we find that we are pretty much on our own. Few couples feel at the outset that they know where this process of choice will lead. There is seldom a clear model available to us ahead of time to provide a sense of what our marriage will be. As we look to other marriages for clues to "what works" between people, we may be disconcerted by the diversity we find or startled by the sense that no one answer is without its costs. Nothing seems to work unambiguously or all the time. None of the alternatives we see seems to have just "good" effects; none seems to be possible without some pain. We may be excited by the diversity "out there." The realization that there is not an already-worked-out-and-guaranteed alternative to the conventional pattern may appeal to our sense of adventure, enlivening us to the special possibilities of our own marriage. We can work out something that is really our own, that uniquely suits us. But the diversity can also strike us as simple confusion. It can leave us feeling quite alone in the process of change. So much is left up to us; it can seem unfair. We are faced with choices that have serious consequences, not only for ourselves but—as we sense—for our children and even for society. And, rhetoric aside, we experience little realistic support in our efforts to evaluate the options and choose responsibly. This is one of the definitions of social alienation—and many couples feel alone and alienated when confronted with the changes and choices surrounding marriage today.

We are learning the costs of choice. It takes time to work things out between us, to explore our values, to learn from one another what each of us needs and wants, to devise patterns that seem to fit who we are, to evaluate the effects of these decisions and, probably, to renegotiate them along the way. We learn, too, that we must take time to celebrate what we are doing together —to acknowledge each other's courage and generosity and to be grateful that our love can stand these tests of change. The new proliferation of choice also makes demands on our emotional resources: we spend our energy and enthusiasm and concern as we try to be responsible to ourselves and our larger commitments in this process of working toward new understandings of how we are together.

Our process of choice is made more difficult by the continuing ambiguities, the mixed messages we hear, from within ourselves as well as from outside, concerning what it is to be "husband" and "wife." On the one hand a wife is told that motherhood is a woman's crowning achievement, deserving her full-time effort. But she also hears that a woman should stay involved in many interests, both so that she does not stagnate in her own development and so that she does not "smother" her children under the force of her undivided concern. A husband is presented an idyllic image of what it is to be a "good father": leisurely weekends spent playing ball with one's growing children. At the same time he is likely to experience pressure at his job (which is, of course, the arena of his "real" responsibilities to the family) to come in on Saturday or to bring extra work home.

There are likely as well to be some mixed feelings within the couple. We may not see eye to eye on how these new roles should work out between us. One of us may be more open to experimentation than is the other. One of us may feel more threatened by the change, judging that "I have more to lose." For example, a wife may be more positive toward her going back full-time to school or to work than is her husband, at least in the beginning. He may appreciate the new possibility of added income to the family as his wife returns to work, but he may feel threatened by her new independence. "She doesn't need me to take care of her anymore." Or a husband may feel easier about his increased responsibility in child care than does his wife. She may feel guilty about turning over these "woman's" responsibilities to him or resent the fact that he doesn't do them well enough to meet her high standards. Cultural factors may contribute to the ambivalence we experience toward one another as we attempt to change together. Over the past two decades the women's movement has influenced American awareness in both practical and symbolic ways. One effect has been a new attention to issues of gender stereotypes and discrimination. As a result, many of us come to marriage today with a good deal of repressed anger toward the opposite sex. As we approach complicated questions of our own roles in marriage we may well feel this anger come into play. A disagreement escalates into controversy; negotiation comes to a halt; compromise is out of the question. My spouse has become "the enemy"—the archetypal "male chauvinist" or the original "strident feminist."

But the most troublesome ambiguities that we are likely to encounter as we attempt to establish a pattern of shared roles in our marriage are the mixed feelings that each of us has within. Most of us carry several different understandings of what it is to be a woman or a man, what it is to be a husband or a wife. Some of these come from family experiences with our own parents, others are influenced by our early socialization in school and church and neighborhood. We have information from our education and from the media as well as the awareness that comes from personal experience. Not all of this information fits together neatly into one consistent understanding. What does it mean to be a wife? Who am I as a husband? On questions of such wide ramification we are likely to hear within us not one clear answer but several, even contradictory responses.

I want to keep my job when our family comes and I want to be a good mother. But a "good mother" is home with her children. But if I stay home full-time I'll go crazy! But a "real woman" would be able to find fulfillment as a mother and homemaker and, even if she couldn't, she would be unselfish enough to put her own interests aside for the good of her child and husband. But today we know that a woman must not sacrifice her identity to that of her husband and children. Not only does she suffer if she does this but they do, too. And on the inner voices go . . .

The multiple voices are heard by men as well. I am proud to have married a strong woman with interests and talents of her own. But I want her to provide the kind of emotional warmth and care for our home that one expects of a wife, the kind my mother provided for our family when we were growing up. It's great to have our two incomes to live on but I wish she could be there when the children come home from school. I can see that she has a lot to do, with her job as well as all the housework, but there are some things that a man just shouldn't be expected to do around the house. I get ribbed by some of my colleagues at work about my extra responsibilities in taking care of the children, now that my wife is working again, but I really do like having this extra time with them. And on the inner voices go . . .

These ambiguities within us and outside us and the strains they provoke in our relationship are expectable in marriage today. To experience these is not simply a sign of personal immaturity or ill will. They are not sure indications that our marriage is "on the rocks" or that a longstanding incompatibility between us has finally been unmasked. They are normal elements in the process of exploring the ways for us to be together, faithfully and well, in a time when many earlier definitions of marriage do not work for us anymore.

These strains and ambiguities may be normal but they still need to be handled well. If they are not recognized for what they are—an inevitable part of a worthwhile but complicated effort—they can negatively affect our marriage. We can attempt to resolve the ambiguity through guilt or blame. We can try to escape the strain by avoiding the troublesome issues. But these approaches seem seldom to be successful for very long. Blame and guilt clutter a relationship, making communication more difficult between us. Avoidance often does no more than delay a problem. The troublesome issues are not resolved; they may even be made worse by a bitterness or mistrust that slowly develops between us.

The Resources of Our Love

As most of us find, it is often easier to talk about the need to move beyond gender stereotypes in marriage than it is to work out new patterns between us. Developing a life in common in which our understanding of who we are together differs from the conventional roles for women and men is a challenge. Our efforts to work toward these new mutually satisfying patterns can be complicated, as we have seen. We may feel there are few models for us to follow. As we experiment with changes in our own patterns we may find it harder than we anticipated. And we are likely to experience unexpected resistance in ourselves.

But the forecast is not all bleak. As challenging as the continuing effort to build a life in common may be, there are also resources in our love that contribute to our success.

At the heart of our efforts to understand our roles in marriage are commitment and trust. There is our genuine desire to work out ways of being together that are more respectful of who each of us really is and more responsive to our best hope for the love we share. Without such commitment—our practical investment in each other and in the continuation of our relationship—and trust—our confident awareness of each other's genuine care—we are not likely to be able to take the risks involved in the struggle toward real mutuality. Trying to work out new arrangements between us will seem too hard or take too much time or generate too much confusion or hostility. It will be easier to stay with our familiar, even if unsatisfying, patterns. Or we will move into a more antagonistic stance, with each of us defending ourselves against what we experience as unacceptable demands from the other. Commitment and trust between us will not do away with the "messiness" of change, but these resources of our love will strengthen us in the struggle and remind us that our life together is worth the trouble.

Next, there must be some breadth and flexibility in what we each understand as acceptable behavior for women and men. If my sense of what is "manly" requires that a husband remain emotionally aloof from the personal problems of his spouse and children; if your appreciation of "femininity" focuses somewhat exclusively on the wife's ability to care for her family and keep house—then it will be difficult for us to consider alternative arrangements in our own marriage. If we are able to see beyond these gender stereotypes and accept the range of talents and limits, of ambitions and opportunities, that are real for each of us, we are more likely to be able to devise shared patterns that suit and satisfy our relationship.

The ability to communicate openly is another resource in developing patterns that work for us. Communication, as we shall see again in Chapter 18, begins in self-awareness and self-acceptance. As we work toward new ways of being together, I must be able to recognize my own confusion and accept my mixed feelings for what they are. I am not always sure of what I need; I am not always consistent in what I want. I don't have to "explain away" these inconsistencies; I don't have to try to relieve myself of responsibility for them by blaming you or someone else for the confusion I experience. Changing together will require that we can confide our hopes, ask for help, deal with conflict and come to shared decisions. There may be the need to face together feelings or hurts that have been long suppressed. There is the sometimes painstaking process of dealing frankly with the discomfort we feel with the changes we are attempting and the accompanying threat that in this process we are losing something more important than what we stand to gain.

There are strengths of personal maturity that contribute to our success in working out new ways to be together. Marriage for a lifetime involves us in a challenging process of change and compromise. Its goal is greater interdependence, a flexible relationship between us where we both have much to give and receive. And, paradoxically, to move toward this mature reciprocity requires that we can each deal well with both dependence and independence between us.

An interdependent relationship depends on the strengths of each of us to stand alone and apart, so that our coming together has about it the power of freedom and choice. But interdependence takes us beyond self-sufficiency: not only can I stand alone, I can stand responsive to you, your hopes, your needs. And, perhaps the greatest challenge, I can stand before you in my own need, trusting you will not exploit my vulnerability, depending on your love to support me as I move toward greater life. Interdependence suggests a balance between us in the give-and-take of love. It takes us beyond the structured dependency of the conventional marriage, where the scope of the wife's independent activity is narrowly circumscribed, where much of her sense of fulfillment must be vicarious, derived from her capacity to rejoice in the successes of others rather than her own. It takes us beyond the defended caution of the "strictly egalitarian" relationship, where we are careful to ensure that neither is asked to give more than the other to our life together. Such self-consciousness may be necessary as we move from one stage of our marriage to another, but few of us find it satisfying. It takes too much energy to maintain this ledger of "gave and got" and ultimately it defeats us. We find that the balance of interdependence is better served as each of us grows in awareness of our own responsibility for this relationship and in a genuine desire not to exploit our partner's generosity or need.

Psychiatrist Mabel Blake Cohen defines interdependence in marriage as "the relationship between two adequate, self-sufficient, successfully dependent adults [in which] the giving goes both ways." For some, the challenge here is to come into a sense of adult adequacy and self-sufficiency—to learn to appreciate one's independence. "I know I can make it on my own, if I have to; I can survive beyond this relationship." For others, the greater challenge is to come into an appreciation of one's continuing needs and how these are to be accepted maturely and satisfied responsibly—to become successfully dependent. "I need this relationship; through it I receive much that is of value to me that I would not otherwise have."

Only when both these realizations are strong—our marriage gives us much but we each have resources to bring to it as well—is there the basis for the flexible and free self-giving that we will need to develop a mature life in common.

The strength that is tested here is self-transcendence—my ability to be moved by a motive beyond myself. For both men and women the capacity to care for more than self is a movement of maturity. The usual route into this ability to love genuinely beyond myself is through the ability to love myself well, to appreciate myself as a worthy (though not exclusive) object of my own concern. Being-for-self and being-for-more-than-self are thus complementary movements of responsible adult living. Many women and men bring to marriage the strength of an acceptance of themselves that opens them to the possibility of mature self-giving. But a good number of us do not. And while this expansion of personality is open to all, its challenge may be experienced differently by women and by men.

A wife, for example, may have learned while she was young that her proper—even exclusive—role as a woman is to be "for others." And she knows well how to do this, undertaking in her marriage a life filled with the activities of generous concern. But, without the strength that accompanies a sense of her worth on her own, she may exercise this generosity "with strings attached." Those around her—her husband, her children, her friends—may experience much of her concern as clinging or intrusive. And she, for her part, is likely often to feel empty or unsatisfied—frustrated by the never-ending demands of others' needs and disappointed that her love seems so little reciprocated.

A husband, socialized to different expectations of what is required of him in marriage, may find it quite natural to be "for himself," to take seriously his own needs and his own goals. The challenge an interdependent marriage brings for him is to learn to be "for others," to develop his capacity for empathy—so that he may be better aware of his wife's experience, her ambitions, her concerns—and his capacity to give himself in decisions and actions that benefit more than just his own goals.

Working out between us our pattern of shared roles in marriage is not done once and for all. Especially in a time when role models are few and social pressures can be strong, we may find that early decisions of how we are to be together need to be modified as we go along. We each learn more about our strengths and needs; we come to a clearer sense of the larger demands to which we are accountable. Our relationship moves to a new level or there are changes in the job or in the family situation. These factors can force us to rethink our relationship once again and to change the patterns that we have only recently established. But this process of reworking and change is not a blemish on our record. It is not a distraction from the otherwise smooth pursuit of our shared roles in marriage. It does not signal that our earlier decisions, which we now want to change, were wrong. The process of growth and change is of the substance of a love that will last. Today the commitment to remain responsive and responsible to this process is at the heart of marriage for a lifetime.

Conclusion

For Christians, the change from conventional male and female roles to more flexible relationships in marriage is assisted by our current realization that human nature is not as stable and finished as we once believed. If women and men differ biologically in ways that determine their respective roles in the generation of children, they no longer appear to differ so clearly in other significant aspects of marriage and family life. The need and resources to nurture, the ability to be strong and decisive, the capacity to both experience and express emotion—these strengths are available to and expected of women and men alike.

Much of what once seemed to be "natural" (and so, ordained by the Creator of nature) often appears today more a result of cultural and historical attitudes than unchanging reality. That women should cover their heads in church is not as natural today as it was for Paul, or even for Catholics only some twenty years ago. That "women are to remain quiet at meetings since they have no permission to speak" (I Corinthians 14:34) strikes many of us as less a religious imperative than a cultural attitude that is today part of an "old self" that is to be put aside (Ephesians 4:22).

From the perspective of contemporary theology, creation is envisioned not as a finished product which has resulted in unchanging natures and fixed roles for male and female but as an unfolding event in which we are to participate. In this continuing creation and revelation we are constantly surprised as we learn more about who we are and what we are called to be. In the journey of Christian marriage many couples experience the need to let go inherited but constricting expectations about what it is to be wife or husband. In this letting go of roles no longer graceful for us, we pray and trust that we are moving toward an ideal, not of unisex life together, but of that radical mutuality described by Paul:

All baptized in Christ, you have all clothed yourself in Christ and there are no more distinctions between Jew and Greek, slave and free, male and female, but all of you are one in Christ Jesus (Galatians 3:27–28).

Reflective Exercise

Today there are many different role patterns that exist among married couples. It may be useful to reflect on some of these differences as they exist among the couples you know best.

First, consider two marriages that you know well and compare how each at this time divides the responsibilities of rearing children, earning a living and maintaining the household and family life. Note both the similarities and the differences that exist, and give some thought to why this is so.

Then consider your own marriage. How are these tasks shared in your home these days? Is this pattern different from, say, five years ago? In what ways? What factors are most responsible for these differences?

Do you anticipate that there will be changes in this pattern over the next five years? the next ten years? If so, what changes do you anticipate? Again, what factors will be most influential in bringing about these changes? If you do not anticipate any real changes, why is this so?

Additional Resources

Sociologist Jesse Bernard has been effective in making available to a larger interested public the findings of recent research concerning roles in marriage and family life. Her *The Future of Marriage* (World Books, 1972) was followed in 1974 by *The Future of Motherhood* (Dial Press) and in 1975 by *Women, Wives, Mothers: Values and Options* (Aldine Press). Most recently she has examined the historical development of the conventional responsibilities of men in marriage in "The Good-Provider Role: Its Rise and Fall," which appeared in the January 1981 issue of

American Psychologist. In *Sex Roles, Women's Work, and Marital Conflict* (Lexington Books, 1978) John Scanzoni provides a significant discussion of these issues, based on empirical research through the 1970s.

In 1979 *Psychology of Women Quarterly* devoted a special issue to questions raised by the changing roles of women in marriage. This resource is now available as *The Motherhood Mandate,* edited by Nancy Felipe Russo. Adrienne Rich offers a provocative analysis of motherhood as an experience and as an institution in *Of Woman Born* (Norton, 1976). Michael Lamb discusses fatherhood in *The Role of the Father in Child Development* (Wiley, 1976).

Judith Fischer Lyness' "Experiential Report of Androgynous Spousal Roles" is part of the larger discussion of changing expectations between men and women in *Exploring Intimate Life Styles,* edited by Bernard J. Murstein (Springer, 1978). Mabel Blake Cohen examines the psychological dynamics of interdependence in "Personal Identity and Sexual Identity," in *Psychoanalysis and Women* (Penguin, 1974), edited by J. B. Miller.

In *The Future of Partnership* (Westminster, 1979) theologian Letty Russell explores the implications of the Christian call to mutuality for marriage and for the larger life of the Church.

17

WORK AND MARRIAGE

Work is a significant part of life. For some of us, work is important primarily for the money it provides. My work is just a job, but through it I generate the income I need to meet my financial obligations and, if I am lucky, to live well. But while income and benefits are important to most of us in our work, they are not always the crucial issues. (For those whose access to steady work is limited by handicaps of race or gender or age or training, finding a job that pays decently may be the *only* crucial issue.) For many of us, it is being good at what we do that matters. In my work I gain competence and a sense of personal achievement; it is these accomplishments that make my job significant to me. For others of us, work is even more central in life. I experience my job as part of a "life's work," a vocation. It is more than "just a job"; it is what I want to do with my life. In many significant ways my work says who I am and who I am called to be.

Work is an important ingredient in the lifestyle of any marriage. Who works, at what kind of job, under what conditions, with what demands and what rewards—these issues help define the kind of marriage we have. In several places in this book we have already noted the close links between "husband" and "worker" in the conventional image of marriage. To be a good husband has meant to be a steady worker—to hold a decent job that has the promise of financial security and, if possible, financial advancement as well. Until recently the roles of husband and worker have been closely enough identified in American society to permit a general tolerance for the increasing demands of "greedy" occupations, those jobs that require open-ended investment of time and energy, often to the detriment of one's family life. Thus it has been understood, even expected, that a man—and especially a responsible married man—should give his first commitment to his job.

There has been much greater ambivalence about women and work. Until recently women have not been considered a part of the stable work force in Western capitalism. Women have always worked but they were considered "reserve" labor. They were available to take up jobs that came only seasonally or at other times when, as in a national emergency like a war, the male work force was not sufficient. This reserve of additional workers was easily turned out of paid employment when they were no longer necessary. Women who work have been praised for such flexibility: commended for their willingness to move into the work force when needed (as in the tributes to Rosie the Riveter in World War II) and, especially, for their willingness to move out of these jobs as soon as male workers were available to fill them.

Not to have to earn a living has been seen as one of the highest privileges of the married woman; being supported by her husband, her most valued right. The conventional response to the wife who *has* to work has been pity. "Poor girl, she has to go to work. It's too bad that her husband can't support her as he should." The response to the wife who *chooses* to work has been blame. "It's unnatural for a married woman to want to work. What's wrong with her that she can't find enough in her own home and family to keep her busy?" If there are children at home, the blame frequently hardens into reproach: "Children need their mother to be at home with them. No wonder there are so many troubled kids around these days." This is especially true if the children are young enough not yet to be in school: "What kind of mother would leave her baby with a stranger?" According to conventional wisdom, a departure from this preferred pattern of the non-working wife has dire consequences:

for her (a woman who works loses her femininity and becomes hardened like a man), for the children (children of working mothers tend to "go wrong"), for her husband (his status as a man and as a good provider are called into question) and for the workplace (married women aren't "serious" workers—you can't count on them to stay with a job).

But conventional wisdom has not caught up with the facts of the working wife. Statistics regarding working women can fluctuate from one report to another, but the trend is clear. Over half of married women today are employed regularly outside the home. Information from the 1980 census suggests that this number is growing. While in most families with preschool children the mothers are not working (only in 40 percent of these families are wives also wage earners), every year more women with small children at home do go back to work, part-time or full-time. Continuing inflation is likely to contribute to the rate of this increase. In some cases working women describe their employment as "necessary." In 15 percent of families with children, for example, women are the chief breadwinners, due to the death or serious illness of the husband or to desertion or divorce. These women cannot remain "in the home" even if they would choose to do so. In other cases the married woman's return to work seems to be more a matter of choice, since hers is a second income for the family. But in many families, and even more so in this era of rising inflation, this second income has become necessary if the family is to maintain its standard of living. So the wife works not so much for reasons intrinsic to the work but in order to bring in additional income.

But increasingly there are factors beyond economic necessity that bring wives to work. More and more women are evaluating work not only as an option but as a right. And their motives for working are intrinsic to the job. Here a wife's work has meaning because it gives her a sense of herself as a capable person or as a contributor to the world. She sees her job as a part of both her personal fulfillment and her commitment to larger values.

In spite of these dramatic shifts over the past several decades in the facts of the American work force, there remains much negative feeling toward the working wife. There is a scale of decreasing acceptance of a woman's motives for working outside the home. For the wife who "has to work," as we have seen, there is pity accompanied by a (perhaps reluctant) acceptance of her place in the paid work force. (This situation changes a bit if the woman is on welfare. Here most Americans do not want mothers, even those with small children at home, to be supported solely through tax-financed benefits.) In this time of inflation, there is growing acceptance of the woman who works to supplement her husband's income or to guarantee important advantages—such as a college education—for her children. By rule of thumb, then, a woman's work beyond the home is valid to the extent that it contributes beyond herself, to the financial needs of the children and the family unit. There is still not much acceptance of the intrinsic value of work to the woman herself. Here her motives (unlike comparable motives in a man) appear selfish. Her paid employment is less clearly an extension of her "wifely" role. She is working not "for them" but for herself and her own satisfaction. And she may even be taking a job away from a man, who is more likely to "really" need it to support his family.

The Integration of Work and Marriage

Work makes demands on marriage. Every person who is employed has to deal with the question of how work fits into his or her larger life. How much of myself do I invest in my job? Does my work always take precedence? Is career advancement worth the demands it makes on my personal life? When a worker is married, there is the added question of how the responsibilities of work and the responsibilities of marriage and family life can be balanced.

The conventional marriage suggests one answer to this question: family life accommodates to the demands of (the husband's) work. The daily schedule of our life at home—when we arise, when we take our meals, when we are together as a family —takes its shape from the structure of the husband's work. Where we live, for how long, when our family may have to move—these are influenced, even dictated, by the husband's job. A pattern of mobility typical in America involves frequent relocation of the family as a result of the husband's job transfer. We move away, perhaps a great distance, leaving behind friends and our established patterns of family and social life.

Life in the family is also responsive to the emotional demands made by the husband's job. Aware of a time of special strain in her husband's work, a wife prepares a particularly nice meal and urges the children to be quiet or to play outside when their father comes home. If the job-related stress continues, the wife may take up some of the responsibilities usually met by her husband in order to free him or help lessen the burden he is experiencing. She may spend more time with the children so he can have weekends free; she may offer to share some of the extra work he is bringing home, typing reports or handling some correspondence; she may cancel her plans so that she can "be there" with him or keep the children from disturbing him when he is home.

This kind of unselfish care is part of the process of accommodation that we see in most successful marriages. My sensitivity to how you are feeling, my concern for the burdens you bear, my creativity in finding ways to support you—these are rich resources of love. No one interested in marriage for a lifetime will suggest that these generous instincts be cast aside. But a troublesome aspect of the pattern of accommodation in many conventional marriages is that the process works in one direction only. The wife (and, more broadly, the pattern of family life) accommodates to her husband; he, in turn, accommodates himself to the requirements of his job. There is little flexibility or "give" in the other direction. Seldom do the requirements of the husband's job shift to accommodate his other interests or his family obligations. Most men would not feel right about taking extra time away from work to spend with their children or about refusing a promotion so that they could have more free time at home. A man who makes these kinds of choices is suspect, both as a worker and as a husband. And, similarly, in the conventional pattern, seldom is a husband expected to accommodate himself to his wife's preferences or needs. He may well be concerned about her and show this concern in his actions and affection. But it is not often—and it is not expected of him—that he will seriously alter himself or his life patterns because of her. For many women, becoming a wife in the conventional mode involves significant personal accommodation. Becoming a conventional husband demands fewer changes of such scope.

Marriage without accommodation is impossible. For most of us, it would also be undesirable. The desire to serve the beloved is part of the dynamic of love. I want to do all I can to make your life fuller, richer, happier—even though this will make demands on me. These costs of love are its proof. And we hold ourselves ready to pay them, sometimes even eager to do so. As we saw in Chapter 16, many couples today are attempting to establish a lifestyle in which these costs of love are broadly shared, where both the rewards and the demands of accommodation in marriage can be mutual. And the issue of work is critical in these attempts.

Patterns of Accommodation

As we have seen, a working wife is increasingly a factor in contemporary marriage. There are many ways in which the realities of both spouses working are incorporated into the lifestyle of marriage. A common pattern is for the husband's work commitment to have priority, often because it is his job that is the principal source of family income. The wife works, part-time or full-time, but her investment in the job may not be as complete as is his. Her education or experience may limit her to a job that holds neither the salary nor the advancement possibilities that his does. She may enjoy her work and the involvement and income it brings, but she is likely to consider her marriage and family her real career. So she is willing to modify her job investment to suit her family life. This may be behind her decision to work only part-time. That way she is able to continue to provide for her family and her home the quality of care that is important to her. Or she may take off from work over the summer months when her children are out of school. Or she may choose volunteer work over a paid job as long as the children are living at home in order that she may stay in greater control of her time and thus be more available for them.

While some women want, and are able to work out, this kind of flexible investment in the world of work, many working wives do not. These women have full-time jobs that carry their own, somewhat rigid, demands—as do the jobs of most men. Like many a man, the woman may see her work as "just a job"—but one that is nevertheless necessary to her family's financial well-being. Because she needs the income she is not in a position to negotiate which of the job's demands she will meet. She is held to the same work requirements as any male co-worker. She is just as likely to suffer the consequences if family problems divert her attention at work or a sick child keeps her away from the job for several days.

Other women, again like many men, consider their work to be more than "just a job." They have prepared for this work over a long time through education and various kinds of apprenticeships. They are aware of the normal patterns of advancement and reward and they expect to participate in these. They may even experience this career as a "calling," an important part of their own identity and of their involvement in the world. It is in such dual-worker and, especially, dual-career marriages that the demands are heaviest for accommodation. Couples have to resolve the many demands of each partner's work and their shared family responsibilities in ways that also mesh with the other's needs.

One way in which the strains of this dual-worker marriage are resolved is in the emergence of the "superwoman." Here the wife continues to carry responsibility for those parts of family life that have been seen "traditionally" as woman's work (child care, meal preparation, housecleaning) and simply adds to these whatever responsibilities come with her job. Sometimes a woman assumes this stance on her own. She doesn't want to be "selfish" and have her work "inconvenience" her husband or her family. Or she wants to "prove" that she is as feminine as the next woman, or as good a mother—so she retains all those family tasks that the "feminine" and "motherly" women do.

Sometimes the "superwoman" stance is forced on her. "I don't mind if my wife goes back to work, in fact I think it will be good for her. But I surely expect her to continue to keep the house in shape and to have supper ready when I come home." This attitude can generate much conflict. But more often—since many wives, already feeling guilty about going back to work, will do anything to avoid conflict over their job—it generates the superwoman.

Sometimes the husband or children agree to take on a larger share of the household tasks when a wife returns to work. Even as they do so, however, it is understood that they are only "helping out" in an area that is still basically the wife's responsibility. But they do these tasks poorly and soon give them up. "You know how to do this so much better than I do. It doesn't take you nearly as much time and, besides, when I do it you just have to do it over." This assessment may well be accurate. Though this is rapidly changing, there are still many men who do not know how to do well or easily the practical chores of home and family life that most women have learned before (or during) their marriage. Knowing this, and faced with the husband's subtle or obvious resistance to learning how to do the chores, some women again find it easier to do the work themselves. Again, the superwoman emerges.

The evidence available from recent research concerning marriage patterns in dual-worker and dual-career families confirms this fact. Working women spend almost as much time in household chores as they did when they were not working outside the home, or as do their non-working sisters. Husbands of working wives do not do that much more work around the house than they did before their wives started working, or than do men whose wives do not work. When husbands do take over tasks that were previously handled by their wives, it is the more "pleasant" tasks of child care and homemaking (some tasks of cooking or entertainment) that the husband is likely to take as his own. The onerous and more monotonous jobs remain for the wife. And often she is grateful even for whatever little she can pass on to others in the family, since she—as they—is likely to feel that really the job is hers and they are just helping out.

The superwoman solution takes a serious toll on the woman who tries it. Her health can be affected as she takes on more and more responsibility and experiences the physical and emotional strain that comes as she tries to accomplish all these things. Her level of anxiety can be quite high. She is faced not only with many concrete tasks but with, often, a continuing ambivalence within herself concerning her right to have a job. She may well adopt unreasonably high standards for herself both in her home responsibilities (to ensure that she is "no less" a wife and mother for having taken on her job) and in her career (to ensure that she is "no less" a worker for the fact that she is married).

The superwoman solution can have a superman alternative. Many men are in careers that, historically, have counted on the unpaid assistance of an accommodating wife for their success. She is sometimes required as hostess or typist or social secretary. She often has to stand in for him in some tasks of parenthood or family life, so that his time is free to meet the greedy demands of his job. A college president or a politician may need his wife at his side in many of the ceremonial aspects of his job. A physician may need the cooperation of an understanding and flexible wife if he is to meet the unexpected demands in his schedule. A man who travels in his work may need a wife who is willing to take over the full responsibilities of householder and parent in his regular absences. A man in these kinds of occupations who wants to support his wife's movement into a work or volunteer commitment of her own may find that he must take on a cluster of new responsibilities of which other men in his profession are free. In doing this he may begin to experience both the ambivalence and the overextension that many married career women know today.

A more useful alternative to the "superperson" solution is the effort to achieve greater mutuality in marriage. This ongoing process touches us not only emotionally, so that we each feel responsible to both give and receive the gifts of compromise, support and respectful challenge, but also in the practical details of daily living.

As we noted, in the superwoman solution the woman is likely to retain most of the "wifely" tasks of the marriage, especially those that are the most menial. For some dual-worker couples the additional income enables them to pay to have others handle some of the negatively valued tasks. Laundry can be sent out, someone may come in regularly to clean the house, meals may be eaten out more frequently. But in most families today in which both spouses work full-time this solution is too costly. Even if we take advantage of some outside services we can't afford to pay other people to do all the less desirable tasks of daily life. We may even be opposed to this solution in terms of the values that are implied. The only way for the spouses to be able to avoid the "superperson" trap is for them (and the children) to work out more equitable ways in which the home and work responsibilities are to be shared. And in working out the ways in which this role shift is to be accomplished we are brought again to patterns of role sharing and interdependence.

As we noted in the previous chapter, an interdependent couple is likely to divide household chores and other recurrent tasks according to interest and skill. Often, but not always, this division of who does what will diverge from the conventional description of "man's work" and "woman's work." Jobs that no one likes will be rotated. But the interdependence is even more evident in the couple's sense that either one of them could do many of the chores that the other has agreed to, and—if necessary—either would be willing to take over for the other. When this sense of interdependence is strong, it becomes much easier for a couple to deal with the inevitable complications that arise in their complex lifestyle. If job-related travel or an unusually heavy workload makes it impossible for one of us to meet our commitment to a task at home, the other is able—and willing—to take over. Family life will not come to a halt if I am too busy to cook this evening or if you have to be away during the week that the baby-sitter is unavailable. Interdependence doesn't mean that these interruptions are always easy to deal with or that they can be accommodated without strain. Instead, it means that we tend to experience them as a challenge for both of us, rather than as simply "your problem," and one that we are both committed to resolve in a way that respects each of us. That such interdependence will demand of each of us both resourcefulness and generosity should be clear. Equally clear, at least in the experience of many working couples, is the contribution that such interdependence makes to the quality of their marriage.

Issues for Working Couples—Child Care

The issue of greatest concern in most dual-worker families is child care. It is working parents of young children who experience the most serious pressures within their marriage and, often, pressures from outside as well. The physical and practical needs of young children are both evident and compelling to parents. In our psychologically conscious society, they are keenly aware of a range of emotional needs as well and of the controversy concerning how these needs are best met. Working parents, especially working mothers, are particularly sensitive to the effects that their complex lifestyle may have on the emotional development of a young child. The evidence, then, is that most working couples are very serious about their duties as parents. They hold these responsibilities in the highest place and manifest both creativity and generous self-sacrifice in their efforts to meet them well.

For all the concern and even prejudice that surrounds the controversy over child care, the evidence that is thus far available from child development research is reassuring. To overstate the case only slightly, it seems that any plan for child care can work, as long as the child's basic needs are met by persons who are caring and generally consistent in the way they treat the child— and as long as the parents feel good about the arrangement. And many types of child care are tried. Seldom does any one couple have a choice among all these options, but all these variations are used, and successfully, by dual-worker families.

The choices include leaving children with other members of the family or having a child-care person in our own home. We may participate in a cooperative program of shared child care among a group of parents or bring our child to someone else's home to be cared for or enroll our child in a formal day-care or

preschool program. Many couples use several of these alternatives. Both the experience of couples and the findings of research
concur that there is no one "right" way. What is best for our
child depends, clearly, on what choices are actually available to
us. But beyond this practical limitation, "what is best" can fluctuate among a number of alternatives, some more useful than
the others, depending on the family work schedule, the child's
age, the travel time and costs involved. In each family situation
several options are likely to be basically acceptable and yet none
is without some residual problems as well. The decision about
child care is seldom made just once. Over the course of several
years we may have to decide several times on the arrangements
that are best. A preferred baby-sitter moves away, our child
outgrows the age limits in one program, the tuition in another
becomes prohibitively high—these and other expected and unexpected changes keep the child-care question active.

Many working couples find that these ongoing decisions about
child care are the most complex challenge of their commitment
to mutual accommodation and shared roles in marriage. We
sense that there is much at stake in these decisions, for our children as well as for each of us. As parents today we operate in a
world where there are few clear guidelines and yet where expectations are high. There is little social or institutional support for
us in becoming parents. "Adults only" housing, the spiraling
costs of education and medical care, the pathological forces of
drugs and violence—these give us pause as we consider what it
means for us to be good parents. There is not much consensus
concerning what is the best way to raise children. Experts disagree, the research findings are often contradictory; we sometimes
catch sight of the inconsistencies in our own values and behavior
as parents. As a working couple we have to cope with these ambiguities, along with the already heavy demands on our time
and energy that come from our jobs.

Couples who decide to work during their children's preschool
years find themselves having to confront not only society's expectations regarding what is the acceptable way to raise children, but their own well-internalized notions of what is expected
of them as parents. They discover they are at odds with cultural

images of "the good family." But, and this is often more disconcerting, they find they are themselves ambivalent about whether
what they are doing is really right. "Maybe we're just being
selfish. Maybe we're just fooling ourselves in thinking that our
children will not be harmed, if not now, then later, by our not
having a more 'normal' family life for them while they are still
so young." Frequently this self-questioning is reinforced by the
concern, even the criticism, of people close to the couple—their
friends, but especially their own parents and in-laws. Working
couples thus find themselves taxed not only by the requirements
of their commitment to both work and family but especially by
the additional strain generated by their efforts to resolve the
emotional controversy over whether what they are doing is the
best thing.

The Balance of Power in Marriage

Beyond the crucial questions of child care, the working couple
can raise questions of image and status and power in marriage.
If the woman's pursuit of a job is experienced as an attack on or
a depreciation of her husband, the larger emotional issues involved here can cloud their attempts to deal with the practical
decisions of child care, household tasks, daily schedule. In some
marriages the very fact of the wife's interest in a job or a career
is threatening. This implies—to her husband, perhaps to others
as well—that she is not satisfied in their marriage or that he
"can't control his wife" or that she does not see him as an adequate provider. The question becomes more complicated if her
job is demanding enough to require accommodation on his part
—some change in his normal patterns of work or leisure or responsibility in the home. The issue here can quickly become one
of power: who will have to "give in" more to the demands of the
other's job. There is often additional tension if the wife's career
is seen as of higher status; if, for example, there is more money
or glamour or prestige involved in her work than in his. These
factors of status and power strain the process of mutual accommodation in marriage.

One response to the power issues in marriage is a posture of mutual self-defense. The process of accommodation focuses here on defining and protecting the rights of each, against the demands that the other might make. We each attempt to protect ourselves, to circumscribe the scope of our duties and to guarantee the range of our rights, lest our privacy or other resources be eroded by our having to take up more than our "fair share" of the tasks of our marriage and family. In some marriages this defines the mutuality we want. For other couples, this is more a stage we find we have to go through as we try to change an earlier lopsided pattern of power, usually one in which the wife carried the chief burden of accommodation.

A second response to the question of power between us takes the posture of autonomy. Its goal is independence, that inner confidence that I can make it on my own resources. Here we are less combative and also less "engaged" than in the stance of self-defense. The focus of our efforts at accommodation is to free each of us for personal fulfillment, to leave each of us less dependent on the other. We learn to make fewer demands and, often, to expect less from our relationship. For some couples, this kind of accommodation is seen as the most realistic goal of a mature human relationship. To ask more is to be disappointed; in fact, it may well be a sign of immaturity or of some neurotic need. For other couples, this more autonomous stance toward one another is an improvement over an earlier, now less satisfying, dependency between us or a welcome relief after the strain of months of unsuccessful struggle to work out a new kind of equality between us.

But for most of us, our goal in marriage goes beyond autonomy. We sense that independence is an important resource to bring to marriage and that integrity is a strength to be cherished and nurtured along the way. But we marry in the hope of mutuality. Our commitment to the rigors of accommodation and the risks of compromise is sustained by the confidence that we may create a lifestyle between us in which, as we saw in Chapter 16, the giving goes both ways. This communal orientation is especially important to the success of our marriage when both of us work. The "we" of marriage here includes the ability of each of us to face the complications of our life as partners-parents-job holders, seeing these as practical problems that we can solve together, rather than as issues of power or status between us.

The Meaning of Work

Many ambiguities remain concerning the influence of work on marriage. Many issues surrounding the working wife and the working mother continue to be unclear. We have much to learn yet from research and from the testimony of those of us—wives, husbands, children—who are involved in the complex lifestyles of the dual-worker and dual-career marriage. One of the hints we have available to us now, however, concerns changing understandings of the meaning of work. Much of our upbringing as Americans, much of our education and professional training, dictates that work is the primary investment in adult life. This has long been true for men, and the pressure is felt today by professional women as well. We have noted frequently to what extent a commitment to the job and a willingness to acquiesce to whatever it demands have been, and still are, taken as signs of mature adult responsibility. The social movements of the 1960s called into question this automatic priority of work in life. The experience of many working couples has brought them to a similar point. As we struggle to mediate among the multiple demands of work and family, we may sense a growing reluctance to give our jobs such influence over the rest of life. We come to the conviction that it is not always our time with our children or our own relationship that must give way before the requirements of our work. Gradually we realize that these job-related demands must themselves be questioned and some of them resisted. We come into more confident awareness of the values in our life that go beyond financial success or professional advancement. And we begin to make choices, choices that are likely to influence our careers even as they shape our marriage.

But even this maturing realization is not itself without ambiguity. The liberating awareness of how work can enslave us can be turned against women, as when it is used as a defense against their fuller participation in society. "Work is just a trap;

women are better off for being protected from its pernicious influence. Truly theirs is 'the better part,' with their lives devoted to the humanistic concerns of affection and nurturance and emotional self-expression—all of which are absent in the harsh world of men's work."

It is true that maturity for many men today involves their ability to move beyond the bind of seeing themselves primarily in terms of their success on the job. But maturity for many women requires that they move into the experience of such competence. For many women, working in a job that is both financially rewarding and personally satisfying is an indispensable part of their growth into an adult identity and self-confidence. We know today that for many, perhaps most, working women their jobs do not hold much intrinsic satisfaction. I work only because I have to and I work at a job that is of little value in itself and that contributes even less to my enrichment. But this unsatisfying pattern of woman's work is more likely to be changed by increasing the participation of women across the full range of employment than by restricting their roles as workers, whatever the motive behind such discrimination.

The question of the meaning of work is thus essentially related to the future shape of family life, to the goals of the women's movement, even—no doubt—to the way in which we understand ourselves as a nation. The break that has been experienced in our previous identification of good worker–good husband and good worker–good citizen has left space for us to ask again questions about the significance, even the spiritual significance, of our work. As Madonna Kolbenschlag reminds us in *Kiss Sleeping Beauty Good-bye*, "Recovery of the spiritual sense of work is imperative if women are to be liberated rather than automated by it." We would extend her words to all of us who work.

Reflective Exercise

What place does work hold in your own marriage (or a marriage that you know well)? Consider the question from several points of view.

Who in the family household is currently involved in the world of work—husband, wife, older children? Give some thought to the shape that this involvement in work takes in each person's life.

How demanding is the work in which family members are involved—in time? in energy? in commitment? Are there other "demands" that the individual or the family experiences from the world of work? Be as concrete as possible here; give examples and instances of what you mean.

What are the benefits that come from this involvement in work—benefits for the individual? for the family? Are there ways in which the work of family members benefits others as well, beyond the family?

If you were able at this point to make one change in the way that work is a part of your marriage, what would that change be? Why is this change important for you?

Additional Resources

A valuable resource covering a broad range of the questions of work and marriage today is the slim volume *Working Couples* (Harper & Row, 1978), edited by Rhona Rapoport and Robert N. Rapoport. Carolyn Bird covers some of the same material in a more popular style in *The Two Paycheck Marriage* (Rawson, Wade, 1979). Frank Mott's analyses in *Women, Work, and Family* (Lexington Books, 1978) are based on longitudinal survey research done for the United States Department of Labor and draw out the economic implications of the changes in women's employment since 1968.

Several of the essays in the *American Psychologist* issue devoted to "Psychology and Children" (October 1979) bring together the current consensus from research on working mothers and child care. Two that are especially useful are Urie Bronfenbrenner's "Contexts of Child Rearing" and Lois Wladis Hoffman's "Maternal Employment: 1979."

The intriguing question of the impact of work on the rest of life has been explored from several starting points. In *Greedy Institutions* (Free Press, 1974) Lewis Coser examines the patterns of undivided commitment that are a part of the world of paid employment. The interaction of work and personal maturity is discussed in several essays in *Themes of Work and Love in Adulthood* (Harvard University Press, 1980), edited by Neil Smelser and Erik Erikson. In her larger analysis of the influence of feminine myths and models in *Kiss Sleeping Beauty Good-bye* (Doubleday, 1979), Madonna Kolbenschlag explores the ways in which women's separation from the world of work has deprived them of many important psychological as well as economic benefits.

18

COMMUNICATION AND CONFLICT

In marriage we see intimacy in both its most inviting and its most challenging face. Our daily patterns of life—living together, working together, sleeping together—these are the substance of intimacy. Here we feel ourselves being tested and getting better at being "up close." To live well these "up close" patterns of marriage we need, as we have seen in Chapter 13, the resources of psychological maturity: a sense of who I am, an openness to others, a capacity for commitment, some tolerance for the ambiguity both in myself and in other people. But these resources may not be enough. Aptitudes for intimacy must be expressed in behavior. We must be able, in the give-and-take of our life together, to develop a lifestyle that is mutually satisfying. Our desire to be close must be expressed in the way we act toward one another. It is encouraging to know that we can get better at being married. We can learn more satisfying ways *for us* to be close; we can learn more effective ways to give and receive the gift of ourselves that is at the core of our married love. And among the most valuable resources for this growth in marriage are the skills of intimate living.

The Skills of Intimacy

Over the past two decades there has been much interest in psychology and other disciplines in understanding better what happens in communication between people. As a result we are more clearly aware today of both what helps and what frustrates understanding in close relationships. Values and attitudes are important in our ability to live up close to others, but so, especially, is our behavior. There are skillful—that is, effective—ways to be with and behave toward one another. Interpersonal skills that are especially important to the intimate life of marriage include empathy, self-disclosure and confrontation. Each involves both attitudes and behaviors; each can contribute significantly to marriage for a lifetime.

Empathy enables me to understand another person from within that person's frame of reference. Empathy begins in an attitude of openness which enables me to set aside my own concerns and turn myself toward you. But this basic openness is not always sufficient. My capacity for empathy can be enhanced by my developing a range of behavioral skills. An accepting posture, attentive listening, sensitive paraphrasing—each of these can contribute to my effective presence to you.

My posture can give you important information about who you are to me and how important I judge your communication to be. If I appear distracted or edgy, if I keep glancing at my watch or rush to take an incoming phone call, I am likely to let you feel that you are not very important to me now. In the midst of the hectic schedules of most married couples today, it is often necessary to take steps to ensure the postures of presence: taking the time to sit down together to talk, finding ways to give each other some undivided attention, learning when to hold a personal concern until later and when to "stop everything" in order to deal with an issue now.

Learning to listen well to each other can be the most important skill of our marriage. To listen well is to listen actively, alert to the full context of the message—the words and silences, the emotions and ideas, the context in which our conversation takes place. To listen is to pay attention: paying attention is a receptive, but not a passive, attitude. If I cannot pay attention, it will be difficult for me to hear; if I do not listen, it will be difficult for me to understand and to respond effectively to you. The skills of active listening are those behaviors which enable me to be aware of your full message. This includes my being alert to your words and their nuances. But equally and often even more important are the non-verbal factors involved. Your tone of voice, your gestures, the timing, the emotional content—these may tell me more than the words between us. To listen actively, then, calls for an awareness of the content, the feelings and the context of our communication.

Sensitive paraphrasing is a skill of empathy as well. I show you that I understand you by saying back to you the essence of your message. To paraphrase is not merely to "parrot"—to repeat mechanically what you have just said. Rather I want to show you that I have really heard *you*, that I have been present not just to your words but to their deeper meaning for you. I go beyond the simple assurance that "I understand" by offering you a statement of what I have understood. You can then confirm that, in fact, I have understood you—or clarify your message so that my understanding may be more accurate. In either case, I demonstrate my respect for you and for your message. It is important to me that I understand what you say, and it is to you that I come to check my understanding.

Empathy, then, is my ability to understand your ideas, feelings and values from within your frame of reference. The goal of empathy is to understand; as such, it precedes evaluation. Empathy does not mean that I will always agree with you; it does not require that I accept your point of view as my own or even as "best" for you. I may well have to evaluate your ideas. We may well have to discuss and negotiate as we move toward a decision we can share. But these movements of evaluation and judgment come later in our communication. My first goal is to accurately understand you and what you are trying to say to me. Judgment and decision are not secondary in our communication but they are subsequent to accurate understanding.

In Chapter 11 we introduced our discussion of the virtues of marriage, those habits of graceful action that enable us to live well this vocation of committed love. In this light we can understand the skillful behavior of empathy in terms of Christian virtue. Empathy is the practical ability to be present to another person. Its exercise is a discipline: if I am distracted by fatigue or agitated by fear I cannot be present to my spouse. As virtuous behavior, empathy depends on a (relatively) strong sense of my identity and vocation. I do not have to defend myself: being aware of and comfortable with who I am, I can give my full attention to another person. Empathy thus is the stuff of intimacy. Without some skill, some virtue here, it will be difficult for me to express my love for my partner. Finally, to speak of empathy as both a skill and a virtue is to remind us again that we can get better at it. A Christian spirituality or asceticism of marriage will include these efforts to learn to be more effectively present to those we most love.

The open stance of empathy does much to enhance communication in marriage. But communication involves more than receptivity. I must be able to speak as well as to listen; to initiate as well as to understand. Self-disclosure thus becomes an essential skill of intimacy. To share myself with you I must be able to overcome the hesitancy suggested by fear or doubt or shame. But these inhibitions overcome, I must be able to act in a way that gives you access to my mind and heart, in a way that is fitting for me and for our relationship. Appropriate self-disclosure can seem complicated. But I am not limited to my current level of success. I can become more skillful, learning better ways to express my values and needs, my ideas and feelings.

Self-disclosure begins in self-awareness. I must *know* what I have experienced, what I think, how I feel, what I need, what I want to do. This knowledge is not likely to be full and finished; an unwillingness to speak until I am completely sure of myself can be a trap in communication. Self-awareness is rather an ability to know where I am now, to be in touch with the dense and ambiguous information of my own life. Beyond knowing my own insights, needs and purposes, I must value them. This need not mean that I am convinced that they are "the best." It means rather that I take them seriously as deserving of examination and respect, from myself and from others as well. My feelings, my perceptions of myself and of the world—these have worth and weight. By valuing them myself I contribute to the possibility that they can be appreciated by others as well. My needs and purposes exist in a context of those of other people, to be sure. But a conviction that my own ideas and goals are of value is basic to mature self-disclosure.

An important skill of self-disclosure is my ability to speak concretely. I must be able to say "I," to acknowledge my own ideas and feelings. Self-disclosure can be thwarted by a retreat into speaking about "most people"; "everybody knows . . ." instead of "I think that . . ."; "most people want . . ." instead of "I need . . ."; "people have a hard time . . ." instead of "it is difficult for me to . . ." Beyond this willingness to "own" my experience, I can learn to provide more specific details about my actions and emotions. To share myself with you in our marriage I will need, for example, a well-nuanced vocabulary of feelings—one that goes well beyond "I feel good" and "I feel bad." To tell you that "I feel good" is to share some important information about myself but not yet very much. What does this mean for me? Is this good feeling one of confidence? or affection? or physical vigor? Does it result from something I have done or something that has been done for me? Are you an important part of this good feeling for me or are you really incidental to it? My self-disclosure becomes more concrete when I can name my feelings more precisely and when I can describe the events and actions that are part of them for me.

Confrontation, too, makes a critical contribution to intimacy in marriage. For most of us the word "confrontation" implies conflict. And, as we shall see shortly, the ability to deal well with conflict between us is an important skill of marriage. But we use the word "confrontation" here in a meaning that goes beyond its narrow and, most often, negative connotation as interpersonal conflict. The ability to confront involves the psychological strength to give (and to receive) emotionally significant information in ways that lead to further exploration rather than to self-defense. Sometimes the emotionally significant information is more positive than negative. To say "I love you" is to share with you emotionally significant information. And many of us know how confrontive it is to learn of another's love for us.

Similarly, to give a compliment is to share emotionally significant information, and there are people who defend themselves
against this "good news" as strongly as others of us defend ourselves against an accusation of blame. But most often, to be sure,
when confrontation becomes necessary and difficult in our marriage, it is because there is negative information we must share
with our spouse. It may be some practical issue of daily life that
we must face—the use of the automobile, our bank balance, plans
for next summer's vacation. The issues, however, may be more
sensitive—the way you discipline the children, my parents'
influence in our home, how satisfying is our sex life.

Skills of confrontation are those behaviors that make it more
likely that our sharing of significant negative information in
these instances will lead us to explore the difficulty between us
rather than to defend ourselves against one another. My ability
to confront effectively is enhanced when I am able to speak
descriptively rather than judgmentally. To tell you that I missed
my meeting because you came home late is to *describe;* to call
you a selfish and inconsiderate person is to *judge.* While both
may be hard for you to hear from me, one is more likely to escalate into a quarrel than is the other. As we have noted before,
judgment is not irrelevant in marriage, but premature judgment
is likely to short-circuit the process of exploration and mutual
understanding. Perhaps there are extenuating circumstances that
caused you to be late; perhaps you are genuinely sorry that you
inconvenienced me and want to do something to make amends.
My attack on your selfishness is not likely to leave room for this
kind of response on your side. It is more likely to lead you to defend yourself against my accusation, perhaps by calling up instances of my own selfishness, perhaps by leaving the scene altogether. In neither case has communication between us been
furthered.

There are other behaviors that make our confrontation more
effective, that is, more likely to further communication between
us. These include the ability to accept feelings of anger in myself and in you and the ability to show respect for you even as I

must disagree with you or challenge your position. These skills become especially important in dealing with conflict in marriage.

Conflict and Love

Conflict is an aspect of Christian marriage about which our rhetoric can be misleading. In ceremonies and sermons about marriage, it is upon images of unity and peace and joy that we dwell. These images of life together in Christian marriage are important and true, but partial. When, as a believing community, we do not speak concretely to the more ambiguous experiences in marriage—experiences of anger, frustration, misunderstanding—we can leave many married people feeling that their marriages are somehow deficient.

Conflict and hostility are not goals of marriage, to be sure. But neither are they an indication that our marriage is "on the rocks." Conflict is a normal, expectable ingredient in any relationship—whether marriage, teamwork or friendship—that brings people "up close" and engages them at the level of their significant values and needs. The challenge in close relationships is not to do away with all signs of conflict or, worse, to refuse to admit that conflicts arise between us. Rather we can learn ways to recognize the potential areas of conflict *for us* and to deal with these issues and feelings in ways that strengthen rather than destroy the bonds between us.

Conflict is normal in interpersonal exchange; it is an expectable event in the intimate lifestyle of marriage. Whenever people come together in an ongoing way, especially if significant issues are involved, we can expect that they will become aware of differences that exist between them. Sometimes these differences will be simply noted as interesting. But often they will involve disagreements, misunderstanding and discord. It is here that the experience of conflict begins.

Marriage engages each of us at a level of our most significant values and needs. My sense of who I am, my convictions, my ideas and ideals, what I hope to make of my life—in our marriage all these are open to confirmation or to challenge and change. In addition, every marriage is a complex pattern of interaction and expectation. We develop our own way of being together and apart; we come to our own understanding of what each of us gives and receives in this relationship. The process through which we develop the patterns of our own marriage is ongoing. We can expect times of relative stability when the rhythms of our life together seem to fit especially well. We can also expect periods marked by significant adjustment and change. The process of marriage includes this continuing exploration, even trial and error, as we attempt to learn more about ourselves and our partner. It is these normal and even inevitable experiences of personal challenge and mutual change in marriage that set the stage for conflict.

Conflict is a response to discrepancy or disparity. "Things are not as I expected or as I want them to be." In interpersonal conflict the other person is seen as somehow involved in, or responsible for, this discrepancy. "You are not as I expected; it is your fault that things are not as I want them to be." Marriage brings us together in so many ways, as friends and lovers, as parents and householders, in cooperation and competition, in practical decisions about our money and our time. These overlapping issues give us many opportunities both to meet and to fail each other's expectations. Thus discrepancy and conflict are predictable.

This predictability of conflict in marriage is not simply a cause for concern. Conflict is not "all bad." Its effects in intimacy are not simply or necessarily destructive. As many marriage counselors know, conflict is as often a sign of health in a relationship as it is a symptom of disease. The presence of conflict between us indicates that we are about something that is of value to us both. Conflict thus marks a relationship of some force. This energy can be harnessed; it need not always work against us. A marriage in which there is nothing important enough to fight about is more likely to die than one in which arguments occur. Indifference is a greater enemy of intimacy than is conflict.

Many of us have grown up assuming that love does away with conflict, that love and conflict are mutually exclusive. But this romantic view of love is challenged by our experience of tension in our own marriage. We come to know conflict as a powerful dynamic in our relationship and one with ambiguous effect. For most of us, it is the negative effects of conflict that we know best and fear. Conflict feels bad and seems to have bad results. To be in conflict seems like a move away from intimacy. I am angry or hurt, you feel rejected or resentful. And most often my own past experience reinforces the unpleasant conclusion that conflict leads to the disintegration of relationships. Sometimes the relationship ends immediately; sometimes it continues, but with a burden of bitterness and unhealed grievances that ultimately leads to its death. In the face of this negative sense of the power of conflict, the evidence that it is expectable and even inevitable in our marriage is likely to strike us with alarm.

Conflict Can Be Constructive

But these negative results of conflict do not give the full picture. Conflict can make a constructive contribution to our marriage. It can bring us to a more nuanced appreciation of who each of us is; it can test and strengthen the bonds that exist between us; it can deepen our capacity for mutual trust.

The experience of conflict points to an area of discrepancy between us. I am uncomfortable with the way you discipline our oldest child; you don't like me to let my new job interfere with our weekends together as a family; I no longer want to be "the perfect housewife and mother," though this is the way you have always seen me; you no longer want to be "the strong and self-sufficient male," though you know it frightens me to see your weakness.

If we are willing to face the conflict, we may be able to learn from the experience of discrepancy that is at its root. Exploring this discrepancy—between what I want from you and what you are able to give, or between who I am and who you need me to be, or between our differing views about money or privacy or sex or success—we can come to know one another more fully. We can grow toward a greater and more respectful mutuality, based on a greater awareness and respect for who each of us really is.

Conflict is not necessarily a part of every development in marriage. Some changes are accompanied more by a sense of fulfillment than frustration. Some couples are open to the processes of mutual exploration in such a way that there is little sense of discrepancy and little experience of conflict between them. But change is frequently a source of confusion and conflict, even if only temporarily. A relationship that cannot face at least the possibility of conflict will soon be in trouble. In order to ensure that conflict will not arise between us, we may decide that our relationship should touch us only minimally, in areas where we are not vitally concerned. Or we may believe that we must be willing to disown our response to the concerns that do matter to us. But to disown conflict does not strengthen a relationship. It tends instead to have us look away from part of the reality that exists between us. But the reality that is there—the troublesome concern that stands beneath the conflict—does not go away. The discrepancy remains, unattended, as a likely source of more serious trouble between us in the future.

We may know from previous experiences that conflict, faced poorly, can lead to resentment and recrimination. But not to face it does not ensure that our marriage will be free of these negative emotions. A more useful stance involves our willingness to face the conflicts that may arise between us, aware of their ambiguous power both to destroy and to deepen the love we share. This willingness to accept conflict as inevitable and even as potentially valuable need not mean that we find it pleasant to be at odds. But it does mean that we are willing to acknowledge and even tolerate this discomfort that conflict brings, in view of the valuable information it provides about our relationship and ourselves.

The experience of facing together the conflicts that arise between us can give greater confidence, an increased security in the strength and flexibility of the commitment between us, since we have seen it tested and found it sufficient to the test. Conflict can have this positive effect in a relationship but it remains a powerful and ambiguous dynamic. Just as the presence of conflict does not necessarily or automatically signal a relationship in trouble, neither does it necessarily or automatically result in new learning or growth. Whether the expectable event of conflict in our marriage will have positive or negative effect is due in large part to how we respond to it. To deal well with the ambiguous power of conflict we must first appreciate that conflict can be more than just negative between us. We must believe that the benefits of working through our conflict are worth the trouble and discomfort that attend. We must both have the resources of personal maturity that enable us to face strong emotion and to look at ourselves anew and possibly change. And we must have the skills that enable us to deal effectively with one another even in the heat of our disagreement.

Avoidance and Engagement

Most couples develop a characteristic way of dealing with the discrepancies that arise in their own marriage. This style is conjoint, in the sense that both partners contribute to its shape. While couples differ in many details of their characteristic styles of communication, there seem to be two basic stances toward dealing with conflict in marriage. These are avoidance and engagement. As we shall see, both of these basic orientations toward conflict can serve a couple; each, as well, carries its own hazards.

In some couples avoidance is the chief pattern for dealing with conflict. They seem unable to face a situation which might arouse strong negative feelings between them. When confronted with a discrepancy in their relationship that might lead to conflict (the wife's decision to go back to school; their relations with in-laws; the husband's devotion to a hobby that excludes the rest of the family) their response is characteristically to look away from the issue. They avoid exploring certain topics or turn away from them quickly as soon as any negative emotions become involved. One or both may characteristically refuse to accept any information that might point to a problem between them. Thus a wife may prefer "not to know" about her husband's extramarital affair or a husband may "not notice" his wife's increasing dissatisfaction with her role as full-time housewife. The partners may simply deny the evidence or at least refuse to accept that it signals anything that is a problem "for us."

Sometimes this avoidance stance may come from a fear of strong emotion. "I am afraid of what will happen—to me or to you—if I let myself get angry." Sometimes it stems from a sense that our relationship itself is fragile. "Things between us are strained enough as it is. We'd better not risk getting into something that might just draw us further apart." In either case the result is that we evade the discrepancy or, more precisely, evade the necessity of dealing with this discrepancy now. It is seldom that the underlying issue will simply resolve itself if we avoid it. More likely it will remain and, unattended, will become more of a problem between us. Some couples are able to achieve a stable and even satisfying relationship with such a pattern of avoiding conflict when it occurs between them. Early on in their marriage they come to a sense of who they are to one another and what modest demands they can make on the relationship. These early and somewhat limited expectations remain unchallenged over the course of their marriage. The partners display little openness in themselves or in their life together. For them, avoiding conflict is an aspect of the larger pattern of a settled lifestyle.

Among other couples avoidance is more a tool of discretion than a lifestyle. The partners are not characteristically unwilling to face discrepancies or the strong emotions that these may provoke. But, respectful of the force that conflict can release, they are careful with it. The wife may sense her own fatigue this evening and so asks her husband if they might postpone their discussion of a touchy topic until the weekend. Or they may realize that it is risky to bring up, when the in-laws are visiting, some area of disagreement between themselves. But they do not let avoidance become their only option. Aware of the discomfort and confusion that conflict can produce, they are nevertheless willing to deal directly with one another when it does arise. But they take steps to ensure that their relationship will survive. And one of these steps can be to avoid or put off dealing with a conflict issue until a more propitious time. Sensitive to factors of time and place and personal vulnerability, they know how—and when—to engage and to avoid.

Most counselors and other analysts of marriage would concur that an openness to the possibility of conflict is essential if a relationship is not only to survive but to develop. There are, however, strong marriages in which conflict is seldom in evidence. The harmony of these relationships is achieved less by the denial of discrepancy than by the quality of their communication. The partners are able to recognize areas of discrepancy early and to respond to these before they generate conflict. The new information that arises in discrepancy is not often experienced as a threat to personal integrity or to the future of the relationship. With personal resources of self-knowledge and self-acceptance, they show little need to defend against each other and a comparative ease in accommodating to change. While their lives intersect in many ways, there are not many issues between them that run the risk of escalating into serious strife. But even these couples need to be able to deal well with conflict. Its very infrequency between them may leave them vulnerable to special guilt or blame when it does arise.

Engaging in Conflict

An alternative to avoidance in conflict is engagement. Engagement, too, may take several forms—some which help and others which harm our relationship. Engaging in conflict is likely to be destructive between us when we "take on" the issues in a way that escalates the tension, that expands the discrepancy between us. This can happen a number of ways. Often a problem that starts out as minor is allowed to expand. Your not getting the car home on time this afternoon causes me to be late for an appointment of my own. As we start to discuss this, the focus shifts from this one event to the many *other* times that you have inconvenienced me or, even, to how generally selfish you are. This attitude on my side is likely to lead you to come up with your own list of how demanding I am or how many times I have inconvenienced you. The conflict has escalated.

Another risky response is to shift the focus from an objective problem to our relationship itself. Here the issue in conflict becomes a sign of something bigger. "If you really loved me, you'd have the car home on time." Or "if you really cared about me, you wouldn't get so upset that I didn't have the car here on time." Interpreting the problem as a test of love makes the stakes much higher. Turning to personal attack or relying on threats can also escalate the conflict between us. "You selfish oaf, if you bring the car home late one more time, I'll . . ." This is more likely to produce counterthreats than to move us toward resolution.

In another style, engagement becomes cyclic. Some couples are able to take up the conflict, even lustily, but seem unable to go anywhere with it. They tend to become polarized quickly, moving to non-negotiable positions, with neither of them able to offer a way out. They are apparently not afraid of the battle but there is little evidence that they learn anything from it that helps them in their relationship or, for that matter, in their next fight. To the outsider, their conflict style may appear especially damaging and bitter. The strife between them seems more to be momentarily quieted than ever really resolved. In fact, conflict itself seems to be a chief form of communication and contact for them.

A third kind of engagement is more useful in the process of resolving conflict between us. It is an engagement that leads to further development of our relationship, by enabling us to explore the difficulty we are experiencing and to learn from it. This stance requires that we are able to acknowledge that there is some problem between us, rather than simply denying our distress. We are willing to explore the problem; there is an underlying openness to the possibility of learning something new and of changing some part of how we have been together. We realize, when caught in the conflict, that things are not as we thought, that there is some divergence between how we have been interpreting things and how things are. This can lead us into panic: we turn away from this disconcerting information, trying to mask it or to fix blame. Or we can see this as an opportunity for growth, a chance to come to a better sense of what is really going on between us.

This stance of flexible engagement helps us to look at the problem that has arisen between us, exploring it for its meaning. We can do this only if we are convinced that a problem between us is not, automatically, a sign that our marriage is in trouble. Rather it is an expectable part of the process of learning more about ourselves, each other and what our marriage can be. Not every conflict between us will require significant change. Some discrepancies, when we examine them closely, turn out to be misunderstandings. When the situation is clarified, we will find that our normal ways of being together are confirmed and reinforced. But sometimes an exploration of the problem will bring to light new information and suggest changes in how we understand ourselves and how we share our life together.

Effective engagement includes both the exploration of the conflict issue and its resolution. In some couples the exploration is not just a way to reach a solution. The process of coming to understand each other better, as we learn from this experience of discrepancy and the accompanying discomfort between us, is itself an important dynamic of our ongoing life. The particular decision we come to, even the determination of "who won," is less significant than what happens between us. How we deal with one another in conflict, and what we learn from this about our relationship—these are more important to our future together than is the concrete solution upon which we finally agree. A year from now I may well have forgotten what we decided today but I am likely to carry with me the sense of whether we are able to work out the problems that exist between us.

To Be Successful in Conflict

Some conflicts in marriage arise over specific issues that require a particular decision. Shall we buy our second car? Where shall we spend our vacation this summer? Who will take the children to the neighborhood party? Often decisions like this can be made without conflict. We tell each other what we think and how we feel about the question; we note our areas of agreement, discuss the points on which we disagree and come to a solution or a compromise that suits us both. If the areas of disagreement are large, however, we may experience trouble. But this kind of conflict, involving a particular decision about a concrete issue, is manageable for most couples. When our disagreement has a clear focus on an issue "out there," we are likely to be flexible and even creative as we try to come to agreement.

Some conflicts in marriage, however, involve issues that are not "out there" but rather between us. These relationship conflicts are more difficult to face and to resolve. I feel that you have become so preoccupied with your work that you have little time for me; you are unhappy that I have invited my parents to spend two weeks with us at Christmas; we don't agree on the response we should make to our youngest child who is doing poorly in school. Many of us who respond well in solving problems "out there" become ineffective when these "up close" conflicts emerge. Responses that are likely to succeed—sharing information and exploring alternatives—are not pursued. We move instead toward coercion, blame and threat. Predictably, the conflict escalates.

We leave the issue behind as we become caught up in an expanding pattern of injury and self-defense. It is not inevitable that a concern in our relationship should degenerate into an attack on "who I am." But many of us feel this pull. Relationship conflicts almost always touch on issues that are close to the core of the self. Belonging, acceptance, security, personal worth, self-esteem—it is these that are at stake if our relationship is troubled. Anxiety is a normal response when these core issues are raised. The presence of this anxiety can alert us to the significance of what is going on. "Tread lightly here. We are on dangerous ground. Somebody might get hurt." As we learn to recognize the signals of this anxiety in ourselves and in our partner, we can become more skilled in recognizing these vulnerable issues and in dealing with them in ways that protect and heal. But anxiety can also interfere, drawing us away from our normal effectiveness into less mature reactions and responses. Overwhelmed with a sense of my vulnerability, I can use my energy to defend myself rather than to reach out to you or toward a solution. I blame you, or try to confuse you, or refuse to recognize your feelings or your point of view. Flexibility on my part will be impossible. It will feel to me too much like capitulation. I must stand firm to protect the fragile sense of self.

In conflict between intimates, then, there is a built-in tendency toward emotional escalation. Issues of practical decision ("what shall we do . . . ?") become tests of our relationship ("if you really loved me . . ."). Discrepancies within our relationship ("this is not right between us . . .") become occasions of personal attack (". . . and it is your fault"). Effective engagement works against this escalation. A central strategy here is to keep the focus of our disagreement both narrow and clear. To do this we must be alert to the areas of personal sensitivity where anxiety is likely to cloud our response, as well as of the "hot" issues between us, where we both feel under attack. We will not always want to or be able to avoid these areas, but when we approach them we will do so with awareness and with care.

Conflict in marriage is likely to generate strong emotions. This brings us back to a consideration of how important it can be to our marriage for us to develop our skills for responsible confrontation.

A capacity for confrontation enables me to face the stress involved when our communication includes emotions as well as "facts." To deal effectively with conflict in our marriage I will need this capacity to face information that has emotional weight and to accept the presence of strong emotions as a part of our exchange. If I am afraid of strong emotion, especially anger, in myself or in you, I will find the conflict situation especially difficult and may defend myself against it. This is not to suggest that anger is to be pursued for its own sake. Anger is a volatile emotion. It can lead to inflexibility and insult; it can escalate a small concern into a bitter battle between us. While anger is an expectable component of conflict, it need not become the dynamic that drives us on, beyond our control. We can learn better ways to be together in conflict, better ways to communicate even under the emotional weight of the discrepancies that concern us.

As we saw earlier in this chapter, a key to effective communication in the midst of conflict is the ability to be direct and specific: direct—we can tell one another what we think and how we feel about the troublesome issue; specific—we can keep our focus on this issue, avoiding escalation into broader questions or emotions that complicate the question at hand.

Flexibility in Resolving Conflict

For conflict to have a constructive effect in our marriage we must, as we have seen, be motivated to deal with the trouble between us. We are more likely to be willing to take on the conflict issue if we sense both its significance (this question is serious enough that we have to face it) and our own strength (this issue is not so weighty that it will destroy us). But our willingness to take on the troublesome issues does not by itself ensure that we shall be successful in resolving them. Without some flexibility in how we respond to one another, we may find ourselves only more frustrated and angry in the battle that results.

For example, our initial exploration of the problem may reach an impasse. I want us to ask my parents to help us make a down payment on a new house. You refuse to do so. I see things one way; you see them another; there seems to be little common ground. To move beyond this deadlock will require that we are able to reformulate the problem. This reformulation often becomes possible as I am able to understand and appreciate what is at stake from your point of view as well as my own. For me, to ask for money from my parents expresses my sense of belonging to them and being secure in their care. Besides, I know they would love to do this for us. But for you, to take money from them seems like an admission of inadequacy in making our own way. Besides, you feel that it just continues my pattern of looking to them first whenever we face a difficulty instead of trying to work things out on our own. This empathic awareness gives me new ways of interpreting our standoff: for you, the problem is not so much one of money as one of independence and self-esteem. Reformulating the problem, we are likely to be able to move beyond the earlier impasse. I am also more likely to be sensitive to the potentially "hot" issues that may be involved here for you.

If flexibility is necessary for me to accept the new information that can lead to reformulating the problem in a more adequate way, flexibility is also required to come to a resolution. We may need to explore a range of options before we reach a solution that satisfies us both. If our anxiety is high in the stress of the conflict, it may be difficult for us to think creatively or to come up with many different ideas. We may feel "stuck," with few possibilities open to us and none of these acceptable. The more ideas we are able to generate in the midst of a conflict, the more likely it is that we shall be able to evolve a decision that respects both of us and also reaches the necessary solution. We will not start with my parents as we look for down-payment money but will explore other possibilities first. Perhaps we can get part of the money we need from several different sources and thus not be dependent so much on my parents. Maybe we should approach them for a loan rather than a gift, or we can ask your parents for help as well as mine. To come up with new possibilities under the stress of conflict requires personal flexibility. I am not totally involved in defending myself and my original plan. I am free to explore other alternatives, generated by you or by me.

I am also flexible enough to compromise, to work toward a decision that is satisfying for you as well as for me, to accept a resolution that may ask something of each of us as well. My sense that our conflict is resolved does not depend simply on my having the last word.

The attitudes of flexibility and exploration do not, of course, find expression only in conflict. They are a part of the larger openness to one another and to change that characterizes most successful marriages. Such personal flexibility would seem to be especially important in the contemporary context of marriage, where change is such a factor. As we experience change, stimulated both by developments within our marriage and by factors

outside, we need to be able to interpret these changes as, at least
potentially, a part of the ongoing movement of marriage. We
need sufficient flexibility in how we see ourselves and how we
understand our relationship so that these changes can be incorporated with integrity, with a sense that they are more a
fulfillment of the promise of our marriage than they are a falling
away from an earlier and finished commitment.

What is most significant about conflict in our marriage, then,
is not whether or not it arises—since some conflict is expectable
between us. It is not even "who wins." What is most important is
the quality of the communication that occurs. What is said and
left unsaid, with what level of skill, how power is shared,
whether healing or hurt prevails—it is these elements that make
up the pattern of our own conflict style. And our conflict style
will influence the possibility of our own marriage for a lifetime
because it is these elements that our hearts remember.

Many of us who are Christians are aware that our religious
heritage has contributed to our reluctance to deal with conflict.
Conflict instead is to be avoided, in line with our other efforts to
be "charitable" and "meek and humble of heart." But another
part of our religious heritage reminds us of a connection between conflict and intimacy. In the story of Jacob struggling
with Yahweh, which we discussed in Chapter 13, intimacy with
God is portrayed in the ambiguous metaphor of wrestling. Jacob
is in conflict with someone whom he loves very much but whose
purposes he does not fully understand. Conflict is one of the
many embraces of marriage. In conflict, as in lovemaking, we are
brought close to each other and become especially vulnerable to
each other's moves. We may be injured—as, indeed, Jacob was,
limping for the rest of his life. In this struggle we have the opportunity to learn important, intimate details about each other;
we test each other's resources and limits. The point of the Jacob
story—indeed, its revelation—may be this opportunity for intimacy in conflict. If we can resist the impulse to run away (an
avoidance provoked by fear) or to control our partner (in ma-
nipulative engagement), we may experience a new intimacy in
the embrace of conflict. Exhausted by the wrestling of our
conflict, we may also be invigorated. Learning to play fair and

fight fair in marriage is learning how to use conflict to draw closer in love. Through our skillful and virtuous behavior, even conflict can be a means to intimacy.

Reflective Exercise

Take some time to consider your experience of communication and confrontation in your own marriage. Begin in a mood of quiet, letting your memory turn back over the past year or so, patiently attentive to the memories that come of the many different kinds of exchanges that you and your spouse have shared. Spend time with this movement of recollection; let the memories come as they will, whether positive or negative, whether satisfying or disturbing.

From these many memories, choose one that is for you an instance of successful or satisfying communication. Let this example come more fully to mind and then examine it more closely. In what ways was this experience satisfying for you? for your spouse? What was your contribution to the success of the exchange? What was your spouse's contribution? How did you feel during the exchange? after? What can you take from this memory to assist the ongoing communication in your marriage?

Then turn to a memory of a difficult or unresolved exchange, perhaps a time of conflict between you. Again, consider the elements that were a part of the event. What was the focus of the difficulty? Was it a "hot issue" between you, one that finds you at odds with one another often? In what ways did your behavior (and that of your spouse) add to the tension? In what ways did you (and your spouse) try to resolve the problem here? How did you feel during this exchange? after? What can you take from this experience to assist your communication in the future?

Additional Resources

Psychologist Gerard Egan has significantly influenced our understanding of the attitudes and skills that contribute to effective communication. Several of his books are helpful for assessing and improving one's skills in communication. Both *Interpersonal Living* (Brooks/Cole, 1976) and *You and Me: Skills of Communicating and Relating to Others* (Brooks/Cole, 1977) are written in a generally available style and include exercises to help the reader develop practical skills. Two useful resources for expanding one's vocabulary of feelings are John Wood's *How Do You Feel?* (Spectrum, 1974) and Willard Gaylin's *Feelings* (Ballantine, 1979). An important analysis of the emergence and effect of conflict in close relationships is found in *Communication, Conflict, and Marriage* (Jossey-Bass, 1974), by H. L. Raush, W. A. Barry, R. K. Hertel and M. A. Swain.

John Shea provides "A Theological Perspective on Human Relations Skills and Family Intimacy" in *The Family in Crisis or in Transition* (Seabury, 1979), edited by Andrew Greeley. The significance of these skills in ministry is emphasized by Joan Chittister in her discussion, "Healing Language," in *New Catholic World* (November/December, 1979) and by Dennis C. Kinlaw in "Helping Skills for the Helping Community" in *Religious Education* (November/December, 1976). Drawing on insight from both Scripture and psychology, David Augsburger takes up the discussion of the role of conflict, anger and trust in relationships in his *Caring Enough to Confront* (Herald Press, 1980).

19

BEYOND THE PARTNER

Much of our discussion so far has focused on the marriage relationship itself. At several places we have mentioned the connections between the couple and the larger social context, the world of work, the Church community. Here we want to examine these connections more closely. In particular, we will consider some of the ways in which marriage can both benefit from and contribute to the network of relationships beyond the family.

Friendship

Married couples today expect to be friends. This was not always the case. This expectation marks the transition from the conventional marriage—with its clearer distinctions between woman's role and man's role in marriage—toward the sense of marriage which is more prevalent today. In earlier norms a wife was not considered to be, and often was not, her husband's social equal. She was almost surely younger than he, less educated, with little experience in the world beyond the household. We know that many such conventional marriages were (and are) marked by genuine affection and care. But they lacked the base of mutuality that friendship requires. Some marriages today, as we have seen, do not carry the demand of mutuality. But more and more couples approach marriage in the conviction that they are and will continue to be friends.

As we noted in Chapter 3, these expectations of friendship correspond to some of the structural requirements of the contemporary institution of marriage. If the world of my work is a competitive and emotionally hostile environment, if geographic mobility takes me away from my extended family and disturbs my previous network of support, then I am truly fortunate that my spouse is also my friend. Without friendship as a part of our marriage, we might both be without any experience of an adult confidant—a companion who is like me in many significant ways and who can be trusted to share in some important parts of my life.

These hopes for friendship in marriage have, until recently, been most characteristic of middle-class couples. Within some working-class and ethnic groups there has been little expectation that spouses have much in common beyond their intersecting responsibilities as wife-homemaker and husband-provider. Husbands spent most of their free time (as well as work time) with other men, in taverns, social clubs, athletic events. Wives spent their time out of the house with women relatives or other married women in the neighborhood. Often these same-sex groupings provided the support and companionship that were not available or even looked for in the marriage. But in middle-class marriages (and these values are now widely accepted beyond the middle class) there has been much greater expectation that wives and husbands provide these resources of companionship to one another.

The expectation that spouses be friends, then, is an important modern alteration in the structure of marriage. This does not imply that "throughout all history until our day" married couples never were friends. But it does mean that the presence or absence of such friendship did not become a central issue in marriage until quite recently—the last generation or so. And the expectation that spouses shall be friends has contributed much to the contemporary experience of marriage. Liking each other as friends, we find that loving each other is a much richer experience. Sexuality, sensitivity and devotion overlap in a lifestyle of mutual support and challenge. Becoming friends can be a part of our movement beyond romance into the experience of committed love. The range of mutual interests and values that we share can help sustain us through the strains we experience in the family years and bring us to the mature years of our marriage with a sense of enthusiasm for this new time we shall now have together.

But this expectation that we shall be friends can make significant demands on marriage as well. Images of what constitutes friendship in marriage can vary. I may expect our friendship to mean that we will spend as much time as possible together, preferring each other's company to that of all others, as we did when we were dating. For you, our friendship may be less a question of how much time we have together and more a conviction that we are "there" for each other in times of stress or difficulty. You want to be able to count on me for solace and support at these times and you expect me to turn to you when I need this kind of help. The requirements of friendship, then, may be expressed in terms of time and presence or they may be seen as demanding that we like the same things or, especially, that we find in each other our principal source of personal support and growth. But today many married couples, as well as many students of marriage, see this emotional restrictiveness as a hindrance rather than a help to marriage for a lifetime.

That spouses should be friends is not in dispute. What is being questioned is the expectation that partners should be, or can be, each other's only significant adult relationship—each other's *only* friend. Sometimes the expectation of emotional exclusivity is related to concern for sexual or genital exclusivity. It is dangerous to make friends, at least friends of the opposite sex. These friendships will inevitably lead to trouble—an affair, even a divorce. The prevailing assumption here is that women and men are drawn together *only* through sexual attraction and that sexual attraction leads *inevitably* to genital expression. If this be the case, then it is safer to restrict my close contact with the opposite sex to my spouse.

But these assumptions are under question today, chiefly as a result of married people's actual experience of friendship. There are many factors involved in attraction between people, of the same or opposite sex. Sexual attraction is part of some, but not all, friendships between people. Sexual attraction sometimes develops toward genital expression but not always and certainly not "inevitably." Within the human experience, sexual expression is much more a matter of choice and preference than it is of instinct or "need." And most extramarital affairs result from, rather than cause, marital troubles.

Friendship, a rich blessing in life, is a benefit to marriage as well. Friends can ease the strain in a marriage that comes from the unrealistic expectations that my spouse should be "all things" to me. In few marriages are the partners so similar that they share all values or interests. The pattern is rather that people marry on the basis of the similarities (and differences) they see between them at that time. Then, over the course of their years together, they learn more about both themselves and each other. They find some earlier "similarities" do not go very deep or are not as important as they once thought. They find other similarities between them which take on greater meaning. And they discover significant areas in their lives where, unexpectedly and sometimes even unhappily, they are very different. Sometimes this discovery will seem somehow unfair. I *need* you to be a certain way, to be interested in certain things that are important to me. My insistence that you be what I need (more than who you are) is likely to be intense if I have no friends who, in their range of interests and in their love for me, can complement the relationship we have together in our marriage.

In a maturing marriage the presence of friends is much more likely to contribute to than detract from a deepening of the relationship of the spouses. Friends expand the resources of support and challenge available to each of us and to us together. Our friends engage us in ongoing relationships of shared affection and mutual influence that, gifts in themselves, also teach us much about that other ongoing relationship—marriage. Our friendships exercise us in the strengths of commitment and compromise, of dependence and autonomy, that serve us as well in marriage for a lifetime. In a time of personal or marital strain, having access to a friend can serve as a safety valve, reducing the pressure without damage to the structure of commitment and confidentiality that is our marriage. For most of us our friendships and our marriage are complementary: neither replaces our need for the other; each gives us resources we bring to the other.

But, as most of us find, it is not very easy to develop friends in adult life. Friendship takes time, perhaps time that, in the face of demands of our family and work responsibilities, we feel we do not have. To develop friends I must have contact with people who share some of my values and interests. As a homemaker I may find my contact with new people especially limited. If I am working I may meet many people, but not many who see the world as I do. And even after contact is made, friendship requires the sometimes lengthy, or at least involving, process of getting to know and trust one another. But beyond these complications of time and availability, perhaps the greatest difficulty in the development of adult friendships today touches on the question of sexuality.

Friendship and Sexuality

Sexuality is a disquieting issue in many relationships today. American culture complicates the development and maintenance of adult friendship by its general assumption that affection between a man and a woman always and inevitably leads to genital expression. The implication here is that while same-sex friendships may be valuable in adult life, friendships between women and men are distractions from the primary relationship with one's spouse and destructive of the marriage commitment. In this, as in most exaggeration, there is some foundation in fact. The human person is marvelously complex. In most of us the connections among attraction, affection, sexuality and love are complicated and not always fully conscious. Over the course of our own adolescence and young adulthood most of us have experienced the dynamics of "falling in love," where we felt irresistibly drawn to someone, with little sense that we had much control of the situation. If this kind of romantic experience is the standard for every relationship between men and women, then perhaps heterosexual friendships are high-risk for a marriage.

But this caution responds to only part of the reality of human relationships. And in its concentration on sex and genital expression as inevitable, the caution can become a self-fulfilling prophecy. "If we really like each other we ought to be sleeping together, or at least struggling with the question. If we are not, maybe we're not being honest with one another." Both history and current experience testify to the reality of significant emotional relationships in which genital sexuality has no part. Attraction and affection are strong, as are mutual concern and care. But the communion of these friendships does not include genital love. It is yet another sign of our generation's preoccupation with sex that we must reassure one another that this is possible.

In a cultural atmosphere as highly charged with sexual expectation as is our own, it is possible that the issues of romance may arise in a friendship. It may arise for me, as I try to be clear within myself concerning my own emotional commitments. It may trouble my friend as well, making us both hesitant to continue a relationship that might become an affair. It may be a concern for my spouse, arising as jealousy or genuine confusion about this friendship and what it means to our marriage. If romance does become an issue in friendship, the strain can be considerable because the stakes are high. Trust, fidelity, commitment—even the possibility of love between people—these weighty issues can be called under review. Sensing that these risks are considerable, some married people choose to avoid them by permitting no outside friendships to develop for themselves or for their spouse. But many married people judge that the fear of an affair is not a sufficient reason to cut off themselves and their marriage from the benefits of friends. As we are open to the development of other relationships, we will be sure that we nurture our own. Our commitment in marriage is not to emotional exclusivity but it is a commitment that involves both priority and permanence. And we sense that these goals, priority and permanence, are not "automatic guarantees" of our marriage; they are rather the fruit of a lively relationship. As a part of our own relationship, they are both confidently expected and carefully tended. And we welcome the opportunity for old friendships to continue and new ones to develop throughout our married life.

A frequent pattern of the conventional marriage has been for the one spouse, usually the wife, to give up many of her previous acquaintances when she marries. The couple then develop a shared social world that includes chiefly persons who are part of the husband's network of contacts. Now, as more women work both before and after marriage, there is more opportunity for wives to develop adult contacts on their own. Some of the persons that each spouse meets through work become friends of the couple but others remain a part of the social world of just one of the partners. But the expanded involvement of married women in the larger social world, through employment and volunteer services, has expanded the possibilities of friendship not only for women but for the couple together.

The Network of Support

Friendship brings rich benefits to adults in their marriage. For most of us, our friends stand at the heart of the network of relationships that sustain and support us. It can be useful to look more explicitly at this network of support and its function in marriage for a lifetime.

Our support network includes the persons and resources we need for our marriage to flourish. Through their encouragement and challenge our close friends are central. They understand us, confront us, inspire us, suffer with us—and call us beyond ourselves. And besides, we have such good times with them. For most couples, as we saw in Chapters 9 and 10, the larger family network is also a source of significant support and mutual assistance over the course of their married life. Relationships with family members and in-laws are not without strain, but the evidence from both experience and research is that American families regularly provide for one another a variety of emotional benefits and practical services across the generations. When a

problem arises, most couples turn first to some member of the
family for advice or assistance. In an emergency or catastrophe,
most feel they can count on the family to come to their aid, over
distance and in spite of personal inconvenience, even if there are
troubles or tensions between family members. Many times, then,
relatives become "good friends" as well.

Family and close friends are central to the support network of
most marriages but there are other people who are important as
well. We may find that we need to know other couples who
share our values about marriage, or other parents who are struggling with how to raise teenage children, or other married people approaching retirement. Being with these people in a supportive atmosphere where we can hear their hopes and failures
and share our own, we come away refreshed and recommitted.
Our contacts with them may not have the depth or duration of
close friendship but we benefit from being with them.

There may be an older friend or a former teacher who is important to one or both of us as a confidant and mentor—
someone we can approach with confidence, both in times of joy
and in times of confusion. We may cherish the special relationship we have, as a couple or as a family, with a priest or
religious. At certain times in our marriage we may need the help
of a counselor or family therapist. All of these relationships can
be considered part of the support system of marriage today.

The resources we need for our marriage to flourish may involve my taking an evening class every semester, your partici-
pating in the YWCA handball team, our firm commitment to
spend one weekend afternoon together with the children and
one evening a week together without them. We may find that
the opportunity to pray together is crucial and cannot be left
just to chance.

The supportive network we need may take the form of a community—an identifiable group of people who have important
values and purposes in common. The visible "we" of a community may take shape for us around our religious values and action, and thus become a place for us to pray with others or
where we can express and reinforce our convictions about action
for justice in the world. It may take shape around other values—

being good parents, being responsible citizens, caring for the ecological resources of the world. But community will engage us at the level of our significant values, with people who share these values with us.

These are, obviously, only a few examples of the resources and relationships that enable marriages to flourish today. Couples differ from one another in the resources they bring to marriage and in the ways in which these strengths need to be reinforced or complemented by others. But all couples need support for their marriage, especially in the face of the complexities and confusions in marriage today. Our suggestion here is that as married people we do not have to be embarrassed by this need. We may expect to spend time together in consideration of what kinds of support and stimulation we need and how these resources can be included in our own marriage. We can expect that the shape of our support network will itself develop and change, looking diffcrent at different points in our life together. And finally, we cannot just wait for things to get better or complain that married people are left so much alone. Rather we have to take up the responsibility to provide for ourselves, and perhaps for other married people as well, some of these resources of support that are needed in marriage today.

The Limits of the Nuclear Family

The couple, the family, needs to be tied into the larger world both to contribute to it and to be in touch with the resources they need to draw from it. From the viewpoint of a healthy marriage, it is necessary for the spouses to be engaged with other people at a meaningful level. In addition to the demand that spouses be friends, there are expectations today of the nuclear family that make more difficult this process of engagement beyond ourselves. As Edward Shorter has noted in *The Making of the Modern Family*, the nuclear family describes more a state of mind than a particular pattern of household arrangements. This "state of mind" is a sense of emotional self-sufficiency and solidarity among mcmebers of the immediate family. "We are for one another, and we are *enough* for one another." The ideal is interpreted to mean that immediate family members—parents and their children—hold the privileged place in each other's emotional lives. The priority of these relationships is to be protected against the intrusion of outside interests or loyalties. "As a family we can take care of our own needs. We don't—or shouldn't—need to turn to outsiders." Family privacy and confidentiality are highly valued. "Whatever problems we have in the family should stay in the family"—sometimes to the extent of isolating the family from broader ties and resources.

The family ideal here is of a closed system with tight boundaries. Those inside are bound more closely with each other than with anyone on the outside. Loyalties within the system are stronger than any loyalties a family member might develop beyond. And family members expect that whatever needs arise, especially emotional needs, these should be met by the resources of the other people within this family system. To have to go "outside" is to admit some kind of basic inadequacy as a family. This sense of the family has obvious strengths but also problems.

This "togetherness" image of the ideal family has been reinforced by another understanding of what the family is for in society. Family life and, by inference, marriage has been seen as a place of refuge from alienation and conflict in the world beyond. The family is a safe haven from the brutal, uncaring or at least utilitarian relationships that characterize the public arena, especially the workplace. This emotionally protective role of family life has become an ideal in terms of which one's own marriage is to be evaluated. To the extent that we are together as a family, with strong and exclusive emotional commitments to one another, our marriage and family life are "good."

Experience, however, often says otherwise. Each couple or family seems to have an optimum range of togetherness. There is usually some flexibility in this pattern over time but at any point in our relationship there is likely to be a balance of being together and being alone that is best for us. Some couples seem to be able to sense the rhythm of privacy and togetherness that works best for them; others may need to work out explicit patterns of physical or emotional separateness. It may be a pattern of time apart: we each take time alone when we get home from work, before we have an evening meal together. Or I want to take my vacation just on my own this year or you really need an evening a week away from home with other friends. There may be a network of people with whom I share interests that my spouse and I do not have in common—hobbies, political involvement, volunteer work.

Separation often serves to lessen some of the inevitable strains in the intense relationship of marriage. Separation also leaves room for and supports family members in their engagement in the larger world. This engagement can distract from marriage and family commitments but need not have this damaging effect. Widening our participation in the world beyond our marriage can, instead, ease the burden that our relationship bears. Our marriage no longer carries the weight of the full emotional agenda of each spouse. Beyond this, our involvement in action and commitment beyond our marriage invites us into the public world of values and social purpose.

Marriage benefits from the partners' engagement in concerns bigger than just themselves. This benefit is not usually the motive for the couple's involvement but it is a frequent result. People need to be for more than themselves. In Chapter 14 we examined the processes of personal growth and maturity that bring people to this point of wanting to, and being able to, move beyond themselves in activity and concern. Similar movements are seen in relationships. A maturing marriage moves beyond itself, not only in children but in engagement with and concern for the larger world. Some marriages do this in quiet ways. Our strong sense of hospitality makes people feel genuinely welcomed when they are with us, even if it is only for a short time. Another family decides together to give their time and goods to help out a neighboring family in an emergency. In some marriages the contribution beyond is more dramatic. A couple takes up a life of witness and service in a developing country. The family buys a home in an interracial neighborhood as a part of their commitment to social justice. Family members decide to join a wider fellowship of people who are committed to simplicity in lifestyle and sharing their financial resources with the poor. It is possible, of course, to find examples of couples whose outside activities seem to be mainly a way to avoid having to deal with each other. But this sense of involvement with a larger world and commitment to its well-being is more often a sign of vitality within the marriage itself. And it is a movement of self-transcendence.

Self-transcendence is admittedly an abstract and, even, grandiose term. Yet it describes movements we have known in our own marriages. As spouses, as parents, we pour ourselves out for people and concerns that go beyond us. We find ourselves challenged to contribute to projects, the benefits of which are not chiefly ours to enjoy. Our children are especially important here. As we care for them and for the future that shall be theirs, we are drawn out of ourselves and our own, more limited, present. We come to care for a world beyond us, a future in which we shall not directly share. We less frequently ask the question "What's in it for me?" as we focus on what is good for them. And, as we become more broadly generative, even our experience of "us" is expanded. More than our immediate family, more than those "like me" as white, or Catholic, or middle-class, "us" comes to mean all of us. This expanded awareness of who is "like me" will have differing results. For some, it will mean a new concern for what is going on in our neighborhood; for others, a new enthusiasm for work in the parish; for others, an interest in making a contribution to the good of the world. In every case it is an expansion of our concern beyond ourselves, and even our nuclear family, to care for others and the future. For Christians, this movement of self-transcendence finds resonance in the gospel's paradoxical challenge to our family loyalty.

The Family and the New Testament

When, as Christians, we turn to the gospel for insight and wisdom about the meaning and purpose of family life, we may be surprised. Instead of affirming the importance of the family, Jesus repeatedly challenges his friends to reevaluate the boundaries of their families in the light of new values. In Mark, Matthew and Luke this challenge is emphatic.

In Chapter 3 of Mark's gospel, Jesus is preaching and healing when his mother and brothers arrive. When he is told that they are present, Jesus asks:

> "Who are my mother and my brothers?" And looking around at those sitting in a circle about him, he said, "Here are my mother and my brothers. Anyone who does the will of God, that person is my brother and sister and mother" (Mark 3:33–35).

This remark might be regarded as overly enthusiastic rhetoric were it not reinforced in other sayings of Jesus. In Chapter 10 of Matthew's gospel we are confronted with a much more forceful questioning of the ultimate value of the family. The atmosphere of this chapter is apocalyptic. There is an urgency in the air; the end may be near and people will have to stand up for what they believe. In this mood Jesus calls his friends to a radical discipleship, to follow their deepest convictions no matter the price.

> Do not suppose that I have come to bring peace to the earth; it is not peace I have come to bring, but a sword. For I have come to set a man against his father, a daughter against her mother, and a daughter-in-law against her mother-in-law. A man's enemies will be those of his own household (Matthew 10:34–36).

A household, a family, is not an absolutely secure place. Christians may be called to choices which put them in conflict with their own families. The text in Matthew continues:

> Anyone who prefers father or mother to me is not worthy of me. Anyone who prefers son or daughter to me is not worthy of me. Anyone who does not take his cross and follow in my footsteps is not worthy of me. Anyone who finds his life will lose it, and anyone who loses his life for my sake will find it (Matthew 10:37–39).

This call to follow Jesus and his values is echoed in Luke's gospel. Fidelity to the values of Christian living may conflict with loyalty even to our own family. Robert Bellah has observed that the presence of "God the Father" in Christianity challenges, for the Christian, the absolute authority of parents as well as political leaders. A human family's absolute importance and centrality is questioned and overturned by Jesus.

This religious questioning of the family's self-sufficiency and importance is reiterated in Chapter 14 of Luke. Jesus tells his surprised dinner host:

> When you give a lunch or a dinner, do not ask your friends, brothers, relations or rich neighbors, for fear they repay your courtesy by inviting you in return. No, when you have a party invite the poor, the crippled, the lame, the blind; that they cannot pay you back means that you are fortunate, because repayment will be made to you when the virtuous rise again (Luke 14:12–14).

A radical following of Jesus breaks the boundaries between families and the distinctions between mine and yours. A new order of community, breaking through family and class lines, invites us to a different sense of those to whom we belong.

Finally, Jesus observes another limitation of the natural family. Those who had watched Jesus grow up, who knew his relatives, "just knew" he could not be a prophet or teacher. He was "the kid down the block." To these people Jesus declares: "A prophet is only despised in his own country, among his own relations and in his own house" (Mark 6:4). The familiarity of families can blind us to each other's gifts, can provide narrow and restricting expectations. Families, meant to foster growth, at times cripple it.

The sayings of Jesus about the human family are confusing and challenging. Their revelation today may be addressing the nuclear family in its temptations toward self-sufficiency, isolation and privacy. As we struggle to develop caring and healthy families, we are reminded that we belong to a larger family whose members come from different cultures, races and economic classes. This broader Christian and human community challenges us to move beyond the confines of our biological family. Such self-transcendence becomes a part of the expectable discipline not only for the individual Christian but for our marriage and our family as well.

Reflective Exercise

To explore involvement "beyond the partner," it may be helpful to chart a diagram of the important relationships in your life, as an individual and then as a couple. Begin with yourself, listing those persons whom you would include among your own close friends, those whose relationship of sharing and support are significant in your life now. Then add those other relationships, close or more casual, which have been regularly a part of your life over, say, the past several years or so.

Next draw a chart that represents in some way the relative significance of these relationships to you at this point in your life. Use your own sense of what "significance" means for you; there is no one "correct" meaning of the term here. And don't be too concerned with the artistic quality of the chart!

Then you may wish to compare your list and chart with that of your spouse. Take time initially for each of you to explain your own chart; then look for similarities and differences between you. Give some time to the question of how satisfied you each are with the current patterns of your involvement beyond the family. You may wish to plan for some personal or joint action to expand or change these patterns.

Additional Resources

Marjorie Fiske and Lawrence Weiss draw from psychological research and theory in their examination of the role of friendship as a resource in adult development in "Intimacy and Crisis in Adulthood," which appears in the valuable collection of essays *Counseling Adults* (Brooks/Cole, 1977), edited by Nancy Schlossberg and Alan Entine. Paula Ripple discusses the central significance of friendship in adult life in *Called to Be Friends* (Ave Maria Press, 1980). For an expanded discussion of support network and community, see Evelyn Eaton Whitehead's "Ministers Need Three Communities" in the July 28, 1978, issue of

National Catholic Reporter and "Clarifying the Meaning of Community" in the Fall 1978 issue of *Living Light*.

The adequacy of the "nuclear family" as a description or explanation of the American family life is under serious question today. A. F. Uzoka, for example, explores the historical background of the development of the nuclear family as a concept for understanding family organization and functioning in "The Myth of the Nuclear Family" in the November 1979 issue of *American Psychologist*. He discusses ways in which this analytic concept, now become an ideal, influences the clinical practice of many persons attempting to assist marriages and families, with more negative than positive result. Peter Berger and Richard Neuhaus underscore the function of the family as a mediating structure in public life in their provocative discussion *To Empower People* (American Enterprise Institute, 1977).

Robert Bellah's illuminating exploration of "God the Father" in Christianity as a challenge to the ultimate authority of the human family and also of the civil state is found in the essay "Father and Son in Christianity and Confucianism" in his *Beyond Belief* (Harper & Row, 1970).

20

DIVORCE AND CHRISTIAN MATURING

A reflection on Christian marriage cannot be silent on Christian divorce. Its sudden frequency (the rate of divorce in the United States doubled between 1966 and 1976) frightens both those approaching marriage and those living this life commitment. More than a psychological and social failure, divorce for Catholics has long been understood as a religious impossibility. Yet today many American Catholics sense they are receiving mixed messages from the Church, in the dramatic increase in marriage annulments granted over the past decade. Is the Church changing its understanding of divorce? If it is, does this represent a loss of conviction or is it a result of a deepening religious insight?

We will examine the contemporary phenomenon of divorce in three parts. First, by reflecting on the very different experiences grouped under this word "divorce" we will attempt to clarify the questions that must be faced. Second, we will analyze the structure of divorce as a crisis of intimacy; this will begin to suggest the shape of an effective ministry to this painful experience. Finally, we will discuss Christian responses to divorce. Here we will reexamine traditional Catholic convictions as well as contemporary insights concerning divorce and religious maturing.

The Varieties of Divorce

Matching the deception of the single word "marriage"—one word used to refer to a whole range of significantly different ways of being together—is the deception of the word "divorce." The failure of a marriage may result from desertion or physical violence; it may also arise as the only solution to what moral theologians describe as an "intolerable marriage." The common element in these very diverse experiences of marital failure is the ending of a powerful hope. In every divorce a life ambition and promise ends. How and when a marriage relationship ends gives to each experience of divorce its own special significance. Only as we clarify these different hows and whens can we understand the causes of divorce and the shape of a more effective ministry to it.

Divorce in Premature Marriage

One useful way to distinguish the varieties of divorce is to discriminate between "premature marriages" and "matured marriages." By a premature marriage we signify a marital commitment chosen by a very young person or one chosen abruptly, with little preparation. These kinds of marriages can, of course, survive and mature. Yet quite often they do not. The likelihood of divorce is twice as great for men marrying before they are twenty than for men marrying in their late twenties; divorce is twice as likely for women marrying before they are eighteen than for women marrying in their early twenties. The younger the age of those entering marriage, the less likely they are to have the self-awareness and resilience required for this complex relationship. Having had less time and experience to gain the strengths demanded in marriage, such a young person—and this youthfulness may be chronological or psychological—may more likely marry for simply external reasons. I marry because others my age are marrying or because my parents expect me to marry.

Or I marry hoping that in the mirror of my partner I may learn who I am. I may marry in order to have a child and so prove my worth and value. Premature marriages often follow premarital pregnancy; a relatively high percentage of such marriages also end in divorce.

A second type of premature marriage is the hasty marriage. A whirlwind courtship following "love at first sight" propels a couple into a life commitment. Such a marriage leaps over the gradual process of learning about intimacy and exploring the roots of deeper compatibility, placing extra burdens on the marriage itself. We are hardly surprised when such a marriage flounders, when the mutual exploration and negotiation of marriage reveal that the partners are not so ideally suited for each other after all. The transition from romance to post-romantic intimacy does not happen and the couple are soon parted.

Premature marriages are not doomed; they are simply quite hazardous. An encouraging trend is discernible in America today: after more than a half century of a descent in the age of those entering marriage (twenty-six years for men and twenty-two years for women in 1890; twenty-two and a half for men and twenty for women in 1956), the age of Americans at first marriage has begun to rise. In 1976 the average age for a man entering marriage was almost twenty-four years and for women it was over twenty-one; since then, the age has continued to climb. Both the hazards of early marriage and the other opportunities for the young adult (extended education for both men and women and increased employment possibilities for women) are gradually influencing the rate of early marriages.

How can the Christian community better care for its young adults in regard to premature marriages? We will examine the Church's ministry in more detail later in this chapter but here we might note that one ministry is to lessen the pressure to marry. A caring community, with its own experience and maturity as its greatest resource, will help its young to see marriage as a life choice but not a "solution." Marriage will not magically resolve loneliness or establish one's worth. Marriage will not automatically deliver me from my parents' control or provide sexual liberation and enjoyment. A Christian community that can,

honestly and forcefully, remind its young people of these truths
gives them the benefit of its own religious wisdom.

Another Christian response to premature marriages might be
to distinguish marriage and the sacrament of Matrimony. Catholic ministers and theologians today are discussing the difference
between marriage as an almost universal cultural choice and the
religious commitment of the sacrament of Christian Matrimony.
Have we not allowed these two choices to become indistinguishable? A legalistic view of Christian marriage has permitted
us to see Baptism—apart from the person's psychological and
religious maturity—as the sole requirement for the sacrament of
Matrimony. And while the legal right to marry is not in question, today we recognize that not every marriage is a sacrament,
a mature commitment of practically believing Christians. The
problems inherent in such a distinction between marriage and
Matrimony are many. Chief among these is the possibility of an
elitist view of marriage: the sacrament of Matrimony becomes a
reward for a life well lived, or for those with greater religious
sophistication. But this distinction could be observed without
urging a discrimination between "first-class" and "second-class"
Christians. For example, a religious blessing could be available
to a young marriage, signifying it as more than a "trial" marriage
or a merely secular event. Yet such a marriage would not be understood as a sacrament. The sacrament of Matrimony would be
available to this couple later in their marriage, as a celebration
of a tested and more mature commitment.

All these are indirect ministries to premature marriages. The
traditional response of the Catholic Church in annulment also
belongs here. In annulling a marriage the Church says that a sacramental marriage has not happened. Some essential element of
this sacrament is found to be lacking, be that personal freedom
or the psychological capacity for a mature commitment. In premature marriages this approach makes much sense. The annulment process reveals that one or both of the partners lacked the
substance of such a life commitment; significant immaturity or
lack of commitment blocked the religious development of this
marriage. The Church's traditional ministry of annulment seems
best limited to such examples of premature marriages. And more

effective than this retroactive ministry will be the efforts we make in our faith communities to provide for our young people other options for intimacy and personal growth. With less external pressure to marry, they may come to trust their own schedule of growth and postpone marriage until it fits both their best hopes and their psychological and religious resources.

Divorce in Matured Marriage

Another category of divorce among Christians, one with more complications, is that of divorce in a "matured marriage." By this phrase we mean a marriage that has survived for some time. Whether marrying young or not, such a couple has shared a life together of some considerable duration. Their life together has matured, at least chronologically. Patterns of interaction—of loving, arguing, making decisions—have been well established. Such a marriage has also, very likely, begun and nurtured a family.

Within this category of marriage the variations are, of course, enormous. Such a marriage may have been experienced over many years as satisfying and life-giving. Or it may have been just tolerated: with no alternatives available (for economic, psychological or religious reasons), the marriage simply endured. In some of these matured marriages, a significant change occurs which threatens or precipitates divorce. Some changes are obvious and painful, as when a partner deserts his or her partner and family. Or violence becomes a part of the relationship: a pattern of physical or psychological abuse of the spouse or the children effectively breaks the love commitment. Historically, a woman often had no alternative to such a broken but continuing relationship. Catholic teaching reinforced the endurance of such a marriage, arguing that the evil of divorce was greater than the impact of violence or a loveless marriage on the spouse and children.

Today a clearer understanding of the destructiveness of such a marriage has made us more aware of those situations in which a person may have a moral obligation to divorce. Many Catholic theologians and ministers argue that other goods outweigh the good of such a marriage commitment and that fidelity as a Christian virtue extends to more than the marriage bond. Fidelity to oneself and to one's children may require ending such a marriage. As a matured marriage, this relationship has been a genuine Christian commitment. But it has died. Annulment does not fit such an event; some more effective and honest ministry is required.

The examples of the end of a matured marriage that we have just given, those involving desertion or violence, are the clearest instances of the need for divorce. More often divorce is threatened by more subtle changes in a marriage. A couple may come to realize, after eight or eighteen or twenty-eight years of marriage, that they have grown in very different directions or at quite different speeds. The decades during which your career has consumed so much of your time and energy have seen you grow into certain ways of thinking and feeling. During these years I have been equally consumed and distracted by the demands of our children and our home. Gradually or abruptly, we recognize that we have become intimate strangers. We think and feel differently—and have done so for a long time. Somewhere in our past, two paths diverged in the journey of our marriage. Unwittingly, unconsciously, we have been traveling apart from each other. No single event can be isolated; no deliberately sinful act seems to have turned us away from each other; no sexual infidelity divides us. But we are, suddenly perhaps, miles apart.

The threat of divorce in such an instance is quite different than in a premature marriage. In this example of a matured marriage, the couple has a long history of survival together. With more resources at their disposal, they have a better chance to heal their relationship and begin the journey back toward each other. Their crisis of intimacy and fidelity can be an opportunity to grow and to improve a stagnant marriage.

But, experience teaches us, this is not always the outcome. Sometimes a couple find they are too far apart, too different in ambition and conviction, to recover from this danger. Sometimes a marriage dies. The couple likely neither foresaw nor planned such an ending. The Christian community mourns this death, both for the individuals and because this threatens the stability and survival of the believing community. The Catholic Church has until recently been especially reluctant to face this death in its midst. It has argued that only sin and selfishness can lead to divorce. Selfishness and sin are certainly involved in many divorces: where are these absent in our own ambiguous lives? Yet more complex changes in individuals and between married couples can lead to the necessity of divorce. We regret and grieve for this, but our regret will not annul it.

Divorce happens, even between couples who have for many years shared a life and struggled for fidelity and maturity. What does this mean when the couple are Catholics? Is there something called a Catholic divorce? How can divorce be a Christian decision?

Traditionally, the Catholic Church's ministry to failed marriages has been one of either annulling or dissolving. Dissolving a marriage was possible when it could be shown that this sacramental commitment had not been fully completed or consummated. Since this situation pertained to few marriages, annulment remained the chief remedy. In annulling a marriage, the Church declares that the marriage did not legally exist. In a premature marriage, where a life commitment has not been fully and maturely undertaken, annulment is an accurate and proper response. For a marriage between Catholics which has survived and grown for many years, annulment is often experienced as both a religious fiction and an insult. Such a marriage has happened and has been genuine . . . and has died. Catholics are challenged today to understand divorce as neither an impossibility nor simply as a failure of fidelity. When, after much effort and reflection, a divorce is necessary and marital fidelity has ended, a divorcing person must be helped to survive, psychologically and religiously. Religious fidelity—to God, to oneself and to one's children—must survive the death of a marriage. Before examining the Catholic Church's rapidly changing understanding of divorce and its ministry to this painful part of contemporary life, it will help to explore the structure of divorce as a crisis and passage of intimacy.

Divorce—A Crisis of Intimacy

If divorce means such different things to different people, does it have any common elements or structure? What are its most expectable challenges and distresses? As we clarify these, we will move toward more effective care for divorcing members of our community. As we turn to this exploration, it may be necessary again to acknowledge the conviction that divorce is a frightening experience of failure and loss. It should never happen; yet it does. Sometimes a divorce results from selfish, sinful behavior; often it is due to more complex psychological and social reasons.

In developmental psychology the word "crisis" refers to a period of significant change and decision in human life. As a time of decision, a crisis is a period of both opportunity and vulnerability. Some of the crises of married life are expectable, "on the schedule" of a maturing relationship. The advent of the first child, for example, will likely induce a crisis of intimacy: with the appearance of a demanding third person in our midst, we are challenged to find new and different ways of being together. Patterns of lovemaking, recreation and work will all have to be adjusted. This is a critical period because a couple's response to these changes can lead to a matured intimacy or to an increasing distance between them. The death of one's spouse is another expectable, "scheduled" crisis in marriage, anticipated by many women in their fifties and older. Research in developmental psychology reveals that for many married women, this anticipation or "rehearsal" prepares them to deal with this critical time and the adjustments and decisions that will be required.

Divorce, traditionally, has not been an expectable crisis in marriage. It has not been on the schedule of a life of marital intimacy. That is changing. With the enormous increase in divorce in the last two decades, it is difficult for a couple not to be aware of this possibility for their own marriage. This awareness itself can be crippling or salutary. We may give ourselves only

t the pain that
ness of divorce
re attentive and
gile relationship
threat.

o resolve a prior
ognize that their
, they may strug-
Changing the pat-
nful, they may re-
tion within their
t be, or is not, re-
sically or psycho-
e revived. To some
olution. When this
rce become, them-

decision. It is a time
erability are present
her the birth of the
or a divorce—is in-
uch a crisis the deci-
f some cherished or
Some specific way of
life together may be threatened, o... tionship itself may be seen as dying. Because divorce entails the loss of the marriage itself, it is likely to be an especially traumatic crisis of intimacy. (This may not be the case when the divorce is a freeing and even exhilarating termination of a relationship long dead.) An accustomed, even if no longer cherished, way of life is being lost. A life commitment of intimacy has failed. We lose not only a partner but a sense of ourselves as capable lovers and companions, as able to sustain a significant relationship. At the heart of this crisis we are likely to experience profound failure, mixed with guilt, blame and anger. An enormously important part of our life has come to an end; where do we go from here? Having failed at this love commitment, are we simply a failure? What chance have we of making another relationship survive?

But a crisis is not only a psychological experience. It is, for Christians, a powerful religious event. Crises are, for a believer, potentially holy times, times of special encounter with God. Christian teaching fails us when it suggests that encounters with God are reserved for "special" holy persons or limited to church-sponsored events. Most of us sense that we encounter God most powerfully in periods of personal crises, when we are being purified, stripped of some part of ourselves. Adult crises, and especially divorce, can be such an opportunity. Divorcing persons die both to their marriage and to much of their sense of ability and worth. Further, divorce is a social event: the person dies publicly. But in this disturbing event are extraordinary opportunities for new life. In such an ending, whatever its failure and sin, lie possibilities for new beginnings. When a divorce is judged, after careful reflection, to be unavoidable, a person is invited not only to let go a former way of life but also to begin a process of reconciliation. Such a reconciliation—with one's divorced partner if possible, but necessarily with oneself—is the central part of the movement that will resolve this crisis.

Perhaps the greatest disservice of the Catholic Church's more conventional stance regarding divorce has been its neglect of this religious potential. Seeming to suggest that God could not be at work in such an event, the Church's official ministry has forced many Catholics to face this crisis alone. By denying the possibility of divorce and of remarriage, the Church gave divorce the appearance of an unforgivable sin. Divorce was a religious dead end: it could lead nowhere and could not be part of a Catholic's religious journey with God.

The religious potential that is a part of this crisis of intimacy can be illumined by a reflection on divorce as a religious passage. A passage is a complex transition with many of the characteristics of a crisis: it is a time of disorientation and vulnerability accompanied by a loss of some cherished possession; a person struggles to *come through* this period into a new stage of psychological and religious maturity.

The transition of divorce entails three different passages. Divorce is a legal passage, negotiated through lawyers and courts; one enters this passage as a married person and emerges as a single person. But divorce is also a psychological and religious passage. We can negotiate the legal passage of divorce without getting through the psychological transition. Too wounded by this loss, I may retreat into myself, convinced I am a failure at love. I do not come through the passage into a new place, healed and restored; I settle down in this passage and stop growing. Instead of coming through, I am overcome.

Another way that I can fail to negotiate the psychological passage of divorce is to refuse the self-assessment and reconciliation (at least with myself) to which divorce invites me. Frightened by the silence in my life or confused by the loneliness, I may plunge hurriedly into another marriage. I marry "on the rebound." Instead of patiently confronting my marital failure and sorting out its causes, I turn to another marriage to take away the pain. With too little learned from the first marriage, the second marriage may experience similar pain and even a similar fate.

Christians believe that in such a significant psychological passage God is present, inviting us forward with special graces and opportunities. In the dynamic of our psychological growth (even through failure and sin) God's grace purifies and matures us. In the religious passage of divorce we are stripped of our confidence and our public success at marriage. We die to an important part of our life. Drawn into the darkness of this passage, we are invited to examine its core: to confess our responsibility (whatever it may be) without debilitating guilt; to acknowledge our partner's responsibility without vindictive blame. In short, a divorcing Christian is called to a passage of reconciliation: this includes sorrow, repentance and forgiveness. It includes, in the Christian dynamic of growth, dying and beginning to live again. Such a passage of pain and grace will leave a person wounded but not crippled. The scars of divorce will make a Christian more sober about intimacy and marriage but will not mark the person as unmarriable. These scars, signs of injury and healing, are not so different from the other scars that mark the body of Christian believers.

What are the signs that a person has come through the psychological and religious passage of divorce? One sign is a clearer

sense of what has happened: the confusion of anger and guilt
has been replaced by some understanding and acceptance of this
part of my life. A sense of forgiveness, of my partner and myself,
begins to grow. More aware of my specific weaknesses (in communicating feelings, or dealing with conflict, or in dependency)
and of the strengths I have and those I need to develop, I gain
an enthusiasm for building new relationships. An important sign
that this passage has been traversed is the absence of our need
to use the children to hurt or defeat each other; thus the grace
of our successful passage is visited on our children.

Divorce, then, has the structure of a crisis and a passage of intimacy. Traditionally an unexpectable and unscheduled crisis, it
has appeared for many Christians as a disguised passage. Personal embarrassment and shame, reinforced by the Church's limited ministry, has kept this passage private. Divorcing Catholics
went their own way, without the rites of passage necessary for
such a dangerous transition. Ministry in the Catholic Church has
only recently begun to develop these rites of passage for divorce.
It has done so as it has been able to acknowledge that God is at
work in this painful crisis of intimacy.

Christian Responses to Divorce

Catholics have sometimes come to believe that their religious
tradition has had only one unchanging response to divorce. Yet
this rich and long tradition has provided many and varying responses. Jesus' own response was to alter the Jewish laws about
divorce. He proposed an ideal of married love and commitment
that would survive every threat and failure. Jesus responds to
those who ask about Moses' allowances for divorce, "What God
has united, man must not divide." When questioned further by
his own disciples, Jesus expands: "The man who divorces his
wife and marries another is guilty of adultery against her. And if
a woman divorces her husband and marries another she is guilty
too" (Mark 10:11–12).

Yet even within the gospels themselves we find a reinterpretation of this ideal: "And I say to you, whoever divorces his wife,

except for unchastity, and marries another, commits adultery" (Matthew 19:9). In his discussion of "New Testament Perspectives on Marriage and Divorce," biblical scholar George MacRae observes that this sentence "seems to reflect a modification within the Matthean community of the absoluteness of Jesus' prohibition" (p. 40). If the Matthean community found it necessary to adapt the saying of Jesus, so did St. Paul. In his first letter to the Corinthians, Paul urged Christians not to seek divorces. But this rule had an exception: if a Christian is married to a non-believer who seeks a divorce, the Christian is free to remarry (I Corinthians 7:15). This exception, which came to be called the "Pauline privilege," sets higher value on the believer's faith than on the bonds of a marriage in which faith is not an integral part. As MacRae notes, two of the five central New Testament passages on divorce (in addition to the three cited in this paragraph he includes Matthew 5:32 and Luke 16:18) show a reinterpretation or adaptation of Jesus' ideal of lifelong marriage. From the outset, then, we have been struggling in the Christian tradition to combine an extraordinary ideal of permanence in marriage with the reality of our complex social lives.

Marriage and divorce continued to be reinterpreted in the first centuries of the Christian tradition. Bishops and communities differed in their understanding of legitimate reasons for divorce. During these first centuries divorce was not yet formally an ecclesiastical matter; it consisted of the act of repudiation of a spouse. John Noonan, in *Divorce and Remarriage in the Catholic Church,* paraphrases one opinion from these early debates: "unilaterally deciding that the *causa adulterii,* ground of adultery, is present, the husband lawfully dismisses, acting as the surrogate of God" (p. 30). Only in the sixth century did the Church begin to establish tribunals where the validity and dissolvability of Christians' marriages would be judged.

In the Celtic Church in the sixth and seventh centuries, a period of extraordinary social upheaval, pastoral provisions for divorce were developed to cover a variety of extreme situations. The break in a marriage occasioned by a partner being lost in war, or entering a monastery, or when one partner was freed from slavery seemed to call for special dispensation. This pasto-

ral principle, developed in a time of turmoil, found lasting expression in the Orthodox Church as the principle of "economy"
(*oikonomia*). In his article in *Ministering to the Divorced Catholic* Lewis Patsavos summarizes the attitude toward divorce in
this part of the Christian tradition: "The Church recognizes divorce in the case of unbearable marital relationships, which she
equates with physical death" (p. 52). This acknowledgment that
marriages can and do die buttresses rather than compromises the
Orthodox regard for Christian marriage:

> Marriage is held in such an exalted degree that a deterioration of
> its sanctifying quality is regarded as intolerable. The moral disin-
> tegration caused thereby thus warrants the means of arresting
> the spread of spiritual decay (p. 52).

Differences among Christian bodies concerning marriage and
divorce were heightened by the Protestant Reformation of the
sixteenth century. Protestant theologians and ministers, reacting
to both the Catholic Church's theology and its political control
of marriage, argued that matrimony was not a sacrament and
that it was not absolutely indissoluble. Since that time bitter
differences and institutional pride have split Catholics and Protestants: as a result, many Catholics remain unable to accept the
pastoral values that permit the dissolving of certain marriages
and many Protestants remain deprived of the richness of a sacramental understanding of Christian marriage.

As the Catholic Church enters the last decades of the twentieth century it is again challenged to interpret the ideal of Christian marriage in the light of contemporary experience. Powerful
reforms in canon law and in Catholic theology itself are assisting
this interpretation. But its success will depend on our ability to
change, to be confident that God is at work in the present as
surely as in our past. The constant reflection and revision that
have consistently been a part of our two-thousand-year-and-
longer tradition have, for many, been masked by the relative rigidity of Catholic practice between the Reformation and the
Second Vatican Council.

Of the many historical developments in Christian reflection on
marriage and divorce, perhaps the most significant has been the

transformation of the religious ideal of a lifelong marriage into an absolute, philosophical reality. As Christian faith spread and became gradually shaped into "Christendom"—an international political and legal organization—legal considerations in Church life began to outweigh pastoral approaches. The scriptural image of marriage as a covenant, a personal and mutual commitment of love and devotion, began to be replaced by the image of marriage as a contract. This clearer, less ambiguous image presented Christian marriage as essentially a non-negotiable legal agreement. This contract was sealed, legally and forever, in the biological act of sexual intercourse.

The necessary flexibility of the Christian ideal of marriage was lost in this legalistic interpretation. The permanence of Christian marriage shifted from the status of an exciting and empowering ideal to that of a metaphysical reality. We came to judge that a Christian marriage, properly begun, could not end. The religious ideal of "should not" had become the legal reality of "can not." The rigid pastoral practice that resulted from this legalism has been experienced by many Catholics. For many, it has been a practice that had little affinity with the tone of the gospel of Jesus Christ. Happily, since Vatican II the Catholic Church is reforming its canon law of marriage and complementing its legal theory with a more lively theology and spirituality of Christian marriage. Before turning to the threefold ministry that this reform has initiated, we will review one other important historical development that has threatened the gracefulness of the Church's ministry to marriage and divorce.

From at least the time of the prophet Hosea in the eighth century before Christ, Jews and Christians have related the ideal of lasting marital fidelity to the image of Yahweh's unending fidelity with Israel. The marriagelike fidelity between Yahweh and Israel was translated by the first Christians as the relationship between Christ and the Church. A powerful, triple relationship emerged around the religious ideal of fidelity:

YAHWEH	CHRIST	HUSBAND
↕	↕	↕
ISRAEL	CHURCH	WIFE

As evocative as these comparisons were, they did have their limitations. The first two relationships exist between God and humans; they are non-mutual and, with God as one of the partners, unbreakable. If we confess one God, where else might we go? Even if we are religiously unfaithful, we have but one place, one God to whom to return. The human relationship of marriage is, of course, quite different. Marriage may strive for the unending fidelity of the Yahweh/Israel and Christ/Church relationship. But both partners of a marriage relationship are human, frail and limited; both are like Israel and the Church, rather than Yahweh and Christ.

Another obvious limitation to these comparisons is their hierarchical structure: Yahweh, Christ and the husband are superior; Israel, the Church and the wife are inferior. If sinfulness in the relationship can only be introduced from the side of Israel and the Church, the subtle suggestion can be that sinfulness in marriage is introduced (most likely) by the wife. This particular limitation of these images of fidelity was less obvious in a patriarchal period when men were assumed to be stronger and even more God-like. In the late twentieth century this limitation stands out in bold relief.

To fully identify religious fidelity—keeping faith with God— with the lifelong survival of a marriage is theologically wrong and pastorally harmful. Unfortunately, this has been and continues to be done. In 1930 in his letter on Christian marriage Pope Pius XI argued that divorce is impossible because the Church "may never be divorced from Him [Christ]." Marital failure is compared with apostasy, "withdrawing as it were from marriage with Christ." In his visit to the United States in the fall of 1979, Pope John Paul II reiterated this complete identification of religious fidelity and marital indissolubility: "The covenant between a man and a woman joined in Christian marriage is as indissoluble and irrevocable as God's love for His people and Christ's love for His Church." The survival of a marriage may be assisted by urging a couple to a fidelity that is *like* God's unending faithfulness with us. But the ending of a Christian marriage is not necessarily the ending of religious faith (though the Church's ministry has, in the past, helped this to be a fact). Divorce is not apostasy. The failure of the human relationship of marriage can and often does lead to a growth in religious faith. This fact does not lead us to encourage divorce or neglect marriage; it does remind us that marital fidelity and religious faithfulness are not identical. The historical comparison of marital and religious fidelity, once so empowering, has come to be a much less useful image. Images are a central part of Christian life; they partly reveal (even as they partly hide) the movements of God in our world. But images are creatures with creaturely limits. To cling to an image, often by making a metaphor into a literal, unambiguous law, comes close to idolatry. A hardened image, turned into an idol, may tell us where God used to be, but also likely distracts us from God's movement today. These two historical developments, the turning of the religious ideal of a lifelong marriage into a legalistic absolute and the identifying of marital fidelity with religious faithfulness, stand today as obstacles to the Catholic Church's healing of its ministry to marriage and divorce.

A Threefold Ministry to Marriage and Divorce

A Ministry of Reform

The first and most basic ministry that faces the Catholic Church in the 1980s is a ministry to itself. This is a ministry of healing and purifying those of its structures that have become rigid and sinful. This is not an especially scandalous stance once we recognize that the Church is both divine and human, that it is a human community but one that God will not leave. This purification of its own structures is always demanded of the Church, but it is required of the Church in regard to marriage and divorce in specific ways today. There must be a theological healing: legalistic biases about absolute indissolubility as well as images that suggest a parallel between God and husband and between sinful Israel and sinful wife need purification. This healing is well under way. Other changes in the Church are contributing to this theological reassessment. One such change is the healing of the still considerable gap between clergy and laity. This long-endured break must be quickly mended, not only because it works out among Catholics as a separation of unmarried and married, but because it enshrines an unsupportable distinction between the "teaching Church" and the "learning Church." The 1980 synod of Catholic bishops on "The Role of the Christian Family in the World Today" included laity and married Catholics as observers, but not as active participants. Certainly one does not have to be married to understand and care effectively for marriage; but a Church which takes seriously its deepest values of mutuality and servanthood must include all segments of the community in its deliberations, decisions and ministry.

Accompanying the theological reform and the healing of the political division between clergy and laity, there will be administrative changes in the tribunal system which treats divorce cases. Happily, this reform too is already begun. Increasingly, pastoral care is assuming a larger role than legal clarification. The ministers of this system (still, in the main, clergy but with some married persons gradually becoming involved) are beginning to understand themselves as facilitators of a religious process instead of judges in a legal proceeding. The next step may be to locate these tribunals more thoroughly in the communities where Christian faith is lived. Ministry in the Catholic Church, once so profoundly separated from the community (by isolated seminaries and a distant hierarchy), is slowly returning to its home. Part of this return will be to locate the Church's ministry to those divorcing in their own communities. The inclusion of lay ministers in the tribunal and greater attention to the couple's own judgment about the viability of their marriage will, expectably, accompany this change. For many Catholics today, the tribunal system is the human face of the Church at the diocesan level: it is here that a divorcing person meets Christ or fails to. It is here that the person learns how the high ideals of Catholic life are matched by a Christ-like care and concern.

A Ministry of Prevention

The Church's ministry to its own structure must be complemented by a more effective *preventive* ministry concerning divorce. This is a ministry to Christian marriage which makes divorce a less likely and less necessary consequence to marriage. As we have discussed several places elsewhere in this book, an effective ministry of marriage preparation is vital. Three specifics of this ministry may bear repeating. First, Christians have to announce what can sound scandalous in our culture: not everyone need marry. Marriage is not an automatic or universal choice for every adult. Certain of us thrive, certain careers are to be pursued, apart from marriage. Not only does our tradition of celibacy remind us of this, but the holy lives—both generous and satisfying—of so many unmarried lay Catholics attest to this option in adult life. If marriage is not to be a part of my own vocation and life, it is best to discover this prior to marriage rather than as a result of it. By announcing this truth, so disconcerting (at least until recently) in a culture such as our own, the Church ministers both to marriage and, indirectly, to divorce. Second, the Church's ministry to marriage might more emphatically urge the delay of marriages. A high percentage of very young marriages end in divorce; hastily entered marriages frequently suffer a similar fate. Catholic dioceses are beginning to insist on a six-month period between engagement and marriage. This administrative decision will be ministerially effective as we use this period to provide opportunities for the couple to learn more about themselves and what Christian marriage can mean for them.

Third, as many theologians and ministers suggest, the Church may become more sensitive to the distinctions between marriage and the religious sacrament of Matrimony. A religiously blessed marriage might come to be the ordinary beginning of this Christian life commitment. As (and if) a marriage matures, this commitment, well begun and demonstrating the virtues required of an enduring Christian relationship, would be celebrated sacramentally. Such a distinction might help us better to recognize that, in the words of theologian Edward Schillebeeckx (quoted by Richard McCormick in *Theological Studies* of March, 1980), "Indissolubility is not a property necessarily following from marriage as an institution but an inner task to be realized." Schillebeeckx further clarifies this developmental view of the sacrament: "Human marriage is not indissoluble because it is a sacrament; rather it is a sacrament because and insofar as it contains the will to develop itself in unbreakable covenant fidelity."

A Ministry to Divorce

The Church's ministry to divorce must be more than preventive. Despite the Church's best efforts—and the best efforts of married persons—divorce happens; marriages die. However much we mourn this fact, still it is so. The Church's ministry begins in admitting that the ideal of a lifelong commitment is not always attainable. Once the Church admits that marriages of Catholics can and do die, it becomes a question of how to minister effectively to those who confront divorce as a necessary choice in their lives. Here graceful ministry is rooted in an awareness of what is happening to the person. When divorce is understood as a dangerous religious passage in adult life, as a time of vulnerability, loss and grace, we can begin to construct rites of passage which assist Christians in this perilous time.

As we suggested in Chapter 7, rites of passage include efforts of educational and supportive care as well as liturgical celebration. The educational and supportive rites of passage for Christians who are involved in divorce include the support groups and counseling opportunities provided by a caring community. Such care, when done with professional skill, can provide the protective context in which a person can recognize both the pain and the grace of this part of life. Psychologist James Hillman speaks of our wounds as the eyes through which we see into ourselves; insight is provided by means of these wounds. Divorce is clearly such a wound. The vision it provides will include insight into God's working within us. We learn from our wounds to the extent that we are supported, by caring friends and other ministers, and thus have the courage to look into who we are and what God is doing with us. In recent years groups for separated and divorced Catholics have emerged throughout the United States. In these and in other ways, some with and others without official sanction, we are learning to care for those in our communities of faith who are traversing this dark passage.

As the Church learns the educational and supportive rites of passage for divorce, it is also faced with the question of liturgical rites of passage for this transition. After much turmoil and with the help of loved ones, a person comes through this passage. A great deal has happened: anger and guilt have been gradually transformed. Some sorrow is likely to remain, but more and more there is a sense of reconciliation, at least with oneself and with God. Confusion and defeat have been faced and have lost much of their power. A new, fragile confidence is beginning. If there remains, emotionally and religiously, much unfinished business, a passage has nonetheless been completed. And as one emerges, after perhaps a year or two in this transition, is not some acknowledgment required? Catholics are liturgical people; we want to celebrate in public acts of prayer and worship the many movements of grace and sin in our lives. If divorce is an important religious passage, it would profit from such a liturgical acknowledgment of its completion. And quietly and informally, there are appearing, in Protestant and Catholic communities in the United States, rites of passage in which a group liturgically acknowledges a member's graceful coming through this passage. This is not a "celebration" in the most popular sense of the word, but it is a celebration in a precise religious sense: we acknowledge in prayer and song and Eucharist that God has brought us through this time. We stop a moment to recognize, if not in the larger community, then among our immediate friends and relatives, the good news that even in this unlikely place of failure and loss, we have been brought through death to life again.

Traditionally, personal reconciliations with the Church after divorce have taken place through what theologians call the "internal forum." These are private reconciliations, intended to avoid scandal. As the Church ministers to its own structures and develops a more honest and effective ministry to the divorced, these acts of Christian reconciliation will be able to be shared in the larger community. In this new light of the community we shall see that the scars of the divorced are not so different from those of all the rest of us. Until then, informal, experimental liturgical rites of passage will continue to assist Christians in this perilous passage.

To some Catholics a change in the Church's laws about divorce and remarriage may seem like a sign of weakness and lack of conviction. To them the choice appears to be between irresponsibility and indissolubility. Pope John Paul II suggested such a choice in his speech in Washington, D.C., in 1979: "When the institution of marriage is abandoned to human selfishness or reduced to a temporary, conditional arrangement that can easily be terminated, we will stand up and affirm the indissolubility of the marriage bond." The urgent focus of Christian ministry that we have addressed in this chapter is the middle ground between irresponsible selfish relationships and marriages that survive a lifetime. Some marriages of mature and committed Christians fail. To care more effectively for these members of the believing community is neither irresponsible nor scandalous. If there is scandal in this regard today, it concerns not the Church's laxity but its inattention to many of its most sincere members. The way out of this scandal leads through a purification of the Church's theology and ministry toward a more graceful response to these members of the Christian body.

Reflective Exercise

Consider what experiences have most influenced your own thinking about divorce. Do you have a close friend or a relative who has been divorced? How has this affected your understanding of the reality of divorce? Be as concrete as you can, listing realizations to which you have come as a result of the divorce in the life of someone close to you. Give some consideration, as well, to the response that the divorcing persons received from you, from family, from friends, from the Church. What have you learned here about the effects of divorce?

To what extent has divorce been a part of your direct experience—perhaps a frightening possibility for your marriage at some point; perhaps a reality that you have moved through as your own marriage has ended? What do you consider to be the most important lesson you have learned about divorce from this personal experience?

Additional Resources

The past several years have seen an explosion of excellent pastoral reflection on divorce and remarriage in the Catholic tradition. Among the most useful are James Young's *Ministering to the Divorced Catholic* (Paulist Press, 1979) and Paula Ripple's *The Pain and the Possibility* (Ave Maria Press, 1979). In the volume edited by Young, the articles by George MacRae, "New Testament Perspectives on Marriage and Divorce," and Richard McCormick, "Indissolubility and the Right to the Eucharist," will be especially helpful for the theologically inclined reader. McCormick's discussion of indissolubility is perhaps the most succinct and cogent on record. This highly regarded moral theologian has provided numerous other discussions of divorce and remarriage: see, in particular, his work in the March issues of *Theological Studies* in 1971, 1975 and 1980. Lewis Patsavos' examination, "The Orthodox Position on Divorce," is also found in the volume edited by James Young.

Two other useful contributions to the recent discussion of divorce in the Catholic tradition are Stephen Kelleher's *Divorce and Remarriage for Catholics?* (Doubleday, 1973) and Lawrence Wrenn's edited volume *Divorce and Remarriage in the Catholic Church* (Newman Press, 1973). In the Wrenn collection, John Noonan examines "Ursa's Case," the first instance of the Church's intervention (at the beginning of the fifth century) in a legal dispute about divorce. See also Noonan's important book *The Power to Dissolve* (Harvard University Press,

1972). Canon lawyer James Provost reviews recently suggested strategies for regularizing some second marriages among Catholics in "Intolerable Marriage Situations Revisited," which appeared in the journal *Jurist* in 1980.

A vital practical resource for divorced Catholics is the North American Conference of Separated and Divorced Catholics. Headquartered in Boston (5 Park Street, 02108), the group sponsors regional organizations and publishes a quarterly newsletter, *Divorce*. "Divorce: The Darkness and the Gift," Patricia Livingston's evocative address to the 1980 annual meeting of the Conference, is available as an audio-tape from Ave Maria Press.

A wide-ranging discussion of divorce from a social science perspective can be found in *Divorce and Separation—Context, Causes and Consequences* (Basic Books, 1979), edited by George Levinger and Oliver Moles. James Hillman traces the connections between our wounds and spiritual insight in his *Revisioning Psychology* (Harper & Row, 1975). In a special issue in 1980 devoted to "Children of Divorce," the *Journal of Social Issues* presents some of the most recent research on the effects of divorce on children.

Part Five:

A CONTEMPORARY
SPIRITUALITY OF
CHRISTIAN MARRIAGE

Spirituality brings us in touch with the power and presence of God and calls for our virtuous response. A spirituality of marriage, both Christian and contemporary, involves virtues that are grounded both in our religious tradition and in the psychological resources required for modern life. Self-intimacy is the virtuous acceptance of myself that enables me to be faithful in our marriage: coming to love the particular person who *I* am, I am better able to love, enduringly, the particular person whom I have married. The virtue of fidelity, necessary for a lifelong marriage, combines commitment and change. As our marriage matures, each of us continues to be faithful both to our continuing commitments and to the new invitations that we discover in our life together. Our Christian values must take root in the lifestyle of marriage. This lifestyle, shaped by our practical decisions about work and money and prayer and play, is part of our family's ministry, our contribution to a more just and loving world. The spirituality of Christian marriage is also shaped by our response to the especially important times in our life the crises in which the Christian dynamic of loss and gain, of death and life is experienced. The discipline or asceticism of our family's use of time influences our attempts to live more gracefully the special history of our own journey together in the Lord.

2 1

SELF-INTIMACY:
THE FOUNDATION OF FIDELITY

Intimacy and fidelity are the central virtues of marriage. Fidelity
is required if our intimacy in marriage is to endure. Yet fidelity
is more than stable endurance. It entails a *process* of being faithful, for both our marriage partner and our God are continually
and surprisingly being revealed to us.

Fidelity in marriage, the survival and growth of intimacy between us, is grounded in another kind of intimacy: my
awareness and love of myself. In marriage we risk ourselves in a
lifelong commitment. But who is this self that I entrust to another? How familiar am I with my inner ambitions and fears,
with my own body and sexuality, with my personal dreams and
doubts? These all go with me into marriage and will powerfully
influence my ability to be faithful.

Self-intimacy—the virtue which allows me to love, care for
and accept myself—is a strength required of every adult. And
for many of us marriage and family are the arenas where we
confront this challenge most concretely. Self-intimacy is at once
a virtue required for marriage and a virtue which is especially
tested and developed in marriage.

Intimacy and a Plural Self

A reflection on the virtue of self-intimacy begins with the realization that we are, each of us, plural. Each of us is an amalgam

of different and even conflicting hopes and fears. We combine within ourselves a variety of ambitions and ideals; there are so many things we would like to be and do. Accompanying the ambitions and dreams within us are our apprehensions and doubts: some of these are momentary or occur only in certain situations; others, we find, endure. They accompany us throughout the years of our life.

This pluralism we find within may seem a scandal and thus remain a secret. We have learned that only "crazy people" have conflicting, ambivalent, unresolved elements inside. "Normal people"—most of those we see around us—appear so stable and balanced. My own interior life, with its abrupt surprises, its anxieties and unfinishedness, is embarrassing. Perhaps it is to be suffered, but hardly to be explored or shared—even with myself. Self-intimacy is a virtue by which I grow in awareness and acceptance of *this particular* human being I am becoming. It adds to the strength of identity, my sense of clarity and confidence about who I am, a tolerance and affection for this specific person. It is a strength of mature self-love which is the ground for my love of and care for others.

The less I need to keep my plural self a secret, the more alert I can be to a crucial task of psychological development and Christian maturing. This is the task of attending to the ongoing revelation of a self that is becoming. Our richly complex selves, created by and inhabited by our God, reveal themselves only over time and only to the careful observer. The self-revelation of God which takes place in nature and in other people, our lovers and enemies alike, also occurs within. The presence and self-revelation of God in our own particular lives leads us beyond narcissism and invites us to religious introspection.

There are two complementary challenges to psychological and religious development in adult life, and in their balance maturity appears. The first has received more attention in the Christian tradition: the challenge to change, to reform, to be converted. We know ourselves to be sinners—selfish, suspicious and often even destructive. In our Christian life we are challenged to change, to respond to God's efforts to transform and heal this wounded self. This is the call to *metanoia*—Christian conversion and change of heart. This requires much effort and a kind of "holy intolerance" with who we are. It is important to note the appropriateness of this intolerance, especially at the beginning of adult life. Young adults are often intolerant of others and of themselves as well. Similarly, in the early stages of their new conviction, converts of many kinds are notoriously intolerant of those who do not share their own clear vision.

Yet there comes a period of maturing when such intolerance becomes less "holy." Then we glimpse the other aspect of *metanoia:* the challenge to be converted to a deeper love and acceptance of ourselves. As we continue to change—to become more virtuous and less selfish, less destructive and untrusting—we are also challenged to come to a more tolerant love of this particular amalgam of strengths and weaknesses that we find ourselves to be. This challenge is essentially an invitation to greater self-intimacy.

The movement of self-intimacy and greater self-love is not a settling into smugness or complacency. It is a call to bring about a deeper harmony and integration of the variety of things that I am. It is an invitation to move beyond the useful self-denial of an earlier stage in life when it was perhaps necessary for me to look away from some ambiguous, humiliating or confusing parts of myself. As we mature, we seem to be asked—and for Christians this is a religious request—to befriend ourselves. We are invited to a new level of comfort with our own particular and peculiar self and to a more appreciative familiarity with what God is doing with us and despite us.

Befriending Myself as Plural Now

We are, each of us, not only plural over time through the history of what we have done and who we have been; we are plural now. This very day I find myself multiple, with enthusiasm for many parts of my life and apprehension about many others. I am, often at once, courageous and afraid, hopeful and despondent. I find my best efforts of care laced with a variety of motives, accompanied by a range of diverse feelings. And I realize as I mature that this variety of motives and feelings does not necessarily make me bad, but it does make me who I am. This particular combination of abilities and limits, of creativity and stubbornness, is who I am. The challenge of self-intimacy is to better understand this plural self and to better love it.

There is much internal information available to us about who we are and how we are doing. At times this information takes dramatic form, in an ulcer or heart attack. Exhaustion and depression may likewise signal an imbalance, a lack of harmony or integration in our life. Psychological and religious maturity entail the ability to attend to both the dramatic and the everyday information available to us. A different kind of discipline, influenced by cultural norms of achievement and self-sufficiency, urges us to push ahead, to keep going and ignore this information. Such a discipline is a form of self-denial in a quite unchristian sense. Its fruit is more often an exhausted and angry "achiever" than a generous and concerned adult.

Self-intimacy begins in attending to the information from within. As we listen, we learn more about both our limits and our best hopes. I can begin to set aside the expectations that others have of me and my own idealistic but abstract goals, replacing these with a clearer and more concrete awareness of what my own life offers. I come into the rhythm of *my* adulthood and into a greater comfort and patience with my own life journey.

Self-intimacy can result in a clearer sense of my motives. More aware of why I overwork, or get angry or depressed, I have a better opportunity to heal these parts of myself—whether this healing entails overcoming or becoming comfortable with them.

The goal of this task of befriending a plural self is "self-possession." Each of us probably knows a few people who are deeply comfortable with who they are. Neither resigned nor over-achievers, they are doing well what they can, quietly aware of their own limits and needs. Such people are at ease with themselves. They have found their rhythm; they have, in the deepest sense, come into their vocation. And perhaps best of all, they like themselves.

I may even sense some of this movement in myself. I find, for example, that I can only work *this* hard; I wish I were stronger and could work as long as some others around me. But I cannot —and that is acceptable to me. I acknowledge that this is how I look—not taller, not more attractive or youthful, not with more commanding presence. I look like this—and it is acceptable, too. Actually, it is better than acceptable; this is who I am and I like it. There are, as well, certain recurring fears and doubts that seem to be me. I once assumed that effort and the years would rid me of them. Now it looks as though they are with me "for the duration." So I will make the best of them. I may even come to embrace these inner demons, these once intolerable weaknesses. St. Paul may have had something like this in mind with his reference to the thorn in his flesh. Certain weaknesses and peculiarities we cannot shake; they are us. Even God seems content not to remove them. Self-intimacy invites us to be more tolerant of even these aspects of who we are.

Finally, self-intimacy allows us to live in the present. Self-acceptance means liking myself *now*, at this age in my life. With growth in this virtue, I am rescued from a cultural obsession with youth, an obsession which would have me apologize for my present age as I grow older. I am more able to be present to every year of my life. I need not deny or hide my age—because I like who I am now.

The religious insight that supports this call to self-acceptance and love is that we cannot wait until we are perfect to love ourselves. A myth of perfection has injured much Christian effort at religious growth. In the pursuit of perfection we have been allowed to hate ourselves as sinners, imperfect, flawed. When we are surprised by human love, we may think that we are loved only because the other person does not really know us. We are tempted to hide our flaws, pretend to be someone else in order to hold on to this undeserved love. But if we are lucky we learn that our friend really loves *us*—all of who we are, flaws and all. It may take this lesson to remind us that God loves us as we are. In God's sight we are lovely now; it is not our good works, our achievements or even our penitence that renders us magically lovely. It is in being loved, to paraphrase Chesterton, that we become lovely. This is true for self-intimacy: I am invited to love myself, not in the light of future improvement, but now as I am. More comfortable with both my particularity and my loveliness, I become better at loving others.

Reconciling Myself as Plural over Time

As the journey of our life proceeds we accumulate a history: we have been many places, lived many roles. The pluralism of this historical self is rarely one of radical or total change. I recognize some continuity in myself from child to adolescent to adult. Enduring memories and hopes bind the journey and identify it, in all its stages, as *mine*. We may meet people who represent extremes of personal change or stability. There are some who cut off their roots, trying to disengage themselves from a hated or intolerable past; they may even change their names in a search for a different identity. At the other extreme we meet people who have refused change, who have held rigidly to what they have always been. But most of us live between these extremes. As we continue to change in response to life's demands and invitations, we find ourselves unfolding, we discover unsuspected interests and unanticipated abilities. And we learn the deception of language. A single word—such as "parent" or "wife" or "worker"—has been used to describe me for the past fifteen or thirty years. Yet I find I have played a multitude of roles under that single category; I have understood myself very differently at different points over those years.

My present self, then, is an accumulation of what I have been and what I have done—successes and failures, promises kept and commitments left behind. This personal history abides in us in various states of consciousness and harmony. By mid-life, however, we can expect this history to demand some of our attention. About this time many adults find themselves invited to reexamine this history and to better integrate certain aspects of it into their lives.

This invitation to a reassessment of my life may arise in a sudden confrontation with a tender part of my past. I am suddenly reminded of the way my parent—or teacher, or superior, or spouse—has treated me. I am surprised by the anger this recollection generates. Blame joins anger: these people hurt me and are to blame for my troubles now. In this anger there is revealed to me an important part of my past, of myself, that has remained unforgiven. I see a part of my life that is ugly and painful, an unforgiven part of myself that I had kept hidden but now demands attention. Or the sore, unforgiven part of my past may be something that I did to myself. Some mistake or poor choice now reappears; guilt and regret flow again within me. The revelation is the same: this is a part of myself that I have hated or denied or been ashamed of. Now I am invited to be reconciled with it.

There seem to be three options when such disconcerting information emerges. I can get busy and try to bury this disturbance from the past. Here the hope is to ignore it. I treat it as a distraction; I repress it (again) and hope it will go away. A second option is to seize, with renewed vigor, on the feelings of blame or guilt and give myself over to the process of punishment—of my parents, or spouse, or myself. This option is to respond to the distress without discerning its opportunity. A third option is to confront the blame or the guilt as an important initial phase of this interior invitation. As I experience these strong feelings about my past, I may eventually experience as well the invitation to forgive. This powerful, negative event really happened and did, in fact, influence my life. But, as I may find, I no longer need to blame my parents or other authorities; I no longer need to carry this guilt about my own actions. This sore and wounded part of my past—part of myself—I can forgive. Perhaps forgiving is too condescending a term; I can embrace this part of myself, welcoming it into my present life. This is not an embrace that magically transforms the past; it does not make either the pain or the scar disappear. But this embrace and reconciliation with my past is a kind of exorcism: this part of myself, with its harbored rage and guilt, loses its power over me. As I come, over some time, to forgive this event of my past, I dissolve its destructive power in my life. I no longer have to deny or avoid this part of me. It cannot hurt me as it used to because I have embraced it, welcomed it home, and in so doing, relieved it of its power.

How is such an extraordinary thing possible? Christians have learned of this in the life of Jesus Christ. The possibility of forgiveness is one of the most startling of Christian revelations. When our hearts harden (even against ourselves) and forgiveness seems impossible or intolerable, the gospel tells us otherwise. Christian revelation tells us we can expect the extraordinary even from ourselves. And it also proclaims the effect of this powerful act of forgiving: the past can be changed. The notion of fate suggests that what is done is done. Forgiveness contradicts this: it gives us power to change the past and the force of its failures. We can forgive what has been done to us—by parents, by the Church, by our spouse, even by ourselves. The past, our personal past, is not as finished as we have been led to believe. It is alive and well, or alive and ailing, in our memories and recollections. At different junctures in life we are invited to explore this lively part of ourselves and to further the continual process of reconciliation and integration that describes our growth in the virtue of self-intimacy.

The reconciliation with a wounded, unforgiven part of my past exorcises its power over me. This important result of reconciliation can be discussed in terms of self-defense and the conservation of energy. Self-defense is not, simply, bad. We all need defenses to survive the demands and assaults of life. Yet we often sense that our tendency is to over-defend. As we catch ourselves repeatedly checking our makeup, or straightening our tie, or smoothing our hair, we can recognize the energy that we expend, daily, in guarding this fragile self. With humor or curtness or credentials, we armor ourself against anticipated assaults, real and imaginary.

As we mature and come to a greater comfort with who we are, we need expend less energy on defense. More comfortable with this particular person that I am, with my many limits and strengths, I have less need to defend or prove myself before others. Having learned about my loveliness, foibles and all, from loved ones and from God, I need give less attention and energy to hiding my weaknesses—showing my best profile and disguising my flaws, physical or spiritual.

This is energy saved, energy conserved and redeemed. Rescuing this energy from the purposes of self-defense, I can invest it in efforts of care for others and concern for the world. My partner, my children, my career—all of these consume my energy. Self-intimacy invites us to a more efficient and virtuous use of this personal power. And this is an ironic sign of its genuineness: by careful, loving attention to my own life I liberate the personal energy formerly given to defense and repression, freeing it for more powerful care for the world beyond myself.

Narcissus and Religious Insight

Christians have learned to be squeamish about "looking inside." Such introspection is often felt to be selfish, distracting us from other persons and from our God whom we should serve. Christian distrust of self is rooted in a theology of the Fall which interprets original sin as a turning in on the self. This theology understands human nature as inclined toward narrow self-absorption; it urges us to learn to avert our gaze. Christian asceticism, in such an understanding, turns our vision away from ourselves—from our bodies, to be sure, but also from our own ambitions and hopes. All are most likely to be selfish. If we are corrupted on the inside, then introspection serves no good religious purpose. Rather it moves toward narcissism. Self-intimacy here is not a virtue but a vice, a form of spiritual self-abuse.

About such introspection, two questions are especially relevant: *how* we inspect ourselves and *what* we expect to see. Narcissus gazed into a pond and saw himself, or thought he did. This watery, insubstantial reflection fascinated him, absorbing his attention. He looked again and again, distracted from other activities.

This same image of gazing into the pond of oneself appears often in the Buddhist religious tradition, but with quite a

different meaning. Each person, according to one Buddhist tradition, is like a pond of murky, agitated water. We are called to
quiet this turbulence, to discipline our lives until the murkiness
settles and the water is clear and still. Then a disciplined look
into the water reveals not the individual's image, but that of the
Buddha nature. Hidden in the depths is not just my private
reflection, but an identity that unites me to all other living
things and, by so doing, tells me who I am. Such introspection
leads not to an obsessive absorption in myself, but to a recognition of who I am and where I belong. Christian introspection, itself undertaken to calm the turbulence that our fears, ambitions
and distractions cause in our life, reveals both our identity and
God's presence. My profoundest identity is not my individualistic, isolated self. This identity is—and here Buddhist and
Christian mystics would agree—a common identity; for the
Christian, this is a oneness with others in God. This is a parable
and an irony: it is by a disciplined introspection that we can find
our community with others. To look within apart from such faith
is to come face to face with only myself; to look within with
faith is to come face to face with God. In this recognition, this
"enlightenment," sudden or gradual, we are rescued from
narcissism because we see both who we are and to whom we belong.

So there are different ways to look within. Narcissism, as a
compulsion and a distraction, has me searching repeatedly and
desperately for a self. Such a search is not a sign of self-intimacy
but proof of its absence. Narcissism is not self-love but an inability to love and be comfortable with myself. The compulsiveness
of narcissistic persons, who must search for "who I am" again
and again in the mirror of every new performance and relationship, reminds us of their discomfort with the self. Their busy
search signals a dis-ease with the self. Narcissistic introspection
arises not from self-esteem, but from its opposite.

Christian introspection is guided by a conviction of an inner
loveliness and an enduring presence. I may not always experience this presence or my own loveliness, but I believe in it. I
look within in response to the invitation to befriend this person
so beloved of God. Self-intimacy as a Christian virtue develops

over many years of patient, tolerant listening to this plural and unfolding self. I come gradually to better distinguish personal limitations that must be changed from those that must be tolerated and embraced. As I come into a more penetrating awareness of myself I see not only my limits and incompleteness, but my loveliness as well. I may even come to a tangible sense of a presence within, a presence that does not distract me from my own identity but encourages me further into it.

Mid-life and Marriage: Where Self-Identity Grows

Knowledge takes time; the self-knowledge that issues in a deeper respect and tolerance for this particular person who I am takes decades.

In the early years of adult life we have as yet only a modest amount of information about ourselves. Possibilities are many; opportunities, ideals and dreams of success abound. Others' expectations still tightly wrap our own hopes. Our energy both excites and distracts us. In young adulthood we necessarily spend much time checking external criteria of how we are doing; we look for ways to "prove ourselves"—to have someone or something testify to our identity and worth.

Maturing describes the process of "finding ourselves"—coming to awareness of how competent we are at what we do, and how limited we are as well. This awareness is less and less founded on external criteria or others' approval. As we find ourselves we realize there is less need to prove ourselves.

What was unavailable to us at twenty-five becomes clearer by forty-five or so: an awareness of strengths we did not earlier suspect; the presence of dreams that previously lay buried under the "shoulds" of others' expectations; the concrete shape of fears only hinted at in our youth. All this suggests that self-intimacy is a virtue that has its special season in mid-life.

Self-intimacy is not a private enterprise. Few of us find it is effective to retreat into isolation in order to learn about and come to love ourselves. For most of us, marriage and family are the arenas for this challenge. It is our marriage partner, our children and our friends and colleagues who reflect back to us information about who we are and what we are becoming. I learn that my spouse frequently sees parts of me before I do; this is both an exciting and a humiliating aspect of marriage. My partner is thus a means of this self-revelation. And my children contribute powerfully to this revelation as they elicit in me tears and angers that I had previously succeeded in hiding even from myself. Penelope Washbourn in *Becoming Woman* describes the invitation to self-intimacy that a child can provide:

> I am terrified by the power she has to unleash emotions in me, my loving and my raging. I don't think of myself as a violent person, but I know through her that I am . . . Our poor children. You have the power to destroy all falsity and reduce us to see us as we are, humble us to see ourselves with all our superficial masks torn away! (p. 125)

This unmasking of myself, performed by my partner and my children, reveals me more surely to myself and invites me both to change and to come to a new self-acceptance.

As a virtue, self-intimacy depends on skills for its practical development. Sensing the disturbances or dreams within, we are challenged to take the time to listen; as we listen we need the ability to name our feelings. Courage and skill are required if we are to share this confusing or exciting information with those closest to us. Such skillful listening, naming and sharing guide the processes of reconciliation and forgiveness that are such an important part of self-intimacy at mid-life.

Loneliness and Solitude

We all spend much time alone. However busy we become, we still live "in ourselves," having to contend always with our inner life. Loneliness and solitude describe two very different ways we are with ourselves; each is related to our maturing in self-intimacy.

Loneliness has many connotations. For us here this word describes the experience of not being at home with myself. I can be lonely in a crowd as well as when alone. Loneliness occurs when I am alienated from my own resources. Distrustful, or frightened, or disgusted by who I am, I cannot be at home with myself. I am uncomfortable with what is inside and need to distract myself; I turn up the music, talk louder, get busy. When we are lonely we find difficulty with recollection or prayer; our aloneness distracts us from ourselves.

Madonna Kolbenschlag, in *Kiss Sleeping Beauty Good-bye*, discusses envy as characteristic of persons who are not at home with themselves. Lacking confidence in myself, I need to be on the watch for others who may be doing better, looking lovelier, getting ahead. With no trust in inner criteria of my worth, I am forced to look outside for indications of my identity and value. This gives a new and sadder meaning to the phrase "looking out for myself." Living in such an other-directed fashion, I am prey not only to envy but also depression. Depression is a serious malaise, a discomfort with who I am. I am dissatisfied with my limits, my shortcomings, my own particularity. Depressed and envious persons wish they were someone else and somewhere else. They are not at home with themselves. Kolbenschlag suggests that envy may be a particular temptation for women. In classic Christian theology, the deadliest sin is pride and self-assertion. Envy, on the other hand, is the sin of those who fail to assert themselves, who fail to find and become themselves. The Christian virtue which strengthens us to overcome the sin of envy, as well as the curse of depression and loneliness, is self-intimacy.

Solitude is another experience of being by myself. Its connotations are different than those of loneliness: solitude suggests not an alienation but a mellow quiet—a comfort, perhaps mixed with sadness, in being alone. Another translation of solitude might be "being at home with myself." We began this reflection with the image of the self as plural, comprising a variety of abilities, shortcomings and ambiguities. The home of the self, then, is peopled with many residents. Self-intimacy and solitude suggest a certain domestic tranquillity. The mellowness of solitude reminds us that presence to myself is not always an experience of delight. Self-intimacy entails not a banishment or denial of every failed or incomplete part of myself, but an embracing of these aspects. Solitude suggests a deep peacefulness with this particular person that I am. To return to the metaphor of the self as a home: every house is, in part, haunted. We speak of families having skeletons in the closet. So with my own interior abode. The lonely person, uncomfortable with many inhabitants of the self, tends to stay away from home. In solitude, I become more aware of, and at ease with, the skeletons and unexorcised ghosts of my inner life. This ease contributes, in turn, to a befriending and taming—the integration of my plural self.

The fruit of self-intimacy, experienced in solitude, is the ability to be alone. I do not need to clutter my life with activity and busywork. I can, at times, stop talking and let the noise settle. This is possible because I know that what I will be left with— just myself—is good. There will be not just agitation and guilt and disappointment to contend with; there will also be gentle humor (how strange I am!) and thankfulness (how blessed my life has been!). In periods of solitude, whether enforced, as with illness, or chosen, as in prayer and days of retreat, I can listen more trustingly to the inner voices. And among these many contending sounds I may hear the voice of God blessing me with new vision and hope.

Reflective Exercise

To grasp more concretely the multiplicity of your own sense of self, it may be useful to return again to a chart or picture. Start by drawing a large circle on a sheet of paper. Within the circle, record some of the roles you fill in your family and job and elsewhere. Place close to the center of the circle those roles that are most significant to you; place others at a distance that shows their lesser importance to you.

Then add within the circle the names of three or four things that you do really well, or aspects of yourself that you especially like. Finally place in the circle three or four personal limitations that you have.

Spend some time savoring this picture of yourself. Note which roles you placed closest to the center and which are further away. Note what you chose to add concerning your strengths and limitations. What does this representation of yourself say to you now?

Now list *outside* the circle some aspects of yourself that you find least tolerable. Consider each in turn: is this a fault or failing that needs to be overcome? Or is it a genuine part of yourself that needs to be befriended, that asks to be welcomed into the larger circle? Reflect on how you might deal with each of these unwanted parts, in a way that contributes to harmony and peace among the many aspects of who you are.

Additional Resources

The development of self-intimacy is discussed under different names and pursued with various strategies. Canadian Jesuit John English, in *Choosing Life* (Paulist Press, 1978), outlines a method of personal reflection and decision making that is grounded in this Christian virtue. The religious task of forgiving part of our past is explored by Dennis Linn and Matthew Linn in *Healing Life's Hurts* (Paulist Press, 1978). For practical reflections and exercises aimed at self-intimacy, see Elizabeth O'Connor's *Our Many Selves* (Harper & Row, 1971). A more comprehensive reflection on this virtue is provided by Louis Dupré in his *Transcendent Selfhood: The Loss and Rediscovery of the Inner Life* (Seabury, 1976). If the reader allows for some anti-Christian bias and jargon from the self-help industry, *The Disowned Self* (Bantam, 1971) by Nathaniel Branden may provide insight into the challenge of self-intimacy.

Henri Nouwen examines the importance and strength of solitude in *Clowning in Rome* (Doubleday Image, 1979). On the experience of loneliness, see his *The Wounded Healer* (Doubleday Image, 1979). In the first part of *The Culture of Narcissism* (Norton, 1978) Christopher Lasch draws on recent psychoanalytic thought to give an excellent description of narcissism. Unfortunately the diatribe that occupies the rest of the book vitiates its overall value.

Penelope Washbourn's *Becoming Woman* (Harper & Row,

1977) traces the struggle of self-intimacy in contemporary women. In *Kiss Sleeping Beauty Good-bye* (Doubleday, 1979) Madonna Kolbenschlag explores envy as a vice to which women may be especially susceptible and which distracts from personal growth and vocation.

22

FIDELITY: COMMITMENT AND CHANGE

Fidelity is the virtue at the core of the lifelong commitment of marriage. In the phrase "lifelong commitment" we begin to glimpse the complexity of this virtue: commitment suggests stability and lifelong implies change. Erik Erikson reminds us of the threat involved in personal change: "To grow means to outgrow others and, in fact, oneself." Marital fidelity combines commitment and change as two persons seek to grow in the same direction; fidelity is the careful tending of both the commitments and the changes necessary in a maturing love.

The complexity of fidelity appears in two features of this strength. It is both an advanced and a mobile virtue. It is advanced because it depends on the already developed strengths of identity and intimacy. Lacking clarity and some confidence in who I am, I will have extra difficulty in being faithful to another person. If my sense of myself frequently shifts in efforts to please others, so will my commitments. Fidelity will be difficult. Likewise with the personal strength and virtue of intimacy: this gradually developed ability allows me to sustain the closeness that is the core of marriage. Lacking this virtue or consistently frightened by the demands of being close to another person, I will have much trouble sustaining a marriage relationship. But without intimacy, marital fidelity has little meaning.

Fidelity is, to be sure, a strength we learn about and develop *in* marriage. It may be only after some years together that we feel this virtue being tested and growing strong. Yet we cannot expect fidelity to grow in marriage if the prior and complementary virtues of identity and intimacy are lacking or remain fragile.

If fidelity is an advanced ability it is also a mobile virtue. We are challenged, in marriage, to be faithful to three changing persons. We quickly learn that our partner is one of these. Such a discovery can be disconcerting. I find you are not the person I thought I married. You are more powerful or more passive than I had thought; you are less ambitious or less affectionate than I had hoped. As our life together develops, I find you are not the person I expected you to be. What can faithfulness mean when I realize I have married the "wrong" person, someone different from what I had expected?

As I find my partner growing in ways that confuse me, I may prefer to be faithful to the person I married rather than to the person I am now married to. I want you to be the one you used to be, or once seemed to be. An important parallel occurs here with the Catholic who insists that the Church not change: I want to be faithful to the Church of 1955, not this confusing Church I experience today. But fidelity, as a human virtue, is a mobile faithfulness: we need be faithful to persons and even institutions that are growing and changing. Fidelity is especially strained when we move at different speeds and in different directions from those with whom we would be faithful.

But if my partner grows in unexpected and unplanned ways, so do I. My own identity is unfinished and my adult vocation is only gradually made clear to me. It is only gradually that I am revealed to myself. The woman who married at age twenty in 1958 may have readily and willingly joined her life not only to her husband but also to his dream and his career. Such a relationship, with him as the decision maker and his goals as the family's chief goals, made utmost sense to her then. In 1981 this woman finds herself changed. With the children out of school, she senses ambitions and hopes previously undreamed of now arising in her. She wants a more assertive role in family decisions about finances and the future. Whence all these changes, unbargained for by either her or her husband when they were first married? Do these new stirrings in her simply threaten her fidelity to her marriage? Are they genuinely part of her growing vocation, however recently born? Are they a part of herself to which she owes some attention and fidelity? Is not the impulse "to be faithful to oneself" just another name for selfishness? How shall I be faithful both to past commitments and to present hopes, when these seem so clearly to diverge?

Fidelity, a mobile virtue, is achieved between moving spouses. Yet, for Christians, a third party is involved in marital fidelity. As we grow and our partner changes, our understanding of God necessarily matures. Even God changes; or, to be more precise, our understanding of who God is changes. As we mature, our adolescent image of God as one whose care is expressed in clear commands and unambiguous answers gives way to a more subtle and complex image. God may appear less exclusively as a powerful parent and more as a partner in life who urges us beyond established defenses and fears into care for others well beyond our family. Maturing in faith may well include outgrowing God, the God of our youth, and growing toward a more ambiguous presence at play in human life. But again the question of fidelity: To which God shall we be faithful? Does not an inflexible fidelity to the God of our youth have another, less virtuous name? Is this not, perhaps, our own attempt at idolatry?

Movement is everywhere. Yet in and despite this movement, itself a sign of life, we recognize an enduring self and a developing vocation. We come to recognize and appreciate the person we married, however different now. And we see, too, and confess the God who is continuously at work in our life. In this interplay of change and continuity we begin to glimpse the intricacy of marital fidelity.

Sexual Fidelity and Marriage

Historically, the commitments of fidelity in marriage have been understood to begin in sexual exclusivity. Often, though, "to be faithful" was interpreted in *simply* sexual terms—as shorthand for genital exclusivity. Focusing the commitment of fidelity on sexual exclusivity is especially characteristic of an early phase of our love. To "fall in love" means that you become my priority, or at least my preoccupation. *This* relationship in fact crowds out all others. Friends and family, obligations at work or school —all these pale in importance. We are each taken up with our romance and the volatile emotions that accompany it—longing, ecstasy, anxiety, jealousy, joy. Romantic love demands emotional priority: nothing is more important to me than you; nothing should be more important to you than me. Genital exclusivity becomes the seal of our special relationship, of this emotional priority. We have no other lovers, we want no other lovers—this is to us a sign that our love seeks the exclusive commitment of marriage.

As our married love grows larger than romance we come to an expanded sense of what the priority of our relationship means. The "we" that is in the process of developing becomes more real and tangible to us. Our lives overlap more and more, our purposes converge. An interdependent life begins to take shape, with our ongoing relationship at its core. I come to sense, perhaps only gradually, how central is this love—to who I am, to what I do, to what I know my life to mean. In some of the actions and choices of our marriage we *express* the centrality of our mutual commitment, in other choices and actions we try to *reinforce* it, to help ensure the continuing vitality of our mutual love.

At this point in our maturing marriage we realize that the priority in which we hold one another and our relationship is more than sexual. Our sexual love is significant to our mutual fidelity but our faithfulness to one another includes much more. Our determination that *this* relationship shall continue and flourish does have ramifications. A commitment to the permanence and priority of our marriage will influence other commitments in our lives—our commitments to work as well as our commitments to kin and other friends. But, as we saw in Chapter 19, priority does not demand social isolation; sexual fidelity does not demand that, emotionally, we must stand apart from all others.

The link between genital exclusivity and the deeper faithfulness required in marriage is not illusory. Sex and love are not identical but they are deeply related in human experience. And love carries a future; it brings with it both mutual obligations and shared hopes. The "simple, casual affair" is not easy to sustain. Genital love is seldom innocent of complications. That, in fact, is part of its fascination. Sex *goes* somewhere—it can take me beyond myself; it can take us deeper in our love; it can also draw me away from past allegiances into new ones.

For many of us sex is fun but we know that it is not to be treated lightly. Sex is a powerful experience in our lives, with intellectual and emotional ramifications that often extend beyond our immediate control. Most of us sense in ourselves what the testimony of others confirms—the larger faithfulness of marriage is not easily sustained without sexual fidelity at its heart.

What, then, of sexual infidelity? How can we—can I—deal with the reality of an affair that has come between us? Whether it is you or I who is "at fault," where do we go from here? How do we restore the larger reality of fidelity between us?

The questions here are complex, to be sure. So many emotions are involved—anger, jealousy, blame, embarrassment, shame, grief, betrayal, loss. There is real pain and real guilt and real sorrow. There can be an impulse to hide from the truth: "If I refuse to acknowledge that anything has happened, maybe it will just go away." There may be a desire for retaliation: "I'll show him (her) that two can play that game!"

The process of healing that must follow if our relationship is to survive may take time. It may bring out other, perhaps even deeper, hurts between us. Here, as in so much else in marriage, we may discover that we are *both* involved, that it is too simple to see what has happened in terms of one "guilty" and one "innocent" party.

Perhaps the most important step in restoring a relationship shattered by sexual infidelity is coming to the realization that healing *can* happen. We can come together again, not just in guarded compromise, but in renewed mutuality and even deepened love. We can, though perhaps only after some time, move beyond recrimination and self-defense. We can each accept responsibility for what we want our future to be together; we can reach out again in trust. As this happens between us, then we can experience in our own lives the power of that love, both human and more than human, that St. Paul proclaimed as a special strength of Christians: a love that remains ready "to trust, to hope, to endure whatever comes," most important, a love that "does not come to an end" (I Corinthians 13:7–8).

But in most marriages the greatest challenge to faithfulness is not an affair but change. Our marriage begins in a conviction that we are compatible. We are similar in many ways, and the ways we are different are interesting and even complementary. We sense ourselves to be well matched and that impression has some truth in it. The next several years of our life together will give us opportunity to test this sense of compatibility and to see more accurately the ways in which we do, and do not, fit together well.

To begin our marriage well matched is to be ahead as we start. But this initial congruence does not guarantee that our lives will always move in rhythm. Each of us will continue to change, and for many of us it is this experience of change in marriage that brings the greatest challenge to our mutual commitment. Here the "crisis of fidelity" involves our attempts to be faithful to one another and to the movement of our love in the midst of the changes and choices that continue to shape our lives.

Crises of Fidelity

Crises of fidelity—events which threaten our commitments and common life—can arise at any point in a marriage. Such crises can cause the breakdown of a marriage: our bond, already weakened, disintegrates and promises are no longer kept. But a marital crisis, as a time of opportunity as well as danger, may also bring about a breakthrough. Confronting a new difficulty in our relationship or acknowledging its stagnation, we may seize the opportunity to resolve long-held differences; we may begin to identify and leave behind outdated expectations and demands. The energetic struggle of such a crisis can invigorate us and renew our marriage.

Although crises arise at different times and with different causes, there is appearing today a pattern of strain characteristic of many marriages in mid-life. Naming these crises may give us a better chance to survive them. "Mid-life crisis" has, unfortunately, become part of the jargon of our time, celebrated in novels and films and regularly discussed in newspaper columns. As jargon, such a term explains away certain experiences, making them banal rather than illuminating them. Yet there does seem to be an expectable pattern to certain crises of marital fidelity that arise only after we have been together over time.

After several decades of adult living—that is, of work and marriage and family responsibility—many people enter a period of introspection and stocktaking. We may expect that in our early forties certain questions about our career, our relationships and even the meaning of life may reappear. The "early forties" is a very general designation; for some of us these questions may have already risen in our mid-thirties, while for others these concerns become prominent only in our fifties. But for very many adults, these questions of personal reassessment begin to arise, and when they do they may trigger a crisis in marriage.

Psychologist Bernice Neugarten describes this period of introspection as a time of increased interiority. What are the events that may usher in this often frightening opportunity for reflection and change? By our early forties (allowing for significant variation in this timing, according to our different schedules of marriage and career) our children are leaving home or, at least, becoming much more independent. Less energy is required in caring for our family. For many women the question arises of how this extra energy is to be spent: Is there life after mothering? What am I to do, what *can* I do over the coming decades as the children need less and less of my attention and energy? These questions belong not just to the wife and mother, but to the marriage and the family.

A shift in mid-life into this new interiority can also be triggered by a career now leveling off. The energy and doubt that surrounded my work in my twenties and thirties may begin to settle. Either success at a career or stagnation with a job may invite me to ask questions about the future: Is this what I want to do the rest of my life? Have the past two decades been a waste? Or have they been good, even though their result is now strangely unsatisfying for me?

These questions about what I can do, or should do, have several characteristics that mark them as mid-life concerns. First, they arise with a new urgency in regard to time. In my forties I may begin to sense that I have more of a past than a future, more yesterdays than tomorrows. If I want to do something different with my life, now is the time to decide. This may be my last chance to change jobs or to seek a more satisfying relationship. Now is the time: this is the inner voice of mid-life. This question of timing may arise as a personal concern but it has significant ramifications for a marriage.

Another characteristic of mid-life questions that can generate marital crises is that they often involve our parents. As we move into our forties, our parents are also growing older. As we noted in Chapter 10, their aging may trigger disconcerting questions about our own aging. In mid-life my own death becomes a less abstract possibility and my mortality becomes a more personal and immediate reality. If our parents' aging warns us that we, too, shall die it may also set off another, equally disturbing, realization. Our parents have, throughout our life, been our advocates and guardians. Kissing our wounds, protecting us from the neighborhood bully, they have taken a place between us and the dangers of the world. Long after we have left home, our parents may still stand as guarantors of meaning for us. As they age and die, this buffer and guarantee is removed. We are, at last, orphaned and left to make sense of the world on our own. This is, admittedly, a subtle and not always consciously perceived experience. Yet for many adults this may be part of an experience of reevaluation and stocktaking in mid-life.

In many different ways this reassessment in our middle years is an effort to disengage ourselves from our parents. As we have suggested, we may seek to prepare ourselves for their death. But also, and this is a more common and conscious experience, we work to disengage ourselves from their expectations for our marriages and careers. In our middle years we may find ourselves in a crisis that is shaped by anger toward our parents. We may come to realize that we have lived out their ambitions for us, to the neglect of our own hopes. Or we abruptly recognize that we married our parents' choice for our spouse instead of our own. This influence can be acknowledged, for example, in a woman's realization that, after much struggle against her father in late adolescence, she has "married her father" in her husband. The anger that often accompanies the mid-life recognition of our parents' influence is reinforced by the realization of our own complicity. We allowed them to choose our spouse or career, and so our guilt reinforces our anger.

Finally, another characteristic of our middle years that is likely to influence our marriage is a shift in the way we want to contribute to the world. This shift is the substance of the challenge to the mother in her forties, who must decide how to rechannel her generative abilities in new directions. In a career this challenge often arises as a desire to contribute in a broader, less specialized way. This is, of course, the natural development of adult leadership: after a decade or more of specialized and highly focused work, a person may well feel drawn to a broader or more comprehensive level of involvement. In *Adaptation to Life,* George Vaillant describes this movement in the lives of the men he studied:

> Almost always, full leadership involves a shift in career focus. Instead of delving progressively deeper into their specialized careers and acquiring progressively more competence, in middle life the men's career patterns suddenly diverged and broadened; they assumed tasks that they had not been trained for. Being truly responsible for others is not a job for the specialist (p. 227).

In the Catholic Church today this pattern of concern for expanding the focus of one's work is taking an intriguing form. Many lay persons are, in their forties and fifties, showing great interest in ministry. Some women, their families grown and gone, see ministry as a way to rechannel their considerable energy and gifts. More and more men find themselves attracted during these years by the idea of the diaconate or lay ministry. Having spent two decades or more pursuing a career, they now feel the desire to expand their concern. They may have experienced these decades as fulfilling; they may have stayed with this work only because it was necessary to do so for their families. In either case, now they would do something else, contribute in a broader and more explicitly religious way to the world. The Church is challenged to respond to this new religious interest and to provide structures for this emerging ministry.

Reconciliations in Mid-life

These, then, are some of the contexts of the crises of marital fidelity. By our forties we are often experiencing changes of enough significance that our marriage commitments may demand serious reevaluation. Fidelity in our marriage includes both change and commitment; these reevaluations of our life, then, must be undertaken in fidelity to our partner, to ourself and to the movements of God in our life.

As our adult identity and vocation take shape initially in response to a dream or life ambition, these may be tested in midlife by a reexamination of that dream. This is really a crisis of fidelity, now to my own growing identity and vocation. Several decades of work and love as an adult have provided much information about who I am and what I can do. This information accumulates as I mature and may, expectably, reach a critical level when I am compelled to stop and evaluate my life. As Daniel Levinson indicates in *The Seasons of a Man's Life*, three types of reevaluation are common at this point in life.

In the first kind of reassessment and reconciliation with a life dream, I am challenged to fit my dream more closely to my own maturing life experience. Levinson uses the term "de-illusionment" to signify this shift from the useful and even necessary illusions of the beginning of adult life to the acceptance of the particular person whom I have become. The bigger-than-life quality of my dream in early adulthood gave me great enthusiasm and energy, propelling me into the adult world of work and love. As I mature through my forties, I have less need of these grander (even grandiose) aspects of my dream. I am invited to let go of illusory parts of the dream (my life is not as glamorous as I had expected) and savor its real, specific development (the way my life has gone is good). This first kind of reconciliation is likely to involve my marriage as well. Our marriage also most likely began with the romantic excitement of a dream. As we mature together we come to see the meaning and shape of marriage *for us*. It will necessarily be different from our earlier, inexperienced expectations for it. A crisis at mid-life may challenge us to come to terms with our marriage. "Coming to terms" does not mean settling for a drab, unexciting relationship, but it does mean embracing and developing the unique, particular relationship that is our marriage now.

The crisis aspect of such a reassessment may arise when we realize we have each assumed roles that never really fit. I expected you to be the kind of wife that my own mother was; you assumed I would be the husband-provider that men "are supposed to be." In a mid-life reevaluation of our marriage we have the opportunity to explore these and other expectations and to share dissatisfactions that until now we have been too busy to notice, much less to share with each other. In such a period of reexamination we have an extraordinary opportunity to make our marriage more genuinely *ours* and to heal difficulties and hurts that have developed over the past decades.

Levinson outlines two other ways that adults at mid-life may be invited to reexamine the dreams of their youth. These are the reconciliations demanded by a dream that is discovered to be a tyranny or by a dream that has been too long ignored.

In mid-life a married man may look up and realize he has "made it." He has achieved what he set out to do. Life has, until now, been very successful. Why, then, he asks, am I dissatisfied? What is missing? Is this really what I wanted from life? Such a reexamination may reveal that he has paid too high a price for his success. He begins to realize that he has worked too hard, driving himself and others around him. He has made extraordinary demands on his family and on himself to get this far. The life ambition that excited him in his twenties has, by now, become a tyranny. It has come to rule him. His crisis in mid-life may focus on how he responds to this painful realization. How is he to turn away from this compulsive, tyrannical part of himself and reclaim other aspects of his life so long neglected—his love for his wife, more time and attention for his growing children, his own playfulness and emotional life?

Such a realization can be traumatic; it may seem that a total change of lifestyle is demanded; a new sexual partner, one unconnected with my compulsive past, may seem a necessary part of this change. The tyranny of a career must now be healed and a person's whole family will be affected by this effort at reconciliation. How can I be faithful to this new, healing insight and also faithful, in a way more profound than in the past, to my marriage and family?

The third kind of reexamination concerns a dream ignored or deferred. This is an experience that is increasingly frequent among women today. I come to realize that I never really had a dream of my own. I grew up knowing that I was going to get married and to raise a family—that's what women do. And that's what I did, never really questioning what I wanted to do with my life. It's not that these years of my marriage have been bad for me or unhappy or a waste. It's more that I now sense I never had a chance to choose my life, and it's this lack of choice that I really regret. I don't want to live my whole life vicariously—supporting my husband's dreams, nurturing the dreams of my children. I want to have a dream that I can pursue as my own—not necessarily apart from my loved ones or in opposition to them, but a dream that is really me. And the most frustrating and frightening realization for me now is that, after all these years of my life, I don't even know what my own dream is. Sometimes I am scared that it may even be too late for me. After all this time I may find that I am unable to plan or to choose or to act for myself. But I am determined to try.

And we see the signs of this determination today in the phenomenal increase in the number of married women returning to school and to work. The choice by married (and, especially, divorced and widowed) women to reengage themselves in the world of work does not always result from a reawakened sense of a personal dream. Often, as we have seen before, it is simple economic necessity that compels a woman to find a paying job. But even among many women who "have to" work there develops a sense of autonomy and self-confidence in being able to make their way in the world larger than the family.

This "awakening of a dream" in the lives of many married women reminds us of the influence of the women's movement in contemporary American life. There is virtually no woman in America today whose life is untouched by the controversy generated by the women's movement. This is not to say that most women identify themselves as feminists; indeed, most do not. But it is increasingly difficult for a woman in our culture to hold herself aloof from the debate over women's role and women's rights. Women (and many men, as well) feel themselves having to take a stand on issues that previously did not come under question. Women differ in their response to these issues and in their identification with "women's liberation." But it is harder and harder for a woman to remain unaffected, one way or the other, by the conflicts and contradictions that the women's movement has brought to light. Whether she resists the movement, is ambivalent toward it or is active in support of its goals and strategies, a woman today sees her own life affected. And many marriages are being profoundly influenced by these broader cultural forces, as well.

The women's movement accelerates the process of self-examination and change. My struggle to understand who I am as a woman and what I should do with my life can call into question all my previous choices and commitments. This reassessment can be invigorating, holding out the promise of a life that is fuller and more richly satisfying for me and others. But it can be frightening as well. I cannot remain as I am, as I have been. I have to change. But at what cost? What are the risks? Do I have the courage? Is it worth the price?

In many instances, one of the central risks of personal change for a woman is the challenge this raises to her husband and their marriage relationship. In a marriage, neither spouse changes without affecting the partner and the intricate pattern of their shared life. These patterns of who we are to each other and how our lives overlap have developed over years, even decades, of being together in "our way." Now this established pattern is called into question. For many married women who are coming

into a new awareness of themselves, the established pattern of
their marriage is seen as the central problem and the most important place in which change must occur. But change here is
not just change "for me," it is also change for my spouse.

Again, for most women this awareness does not appear immediately as a decision for divorce, but rather as a conviction that
"we cannot go on together as we have in the past." The challenge is then for us to come to a new understanding of who we
are together, an understanding which will be expressed in
changes in our daily patterns and our shared lifestyle. But these
changes will not simply mean that I want to be different, they
will also demand that you be different as well.

Dealing with the changes in marriage that are provoked by
these movements in women's consciousness will be the challenge
of marriage over the foreseeable future. Couples marrying now,
couples already married, couples approaching marriage can expect their own marriages and those of their friends to be
affected. We will all be engaged in the process of working out
new patterns of mutuality and differentiation in our own marriages and in sharing in the larger cultural revolution of marriage around us.

It is expectable, then, that in our middle years we may be invited to reexamine our dream. Whether we need to reconcile a
youthful dream with its mid-life realization or deal with the tyranny of our life ambition or pay attention to a dream long
deferred, each of these reassessments will powerfully affect our
marriage. We may feel the need to blame our partner for his or
her part in our ignoring of a dream or in its tyranny over us. The
dissatisfaction with our past may include discontent with how
we have been together in marriage.

Yet these expectable crises of mid-life are not just times of
trouble. They can be opportunities for extraordinary growth,
both in our personal lives and in our marriage. The nature of
these crises is that they bring together several decades of information about ourselves. They invite us to reexamine our life in
the light of this information, this gradually unfolding revelation
about who we are. Such crises are destructive of a marriage

when this information cannot be shared. When a person is too frightened or angry to share these questions and their distress, a communal solution of the crisis is blocked. When couples have the courage to learn new skills that assist them in communicating concretely and without blame, this sharing—even of grief and confusion—can deepen their intimacy. Perhaps for the first time in many years we are facing our doubts and fears together. Ironically, then, a crisis arising over a job or career or even an affair can force us to examine our relationship and make the changes that are necessary for our survival together.

Marital fidelity at mid-life is, as we have seen before, rarely a question of sexual fidelity alone. It is even more rarely a matter of holding, determinedly, to our former way of being together. Most often it entails a faithful response to the challenges that invite us to outgrow our past and mature into a new, more satisfying way of life together. Such a challenge raises many frightening questions. What will be required for us to move beyond our past expectations? Do we each have the courage and honesty to accept our responsibility for where our relationship is now? Do we each have the stamina to try again, the creativity to find a way for us to be together beyond our past? Can we forgive— ourselves and each other—and take up again the delicate task of weaving together our diverse hopes and fears and purposes into the fabric of a shared life? For some couples at this point the price of renewing a marriage seems too high. Divorce seems the "easier" or even the only answer. But other marriages take up the challenge. We attempt, in this vulnerable time when we are aware of our own limits, to determine anew how we shall be together and how our love may once again flourish.

If these times of crisis do not always lead to solutions that save and mature a marriage, they do provide an extraordinary grace moment in adult life. Frightening and disorienting as they are, these are sacred times, periods of special insight and revelation. Aware of this, the Church is beginning to respond to these times with rites of reconciliation which help Christians live through these crises more gracefully.

Crises, Fidelity and Rites of Reconciliation

Marriage as a lifelong journey necessarily has many junctures and possible detours. It is becoming clearer how this journey is challenged in our middle years. Certain expectable questions may arise, inviting our marriage in new directions that demand healing and change. If these questions are an expectable part of a maturing marriage, we must learn not to be embarrassed by them. For many of us in our forties and fifties even the emergence of these questions seems inappropriate and immature. We should have settled these concerns long ago. Others do not seem to be puzzled by them, why then are we? What is wrong with *me?* Interpreting these concerns as immaturity instead of as opportunity, we try to hide them from our loved ones and even from ourselves.

Yet if these crises of mid-life are an important part of our growth, if they are, in fact, how God leads adults into holier lives and more mature marriages, then more attention must be paid to them. They must be recognized as religious passages of marriage and adult life, as God's work which demands a response in the Christian community.

Such a response will likely be in the form of rites of reconciliation which fit the challenges of our middle years. The vagueness of the words "ritual" and "rite" requires some clarification. Rites are, simply, ways that a community pays special attenton to key moments and movements in life. Birth, entry into adult life, marriage and death are the most universal and crucial movements to which religious faiths and cultures have given attention. In these movements the Christian community celebrates God's presence and activity. In these key transitions the Christian sacraments provide healing and protection. This protection is not meant to be a distraction from what is taking place, a way to avoid the danger of the transition. Rather it is a protection *for* what is happening: an individual is surrounded by a caring community, supported by its religious heritage and its accumulated experience of the danger and possibilities that are here. This protection allows the person to look into the heart of this difficult challenge. The wisdom of the community speaks to us at these times: expect to lose some cherished part of yourself (the carefree irresponsibility of childhood or the independence of an unmarried life or even your life itself); but know that in this loss you will gain something new, something that will speak to you of the love of God.

The ritual celebration of marriage which marks the first stages of this journey acknowledges the loss and gain of this important transition. But, as we discussed in Chapter 7, a community has more rites available to it than just the rituals it celebrates in church. The word "rite" may be used not only to mean the liturgical celebration of marriage but also to describe the educational efforts of a community to support and guide persons in these crucial passages in life. Thus, in regard to marriage, the liturgical ritual of the marriage ceremony must be complemented by other educational rites. These rites are structured opportunities for the couple to pay special attention to what is happening in their lives. The rites of marriage preparation in a parish or other community can provide an opportunity for the couple to explore their expectations and motives as they move toward this life decision. Such educational rites might well include training in the skills of self-awareness and the virtues of communication so necessary for this long and complex journey.

But the activities surrounding the first stages of marriage must be complemented by similarly protective and graceful rites for the transitions to be expected as a marriage matures. Such rites already exist implicitly in the ministries of marriage counseling and other social services. As we gain clearer information about the psychological patterns of change and challenge in mid-life marriages, we must elaborate and better focus these "marital rites." Both in counseling contexts and in carefully structured group sharing, married Christians can learn to pay special attention to the challenges and graces of their own marriages. Christian ministers to marriage—not just religious professionals but skilled married couples as well—might be especially alert to the reconciliations expectable in marriage in mid-life. Marriage Encounter, a prayerful guided group experience for improving communication in marriage, is one example of the efforts in the Catholic Church to respond more effectively to the challenges of marriage today. It is an instance of the rites which may be devised to assist Christians through the crises of their lives into more graceful and satisfying marriages.

The various educational rites of marriage at mid-life will, at times, be accompanied by liturgical celebrations of a passage completed. When a couple or family has struggled through a reconciliation with a dream, or dealt, painfully but effectively, with a problem in the family, this movement demands celebration. They have come through a perilous time. Through confusion and doubt and anger, they have survived. Believers have always celebrated such survival by praising and thanking God. Such a ritual celebration—shared perhaps with a number of persons close to the family—may include sorrow for past sinfulness, mourning for what we have lost or had to set aside and praise for the God who has led us through this dark passage. This celebration both concludes our crisis and publicly acknowledges God's presence in our distress and confusion. It signals to others to expect and embrace these ambiguous movements in their own lives, since this is how our God works with us.

The educational rites for mid-life marriages will, of course, include strong, effective care for individuals and families whose marriages do not survive the crisis. Care for those in our communities who are separated or divorced is a recent but rapidly growing ministry among Catholics. As we discussed in Chapter 20, the counseling and educational rites which assist a divorcing person need to be complemented by a liturgical acknowledgment of what has happened. Such a "rite of divorce" is neither a joyful celebration of this tragedy nor a belittling of marriage. It is, rather, a celebration in the precise religious sense of this word: we acknowledge together God's presence and activity in this most painful passage. As in the liturgical celebration of a marriage crisis successfully negotiated, here we acknowledge sinfulness and guilt, we mourn what has been lost and we praise God for bringing us through the valley of this death. Divorce ends some crises of marriage and with it ends marital fidelity. The marriage dies, but the divorcing persons do not, or should not. Divorcing persons must endure and grow—in fidelity to God and to their own vocations. A strong, effective ministry to divorce allows the survival and even flowering of this fidelity.

Marital fidelity is a most complex virtue. In the midst of past commitments and present changes we try to grow more faithful —to our marriage and family, to God and to our own vocation. This growth will be fostered by the Church's ministry in rites of reconciliation at mid-life.

Reflective Exercise

At the end of Chapter 12 we reflected on the dream at the outset of our adult life and its influence on our maturing. We return to this assessment now in the context of fidelity in mid-life.

Spend some time recalling the exercise in Chapter 12. How has your dream grown and changed over the past years? How is it different now than at twenty-one? Listen for what has been lost and what has newly appeared.

For those of us in mid-life it is important to ask: What reconciliation with the dream may be required now? Are you being invited to a mellow adjustment of an earlier, more romantic ambition to what you are now actually able to accomplish? Is your reconciliation the more difficult challenge of dealing with a dream that was too aggressively pursued? Or have you now to confront a dream long deferred, a dream all but lost in the busy years of your marriage?

Marital fidelity includes being faithful to your own dream and also supporting the dream of your spouse. As these two dreams in your marriage develop, how can you guide them so that they grow together? What care and compromise are needed, in your marriage, to heal wounded dreams and to harmonize different and new dreams?

Additional Resources

The particular challenges to fidelity as marriage matures become clearer as we better understand the dynamics of personal development and change through adult life. Fortunately there are many resources now available to assist this understanding. The issues that are critical for development among adult women are explored by Maggie Scarf in *Unfinished Business* (Doubleday, 1980) and by Lillian Rubin in *Women of a Certain Age* (Harper & Row, 1979). Significant research into patterns of development among adult men is reported in George Vaillant's *Adaptation to Life* (Little, Brown, 1977) and Daniel Levinson's *The Seasons of a Man's Life* (Knopf, 1978).

James Zullo examines "Mid-Life: Crisis of Limits" in his audio-tape series available from NCR Cassettes, Kansas City, Missouri. The collection of essays in *Mid-Life: Developmental and Clinical Issues* (Brunner/Mazel, 1980), edited by William Norman and Thomas Scaramella, includes discussions of marriage and family interaction, sexuality and divorce.

Bernice Neugarten's contribution to the understanding of adult development spans several decades. Some of her recent articles are useful to an appreciation of the movements of interiority and reconciliation in adult life. See, for example, "Adaptation and the Life Cycle" in the Schlossberg and Entine edition of *Counseling Adults* (Brooks/Cole, 1977), "Time, Age, and the Life Cycle" in the July 1979 issue of the *American Journal of Psychiatry*, and *Personality Change in Adulthood* (American Psychological Association, 1978).

Chuck Gallagher's discussion of *The Marriage Encounter* (Doubleday, 1975) is a useful introduction to this significant movement in marriage enrichment.

23

SPIRITUALITY AND LIFESTYLE

The choices that influence our lifestyle are part of the spirituality of our marriage. It is in these choices that we express the values that shape our life together. And we sense that Christianity's most significant contribution to our marriage is in the values to which it calls us. That unselfish love is possible, that sacrifice can have value beyond itself, that pleasure is to be celebrated but not idolized, that I am not for myself alone—these profound truths of human life are not always apparent. There is much in contemporary society, perhaps even much in our own experience, to suggest that these convictions are illusory or naïve. Alone, we may feel how fragile is their hold on us. In community with other believers, we can face our doubts with less fear because we do not face them alone. We can nourish the religious vision of life that sustains us in our journey of marriage for a lifetime.

Christianity does not give married love its value; rather it celebrates the deeper meaning of married love that can sometimes be lost or obscured in the hectic pace of life. Christianity gives us insight, vision into what is ordinarily invisible—the power and presence of God's redeeming love all around us and especially in certain privileged, sacramental experiences. And for most Christians, married love and the life commitments that flow from and surround this love are instances of this privileged experience of the power and presence of God. In this chapter we

will explore several of the values which help to shape the lifestyle of Christian marriage.

The lifestyle of our marriage is influenced by many forces.
Some of these seem beyond our immediate control—economic
factors that bring inflation, political factors that shape national
policy on child care, cultural factors that affect what is "expected" of women and men. In some marriages the influence of
these external factors is so strong that there seems little room for
choice. If I am poor, undereducated or chronically unemployed,
it will be difficult for me to feel that I am in control of my own
life. These burdens of social inequity weigh heavily on many
Americans, adding stress in their marriages. A high incidence of
divorce and desertion results.

But for most Americans, the lifestyle of marriage is not simply
a product of external forces. We are conscious of ourselves as
agents. Within certain limits we choose how we shall live. Some
of our "choices" may be illusory, more influenced than we would
like to admit by factors outside our awareness, but we are nevertheless conscious of ourselves as making decisions that influence
the shape of our marriage.

The choices that are most important for our lifestyle are those
that touch on the use of our resources. Our resources of concern,
of time and of money are the "stuff" of our life together. The
choices we make about these resources are not incidental; they
are close to the substance of what our marriage is. What do we
care about together? What is our money for? How do we spend
the time of our life? It is in our response to these questions that
we discover the values of our marriage and express them in our
lifestyle.

Prayer and Justice

Prayer is part of the lifestyle of Christian marriage. This will
include the ways that we as a couple, as a family, participate in
the prayer of the Church, especially the celebration of the Eucharist. But it will involve as well our developing suitable ways
for us to pray together, to share—sometimes as a couple, some-

times with the children as well—the intimate experience of coming into the presence of God in prayer. In recent decades the devotional life of many Catholic homes included the family rosary or prayers honoring the Sacred Heart. Family prayer today is more likely to focus on the reading of Scripture, reflecting together on its meaning for our lives and our actions in the world. In Chapter 24 we will return to a discussion of the role of family prayer and religious celebration.

Prayer has been urged in marriage as one of the ways for the family to deepen its own unity: "The family that prays together, stays together." To pray together as a couple and as a family can reinforce, sometimes powerfully, our experience of being together in the ways that matter most. But the prayer of Christians is not simply about unity among us; it is about our community with humankind in the presence of God. Liturgical prayer especially celebrates this larger awareness. It is as the people of God that, in the name of Jesus and through the power of his abiding Spirit, we pray. But family prayer, too, should open us beyond "just us." The needs of the world, concretely the ways in which pain and loss and injustice are part of the world that we can influence, are part of our prayer.

In fall 1978 Archbishop Jean Jadot delivered an address on the implementation of the pastoral plan for family ministry that had been developed by the bishops of the United States. In his talk he spoke of prayer, faith and justice as these touch the family. He said, "The prayer I am speaking about is not so much the recitation of prayers as a shared experience of prayer. This finds its origins in a common reading of the Holy Scriptures and in a concern for those who are in need, for justice and peace in the world, for the coming of the Kingdom of God . . . such prayer quite naturally evokes an awareness of the family's mission to service. It also raises the family's social consciousness."

The conviction that we are for more than ourselves is basic to the Christian world view. This value must find its expression not only in our prayer but in our lifestyle. Most of us know, as we saw in Chapter 19, that our marriage is about more than "just us." We need more than "just us" if our family is to thrive. We are aware of how much, as a couple and as a family, we depend

on contact with certain relatives and support from special
friends. But as Christians we go beyond ourselves not just in
what we need but also in what we contribute.

Our life as a family and especially our children carry us into
the larger world. As our children grow, we sense how much
more they belong to the world and its future than they do to us.
Thus, our care for them cannot end at our doorstep. Our first
movements to contribute to the world beyond may well be for
their sake—to make the world a better place for them, a place
worthy of their hopes and conducive to their growth. But it is
possible for this initial impulse of generative care, our concern
for our children and their future, to stagnate. Our preoccupation
with what is good for our family can become a new form of
selfishness. The boundaries may be broadened slightly, but it is
still "us" against "them."

But for many of us the movement of concern for our children
invites us into a concern for the children of the world, for the future of humankind. I become more deeply aware that, by emotion and by action, I am involved in the lives of others. As parent, as worker, as citizen, I am in my own way somehow
responsible for the future. The world—its hopes and problems—
has a claim on me.

As Christians we hear this invitation to generativity reinforced
in the call of Jesus. I am not only my brother's keeper; the category of brother and sister has expanded to include whoever is in
need. "I was a stranger and you made me welcome, naked and
you clothed me, sick and you visited me, in prison and you came
to see me" (Matthew 25:35–36). Christianity expands the
boundaries of our concern. We find we belong to a larger community. We hold our resources as stewards: these are not simply
our "possessions," but the means of our contribution to a more
just world.

Most of us sense, increasingly, that the issues of social value
and justice that we face in our own lives are complex. There are
not many questions where the "one right answer" emerges
quickly and clearly. In any particular case, persons of good will
and intelligence may come to different conclusions about what
should be done. When the issues at stake touch directly on our

own lives or our family's welfare—as in questions of job security or property values or tax reform—it can be even more difficult to determine the just response.

In these situations Christian awareness does not give easy answers but it does give us a starting point. We are not for ourselves alone. Action for justice and the transformation of the world is, as Pope Paul VI proclaimed, constitutive of our response to the gospel. We stand under the gospel challenge that we share the burdens of humankind and participate in its liberation. The way in which we, as a couple and as a family, participate in this mission of Christ may well have to be worked out on our own. But it can be expected that our maturing as Christian adults will involve our developing a lifestyle which expresses our understanding of the mission to which Jesus calls us and supports us in our response.

The Meaning of Money

Money is a central issue in marriage. What money means to us influences our relationship; how we use money shapes our lifestyle. And in many marriages decisions about money are among the most complex the couple face. Disagreements about money (how to manage it; how to spend it; who should make these decisions) and distress over money (living beyond our means; bills coming due; not having enough money to meet an unexpected expense) are significant sources of marital strain.

Money issues in marriage are troublesome in part because money carries so many different meanings. What is money for? My response here influences the way I answer the other questions. How much money does our family need? Can we ever have enough? How would we even go about determining what would be "enough" money for us?

For some of us, money is mainly for the practical necessities of life—food, clothing, shelter. For others, it is for enjoyment—for leisure or luxury or fun. Sometimes money is for our children's future, their education or financial security. Sometimes it is for self-esteem: "Surely I am worthwhile, just look at how

much money I make." Sometimes money is for power: "I can
buy anything and anyone I need." And sometimes it is a resource we have to be used for the good of the world.

Most practical decisions about money carry some larger emotional significance. These decisions say something important to
us about who we are in the world. If, as a couple, we see money
differently, if we each act out of a different sense of "what our
money is for," we can anticipate that money issues will be troublesome to bring up between us and difficult to resolve.

The emotional significance of money is not the only source of
strain. Inflation and the threat of economic recession are very
real factors in the lifestyle of most families. Young couples find
they can no longer afford to buy a house and so delay their decision to have a child. Couples with children realize that they both
must bring in a paycheck if they wish to send their children to
college. Couples who had resolved to retire early now plan to
continue to work, unsure that their retirement benefits will
remain adequate to living costs. Faced with rising prices, high
interest rates and, for some, even unemployment, many families
must make difficult decisions about money—decisions that
significantly influence the lifestyle of their marriage.

But admitting the reality of these financially uncertain times,
the money strain in many marriages is as much influenced by
consumerism as by inflation. Even in this inflationary period,
American families enjoy one of the highest levels of affluence in
the world. We want and expect "the best that money can buy"
for ourselves and our families. Advertising expands our sense of
what we need, assuring us that "we owe it to ourselves" because
"we're worth it." Perhaps especially as Americans we find ourselves susceptible to the temptation to judge our value by what
we have—our material possessions, our standard of living, our
buying power. This preoccupation with "the things of this
world" has always been in tension with deeper religious intuitions: being is more than having; our worth is not grounded in
our wealth; we are not "saved" by what we accumulate. The
Christian vision has always called us to a certain detachment
from wealth. As believers, we know we hold the goods of this
world as stewards. Our responsibility is to care for the person in

need, even out of our own substance. Today we see that this challenge has even broader scope. We are more aware of the connections between the prosperity of the United States and the poverty that exists elsewhere. It is often at the expense of other peoples that we have enjoyed, as a nation, the abundant resources of food and energy and technology that constitute "the good life." The patterns of this structural injustice are complicated, to be sure. It is not easy to trace our personal responsibility in this or to determine what we, as a family, can do to right the balance in world economics. But the complexity of the problem does not relieve us of responsibility. As Christians, we need to examine our family's standard of living not only in view of the shrinking dollar but in view of our accountability in the world. How we spend our money and where we invest our savings—for the Christian today these are more than practical financial questions to be resolved in terms of prices and interest rates alone. They are issues of religious significance that give shape to a Christian lifestyle.

Marriage and Ministry

For us as Christians, the question of lifestyle ultimately brings us to a discussion of ministry. Ministry is the action of believers undertaken in pursuit of the mission which Jesus entrusted to the Church—the coming of the Kingdom. Formal ministry is activity that is recognized or commissioned by the community of faith. Alongside this formal ministry is that ministry expected of all believers—the daily efforts to shape the world according to Christian values of love and mercy. Some Catholics who are married are part of the Church's formal ministry. The expanding involvement of lay persons in roles of official ministry is a fruit of the new vitality in the Church since the Second Vatican Council. Lay women and men serve in liturgical ministries in parishes as lectors and musicians and ministers of communion. Increasingly, the teaching ministry of parishes and dioceses is carried out by lay persons, some through full-time careers in religious education programs or Catholic school systems, others serving in a volunteer capacity as catechetists, conveners of an adult discussion group or members of the parish school board. There has been a comparable increase in the number of lay persons staffing the service agencies and social policy programs that operate under Church auspices or support.

This expansion of "approved" or "recognized" ministries over the past two decades has blurred many of the earlier distinctions among religious, clergy and lay persons in our Church. Married men ordained to the permanent diaconate, women religious serving as pastoral associates in parishes, women and married men studying in Catholic seminaries in preparation for careers of full-time ministry—these persons do not fit easily into former categories. In some cases the openness to lay persons in roles of service and leadership has been more a response to personnel shortages ("There just aren't enough brothers, sisters and priests to go around anymore!") than a sign of a deeper appreciation of the scope of the Christian call to ministry. But in any case, a significant number of Catholic lay persons—both married and single—understand their life vocation to be in the formal ministry of the Church.

The involvement of married Catholics as formal ministers in the Church's ministry *to* marriage—as planners and leaders in programs of marriage preparation, marriage enrichment, marriage counseling, and as part of the liturgical celebration of marriage—is on the increase and is good. In our discussion here, however, we wish to look at the relationship of marriage and the general Christian call to ministry.

For some Christians, both those ordained and others who are not, the immediate focus of their own religious action is within the community of faith, a ministry to and through the formal Church. But for most believers the call to live and act in response to the Christian vision will find expression in their family and their work and their other involvements in society. How is the religious experience of marriage related to the religious action or ministry of an adult Christian life? At several places in this book we have discussed this ministry of the mature Christian in terms of religious generativity. Psychological maturity leads me beyond myself and my intimates toward genuine care for the world. So, too, religious generativity leads me beyond the celebration of the "Good News" for myself, toward religious action—ministry—for a world beyond myself and my religious "intimates." We have seen that intimacy can either contribute to generativity (when the experience of our love releases in each of us the psychological resources we need for generosity and self-transcendence) or detract from it (when our love seems so fragile that we must spend our energy and other resources on ourselves, with none to spare for the world beyond). So marriage can have an ambiguous effect in Christian maturity and ministry. There are Christians for whom their own marriage and family occupy their full concern, not only in moments of crisis such as serious illness or the loss of a job, not just during periods of predictable stress like the birth of a child or, for some, the event of retirement—but characteristically. "We are for ourselves—alone." They may take quite seriously their responsibilities as spouses and parents. Their marriage is stable, their children have as many educational opportunities and social advantages as the couple can afford. They may participate actively in the parish. They are regular churchgoers who contribute financially and see to it that their children take part in the religious education program. But through it all, they are "for themselves." They may see the parish in terms of what it has to give them—a satisfying experience of worship, a program of moral education for their children, perhaps even a sense of security and some status in the community. But to be an adult Christian has not brought with it for them the motivating conviction: I am, our family is, for more than ourselves.

Among many other Christians marriage is just such an opening to God and to the world. The lessons of our marriage teach us to care beyond ourselves; our concern for our children links us to the concerns of the world. We sense that our life together as a family not only "uses up" our strengths, but also generates new resources that we can share and spend beyond ourselves. Our home, our love, our joy together, our time, our insights, our concerns, even our money—these resources of our life together do not exist for ourselves alone. At any one point in our marriage we may be overwhelmed with a sense that there is not enough of us to go around, that our resources are deficient, not just in the face of the needs of the world but even for the needs of our own family. But over its life course, if not at every moment, our marriage as maturing Christians will be marked by openness to needs beyond the family and by an active sense of our own contribution to the coming of the Kingdom, the presence of God in justice and love.

There are, of course, many different ways in which this ministry of maturing Christians will be expressed, and so many ways in which the relationship between marriage and ministry will be seen. For some couples, their ministry is through their family life. They open their home to foster children or adopt a handicapped child. In another family the kitchen is always open to the teenagers in the neighborhood and the couple have time to listen to the concerns of their neighbors and friends. A third couple decide in retirement to devote two days a week together to visiting shut-ins or to welcome a recently widowed neighbor to live with them until she can make other plans. Other couples will sense that their involvement in issues of social concern is crucial to the religious education of their children. To take an unpopular stand on a question of racial justice, to become involved in a political campaign, to use part of their family's vacation money to assist those who have suffered in a disaster—these couples see such actions as of religious significance and encourage their children to share this practical understanding of faith.

For many lay Christians the arena of their ministry is the world of their employment. In my professional responsibilities, in my union activities, in a business decision I can influence, in the way I deal with my company subordinates and superiors, I try to bring to bear the convictions of my religious faith. On the job I take a stand that I know is right, even at the risk there may be repercussions. Or as a couple we decide to change jobs and move across country, so that we can participate in a project for economic justice. For many of us, then, our efforts to contribute to the world and to justice among people happen here, in the work that we do in the world. It is here that a sense of personal vocation takes shape. It is here that we work to hasten the coming of the Kingdom.

A Playful Marriage

The lifestyle of our marriage has much to do with how we are involved beyond ourselves. But our lifestyle also influences and expresses how we are together. Many of the values of Christianity contribute to the way we live our life together by urging us to take marriage seriously. Marriage is for grown-ups; its responsibilities are significant; the honeymoon does not last forever. These sober truths are important for us to hear and the Church serves us well in giving voice to this wisdom. But Christian wisdom also speaks to another side of marriage—the intimate connections between love and play. As our marriage matures, it becomes more playful. Here we will consider several elements that are part of the lifestyle of a playful marriage.

The Time of Our Life

A playful marriage depends on how we spend time together. The demands of careers, children and other involvements can easily overwhelm a marriage relationship. The fatigue and distraction that result can seriously erode our presence to each other. We learn that the playfulness that marked our carefree relationship at the start of our marriage does not endure easily or automatically. We learn, paradoxically, that if we would have a playful marriage we must work at it. Playfulness between us, like our other experiences of intimacy, will have to be cultivated. It will require a discipline in our lifestyle, especially a discipline of our time.

If marriage is a vocation that begins in a resounding "yes," it matures in many "no's." To have quality time for my partner and our family I find I have to say "no" to many outside demands and requests. This discipline, which we discuss in Chapter 24 as an "asceticism of time," helps us structure time for these central commitments of our life. Such disciplined planning and foresight can be experienced as cold calculation or as a canny response to life's multiple demands. Without such an asceticism, we become subject to the endless demands (all of them "worthwhile") of contemporary married life. Gradually exhaustion takes the play out of our marriage, both its flexibility and its fun. Our playfulness can be fostered by planning special times for just the two of us. We set aside times and places with protective boundaries. On our vacation, in days of rest or retreat, we give ourselves permission to play again. Apart from the seriousness of the rest of our life, these occasions invite us to play together and enliven our love.

Competition and Play

A playful marriage also recognizes the connection between competition and play. Our competitiveness can be acknowledged. We can accept the fact that marriage is a contact sport, one in which injury, anger and even loss are sometimes to be expected. But our competitiveness can also enliven us. As we identify together how and when we feel competitive toward one another, these feelings lose some of their force over us. We can share more concretely some of our fears about conflict between us and even feel some of the exhilaration of our struggles.

Competition, as we have seen in Chapter 13, is often an act of intimacy. It brings us "up close" and engages us with one another, however ambiguously. In competition, as in wrestling, we can come in touch with each other in ways that both excite and threaten us. In our competitive encounters we can learn much about ourselves and each other. We can find unsuspected strengths; we can also come upon unacknowledged weaknesses. To compete does not mean that we must use these strengths to dominate or must exploit these weaknesses. My awareness of your weakness can help me love better, help me to protect or at least not take advantage of your vulnerability. Awareness of a strength can help me love better as well, enabling me to use it to foster rather than control our marriage.

The thought of competition in marriage may still disturb us. It may conjure up images of the professional athlete, concerned only with performance and rating, and with coming out ahead in this encounter. But this is only one narrow interpretation of competition. We may also see competition in our marriage as not necessarily setting us against one another but as bringing us closer together. This "closer together" is, of course, threatening. It may well, on occasion, produce hurt and injury. In love and in competition we take the risk of a very close encounter, trusting that we will both play fair. But when we do—overcoming our fear of being crushed and our need to dominate—we are exhilarated *together;* the winner is our marriage and our intimate lifestyle.

Playful Sex

Our sexual life together will be part of a playful marriage. Here the Christian tradition has not always been helpful. A central characteristic of play is its uselessness; it is "just for fun." Christians have learned, on the other hand, that sex is very serious business. It has a specific and (even) exclusive purpose: the begetting of children. Only when this goal is dutifully pursued is our sexual activity to be enjoyed. Thus the seriousness and sacredness of sexuality has, for many Christians, overpowered its playfulness. Is not "playful sex" for playmates and libertines? The ambiguity here parallels that of competition. As competition is neither simply destructive nor simply creative, human sexual activity is neither simply purposeful nor simply playful. As Christians we know that sex is sacred: in our sexual sharing we create more life; through it we confirm and increase our love for one another. But this sacredness does not exclude its playfulness. Sex is for Christians very responsible play. The sexual embrace, sometimes generative of new life and much more often generative of our own love, is also fun. Christianity has, to be sure, been cautious in recognizing the value of playfulness in sex. Only recently and even then reluctantly have many of the official voices within the Church been willing to acknowledge the legitimacy of a sexual love whose every act is not intended to bring children into the world. But these developments are happening in our time, in part through the testimony of married Christians. And as they do, it becomes easier for us to celebrate in the lifestyles of Christian marriage the variety and playfulness of sexual love. Sex is not the only place for play in a maturing marriage. But if there is little or no play in our sexual sharing we are likely to find it more difficult to play in the other areas of our common life.

Learning to Play Fair

Another element of a playful marriage is learning to play fair. This means learning the rules that can help our competitiveness and our other intimacies contribute to our marriage, not destroy it. A first rule is that we *need* to contest with one another. To regularly repress our anger, our confusion or disagreement will not reduce these feelings but only store them for later use. Being "a good sport" in our marriage does not mean choosing not to compete with or confront my partner. It means actively engaging in this relationship. "Poor sports" are those who choose not to contest anything with their partners. They may stand on the sidelines and complain, but they do not compete. A marriage in which the partners no longer contest, no longer struggle with each other in any significant way, can be called a stalemate. The partners in such a marriage are likely to experience each other as "stale mates."

If the first rule is simply to play—to compete, to get engaged —the second rule is to play fair. This means playing skillfully, knowing when and how to confront my partner. In marriage, as in every other kind of play, timing is important. And our experience of each other in marriage, the years we have been playing together, should help us to determine the timing of our confrontations. I bring up a sensitive issue when I sense the time is right: when *we* can handle it, not just when I want to take it on. Playing fair is likely to be a part of our lifestyle in marriage the more we are each able to display the skillful behaviors of communication and conflict resolution that we discussed in Chapter 18.

Learning to play fair is a complex virtue, one that most of us acquire only gradually as we mature. Its growth is likely to include the discipline of identifying and cutting away habits of ours that are destructive in our marriage—belittling the other person, striking back indirectly rather than confronting a troublesome issue, using the children as weapons in an effort to win or be right. Finally, play can teach us the importance of compromise and the value of being a good loser. Compromise means finding our way around questions and concerns that threaten a standoff or seem insoluble. The strategies of barter and negotiation will, at times, help us sustain our love and commitment. Learning how to be a good loser is also a sign of maturity. Each of us can expect to fail, even repeatedly, in our efforts at love and mutuality. Play reminds us that we need not be ashamed. Love does not mean never having to say I'm sorry; it means becoming good at it.

In all these ways we mature in love. We learn that play is not just for kids, that being able to trust one another is more important than always being right. In his study of adult maturity, *Adaptation to Life,* George Vaillant summarizes these connections among love, trust and play:

> It is hard to separate capacity to trust from capacity to play, for play is dangerous until we can trust both ourselves and our opponents to harness rage. In play, we must trust enough and love enough to risk losing without despair, to bear winning without guilt, and to laugh at error without mockery (p. 309).

In our own marriage we can expect to know winning and losing, risk and error, laughter and love. These are the stuff of a playful marriage, the building blocks of a lifestyle of marriage for a lifetime.

Reflective Exercise

Listed below are several of the elements of lifestyle that were
discussed in this chapter. Reflect on each of these, considering
how each is a part of your own life now. In regard to each, note
first what you find satisfying in your life and marriage now, and
then whatever changes you would like to initiate.

Playfulness in our marriage . . .

Our prayer together . . .

Our action for justice . . .

Our use of time . . .

Our use of money . . .

Our participation in the life of the Church . . .

Our contribution to the ministry of the Church . . .

Additional Resources

The Catholic bishops of the United States at their fall meeting
in 1980 issued a "Pastoral Statement on the Laity" to commemorate the fifteenth anniversary of the Vatican II Decree on the
Apostolate of the Laity. In this statement, the text of which is
available in the November 28, 1980, issue of *National Catholic
Reporter,* the bishops reiterate their awareness of the multiple
ministries of Christian adults both within their own families and
beyond.

There is a growing fund of valuable resources for couples and
families who wish to explore the justice dimensions of their own
lifestyle. "Parenting for Peace and Justice" by James and Kath-

leen McGinniss is currently available as an audio-tape series from NCR Cassettes, Kansas City, Missouri, and will soon be published in book form by Orbis Press. In conjunction with the interdenominational Christian movement Bread for the World, Ronald Sider has edited *Cry Justice: The Bible on Hunger and Poverty* (Paulist Press, 1980) as a prayer and study guide for individuals, families and prayer groups. The Inter-Religious Task Force for Social Analysis has prepared *Must We Choose Sides?*, a practically useful study and action guide for Christian commitment in the 1980s. Two Washington, D.C.-based organizations that provide analysis from a Christian perspective of significant current issues of social concern are Center of Concern (focusing on international issues) and Network (focusing on national legislation). Each provides a quarterly newsletter along with other publications for a modest annual membership fee.

The range of resources available for marriage and family enrichment is also wide. David and Vera Mace have long worked with the Christian churches for more effective ministry to marriage. A good example of their continuing contribution is *How to Have a Happy Marriage: A Step-by-Step Guide to an Enriched Relationship* (Abingdon, 1977), designed for use by a couple or in a group setting. Herbert Otto has edited *Marriage and Family Enrichment: New Perspectives and Programs* (Abingdon, 1976), an excellent guide to resources, programs and agencies available in support of marriage. M. C. Howell returns the focus to the resources available within the family in *Helping Ourselves: Families and the Human Network* (Beacon, 1975).

24

A CHRISTIAN ASCETICISM OF MARRIAGE

Asceticism, a word which may conjure up images of fasting monks and dour hermits, can be applied to a much more ordinary and everyday aspect of Christian life. Asceticism in the contemporary translation that we suggested in Chapter 1 refers to the expectable discipline of a Christian life. The suggestion, not so radical, is that we must *do something* to become Christian. What is one to do? How do we act in order to mature as Christians? What is the discipline required of a contemporary Christian marriage and family? We know that something more than the sacrament of Baptism is required; something more than attending church regularly.

The spirituality outlined in this book begins with the conviction that Christians *see* something different in life and *respond* to this insight in certain ways. A spirituality of Christian marriage and family begins with recognizing and attending to a presence—the presence of God in our life, supporting us and challenging us and inviting us beyond where we are now. Such a spirituality begins in presence and matures in our response to this presence. Presence involves a discipline because being attentive and aware are often difficult tasks. It does not take us long to realize that without discipline and care our job responsibilities and the routines of family life can distract us from rather than manifest to us God's presence at work in our lives.

The notion of presence does not refer to extraordinary apparitions or visions; it does refer to the ordinary, everyday appearances and encounters that constitute our marriage and family life. Consider our presence to one another. Begun in the initial exciting experience of romance, this presence must continue to be realized and clarified. A Christian asceticism of marriage is concerned with continuing and maturing this early romantic presence. There are many forces in marriage today that can impede this development: the demands of a career, the arrival of our children, the difficulty of sharing new ambitions and fears as these arise within us. There are also invitations and opportunities for deepening our awareness of one another and of God, both in the normal movement of our family life and in special, more perilous times.

If we were to chart our marriage and family life, most of us would probably depict a pattern of stable "normal" periods broken at places by certain very special events. The severe illness of a child, an unanticipated promotion, a serious difficulty in our relationship—all these share a peculiar quality which marks them as potentially religious and as important for a Christian spirituality of marriage. In times of crisis, such as these, we can experience ourselves becoming especially present to each other and, potentially, to God. It may be useful, then, to explore the connections between crises and presence.

Crisis and Presence

Crisis, in the developmental psychology of Erik Erikson, denotes an ambiguous time, a period of decision and opportunity. In such a time of increased vulnerability and heightened potential, as Erikson notes, we enter "a critical period in which a decisive turn, one way or another, is unavoidable." We are brought to special attention and given an opportunity to make a choice that will be decisive for the future.

Before examining the psychological and religious features of crises in marriage, it will be helpful to recall some common examples of such challenges. The illness of a child frightens us and brings us to attention; we become suddenly present to each

other and to God in a new and different way. Or I lose my job
and with it my sense of our family's security. This feels like a defeat and makes me question who I am and what I am worth. Or
our family moves to a new house in a new city. At first excited,
we begin to feel uneasy. In this new neighborhood we feel
disoriented. Further, we may be embarrassed by these "immature" reactions.

All of these experiences are disruptive: they interrupt the
smooth flow of our life. More deeply, they challenge the control
we exercise over life. We become, to differing degrees, disoriented. The criteria that used to make for "a good day" do not
apply; the accustomed patterns of life are broken. Expectably
we feel threatened at a time like this. Sometimes we flee into activity, hoping that if we keep busy the confusion will subside.
Sometimes we ask God to make it "all better."

Psychologically, these crises represent an extraordinary opportunity. Deprived of the usual patterns and values of our daily
life, we have the chance to discover or recover other values. We
are offered an opportunity for reassessment: How have we cared
for this sick child in the past? What did that job mean to us?
How would we like to live differently in this new city? These
important questions are often smothered under the press of daily
tasks and distractions. Crises disrupt, break open daily life and
allow us to look inside. They invite insight.

Such opportunities also have extraordinary religious import.
The Greek word *krisis* in the New Testament means judgment or
decision. Most often it refers to a time of crucial decision making. When *krisis* is a time of God's judgment it is also a time of
God's special presence; crisis is a time for coming into the presence of God. This means it is a time of special grace, a sacred
time. And the ambiguity of the psychological notion of crisis as
a time of both threat and promise appears in the New Testament also. Crisis is an end-time: it heralds the conclusion of
something, the loss of something. In every religious crisis there is
a dying to something—one way of being with another person, an
attachment, life itself—and a hoped-for coming to life.

In New Testament terms, a crisis is thus a time of decision in
which we may expect to lose something and to enter into God's

presence. Crises as religious disruptions are how God gets into our life. In the busyness of our family life, our marriage and work, God's presence is constant but often not easily discerned. Worse, we may clutter our life with distractions or fill it with control until there is no space, no gap in which God may intrude or be heard. Our life may be compared to a garment we are weaving: we work a pattern in it daily, a pattern that identifies it as ours. Crises are God's breaking into this patterned design; they are like seams or tears in the life we are fabricating. Habits and distractions are broken along with the pattern. We are forced to pay more attention to our life and our loved ones. And the pattern is likely to change as we realize our life is more than our own fabrication.

Crisis and Story

Another metaphor for our life is that of a story being told. Telling this story over decades, we come to think of ourselves as the sole authors. Within this story, a crisis appears as a parable. A parable, as in the New Testament, is a special kind of tale: it goes against the grain and disrupts our story, overturns it. We are stumped by an unexpected turn in life. Again we are forced to pay closer attention to our story and are reminded that it is part of a larger tale of which we are not the sole authors.

Crises often come in strange, unanticipated ways—the illness of a previously healthy child, sudden dissatisfaction with a successful career, a seemingly harmless remark about our marital relationship. Whatever the cause or the trigger, Christians believe there are no strictly secular crises. Every disruption of our life, every break in our control and defenses, is a religious opportunity. In that gap we are invited to see what had always been present—God's supporting and challenging love telling the surprising story of our life.

In a family, multiple stories are unfolding and so, many different crises can be expected. A Christian asceticism of marriage and the family will include the resolve and the growing skill of attending to these holy if sometimes threatening events.

Not frightened off by the threat of loss, we will recognize that
crises are not always to be avoided or skirted. Some are to be
gone through, looked into. We can expect disorientation here,
but also the voice of God beginning an unanticipated new chapter in the story of this family.

Crisis and Patience

The expectable discipline of a Christian life includes the continuing effort to be present to ourselves, to our loved ones, and
to God at work in these lives. Is there a Christian virtue that is
related to this task, so difficult in today's busy lifestyles? In his
study *Young Man Luther* Erikson offers a clue in his reference
to "those crises . . . which make patients out of us." Erikson
does not mean these crises put us in hospital beds. He uses the
word "patient" in its root sense: we are forced to undergo, to
suffer these unavoidable events. For Erikson, patience is the psychological ability to allow such events to happen and to learn
from them. Paradoxically, this patience is a very active ability:
with it we are able to hold ourselves attentive to what is happening in our lives and with our loved ones. Patience, as a psychological strength, overcomes our uneasiness and fright in the
face of crises. It allows us to look into the face of a crisis, rather
than hide from it in activities that distract and exhaust us.

How is this psychological ability transformed into the Christian virtue of patience? The virtue of patience has sometimes
been understood in an overly passive fashion. Rather than referring to our posture before God, it became at times a political
prescription for certain classes of Christians. Wives, for instance,
should have patience; it is their task to be submissive and accepting. Subjects should have patience with leaders, secular and
ecclesiastical. Obedience and acceptance of their subservient position is in the natural order of things. But there is little patience
today with this understanding of the virtue.

Patience, as a Christian virtue, is the ability to attend to God's
working in my life and in the world. This is a highly active
strength, reminding me that I cannot delegate the responsibility

for my own life. I cannot "patiently" wait for others to interpret my life and tell me what it means. Patience is an adult virtue that calls me to attend to my life and to respond to the revelation I find there.

Patience is grounded in trust. We can pay attention to the particular movements of our own lives only if we can trust ourselves. If we do not know who we are or cannot trust our feelings, we cannot be patient. And patience is rooted in another kind of trust—in the presence and purpose of God in life. When we do not believe that God is at work in this confusing world, when we cannot trust that God is leading us somewhere, we can no longer be patient. We become impatient, either despairing or taking the future into our own hands. Christian involvement in the world combines an intense engagement with expectant attention. Patience, as a Christian virtue, is not at all passive. It does not mean giving the responsibility for our lives to others, even if these others are said to know what is best for us. Assuming responsibility for our own lives and our world begins in awareness of what is happening. This awareness arises in patience—the ability to be present to the continually surprising events of our lives.

Impatience, as a failure of this virtue, takes various shapes today. Sometimes impatience is seen in our efforts to force our lives to go a certain way: refusing to listen to our own particular limits and strengths, we impatiently pursue a myth of the ideal wife or perfect parent or dutiful husband. We follow these abstract ideals because we are too impatient to listen to the special, if not yet clear, information that comes in our own vocation and our experience of *this* marriage. Perhaps the most common form of impatience today is the difficulty in being still. We are used to being busy ("Idleness is the devil's workshop"), used to noise and distraction. All these have a certain usefulness: they keep our minds off unsettling invitations that arise from God, or from our marriage partner, or from our children as our family grows. As Americans, we especially suffer the temptation to lose ourselves in frantic daily schedules of work and commuting, in the noises of our television and stereo sets. All these contribute to an inability to be still and attentive to quieter and more fragile revelations. Patience, as a virtue important for a Christian family, gives us the discipline to listen carefully to the lives around us. Trusting ourselves and God, we listen for the movements of God, the revelation of God in our daily life. An asceticism of Christian marriage begins here.

An Asceticism of Time

Our efforts to be present to one another occur in time. No problem is more prevalent for families than that of time—where does it go, how can we save it? We regret being too busy to spend time with our loved ones; there is not enough time in the week for all we want to do. Compounding these daily troubles with time is our experience of growing older: time is running out.

Is the time of our life just a given? Is it just a boundary of life within which we do the best we can? Or is there some way we can assertively "make more" of our time? Is our use of time—how we as a family decide to use our time—related to our Christian values? How might a contemporary Christian spirituality confront the question of time?

Christians have always been aware of the potential holiness of time. Christianity is a historical religion: we believe in a God who enters time to change it and sanctify it. Christians have sometimes in their history come to believe that God lives apart from time in a quiet, still moment of eternity. With such a view of God, our religious task becomes that of escaping time, an effort to "shrug off this mortal coil" and find our way to this truly holy existence. A more genuinely Christian conviction is that God abides here and now in our lives. We encounter God, receive God's grace and experience the bitterness of God's absence within the changing times of our lives. A Christian spirituality of time will have to do with how present we allow ourselves to be to our God in the midst of the excitement and distraction of time.

Early Christians borrowed two words from the Greek world to describe their experience of God in time. The Greek word *chronos* described ordinary time, the everyday flow of life. This is day-in-and-day-out time with no special focus or meaning. The word *chronos* survives in English in such words as "chronological" and "chronic." The word *kairos* referred to a very different experience of time: a time of special urgency or potential; a time when something is about to happen, a time of particular opportunity, danger or vulnerability. *Kairos* referred to the "right time" or the favorable moment for a decision or action.

The translators of the Hebrew Old Testament and the writers of the New Testament often used these two words to capture their experience of time as holy and time without God's special presence. In the New Testament *chronos* appears in reference to the long period of history before God's self-revelation in Jesus Christ (Romans 16:25). This word is also used to describe lengthy periods of illness before Jesus' healing intervention, as in the story of the man who had lain by the pool in Jerusalem for many years (John 5:6). *Chronos* is used in Jesus' questioning about the duration of the illness of a possessed person: "How long a time (*chronos*) has this been happening to him?" (Mark 9:21). Although the word *chronos* is not always used in this special way, often it does suggest a kind of time in which God's absence is felt or illness prevails, a time of non-salvation. This kind of time suggests life as "chronic"—either ill or aimless, my life is not experienced as challenged or healed by the presence of God.

Kairos in the Old Testament often translates times of special importance, whether these be tribulations (Isaiah 33:2 and Jeremiah 2:27) or joyful celebrations (Exodus 13:10; 23:14; 34:18). One of the most poignant passages in which *kairos* appears is in Psalm Seventy-one, the prayer of an aging person: "Cast me not away in the *kairos* of my old age." Old age is not an ordinary time, but one of special vulnerability. It is a time when the presence or absence of God is especially felt.

In the New Testament *kairos* is the special time of Jesus' public life: "The time (*kairos*) has come . . . and the kingdom of God is close at hand" (Mark 1:15). It is also the frightening period of his impending death: "My time (*kairos*) is near" (Matthew 26:18). *Kairos,* for Christians, refers to times of God's special presence in life. It may be a presence which challenges

us in crises or difficulties; it may be a presence which heals and
consoles us. But it is always a time transformed by God's breaking into our lives. It is a time when God gets our attention,
whether by disaster or by insight. It is also a time of decision:
we are called to change ourselves in response to this presence.

Kairos *and* Chronos *Today*

Christian spirituality always involves the confrontation of our
lives by the gospels, by the Good News celebrated in the Christian tradition. Thus, a contemporary spirituality of time will
explore how *chronos* and *kairos* are experienced in our lives
today. There seem to be two common experiences of *chronos*
time in American life. In the first, we experience life as just continuing day after day with no special point or purpose. Adolescents often have this experience of time: as yet without a goal or
focus, they may experience life as pointless and begin to wonder
why they should continue. The hero of Albert Camus' novel *The
Stranger* illustrates this experience of time: there is no place to
go and nothing to do. *Chronos,* in this sense, describes life as
boring, "chronic"—without the special purpose of a cause, or
lover, or God.

A second, very different experience of *chronos* is that of a
compulsive lifestyle. Parallel to the possessed persons in the
New Testament, we at times experience ourselves as driven,
obsessed with things to accomplish and goals to attain. Life then
has a great deal of energy and focus, but little freedom. We are
possessed by compulsive ideals or "shoulds." In such moods we
hurry through life, too busy and distracted to be present to our
loved ones. We experience time running out and accelerate our
lives to stay ahead of it. Time becomes an enemy, a commodity
in short supply; in such an atmosphere a marriage can hardly
flourish.

However we find our life as *chronos*, we also can find *kairos*
there, too. *Kairos* refers to those special times in our marriage
and our family: the extraordinary time around our wedding, the
birth of our children, a special vacation together. And *kairos* can

also refer to the painful, trying periods around illness or a death or the months during which our marriage seemed in jeopardy and we were forced to pay particular attention to it. In each of these times—sometimes a few days, sometimes many months in duration—God was breaking into our lives, into our time. This in-breaking disrupted the chronology of our daily lives, the patterns of our control or distraction or boredom. Time took on a different quality as we were compelled to give more attention to life. When we look back on this time we see that we were broken or healed or both: we know that we were changed.

There is also a more ordinary experience of *kairos* in our life. Examples here are less crisis-oriented but equally holy. This is the experience of a period of time as especially focused, concentrated and effective. During such a period we find ourselves working effectively and non-compulsively; we find ourselves more than usually attentive to our loved ones, as well as to the movements of our own heart. It is a time of living gracefully—loving and working with vigor and concentration.

A Spirituality of Time

To this point we have talked of *kairos* as God's time, as God's invading our time. An asceticism of time is concerned with an awareness of this *kairos* in our own histories but is also concerned with our response to it. Asceticism is not simply about waiting for God to redeem us; it is an assertive effort *to shape the time of our life to allow God greater access to it*. Christian asceticism is about our daily efforts to shape our lifestyles so we can live more consistently in the presence of God and of one another. Spirituality is about the transformation of *chronos* into *kairos*.

How do we do this? Such an asceticism may begin in "taking the time" to reflect on how we as a family spend our time; it matures in the honest and careful examination of the compulsions that distort our lives—the need to be successful, or to accumulate possessions, or to be responsible for the entire world. A reflection on our own concrete experiences of *chronos* and *kairos*

will help: the more we savor these past experiences of time, the
more we are motivated to change "chronic" patterns of living for
more balanced, "kairotic" ones.

An ascetical restyling of our life is rooted in a conviction
about our own responsibility and agency. No one else can tell
our family how we are best to live—how to balance work and
play, how and when to pray together, how to best use our weekends. Our own Christian responsibility leads us to these choices.
Adult maturity means not being a victim of other people's decisions or our own compulsions; Christian maturity means taking
responsibility for the time of our life and shaping it so that love
and justice have an opportunity to flourish. Finally, a family's
reflection on its use of time will best take place in a mood of
mutuality. Decisions about our shared time are not easily legis-
lated. But coming to an appreciation of how each of us has
different needs, we can build a consensus and compromise about
our family's best use of time.

In Paul's letter to the Ephesians (5:16) we read the injunc-
tion: "Make the most of your time." This is not a capitalistic
counsel for productivity but a religious insight urging us to live
more thoroughly in the presence of God. Making the most of our
time means rescuing ourselves from exhaustion and distraction,
especially as these become chronic. To live regularly with exhaustion and distraction is to fail at loving well and working
well; it is most often to fail as well at our tasks of mercy and justice in the world. The process of a contemporary asceticism of
time may be described as an effort to befriend time. Time is an
enemy drawing us to the final destruction of death only if we do
not believe in God. Time is a neutral medium only if we do not
expect to meet God there. Yet we have experienced that it is in
time that we fall in love, serve our neighbor in need, meet God.
Time is the habitat and terrain in which our love grows and our
family matures. Time is a holy place—but only if we can recognize it, only if we befriend it.

The New Testament phrase "Make the most of your time" can
also be translated: "Redeem the time." This is the point of an asceticism of time. Ordinarily we waste time, squander it or
rigidify it by living compulsively. As we allow God to rescue us

and our family from dissipation and from obsessive living, we participate in the redeeming of time. We become more present to each other, able to love better and more alert to our deepest beliefs. Redeeming the time of our lives, we do what everyone is always working at—we save time. We participate in the salvation of time.

Celebrating the Times of Our Life

Every marriage, every family has special times. There are the very special times around the birth of a child, serious sicknesses, the resolving of a long dispute. We often look back on these, wishing we had paid more attention, had found a way to celebrate these events. It is often only in retrospect that we realize how these times have shaped and matured our family. And there are special times of a more ordinary variety: Saturday afternoons, August vacations, Christmas time and other days of special importance just to our family. These are all times of special presence—sometimes in easy togetherness, sometimes in quarrels and hostility, sometimes in fear and uneasiness. How can a family respond to these times in a genuinely Christian way? How can we celebrate these times—whether "celebration" means a gala party or a mellow reconciliation?

There seem to be two major reasons that families find it so difficult to celebrate, in an explicitly religious and Christian way, the times of their lives. The first reason has been much discussed here: the frenzied busyness of our daily lives. Busy getting ahead and responding to the multiple "shoulds" of American society, we lack the time to spend together. Supper occurs in platoons; evenings are shrouded in fatigue; weekends disappear in meetings, ball games and errands. Quality time together is hard to find. And here a genuine asceticism emerges: we must decide how to spend our time, how to "save time" for tending to each other. Our adult assertiveness is sorely tested in the effort to slow and focus our lives. Only as we ascetically save time for each other can we begin to celebrate the joy and the sorrow which are so deeply a part of our family.

If this first reason has to do with how we spend time, the second reason has to do with how we imagine ourselves. Christian lay persons generally and especially Catholics have learned well the lesson that they are not celebrators. A kind of religious impotence has been taught to the laity: religious celebration belongs to the clergy and its place is in church. When religious celebration is restricted to the sanctuary and to Sunday morning, and when the laity "attend" Mass and "receive" the sacraments, a profound passivity results. Parents should say a prayer before supper, but that is about it. Such a religious understanding of the laity contributes to stability and "good order." Great control and uniformity result from celebrations being restricted to the church building. Celebrations in the home, it was felt, are likely to be highly individualistic and even unorthodox. But the price of our uniformity has been a religious impotence and passivity among many of the faithful.

The hint of a recovery of the religious potency of Catholic lay persons lies in the sacrament of Matrimony itself. Here the couple are the chief celebrants. If they celebrate their marriage in the wedding ceremony, must they not continue to celebrate it as it matures through its own special times and crises? Changes in our understanding of the sacrament of Reconciliation and the Eucharist suggest directions for religious celebrations in the family. Forgiveness for our failures is not simply an affair with God in a confessional; we need forgiveness both from God and from those (most often loved ones) whom we have offended. Communal celebrations of Reconciliation, introduced in the Catholic Church since Vatican II, acknowledge this more public and familial aspect of forgiveness. Many Catholic families today are attempting to find a religious way to share this sorrow and forgiveness *within* the family. As Christians we also celebrate the presence of the Lord among us not only in the formal liturgy of the Eucharist but in the family as well. An important meal for the family is not identical with the Eucharist celebrated in the larger community, but it is not as distant as we had come to believe. As families recognize both the need and the joy of such celebrations of the Lord's presence and of reconciliation, they will recover their own religious responsibility. The result will not be to replace or devalue the Eucharist and the sacrament of Reconciliation but to enhance them by complementing them with familial exercises in these two core Christian acts. It also makes sense that as parents assume a greater role in the religious education of their children, this education be rooted in these two central Christian rituals. But again, a double challenge arises: Do we as parents have time enough to care for our children's religious growth? Do we consider ourselves sufficiently able to share our faith with our children?

This recovery of the religious potency of a family—its ability to celebrate its own holy times—will include a sensitivity to the new goals of mutuality in marriage. Today, leading us in celebration is not the sole prerogative of the male "head of the family." Indeed, as headship gives way to partnership, our family religious celebrations will be planned by those who feel most comfortable and capable in this. As parents we will share responsibility for these family celebrations between us, and often with the children as well.

But if this is to happen, a double discipline is involved. We must take the time to be present to each other so that we may be aware of our special times and crises. Then we must appreciate sufficiently our own religious potency and the holiness of our family so that we can be moved to celebrate the sacred moments of joy, distress and healing that mark our own family's journey with God.

Reflective Exercise

Think back to a recent special time in your family. It may have been a celebration of some success or a troubled time for a child. How did your family respond to this time? Were you able to pay full attention to it, to talk about it and maybe even pray about it? Were you too busy to appreciate its importance at the time? As you look back at it, what was its religious meaning, its special value for your family?

Looking back over the past year of your life, become aware of its many events: the people, the work, its successes, failures and distractions. As you recall this year, try to identify some one period—perhaps several weeks, perhaps several months—that you would describe as *chronos* time for you. It may have been a period of boredom or disappointment or a time of very little energy. Or it may have been a very different experience of *chronos* —an overly busy, distracted and compulsive time. Whatever it was, revisit it now and become aware again of its feelings and moods, and its duration.

Then listen for a period, in this same year, of *kairos* time in your life. Perhaps it was a time of insight or reconciliation in the family. Or perhaps a period of special attention, when you seemed especially alert and present to others at home and at work. Again, revisit this time and savor the feelings that accompanied this experience of holy time or *kairos* in your life.

Additional Resources

A contemporary asceticism of marriage, grounded in the virtue and skills of intimacy, is urged by Archbishop Joseph Bernadin in his address to the 1980 synod of Catholic bishops meeting on the family. The text, "Toward a Spirituality of Marital Intimacy," is available in the October 16, 1980, issue of *Origins*. Catholic couples are becoming increasingly active in expressing their religious awareness and practice within the larger conversation concerning Christian spirituality today. See, for example, Jerry and Marilyn Sexton's audio-tape series "Marital Spirituality," available from NCR Cassettes, Kansas City, Missouri.

Erik Erikson defines a developmental crisis in *Identity: Youth and Crisis* (Norton, 1968), p. 96, and in *Insight and Responsibility* (Norton, 1964), p. 139. In *Identity: Youth and Crisis* he distinguishes normative crises, those developmentally significant events that lead to growth, from neurotic crises, which are more likely to lead to illness and stagnation (p. 163). We have examined the religious characteristics of adult crises in Chapter 2 of our *Christian Life Patterns* (Doubleday, 1979). In his perceptive discussion of pastoral counseling in *Crisis Experience in Modern Life* (Abingdon, 1979), Charles Gerkin gives useful examples of the kinds of marital and family crises ministers are likely to experience in their pastoral work. John Dominic Crossan relates story, myth and parable to crises and human growth in *The Dark Interval* (Argus, 1975).

For a more extended exploration of time management and Christian spirituality, see James D. Whitehead's "An Asceticism of Time" in the January 1980 issue of *Review for Religious*. This article appears in a slightly different form as Chapter 10 in our *Method in Ministry* (Seabury, 1980). For a different approach to time and Christian spirituality, see Niels-Erik Andreasen's *The Christian Use of Time* (Abingdon, 1978). Two practical resources in regard to time management are Alan Lakein's *How to Get Control of Your Time and Your Life* (Wyden, 1973) and James Davidson's *Effective Time Management: A Practical Workbook* (Human Sciences Press, 1978).

Mary Reed Newland has long assisted Catholic families and others in their efforts to celebrate the religious significance of events within the life of the family. See, for example, her early work *The Year and Our Children* (Doubleday Image, 1964) and her more recent *The Saint Book for Parents* (Seabury, 1979). In *Liturgy and Learning Through the Life Cycle* (Seabury, 1980) John Westerhoff and William Willimon discuss the connections between Christian living and liturgy.

25

THE MINISTRY OF MARRIAGE

In this book we have been exploring the religious meaning of marriage. The religious reality of marriage touches on both its inner life of mutual love and commitment and its participation in the larger mission of Jesus. It is the inner life of our marriage that can manifest to us the power and presence of God. We marvel at the mysterious process of devotion and frustration, of joy and compromise, and doubt and happiness that holds us together in our love. We know, sometimes with frightening clarity, that this intricate and often fragile figure of our life together depends altogether on us, and altogether on more than us. It is our responsibility, and yet we receive it as gift.

To be married in the Lord is to be able to experience this power and presence of God in our life together: God's healing love, in your love for me; God's mysterious call, in the challenge of development and change in our life together; God's delight, in the joy we share in sex; God's fecundity, in the wonder of our children. But here as always the Christian vision is not self-contained. We see in order that we may live transformed by this vision. To be married in the Lord is to have eyes to see a deeper meaning and presence in our love. It is also to respond to this presence—a presence which calls us, together, beyond "just ourselves," into an awareness of our involvement in the work of God in the world. As believers, we participate in the mission of Jesus: by our acts of faith and justice we proclaim to the future generations that our God is the Lord. For many of us, our marriage is central to this larger religious purpose of our lives. Marriage tests and reinforces the basic value commitments that give shape to our lives. It is in our marriage and our life as a family that our experience of God is deepened and purified. Our children particularize and expand our sense that we are connected with the human community and responsible for its future.

Marriage as a Source of Ministry

The community of faith is involved in the religious reality of marriage. The Church has a ministry to marriage—to support the relationship, the commitment and the lifestyle of Christian marriage which serves as a central context of the religious experience and maturity of so many believers. But this service *to* marriage is not the only connection between marriage and the ministry of the community of faith. There is the ministry *of* married Christians as well. Ministry is a sign of religious maturity. It is, or should be, expected of all adult believers—not just those few who are identified as professionals but the majority within the community of faith, most of whom *are* married and *are not* in religious careers. There are signs that the Church today is beginning, again, to expect this ministry of the adult believer. That is an important first step. If married Christians are seen mainly as the objects or recipients of the Church's ministry (*we* have to figure out better ways to help *them*) the programs that result will reinforce passivity and will not be likely to contribute to the religious maturity of married Christians. Self-definition, autonomy and personal agency are signs of mature action. The Church today stands challenged to develop ways in which married Christians—and, more generally, lay Christians—can bring these strengths of self-determination, autonomy and personal agency into the ongoing dialogue of the community of faith. The indications are that this will not be easy, but religious maturity will happen no other way.

Marriage and family, then, are not just the objects of Christian ministry as relationships to be cared for and ministered to. A marriage and family is itself a resource to a community of faith, a source of energy and vision, a source of Christian ministry. In this final chapter we would like to bring together a number of this book's themes, now under the rubric of the ministry of Christian marriage and family. We are concerned here with the religious agency and power of a marriage.

This ministry of marriage goes in two directions—caring for itself and caring beyond itself. That a Christian marriage and family is meant to minister to itself, and not simply wait for an officially designated minister to care for it, is seen in the sacrament of Matrimony: the couple are the ministers, the celebrants of this sacrament. And since the sacrament of Matrimony is not exhausted in a single ceremony but continues as the marriage matures, we must ask how the couple continue to administer this sacrament. How does a couple continue to minister to their own relationship and their growing family?

The Purification of Expectations

Summarizing the many suggestions included in our long discussion, we would point to two especially important kinds of family ministry. The first concerns our inherited assumptions about marriage; we might name this the ministry of purifying our expectations. When we marry we bring with us a rich and complex set of assumptions of what marriage "should be like." These assumptions are most often unspoken, perhaps even to ourselves. They have been inherited from our experience of our own parents and family, from our Christian education and from the depictions of marriage in our cultural life. We "know," unreflectively, what a marriage is, how husbands and wives are supposed to act, how children are to be raised. Some of these expectations are good and valuable; others may be destructive or simply inappropriate to our own marriage. Most importantly, they are likely to be, at least in early adult life, external to us. They are more someone else's expectations than our own but they are the inheritance we bring with us into marriage.

As our marriage grows, we come into a deeper knowledge of

who we are, of what *this particular* marriage and family is becoming. We begin the necessary process of reflecting together on our expectations and evaluating which ones fit our life together and which ones do not. This process is the journey into the authority and uniqueness of our own marriage. We may have begun our life together with the assumption that conflict has no place in marriage. Conflict and competition are simply destructive, we had learned, and so shall have no place in our home. When conflict does arise, as it must, we are confused and embarrassed: our experience does not fit our expectations. This can be humiliating and lead us to suppress conflict. We try to ignore it because we sense it should not be here. Another response, and one which exemplifies an effective ministry to our relationship, is to examine this supposition about conflict. Where did we learn this and how valid is it? Do not our Christian tradition and psychological research indicate that conflict is a part of every significant relationship and that it can be a powerful means of growth, even of a greater intimacy between us? Is not our expectation about conflict a naïve and unuseful assumption? Such a reflective process, undertaken together, perhaps in some confusion, is a purification of expectations. It is part of an important ongoing asceticism of Christian marriage, an asceticism for which we are responsible.

Another expectation carried with us into marriage was, perhaps, that we would fully satisfy every need for one another. Friend, lover, companion: our mutual love was such that neither of us would have need for any others. As our marriage matures, we may find this is not so. We cannot, and do not choose to be, all things for each other. Does this mean we are falling out of love or that our marriage is failing? It may, but it may also indicate that a youthful romantic expectation is being purified. A general assumption about marriage is being tested and reshaped by our marital experience. This is a purification and a discipline because it challenges cherished ideas and ideals that we carry within us. Yet we know that simply to live out our marriage and family life according to the expectations visited on us from outside, or even from within, is to ignore and neglect the particular gracefulness of our love.

When we begin this reflection on the assumptions we have brought to marriage, we may find their number is legion: assumptions about you as husband-provider, myself as wife; expectations about how we should make love and how often; assumptions about how many children a "good Catholic couple" ought to have. We find, too, that our marriage is an intersection of expectations, yours and mine; our implicit assumptions emerge in the subtle and not so subtle demands we make on each other.

The purification of expectations is a specific ministry to which a couple is called; it is a work that will test the resiliency of their marriage. We can expect confusion and disorientation when long-cherished assumptions come under attack. We can expect pain and mourning when we are forced to let go expectations long held but no longer fitting for our marriage. But we can also look forward, in this purification, to a refining of our love. In this ascetical process, of which we are the chief ministers, we make our marriage more thoroughly *ours*. It remains an American marriage and a Christian marriage because this is not a journey into privacy. But a Christian and American marriage becomes more thoroughly *ours,* with the expressions of love, the style of conflict and communication, and the patterns of family life and social involvement that fit our particular vocation of marriage.

The ability to perform this ministry, as well as the other ministries to which a married couple is called, is itself based on an expectation. This is the expectation that a couple is religiously responsible for the maturing of their marriage. Our life together will not unfold automatically or naturally, nor can we expect a designated Christian minister always to be standing by to assist our growth. As we are the ministers of the sacrament of Matrimony, we continue to be the ministers of this ongoing sacramental process. This expectation of our own religious potency is one that the Christian Church and its ministers might more powerfully make available to those of us who marry.

Both vision and virtues are required for this internal ministry to marriage and family. We can say that this ministry of the purification of expectations begins in vision—a couple seeing that they can expect to face this challenge together. This ministry is then pursued through virtue; that is, the couple must be equipped for this demanding task. Specific skills which help couples share their feelings concretely and without blame and skills that assist their dealing with conflict will give this ministry practical shape.

Celebration in the Family

A second way that a family ministers to itself touches on the central realities of the Christian faith: forgiveness and celebration of the Lord's presence. In our recent past the sacrament of Penance and the Eucharist have been understood as clearly separated from everyday family life. Penance became a totally private affair between God and the soul, performed in church. The connections between the sacrament and forgiveness as it is required and experienced in our life as a family became easily ignored. The reform of the sacrament of Reconciliation has stressed the communal and public aspects of this action of sorrow and forgiveness. A next step, as we noted in Chapter 24, is likely to include efforts to find simple and effective ways for families to share directly in the celebration of Christian forgiveness. If a marriage and family is called to minister to itself, this calling will certainly include learning ways to forgive each other. A simple family rite would allow couples and families to participate more powerfully in this central Christian act. Such a development, already happening in many Christian homes, will not devalue the sacrament of Reconciliation but, on the contrary, will help revitalize it.

The second central religious act of any Christian group is the celebration of the Lord's presence. The liturgical reforms in the Catholic Church in the past twenty years have brought this experience from "the Mass said by the priest" to "the Eucharist celebrated by the community." The increased participation of the laity points to an as yet underdeveloped part of Christian ministry: the celebration of the Lord's presence in the family. Complex historical reasons have led to the restriction of the

Christian sacraments of Reconciliation and Eucharist to the church building and to the activity of the clergy. As Christian reconciliation is moving beyond the confessional box, the celebration of the Lord's presence is also being exercised beyond the sanctuary. The celebration of a "home Mass" by a priest suggests that similar celebrations by the family itself might be expected. One might compare the Jewish Seder celebration by the head of the house with future Christian celebrations of the Lord's presence in the family. The shriveled state of this family ministry can be glimpsed in the meek prayer sometimes offered before the family dinner. But already in many places families are trying simple ways of celebrating both joyful and painful occasions in their common life. Such celebrations of the Lord's presence in the significant events of a family's life will not displace the common Eucharist in a parish or other community but will complement and strengthen it.

Catholics are learning that there are many different ways to celebrate both forgiveness and the Lord's presence. Some of these are to be in our larger official community with celebrants who represent both the community and the larger Church. Other celebrations belong in the home and the couple seem the proper celebrants of these religious events. This ministry within the family has another powerful function: it teaches our children how Christians live. As the influence of Catholic schools declines in many areas, parents are increasingly invited to this ministry. No longer do we have others to train our children in the faith. Once again the home becomes the site for this religious formation. What better focus for this education than family exercises in forgiving and celebrating the Lord's presence in the events of their own life? As with the ministry of the purification of expectations, this ministry of a family to itself depends on vision and virtue: we must come to expect this of ourselves and we need help in developing some basic skills of sharing and celebrating.

The ministry of marriage is also directed beyond itself. A Christian family is a resource to itself and also to the larger community. But this ministry also begins in vision and expectation: we must imagine our family as being for more than itself. There are dynamics in American life—including such different forces as our need for our children to excel and the need to defend our family against crime and violence—that are sufficient to turn a family in on itself. It is "us against the world." It will take all our efforts to give our children the very best; we have little left over, either energy or money, for anyone else. Many Christian families feel acutely today this temptation of the nuclear family: it is a temptation to a collective narcissism. This turning in on ourselves which seems so necessary at times separates us from others, especially those who are not "our kind"—strangers, the dispossessed, the marginal people of whom the Old and New Testaments speak. Many of us are torn between the consuming demands of our families ("Charity begins at home," we tell ourselves) and the repeated, disturbing remarks of Jesus: "Anyone who prefers father and mother to me is not worthy of me. Anyone who prefers son or daughter to me is not worthy of me" (Matthew 10:27). "Anyone who does the will of God, that person is my brother and sister and mother" (Mark 3:35). The solution to this challenge is for a family to find its way between guilt and neglect. How are we as *this* family called to contribute to the larger world, to care for the poor and the disadvantaged? The maturity of our response depends on our journey into the authority of our own marriage and family: knowing who we are gives us a better sense of how we are to give of ourselves.

This ministry of Christian marriage is not some new discovery. It has always been a rich part of Christian communities, a fact that perhaps needs to be more celebrated today. Whether it is a retired couple working for a St. Vincent de Paul soup kitchen or a family welcoming a refugee couple and their children, Christians have always and emphatically ministered beyond "their own kind." An aspect of this ministry that is new is the change in relationship between clergy and laity. When a sharp distinction between these two groups prevailed, it was easy to consider ministry the province of the clergy and financial support of this ministry the only obligation of the laity. As this distinction between clergy and laity becomes less rigid in its expression, Christians recognize that they must give more than money. This is not simply because there are no longer "enough" priests or religious to do the job but because their own religious growth demands more than a pocketbook involvement in the mission of justice and mercy. The growing interest in this ministry among married

Catholics challenges the Church to develop new channels for this service.

This ministry of a family beyond itself is exercised not only in its actions of care, healing and confronting injustice, but also in a more ordinary but powerful witness. Christian marriage is a sacrament: this means it is to be a sign. A marriage and family which is living out its special vocation will stand out in the world. Its decisions about money and possessions, about how to spend its energy and its time, will not simply duplicate cultural values and so be lost from sight. A Christian family's conviction about who belongs to "its kind" will give it a different look; its love between wife and husband and its respect between parents and children will have a special shape. A family's ministry here is performed by this almost unconscious witness: this is the meaning and hope of Christian marriage as an ongoing sacrament.

Change and the Future of Christian Marriage

Finally, this book has been about change: the survival of our marriage commitments in a changing world; our own changing expectations about marriage, sexual sharing, conflict and many other aspects of our life together. Change can be seen as an enemy: it threatens what we have achieved and now cherish. But, we have argued, change can also be a very good friend. It brings us new opportunities and invitations; it forces us out of rigid patterns of behavior and stagnant relationships into possibilities that hold new life.

The Catholic Church itself is in the midst of profound changes in its understanding of marriage. We may sometimes feel ourselves threatened by many of our culture's values which contradict our deepest religious hopes. We are also imperiled by what we as Christians have done to human sexuality and marriage. By interpreting sexuality as our most likely way to fail, as the most sinful part of us, we have cast a heavy shadow over this lovely, if sometimes unruly, part of human life. As Christians we confess that God was *enfleshed*, become one of us. But then we interpreted this enfleshing as non-sexual and non-genital, handing on an Incarnation compromised.

But even this can give us hope. If as Christians we have given these darkened interpretations to sexuality then we can, following both our deepest experience of married love and God's guidance, reform this view of sexuality as well. So it is with marriage. As Christians we have at times interpreted marriage rigidly and harshly. The wondrous ideal of an enduring bond of love we have hardened into a metaphysical reality that cannot know change. Such an interpretation has too often led to an intolerance for those whose marriage bond was not just fragile, but broken. And having imagined the marriage relationship of husband and wife as a hierarchy of superior and inferior, we have been reluctant to set aside the image now when it no longer fits. But here again there is hope in the changes in our religious imagery of marriage and in the movements toward mutuality already begun in our liturgical practice and our pastoral care.

These changes in our religious understanding of marriage give hope to many couples today. And they bring with them, to many of us, a deeper realization of our own responsibility. In our marriage we tell the next generation what sex and marriage and fidelity look like to Christians. We are prophets, for better and for worse, of the future of Christian marriage. We are "traditioners," handing on our faith. This handing on does not happen abstractly; it takes concrete form in our intimate and faithful actions toward each other. We strive for a fidelity which is necessarily twofold: a fidelity to our religious past and its rich revelation and a faithfulness to the present journey and its own revelations, often as yet still unclear. Being realistic, we may expect to err as often as our religious ancestors. In this aspect of our life we do not look for significant change! But believing that our God is present with us, we anticipate that in the journey we shall continue to encounter God's love—in the delight of our shared sexuality, in the tougher intimacy we face in conflict, in the sorrow of our continuing sinfulness, in the strength of our devoted love. And as the journey of our marriages goes on, Christian marriage continues to be revealed.

BIBLIOGRAPHY

Abbott, Walter M., ed. *The Documents of Vatican II*. New York: America Press, 1966.

Aging in a Changing Family Context. Special issue of *The Family Coordinator*, journal of the National Council of Family Relations. Volume 27, number 4, October 1978.

Andreasen, Niels-Erik. *The Christian Use of Time*. Nashville: Abingdon, 1978.

Anzia, Joan Meyer, and Mary G. Durkin. *Marital Intimacy: A Catholic Perspective*. Kansas City: Andrews and McMeel, 1980.

Aquinas, St. Thomas. *The Basic Writings*. Anton Pegis, ed. and trans. New York: Random House, 1945.

Arico, Carl. "Ministry to the Engaged." *Chicago Studies* 18 (1979): 279–98.

Ariès, Philippe. *Centuries of Childhood*. New York: Vintage, 1962.

Augsburger, David. *Caring Enough to Confront*. Scottsdale, Pa.: Herald Press, 1980.

Augustine of Hippo. "On the Good of Marriage," Volume 27, and "On the Trinity," Volume 45. *The Fathers of the Church*. New York: Fathers of the Church, Inc., 1955.

Bane, Mary Jo. *Here to Stay: American Families in the Twentieth Century*. New York: Basic Books, 1976.

Basow, Susan A. *Sex-Role Stereotypes: Traditions and Alternatives*. Monterey, Calif.: Brooks/Cole, 1981.

Bellah, Robert. *Beyond Belief*. New York: Harper & Row, 1970.

Benoit, Pierre. "Christian Marriage According to St. Paul." *Clergy Review* 65 (1980): 309–21.

Berger, Peter, and Richard Neuhaus. *To Empower People: The Role of Mediating Structures in Public Policy*. Washington, D.C.: American Enterprise Institute, 1977.

Bernadin, Joseph. "Sexuality and Church Teaching." *Origins* 10 (1980): 260.
———. "Toward a Spirituality of Marital Intimacy." *Origins* 10 (1980): 286–88.
Bernard, Jesse. *The Future of Marriage*. New York: World Books, 1972.
———. *The Future of Motherhood*. New York: Dial Press, 1974.
———. "The Good-Provider Role: Its Rise and Fall." *American Psychologist* 36 (1981): 1–12.
———. *Women, Wives, Mothers: Values and Options*. Chicago: Aldine Press, 1975.
Bird, Carolyn. *The Two Paycheck Marriage*. New York: Rawson, Wade, 1979.
Bird, Joseph, and Lois F. Bird. *The Freedom of Sexual Love*. New York: Doubleday Image Books, 1970.
———. *Marriage Is for Grownups*. New York: Doubleday Image Books, 1971.
Block, Marilyn, Janice L. Davidson and Jean Dresden Grambs. *Women over Forty: Visions and Realities*. New York: Springer, 1980.
Bouscaren, T. Lincoln, and Adam C. Ellis, eds. *Canon Law: A Text and Commentary*. Milwaukee: Bruce, 1946.
Branden, Nathaniel. *The Disowned Self*. New York: Bantam, 1971.
Bronfenbrenner, Urie. "Contexts of Child Rearing." *American Psychologist* 34 (1979): 844–50.
Butler, Robert N. "The Life Review: An Interpretation of Reminiscence in the Aged." In Bernice Neugarten, ed., *Middle Age and Aging*, pp. 486–96. Chicago: University of Chicago Press, 1968.
Calderone, Mary S., and Eric W. Johnson. *The Family Book About Sexuality*. New York: Harper & Row, 1981.
Carmichael, Carrie. *Non-Sexist Childraising*. Boston: Beacon Press, 1978.
Catholic Archdiocese of Chicago. *A Special Kind of Marrying*. Chicago: Buckley Publications, 1980.
Chapman, J., ed. *Women into Wives*. New York: Sage Publications, 1977.
"Children of Divorce." Special Issue of *Journal of Social Issues*. Volume 35, number 4, Fall 1980.
Chittister, Joan. "Healing Language." *New Catholic World* 222 (1979): 257–60.
Chuang Tzu. *The Complete Works*. Burton Watson, ed. New York: Columbia University Press, 1968.
Cohen, Mabel Blake. "Personal Identity and Sexual Identity." In J. B. Miller, ed., *Psychoanalysis and Women*, pp. 129–45. London: Penguin, 1974.
Cohler, Bertram, and Henry Grunebaum. *Mothers, Grandmothers and Daughters*. New York: Wiley, 1980.

Coser, Lewis. *Greedy Institutions*. New York: Free Press, 1974.

Crossan, John Dominic. *The Dark Interval*. Chicago: Argus, 1975.

Datan, Nancy, and Nancy Lohmann, eds. *Transitions of Aging*. New York: Academic Press, 1980.

Davidson, James. *Effective Time Management: A Practical Workbook*. New York: Human Sciences Press, 1978.

Degler, Carl. *At Odds: Women and the Family in America from the Revolution to the Present*. New York: Oxford University Press, 1980.

Doherty, Denis. "Childfree Marriage—A Theological View." *Chicago Studies* 18 (1979): 137–45.

——, ed. *Dimensions of Human Sexuality*. New York: Doubleday, 1979.

Dupré, Louis. *Transcendent Selfhood: The Loss and Rediscovery of the Inner Life*. New York: Seabury, 1976.

Egan, Gerard. *Interpersonal Living*. Monterey, Calif.: Brooks/Cole, 1976.

——. *You and Me: Skills of Communicating and Relating to Others*. Monterey, Calif.: Brooks/Cole, 1977.

—— and Michael Cowan. *Moving into Adulthood*. Monterey, Calif.: Brooks/Cole, 1980.

English, John. *Choosing Life*. New York: Paulist Press, 1978.

Epstein, Barbara Leslie. *The Politics of Domesticity*. Middletown, Conn.: Wesleyan University Press, 1981.

Erikson, Erik. *Childhood and Society*. 2nd ed. New York: Norton, 1963.

——. *Dimensions of a New Identity*. New York: Norton, 1974.

——. *Gandhi's Truth*. New York: Norton, 1969.

——. *Identity: Youth and Crisis*. New York: Norton, 1968.

——. *Insight and Responsibility*. New York: Norton, 1964.

——. "Dr. Borg's Life Cycle." In E. Erikson, ed., *Adulthood*, pp. 1–28. New York: Norton, 1978.

Fiske, Marjorie, and Lawrence Weiss. "Intimacy and Crisis in Adulthood." In Nancy Schlossberg and Alan Entine, eds., *Counseling Adults*, pp. 19–33. Monterey, Calif.: Brooks/Cole, 1977.

Gallagher, Chuck. *The Marriage Encounter*. New York: Doubleday, 1975.

Gaylin, Willard. *Feelings*. New York: Ballantine, 1979.

Gerkin, Charles. *Crisis Experience in Modern Life*. Nashville: Abingdon, 1979.

Good, Mary. "Stages of Family Development." NCR Cassettes. Kansas City, Mo.: National Catholic Reporter, 1980.

Gordon, Thomas. *Parent Effectiveness Training*. New York: NAL, 1975.

Greeley, Andrew. *The Young Catholic Family*. Chicago: Thomas More Press, 1980.

——, ed. *The Family in Crisis or in Transition*. New York: Seabury, 1979.

Green, Thomas. "The Revision of Canon Law: Theological Implications." *Theological Studies* 40 (1979): 593–679.

Grossman, Frances Kaplan, and associates. *Pregnancy, Birth, and Parenthood*. San Francisco: Jossey-Bass, 1980.

Häring, Bernard. *Marriage in the Modern World*. New York: Newman Press, 1965.

Hart, Thomas. *Living Happily Ever After: Toward a Theology of Christian Marriage*. New York: Paulist Press, 1979.

Haughton, Rosemary. *The Theology of Marriage*. New York: Fides, 1971.

Hengel, Martin. *Christ and Power*. Philadelphia: Fortress, 1977.

Hildebrand, Dietrich von. *Marriage*. London: Longmans, Green, 1942.

Hillman, James. *Revisioning Psychology*. New York: Harper & Row, 1975.

Hoffman, Lois Wladis. "Maternal Employment: 1979." *American Psychologist* 34 (1979): 859–65.

Howell, M. C. *Helping Ourselves: Families and the Human Network*. Boston: Beacon, 1975.

Huyck, Margaret, and William Hoyer. *Adulthood and Aging*. Monterey, Calif.: Brooks/Cole, 1981.

Inter-Religious Task Force for Social Analysis. *Must We Choose Sides? Christian Commitment for the '80s*. New York: Episcopal Publishing, 1979.

Jacobs, Ruth Harriet, and Barbara H. Vinick. *Re-Engagement in Later Life: Re-Employment and Remarriage*. Stamford, Conn.: Greylock Publishers, 1979.

Joyce, Gerald, and James Zullo. "Ministry to Marital Growth: A Developmental Perspective." *Chicago Studies* 18 (1979): 263–78.

Kasper, Walter. *Theology of Christian Marriage*. New York: Seabury, 1980.

Kelleher, Stephen. *Divorce and Remarriage for Catholics?* New York: Doubleday, 1973.

Keniston, Kenneth. *All Our Children: The American Family Under Pressure*. New York: Harcourt Brace Jovanovich, 1977.

Kinlaw, Dennis C. "Helping Skills for the Helping Community." *Religious Education* 71 (1976): 572–83.

Kolbenschlag, Madonna. *Kiss Sleeping Beauty Good-bye: Breaking the Spell of Feminine Myths and Models*. New York: Doubleday, 1979.

Kosnik, Anthony, and associates. *Human Sexuality: New Directions in American Catholic Thought*. New York: Paulist Press, 1977.

Lakein, Alan. *How to Get Control of Your Time and Your Life*. New York: Wyden, 1973.

Lamb, Michael. *The Role of the Father in Child Development.* New York: Wiley, 1976.

Lasch, Christopher. *The Culture of Narcissism.* New York: Norton, 1978.

———. *Haven in a Heartless World: The Family Besieged.* New York: Basic Books, 1977.

Lester, Andrew D., and Judith L. Lester. *Understanding Aging Parents.* Philadelphia: Westminster, 1980.

Levinger, George, and Oliver Moles, eds. *Divorce and Separation—Context, Causes and Consequences.* New York: Basic Books, 1979.

Levinson, Daniel. *The Seasons of a Man's Life.* New York: Knopf, 1978.

Lidz, Theodore. *The Person: His and Her Development Throughout the Life Cycle.* Rev. ed. New York: Basic Books, 1976.

Linn, Dennis, and Matthew Linn. *Healing Life's Hurts.* New York: Paulist Press, 1978.

Livingston, Patricia. "Divorce: The Darkness and the Gift." Ave Maria Cassettes. Notre Dame, Ind.: Ave Maria Press, 1980.

Lopata, Helena. "The Widowed Family Member." In N. Datan and N. Lohmann, eds., *Transitions of Aging,* pp. 93–118. New York: Academic Press, 1980.

Lowenthal, Marjorie Fiske, Majda Thurnher and David Chiriboga. *Four Stages of Life: A Comparative Study of Women and Men Facing Transitions.* San Francisco: Jossey-Bass, 1976.

Lyness, Judith Fischer. "Experiential Report of Androgynous Spousal Roles." In Bernard J. Murstein, ed., *Exploring Intimate Life Styles,* pp. 19–30. New York: Springer, 1978.

Maas, Henry, and Joseph Kuypers. *From Thirty to Seventy.* San Francisco: Jossey-Bass, 1975.

Mace, David, and Vera Mace. *How to Have a Happy Marriage: A Step-by-Step Guide to an Enriched Relationship.* Nashville: Abingdon, 1977.

MacRae, George. "New Testament Perspectives on Marriage and Divorce." In James Young, ed., *Ministering to the Divorced Catholic,* pp. 37–50. New York: Paulist Press, 1979.

Marriage. Reprint of three articles which originally appeared in special issue devoted to "Ministry to Marriage." *Chicago Studies* 18 (1979): 239–77.

May, Rollo. *Love and Will.* New York: Delta, 1973.

McClelland, David. *Power: The Inner Experience.* New York: Irvington, 1975.

McCormick, Richard. "Indissolubility and the Right to the Eucharist." In James Young, ed., *Ministering to the Divorced Catholic,* pp. 65–84. New York: Paulist Press, 1979.

———. "Notes on Moral Theology." *Theological Studies* 32 (1971):

107–22; 36 (1975): 100–17; 41 (1980): 123–38; 42 (1981): 110–21.

McGinniss, James, and Kathleen McGinniss. "Parenting for Peace and Justice." NCR Cassettes. Kansas City, Mo.: National Catholic Reporter, 1980.

Miles, Margaret. *Augustine on the Body*. Missoula, Mont.: Scholars Press, 1979.

Money, John. *Love and Love Sickness*. Baltimore: Johns Hopkins University Press, 1980.

Morrissey, Francis. "Revising Church Legislation on Marriage." *Origins* 9 (1979): 210–18.

Mott, Frank L. *Women, Work, and Family*. Lexington, Mass.: Lexington Books, 1978.

Murphy, Francis X. "Of Sex and the Catholic Church." *The Atlantic Monthly* 247 (1981): 44–57.

National Council on Aging. *The Myth and Reality of Aging*. Washington, D.C.: NCOA, 1975.

Nelson, James B. *Embodiment: An Approach to Sexuality and Christian Theology*. Minneapolis: Augsburg, 1978.

Neugarten, Bernice. "Adaptation and the Life Cycle." In N. Schlossberg and A. Entine, eds., *Counseling Adults*, pp. 34–46. Monterey, Calif.: Brooks/Cole, 1977.

——. "The Future of the Young-Old." *The Gerontologist* 15 (1975): 4–9.

——. *Personality Change in Adulthood*. New York: American Psychological Association, 1978.

——. "Time, Age, and the Life Cycle." *American Journal of Psychiatry* 136 (1979): 887–94.

Newland, Mary Reed. *The Saint Book for Parents*. New York: Seabury, 1979.

——. *The Year and Our Children*. New York: Doubleday Image Books, 1964.

Niebuhr, Richard. *Experiential Religion*. New York: Harper & Row, 1972.

Noonan, John. *The Power to Dissolve*. Cambridge, Mass.: Harvard University Press, 1972.

——. "Ursa's Case." In L. G. Wrenn, ed., *Divorce and Remarriage in the Catholic Church*, pp. 29–40. New York: Paulist Press, 1973.

Norman, William, and Thomas Scaramella, eds. *Mid-Life: Developmental and Clinical Issues*. New York: Brunner/Mazel, 1980.

Nouwen, Henri. *Clowning in Rome*. New York: Doubleday Image Books, 1979.

——. *The Wounded Healer*. New York: Doubleday Image Books, 1979.

O'Connor, Elizabeth. *Our Many Selves*. New York: Harper & Row, 1971.

Orsy, Ladislas. "Christian Marriage: Doctrine and Law *Glossae* on Canons 1012–1015." *Jurist* 40 (1980): 282–348.

Otto, Herbert, ed. *Marriage and Family Enrichment: New Perspectives and Programs*. Nashville: Abingdon, 1976.

"Pastoral Statement on the Laity." Issued by the Catholic Bishops of the United States. Washington, D.C.: United States Catholic Conference, 1980.

Paths of Life. Family Life Series. New York: Paulist Press, 1979.

Patsavos, Lewis. "The Orthodox Position on Divorce." In James Young, ed., *Ministering to the Divorced Catholic*, pp. 51–64. New York: Paulist Press, 1979.

Paul VI, Pope. "Christian Witness in Married Life." *The Pope Speaks* 15 (1970): 119–28.

Pennington, M. Basil. *Centering Prayer*. New York: Doubleday, 1980.

Peterson, James, and Barbara Payne. *Love in the Later Years*. New York: Association Press, 1975.

Pius XI, Pope. "On Christian Marriage." In *Seven Great Encyclicals*, pp. 77–116. New York: Paulist Press, 1963.

Place, Michael. "The History of Christian Marriage." *Chicago Studies* 18 (1979): 311–26.

Pope, Kenneth, and Associates. *On Love and Loving*. San Francisco: Jossey-Bass, 1980.

Powell, Cyril. *The Biblical Concept of Power*. London: Epworth, 1963.

Powers, David, and Luis Maldonado, eds. *Liturgy and Human Passage*. New York: Seabury, 1978.

Provost, James. "Intolerable Marriage Situations Revisited." *Jurist* 40 (1980): 141–46.

"Psychology and Children: Current Research and Practice." Special issue of *American Psychologist*, journal of the American Psychological Association. Volume 34, number 10, October 1979.

Quinn, John. "'New Context' for Contraception Teaching." *Origins* 10 (1980): 263.

Rahner, Karl. "Considerations of the Active Role of the Person in the Sacramental Event." In his *Theological Investigations*, Volume 14, pp. 161–84. New York: Seabury, 1976.

——. "Marriage as a Sacrament." In his *Theological Investigations*. Volume 10, pp. 199–221. New York: Seabury, 1973.

Rapoport, Rhona, and Robert N. Rapoport, eds. *Working Couples*. New York: Harper & Row, 1978.

Raush, H. L., W. A. Barry, R. K. Hertel and M. A. Swain. *Communication, Conflict, and Marriage*. San Francisco: Jossey-Bass, 1974.

Rhodes, Sonya. "A Developmental Approach to the Life Cycle of the Family." *Social Casework* 58 (1977): 301–11.

Rich, Adrienne. *Of Woman Born: Motherhood as an Experience and an Institution.* New York: Norton, 1976.

Ripple, Paula. *The Pain and the Possibility.* Notre Dame, Ind.: Ave Maria Press, 1979.

———. *Called to Be Friends.* Notre Dame, Ind.: Ave Maria Press, 1980.

Rubin, Lillian. *Women of a Certain Age.* New York: Harper & Row, 1979.

Russell, Letty. *The Future of Partnership.* Philadelphia: Westminster, 1979.

Russo, Nancy Felipe, ed. *The Motherhood Mandate.* New York: Psychology of Women Quarterly, 1979.

Scanzoni, John. *Sex Roles, Women's Work, and Marital Conflict.* Lexington, Mass.: Lexington Books, 1978.

Scarf, Maggie. *Unfinished Business: Pressure Points in the Lives of Women.* New York: Doubleday, 1980.

Schillebeeckx, Edward. *Marriage: Secular Reality and Saving Mystery.* New York: Sheed and Ward, 1965.

Sennett, Richard. *The Uses of Disorder: Personal Identity and City Life.* New York: Vintage, 1970.

Sexton, Jerry, and Marilyn Sexton. "Marital Spirituality." NCR Cassettes. Kansas City, Mo.: National Catholic Reporter, 1980.

Shanas, Ethel. "Older People and Their Families: The New Pioneers." *Journal of Marriage and the Family* 42 (1980): 9–15.

Shea, John. *Stories of Faith.* Chicago: Thomas More Press, 1980.

———. *Stories of God.* Chicago: Thomas More Press, 1978.

———. "A Theological Perspective on Human Relations Skills and Family Intimacy." In A. Greeley, ed., *The Family in Crisis or in Transition,* pp. 89–99. New York: Seabury, 1979.

Shorter, Edward. *The Making of the Modern Family.* New York: Basic Books, 1975.

Sider, Ronald. *Cry Justice: The Bible on Hunger and Poverty.* New York: Paulist Press, 1980.

Smelser, Neil, and Erik Erikson, eds. *Themes of Work and Love in Adulthood.* Cambridge, Mass.: Harvard University Press, 1980.

Sporakowski, M. J., and G. A. Hughston. "Prescriptions for Happy Marriage: Adjustments and Satisfactions of Couples Married for 50 or More Years." *The Family Coordinator* 27 (1978): 321–28.

Taylor, Michael J., ed. *The Sacraments.* New York: Alba House, 1981.

Thomas, John L. *Beginning Your Marriage.* Chicago: Buckley Publications, 1980.

Tournier, Paul. *Learn to Grow Old.* New York: Harper & Row, 1972.

Tracy, David. "The Catholic Model of Caritas: Self-Transcendence and Transformation." In A. Greeley, ed., *The Family in Crisis or in Transition*, pp. 100–10. New York: Seabury, 1979.

Troll, Lillian. "Intergenerational Relations in Later Life." In N. Datan and N. Lohmann, eds., *Transitions of Aging*, pp. 75–92. New York: Academic Press, 1980.

Tufte, Virginia, and Barbara Myerhoff, eds. *Changing Images of the Family*. New Haven, Conn.: Yale University Press, 1979.

Turner, Victor, "Passages, Margins, and Poverty: Religious Symbols of Communitas." *Worship* 46 (1972): 390–412, 482–94.

——. *The Ritual Process*. Ithaca, N.Y.: Cornell University Press, 1969.

Uzoka, A. F. "The Myth of the Nuclear Family." *American Psychologist* 34 (1979): 1095–1106.

Vaillant, George. *Adaptation to Life*. Boston: Little, Brown, 1977.

Von Rad, Gerhard. *Genesis, A Commentary*. Philadelphia: Westminster, 1961.

Washbourn, Penelope. *Becoming Woman*. New York: Harper & Row, 1977.

Westerhoff, John, and William Willimon. *Liturgy and Learning Through the Life Cycle*. New York: Seabury, 1980.

Whitehead, Evelyn Eaton. "Clarifying the Meaning of Community." *Living Light* 15 (1978): 376–92.

——. "Ministers Need Three Communities." *National Catholic Reporter*, July 28, 1978, p. 8.

—— and James D. Whitehead. *Christian Life Patterns: The Psychological Challenges and Religious Invitations of Adult Life*. New York: Doubleday, 1979.

—— and J. D. Whitehead. "Retirement as a Religious Passage." In William Clements, ed., *Ministry with the Aging*, pp. 124–36. New York: Harper & Row, 1981.

—— and J. D. Whitehead. "Sexuality and Christian Intimacy." NCR Cassettes. Kansas City, Mo.: National Catholic Reporter, 1980.

Whitehead, James D. "An Asceticism of Time." *Review for Religious* 39 (1980): 3–17.

—— and Evelyn Eaton Whitehead. *Method in Ministry: Theological Reflection and Christian Ministry*. New York: Seabury, 1980.

——. E. E. Whitehead and J. G. Myers. "The Parish and Sacraments of Adulthood: Accesses to an Educational Future." *Listening: Journal of Religion and Culture* 12 (1977): 83–100.

Willing, Jules Z. *The Reality of Retirement*. New York: Wm. Morrow, 1981.

Wilson, Janice. *Sexpression*. New York: Prentice-Hall, 1980.

Witkin, Ruth, and Robert Nissen. *Good Sex After 50*. Port Washington, N.Y.: Regency Press, 1980.

Wood, John. *How Do You Feel?* New York: Spectrum, 1974.

Wrenn, Lawrence, ed. *Divorce and Remarriage in the Catholic Church*. New York: Newman Press, 1973.

Young, James, ed. *Ministering to the Divorced Catholic*. New York: Paulist Press, 1979.

Zullo, James. "Mid-Life: Crisis of Limits." NCR Cassettes. Kansas City, Mo.: National Catholic Reporter, 1977.

INDEX

EVELYN EATON WHITEHEAD is a developmental psychologist, with a doctorate from the University of Chicago. She writes and lectures on questions of adult development, aging, and the analysis of community as a style of group life. JAMES D. WHITEHEAD is a pastoral theologian and historian of religion. He holds a doctorate from Harvard University, with a concentration in Chinese religion. His professional interests include issues of contemporary spirituality and theological method in ministry.

The Whiteheads are authors of *Christian Life Patterns*, published by Doubleday in 1979 and chosen as a selection of the Catholic Book Club. In addition, they have written *Method in Ministry* as well as numerous articles for professional and pastoral journals. In 1978 they established Whitehead Associates, through which they serve as consultants in education and ministry. They are members of the associate faculty of the Institute of Pastoral Studies at Loyola University in Chicago and consultants to the Center for Pastoral and Social Ministry at the University of Notre Dame.

The Whiteheads were married in 1970 and currently make their home in South Bend, Indiana.